A Short History
of
Renaissance and Reformation
Europe

A Short History
of
Renaissance and Reformation Europe

Dances over Fire and Water

Second Edition

Jonathan W. Zophy
University of Houston Clear Lake

PRENTICE HALL, UPPER SADDLE RIVER, NEW JERSEY 07458

Library of Congress Cataloging-in-Publication Data
Zophy, Jonathan W.
    A short history of Renaissance and Reformation Europe : dances
over fire and water / by Jonathan W. Zophy. — 2nd ed.
        p.   cm.
    Includes bibliographical references and index.
    ISBN 0-13-959362-4
    1. Europe—History—476–1492.   2. Europe—History—1492–1648.
3. Europe—History—1648–1715.   4. Renaissance.   5. Reformation.   I. Title.
D200.Z665   1998
940.2—dc21   98-11028
                                                              CIP

Acquisitions Editor: Todd Armstrong
Editorial Assistant: Holly Jo Brown
Editor-in-Chief: Charlyce Jones-Owen
Marketing Manager: Sheryl Adams
Production Editor: Louise Rothman
Manufacturing Buyer: Lynn Pearlman
Manufacturing Manager: Nick Sklitsis
Cover Design: Bruce Kenselaar
Cover Art: Albrecht Dürer, *Dancing Peasants,* Giraudon/Art Resource

This book was set in 10/12 Palatino by The Composing Room of Michigan, Inc.,
and was printed and bound by Hamilton.
The cover was printed by Phoenix Color Corp.

© 1999, 1996 by Prentice-Hall, Inc.
Simon & Schuster/A Viacom Company
Upper Saddle River, New Jersey 07458

Printed in the United States of America

10   9   8   7   6   5   4   3   2   1

ISBN 0-13-959362-4

Prentice-Hall International (UK) Limited, *London*
Prentice-Hall of Australia Pty. Limited, *Sydney*
Prentice-Hall Canada, Inc., *Toronto*
Prentice-Hall Hispanoamericana, S.A., *Mexico*
Prentice-Hall of India Private Limited, *New Delhi*
Prentice-Hall of Japan, Inc., *Tokyo*
Simon & Schuster Asia Pte. Ltd., *Singapore*
Editora Prentice-Hall do Brasil, Ltda., *Rio de Janeiro*

Contents

5   *The Culture of Renaissance Humanism in Italy*   69

6   *Painting in Renaissance Italy*   85

11   The Spread of Lutheranism   184

12   Zwingli, Swiss Reform, and Anabaptism   203

13 *John Calvin and Calvinism*   217

16 The Catholic Reformation 257

17 An Age of Religious Warfare, 1546–1660 272

18   The Legacy   299

Preface

This book originated from the concerns of my students that my course in Renaissance and Reformation Europe needed a different textbook. They argued that the various texts I have been using over the past three decades are too detailed, too boring, and do not pay sufficient attention to the roles of women. Although I do not agree with them about some texts being either too lengthy or insufficiently stimulating, student suggestions did remind me how much of a gap there is between those of us who have studied a period intensely for a number of years and those who are learning about it in some cases almost for the first time. This text is an effort to provide a bridge between the often different worlds of the professor and the student.

I seek to make the Renaissance and Reformation more accessible to students, many of whom have not had much prior exposure to the subject. Deliberately adopting a conversational tone in my prose, I have attempted to write what might be called a student-friendly text by, for example, avoiding technical and foreign language terms as much as possible and attempting to introduce historical figures and concepts as they appear in the narrative. Because this is a "short" history, it is more representative than comprehensive. This means, for example, that some important Renaissance painters are not discussed in great detail. This is somewhat compensated for by the greater coverage given to important women artists and thinkers, who are not always found in traditional Renaissance and Reformation textbooks.

This book is organized around general topics such as Italian Renaissance art (Chapters 6 and 7) and religious warfare (Chapter 17). However, topics are presented roughly in a chronological order throughout the book. Hence, the Black Death of 1347 to 1350 appears in Chapter 3 of the book and the seventeenth-century constitutional crisis in England is discussed in the last chapter. Subtopics are presented in chronological order in each chapter.

All but the second chapter on "The Peoples of Europe" feature a chronology of important persons and events. My students have found these chronologies to be a helpful review aid in preparing for examinations. Even though I do not test them on their recall of specific dates, I want them to attain a relative sense of sequence: to know, for example, that Giotto lived before Artemisia Gentileschi or that Jan Hus preceded Martin Luther. It seems to me that to tell a good story it is usually a sensible notion to begin at the beginning and proceed to the end even if life itself is a seamless web.

Each chapter also ends with a list of suggestions for further reading. These are meant to recommend some of the best and most recent English-language scholarship on various topics covered in each chapter and in some cases throughout the book. Usually, I have selected books and collections of translated sources that I think serious students will enjoy reading, although I do not include novels or nonfiction works written by nonprofessional historians. In the interest of brevity, the lists have been kept relatively short with only limited annotation. They are not at all comprehensive bibliographies. I do refer readers to some of the bibliographical literature such as John O'Malley's *Catholicism in Early Modern Europe: A Guide to Research* or my own *Annotated Bibliography of the Holy Roman Empire.* Obviously, the scholarly monographs included have a wealth of citations in their notes and bibliographies.

Although I try to give some attention to the intellectual developments of the era, my emphasis for the most part has been on people of all ages and both genders. My experience is that the ideas of the period can best be learned by small group discussions of documents and texts. This brief text is meant to be used in conjunction with collections of documents such as Kenneth Atchity's *The Renaissance Reader,* David Englander's *Culture and Belief in Europe,* or G. R. Elton's *Renaissance and Reformation Europe, 1300–1648* and supplemented by more specialized monographs. It is meant solely as a brief introduction to some of the major personalities, issues, events, and ideas of the age of Renaissance and Reformation. It is not a compendium or a grand *summa.* My hope is to capture your attention and interest and stimulate you to make additional explorations of this rich and complex period in human history.

Acknowledgments

Since this book has grown out of more than twenty-five years of teaching college and university courses on Renaissance-Reformation Europe, I want to begin by thanking my students and colleagues at eight different institutions for their advice and their enthusiasm. I have learned more from them than they have from me and have taken their specific suggestions for this book seriously. I particularly want to thank the students of History 3332 (fall of 1994) at the University of Houston Clear Lake. They graciously consented to serve as "guinea pigs" in using a draft of this text. Their comments and criticisms have been invaluable as have those of students from the past several years.

I also dared to assign the draft text to my graduate seminar in the fall of 1994 for their oral and written criticisms. They had great fun critiquing the work of their genial professor and in the process helped make this a much more usable text. I was particularly pleased that they succeeded in using their imaginations to criticize the book as a text not for their own interests but for undergraduates. I want to mention the following students in particular for going beyond my assignment and providing detailed suggestions for the improvement of the text. Those stalwarts include Carolyn Bardin, Mary Demeny, Diane De Vusser, Lisa Edwards, Gloria Flores, Deborah Goldman, Sue Grooms, Haydn Hutson, Piper Madland, Sandra Petrovich, Rita Starostenko, and Sasha Tarrant. One of them, Karen Raines-Pate, deserves special mention for she had helped me with the text for several years as my research assistant. Her work on this project has been exemplary and invaluable. She is already a student-sensitive teacher.

As with my previous books, I received

a great deal of help and inspiration from a variety of colleagues, friends, and family members. Several colleagues at the University of Houston Clear Lake went over all or parts of the early drafts, including Vivian Atwater, Marjolijn Avé Lallemant, Roger Bilstein, and Gretchen Mieszkowski. Lawrence Buck (Widener University), John Patrick Donnelly, S.J. (Marquette University), and William Wright (University of Tennessee-Chattanooga), experienced teachers of courses on Renaissance-Reformation Europe, all went painstakingly over drafts of the manuscript and made incredibly useful corrections and suggestions for further improvement. Colleagues at various meetings of the Renaissance Society of America, the Sixteenth Century Studies Conference, and the Society for Reformation Research have also offered various forms of aid and encouragement. My late mentors Harold Grimm and John Harrison taught me a great deal about the importance of textbooks as teaching tools. Such is the cooperative spirit of Renaissance and Reformation scholars and teachers. Readers for Prentice Hall also wrote perceptive comments in evaluating an earlier version of the manuscript: James R. Banker, North Carolina State University; Carl Christensen, University of Colorado at Boulder; Merry Wiesner-Hanks, University of Wisconsin at Milwaukee. Several anonymous colleagues made valuable suggestions for the second edition of this text. Other scholarly debts are hinted at in the narrative, in the suggestions for further reading, and in the notes.

At Prentice Hall, I owe special thanks to former executive editor Steven Dalphin for his wise counsel and support for this project. Carmine Batsford first persuaded me to approach Steve Dalphin about doing this book. Todd Armstrong, Holly Brown, Sally Constable, Louise Rothman, and many others at Prentice Hall have done an excellent job in putting this text together. Both Annette Weir and Eric de Bruyn of Art Resource in New York deserve a special mention for their good taste and help in securing illustrations. The various art galleries listed with the illustrations throughout the text are also thanked for their help as is the library staff of the University of Houston Clear Lake.

Finally, I must again thank the members of the Howard and Zophy families for their continued support and encouragement. My special colleague-friend, Dr. Angela Howard, who teaches Women and U.S. History in superb fashion at the University of Houston Clear Lake, continues to provide me with great joy, inspiration, and character-building lessons. I have dedicated a previous book to her so this book is in honor of two other wonderful teacher-scholars: Gretchen Mieszkowski of the University of Houston Clear Lake and Randall M. Miller of St. Joseph's University. They are two of the best friends and role models that anyone could ever know.

1

Introduction:
The Best and Worst of Times

". . . as if on a given signal, splendid talents are stirring."
Erasmus, 1517

"This is the worst age of history."
Erasmus, 1536

The Problem of the Renaissance

The conflicting attitudes toward his age expressed by the influential humanist scholar Erasmus of Rotterdam in the preceding quotations suggest something of the fundamental problem of Europe in the time of Renaissance and Reformation. It truly was one of the best and worst of times. In painting, for example, between 1300 and 1700 many parts of Europe experienced an incredible era of superb achievement with such luminaries as Jan van Eyck, Botticelli, Albrecht Dürer, Raphael, Michelangelo, Titian, Artemisia Gentileschi, and many others all producing masterpieces in abundance. Seldom in history have so many artistic geniuses appeared at one special moment in time on one continent.

Artists such as the Italian master Leonardo da Vinci used newly perfected techniques in oil painting, perspective, and the use of light and shade to produce revolutionary paintings such as his *The Virgin of the Rocks*,

of which he painted two versions. This work reveals the left-handed Leonardo as a man fascinated by nature, who painted scientifically accurate versions of human anatomy, plant life, and rock formations. Da Vinci is a man in love with nature and nature's God. His Virgin Mary, baby Jesus, and John the Baptist are depicted as both heroes of the Bible and yet touchingly human. *The Virgin of the Rocks* represents a culminating manifestation of many important Renaissance trends including the rise of humanism and scientific naturalism in art.

The accomplishments of Leonardo da Vinci and his colleagues in painting and other fine arts were paralleled by the almost equally spectacular developments in letters, music, science, theology, and other areas. As the fifteenth-century philosopher Marsilio Ficino expressed it, "This age, like a golden age, has restored to light the liberal arts that were almost extinct: grammar, poetry, rhetoric, painting, sculpture, architecture, music."[1] Many intellectuals of the period

Leonardo da Vinci, *The Virgin of the Rocks*.
National Gallery, London, Great Britain. Photo
courtesy of Alinari/Art Resource.

had the sense that they were living at a special moment in history. We moderns share the sense that something unique was going on during the Renaissance partly because of the rich cultural legacy it has left us.

In literature, the Renaissance was also the age of such cultural giants as Boccaccio, Cervantes, Marguerite of Navarre, Petrarca, Rabelais, and Shakespeare, to drop only a few of the greatest names. Important thinkers such as Christine de Pizan challenged many of the medieval world's fundamental notions about the roles of women in society. Others such as Niccolò Machia-

velli boldly questioned the traditional understandings of the connection between ethics and politics. The great classical scholars and humanists of the period such as Erasmus and Lorenzo Valla helped to revive the wisdom of classical Greece and Rome and strengthen our understanding of the Judeo-Christian tradition. Classical models and humanist ideas also helped Renaissance artists with their pathbreaking work. The word *renaissance* means literally "rebirth" and refers to the revived interest in classical and Judeo-Christian sources. The humanist slogan *ad fontes* (to the sources) sums up this attitude nicely. Many of the humanists urged their followers to immerse themselves in ancient languages and literature as a means of individual and societal improvement.

Some of the extraordinary accomplishments of the time also challenged the ideas of revered ancients. In science, for example, the notions of the universe developed by Aristotle and Ptolemy were discredited to some degree by the Pole Nicholas Copernicus and the Italian Galileo. The Fleming Andreas Vesalius respectfully revised some of the time-honored notions about anatomy put forth by the Greek physician Galen in the second century A.D. Indeed, during the Renaissance we find the beginnings of the Western scientific revolution. Inspirational religious leaders such as John Wycliffe, Jan Hus, Savonarola, and others also confronted many existing traditions while reviving others. Similarly, the writing of history and political theory would never be the same after Guicciardini and Machiavelli.

Yet the Renaissance was also a period of almost incessant warfare, periodic famine, high infant mortality, rapid aging, widespread epidemics, peasant and artisan revolts, intolerance of any form of diversity, grinding poverty, massive illiteracy, forced conversions and migrations, cruelly elaborate public executions of ethnic and religious minorities, and a ferocious witchcraft craze that occurred mostly after the 1590s. For much of the fifteenth century, the European economy suffered a serious depression. The Renaissance began against the background of a series of natural and human disasters and ended in the bloody religious conflicts of the Reformation Era. Women, for the most part, did not have much of a "renaissance," as the modern historian Joan Kelly has noted. The age started with females generally subordinated to males and restricted by law and custom. It

ended up much the same way because patriarchy (the rule of the father in the family and society) continued and in some ways was enhanced. Those relatively few people who consumed the dazzling higher culture of the period were supported by the drudgery of the masses. For many Europeans who lived through it, what we call the Renaissance must have often seemed like the worst of times, as the influential humanist Erasmus called it shortly before his death in 1536.

This book will use the label *Renaissance* to refer both to a period of European history and to the international cultural movement which emerged during the fourteenth century in Italy and spread to much of the rest of the world by the seventeenth century. Although we may have ambivalent feelings about the period or even the use of the term *Renaissance*, there is little doubt about the historical and cultural importance of the years between the lives of the painter Giotto (c. 1267–1337) and the naturalist Maria Sibylla Merian (1647–1717). For the nineteenth-century Swiss historian Jacob Burckhardt, the Italian Renaissance brought forth the triumph of "individualism" and helped usher in the modern world. The twentieth-century historian Richard Goldthwaite recently paid homage to Burckhardt's modernity thesis by describing Renaissance Italy as the birthplace of modern consumer society, such was the obsession with material things among the wealthy elites of the time. This lust for acquisition also helped to fuel the rise of capitalism and the movement toward a world economy.

During the fourteenth through the seventeenth centuries, merchants learned to make better use of international banking and found new ways to raise capital. Simple innovations such as the use of double-entry bookkeeping and bills of exchange greatly improved business practices. Navigational techniques became more sophisticated and ships were made bigger and better. Trade expanded and the standard of living improved greatly, at least for the prosperous. Capitalism also helped lead to an expansion in the horrific practices of the slave trade and to the voyages of discovery, which in turn led to the creation of vast colonial empires and the spread of lethal diseases throughout the so-called "New World." The controversial navigator Christopher Columbus was a child of the Renaissance as was Francisco Pizzaro, who conquered and looted the Inca Empire in Peru. Although life for most Renaissance people changed little, for others it was an era of transformation.

Even though many things about the Renaissance, including the term itself, are subjects of great debate among modern scholars, the period clearly featured the rise of the modern territorial state as feudal monarchies in Europe gave way to more bureaucratized and centralized power structures. Even a massive state like the Holy Roman Empire, which remained largely decentralized and supranational, attempted to regularize its medieval organizational structure. In 1356 the empire codified its tradition of electing its monarchs in a document known as the Golden Bull. Some even thought divided Italy should be made into a unified kingdom. Feudal levies were frequently replaced by mercenaries, who fought for anyone who would pay them. The lance and sword became more and more obsolete, challenged first by the bow and arrow and then by new gunpowder weapons. A military revolution ensued, which was to have profound consequences as general superiority in warfare allowed Europeans to dominate and exploit the rest of the world economically until well into the twentieth century.

The Reformation

The term *Reformation* is another controversial historical fiction created in the nineteenth century to describe the movements for religious reform that followed from the friar Martin Luther's attack against indulgences in 1517 to the close of the age of religious warfare in the middle of the seventeenth century. Obviously, the Reformation as a historical period overlaps with the time of the Renaissance, and many of the same figures were intimately involved in both movements. The reform movement in the Catholic Church has often been called a Counter Reformation, but since the concern for reform predates Luther, the more inclusive term *Catholic Reformation* would seem more appropriate. While both the terms *Renaissance* and *Reformation* have lost some of their power, they still are more descriptive and evocative labels than the prosaic phrases "Europe between 1300 and 1700" or "Early Modern Europe."

Dances over Fire and Water?

Regardless of what one calls this age in history, it was, indeed, the best and worst of times, which is why we can think of it as a series of dances over fire and water. The modern historian and novelist Sydney Alexander first used that stimulating image to refer to the Renaissance. "Dances over fire and water" may be a useful way to think about certain aspects of the period. After all, most of its intellectuals still believed that the world was made up of four basic elements: earth, fire, air, and water. Although firmly rooted in the soil that most of its people farmed for an often meager living, this era seemed to soar above most earlier periods in terms of its cultural achievements. Some of its major figures such as Botticelli, Machiavelli, Michelangelo, William Shakespeare, and Elizabeth Tudor appear nearly superhuman at times. One can imagine them capable of doing anything, including dancing over fire and water. Not since classical Athens or Rome of the first century had Europe witnessed such an age of stunning artistic and intellectual accomplishments set against a background of incredible suffering.

Although the Middle Ages was hardly like "a thousand years without a bath," even its great Gothic cathedrals and magnificent theological summas seem to moderns to be overshadowed by the series of dances over fire and water that was Europe in the age of the Renaissance. These images of fire and water also conjure up horrific aspects of the period. The public burning of religious minorities and dissenters in the elaborate ceremonies called *autos de fé* (acts of faith) by the Inquisition sums up much of the worst about the age. So does the torture and torching of those victims caught up in the agony of the witchcraft trials by both Protestant and Catholic states at the end of the era. Catholics and Protestants also agreed upon the need to drown and burn Anabaptists, those who believed in baptism only for adults and, therefore, had to be "rebaptized." These persecutions occurred in a world almost consumed by the continuing flames of war, which raged on and off throughout much of Europe. The new gunpowder weapons had substantially increased the firepower available to the period's military. So much waste and misery in an age of astonishing beauty, penetrating insights, and fervent piety! Yet the movement known as the Reformation was also a dance of death and destruction. With these cautions in mind, let the dances begin!

General Chronology

c. 1267–1337	Life of the painter Giotto.	**1415**	Death of Jan Hus.
1304–1374	Life of the humanist Petrarca.	**1431**	Death of Joan of Arc.
		1441	Death of Jan van Eyck.
1305–1376	The Babylonian Captivity (the popes at Avignon).	**1449–1492**	Life of Lorenzo de' Medici.
1313–1375	Life of the humanist Boccaccio.	**1453**	Fall of Constantinople to the Ottomans.
1337–1453	The Hundred Years' War between England and France.	**1454**	Johann Gutenberg prints a Bible at Mainz.
		1455–1485	War of the Roses in England.
1347–1350	The Black Death (plague epidemics).	**1469**	Marriage of Isabella of Castile to Ferdinand of Aragon.
1356	Peasant Revolt in France.		
1364–1430	Life of Christine de Pizan.	**1471**	Birth of Albrecht Dürer in Nuremberg.
1378–1417	Western papal schism.		
1384	Death of John Wycliffe.	**1492**	Christopher Columbus's first voyage to the Americas; birth of Marguerite of Navarre.
1414–1418	Reform Council of Constance.		

(continued)

1494	King Charles VIII of France invades Italy; birth of Rabelais.	1558–1603	Reign of Elizabeth I of England.
1495	Leonardo da Vinci begins *The Last Supper*.	1567	Revolt of the Netherlands begins; birth of Monteverdi.
1512	Michelangelo completes the Sistine Chapel ceiling.	1571	Battle of Lepanto.
1513	Machiavelli writes *The Prince*.	1572	Massacre of Saint Bartholomew's Day; death of John Knox.
1515	Birth of Saint Teresa of Avila.	1576	Death of Titian.
1516	Erasmus's edition of the Greek *New Testament* and Thomas More's *Utopia* published.	1580–1640	Peak period for witchcraft trials.
		1587	Death of Mary, Queen of Scots.
1517	Martin Luther's "Ninety-five Theses against Indulgences."	1588	Defeat of the Spanish Armada.
1519	Charles V of Habsburg elected Holy Roman Emperor; Cortés begins the conquest of Mexico.	1589	Death of Catherine de' Medici.
		1598	King Henri IV issues the Edict of Nantes.
1524–1526	Peasants' revolts in Germany and Austria; beginnings of Anabaptism.	1602	Shakespeare's *Hamlet*.
		1605	Cervantes publishes *Don Quixote*.
1526	Ottomans under Süleyman the Magnificent conquer much of Hungary.	1614–1702	Life of Margaret Fox.
		1616	Artemisia Gentileschi admitted to the Florentine Academy of Art; deaths of Shakespeare and Cervantes; Galileo ordered to cease and desist his new astronomy.
1527	Sack of Rome.		
1530	The Augsburg Confession.		
1531	Death of Zwingli; Parliament recognizes Henry VIII as "Supreme Head of the Church in England."		
		1618–1648	Thirty Years' War in Germany.
		1625	Death of Sonfonisba Anguissola.
1536	First edition of John Calvin's, *Institutes of the Christian Religion*.	1642–1649	English Civil War.
		1647–1717	Life of Sibylla Merian.
1540	Paul III authorizes the Jesuits led by Ignatius of Loyola.	1685	Revocation of the Edict of Nantes by King Louis XIV.
1543	Publication of Copernicus's *On the Revolution of Celestial Spheres* and Vesalius's *On the Fabric of the Human Body*.	1688	Bloodless revolution brings William and Mary to the throne in England and marks the triumph of Parliament.
1545–1563	Council of Trent.		

Further Reading

GENERAL SURVEYS

Sidney Alexander, *Lions and Foxes: Men and Ideas in the Italian Renaissance* (1974). Written by a novelist.

Ernst Breisach, *Renaissance Europe, 1200–1517* (1973).

Jacob Burckhardt, *The Civilization of the Italian Renaissance* (1860). This highly influential study has been frequently reprinted.

Peter Burke, *The Italian Renaissance: Culture and Society in Renaissance Italy* (1987).

Wallace Ferguson, *Europe in Transition, 1300–1520* (1962).

Richard Goldthwaite, *Wealth and the Demand for Art in Italy, 1300–1600* (1993). Emphasizes material culture.

John Hale, *The Civilization of Europe in the Renaissance* (1994).

Denys Hay, *The Italian Renaissance in Its Historical Background*, 2nd ed. (1976).

De Lamar Jensen, *Renaissance Europe: Age of Recovery and Reconciliation*, 2nd ed. (1992). A first-rate, comprehensive text, which includes some material on women and a very useful set of bibliographical essays.

Joan Kelly, "Did Women Have a Renaissance?," in *Becoming Visible: Women in European History*, 2nd ed., Renate Bridenthal, Claudia Koonz, and Susan Mosher Stuard, eds. (1987). An important essay in a valuable collection of essays. See also the 1977 first edition.

Robert Kingdon, ed., *Transition and Revolution: Problems and Issues of European Renaissance and Reformation History* (1974). Important essays by the editor and others.

Lisa Jardine, *Worldly Goods: A New History of the Renaissance* (1996). Emphasizes consumerism.

Theodore Rabb, *Renaissance Lives: Portraits of an Age* (1993). Handsomely illustrated character sketches of such diverse figures as Petrarca, Hus, Dürer, Artemisia Gentileschi, Teresa of Avila, and others.

Eugene Rice with Anthony Grafton, *The Foundations of Early Modern Europe, 1460–1559*, 2nd ed. (1994). A valuable synthesis.

Lewis Spitz, Jr., *The Renaissance Movement*, 2nd ed. (1987). A lively text.

Bard Thompson, *Humanists and Reformers: A History of the Renaissance and Reformation* (1996). Engaging survey.

Jonathan W. Zophy, *A Short History of the Renaissance: Dances over Fire and Water* (1997). An expanded version of the first half of this text.

REFERENCE WORKS

Catherine Avery, ed., *The New Century Italian Renaissance Encyclopedia* (1972).

Thomas Bergin and Jennifer Speake, eds., *Encyclopedia of the Renaissance* (1987).

Thomas Brady, Jr., Heiko Oberman, and James Tracy, eds., *Handbook of European History, 1400–1600*. 2 vols. (1994 and 1995). Important essays and bibliographies by leading international scholars on diverse topics such as "Population," "Trade," "Family," and various political entities.

Paul Grendler, ed., *Encyclopedia of the Renaissance*, 6 vols. (forthcoming). When completed will be the most important reference work on the subject.

John Hale, ed., *A Concise Encyclopedia of the Italian Renaissance*, 2nd ed. (1992).

New Cambridge Modern History, vol. 1, *The Renaissance, 1493–1520* (1957); vol. 2, *The Reformation*, 2nd ed. (1990).

COLLECTIONS OF SOURCES

Kenneth Atchity, ed., *The Renaissance Reader* (1997). Wide range of sources.

Kenneth Bartlett, ed., *The Civilization of the Italian Renaissance: A Sourcebook* (1992). Includes more well-selected materials by and about women than is usually the case.

Julia Conaway Bonadella and Mark Musa, eds., *The Italian Renaissance Reader* (1992).

Eric Cochrane and Julius Kirshner, eds., *The Renaissance* (1986).

G. R. Elton, ed., *Renaissance and Reformation, 1300–1648*, 3rd ed. (1976).

David Englander, et al., eds., *Culture and Belief in Europe, 1450–1600: An Anthology of Sources* (1993).

Werner Gundersheimer, ed., *The Italian Renaissance*, 2nd ed. (1993).

Benjamin Kohl and Alison Andrews Smith, *Major Problems in the History of the Italian Renaissance* (1995). An excellent selection of source materials and essays by leading modern scholars concerned with family, gender, and cultural issues.

James Bruce Ross and Mary Martin McLaughlin, eds., *The Portable Renaissance Reader* (1967). Excerpts from the writings of 100 fifteenth- and sixteenth-century thinkers from all over Europe.

Donald Weinstein, ed., *The Renaissance and Reformation, 1300–1600* (1965).

There are also useful English translations of the works of many of the writers discussed in the pages that follow.

Note

1.   Cited in John Hale, *The Civilization of Europe in the Renaissance* (New York: Atheneum, 1993), p. 586.

2

The Peoples of Europe

The Peasantry

Europe of the Renaissance and Reformation was much like Europe of the present in languages and weather, but that is about all. In sharp contrast to today's highly populated, polluted, and urbanized world, the world of the fourteenth through seventeenth centuries was thinly populated and mostly rural and agricultural. If only 1 to 2 percent of a modern, industrialized country's workforce is necessary to feed the rest, nearly the opposite was true during the Renaissance. Crop yields were still minimal by modern standards despite the wider use of horse collars and oxen yokes, iron-tipped plows, and a greater reliance on the three-field system than had been the case in the early Middle Ages. The three-field system allowed a farmer to plant one field with wheat in the fall and barley or rye in another in the spring, while letting one field lie fallow each year. Even though this system improved the yield over the two-field system, agricultural production was less than abundant. The result was that every able-bodied person in a Renaissance farm family, including women and children, had to work the land intensively. Toddlers under seven were allowed to play at home and were looked after by the disabled or older children.

A CULTURE OF POVERTY: VILLAGE LIFE

Most Europeans in the sixteenth century lived in small farming villages of 500 to 700 inhabitants and were generally connected to self-sufficient agricultural estates called *manors*. Typical villages would be filled with windowless, thatch-roofed huts with dirt floors. Usually peasant huts had only two rooms plus an attic and a barn or a cowshed. Privacy as we know it today was unheard of. Furthermore, lice and vermin abounded, ventilation was poor, and the smoke of the central fire of the hearthstone mingled with the smells of humans and animals.

In addition to the peasant huts and sheds, a village might have a miller to grind grain, a tavern, a blacksmith shop, perhaps a general store, a parish church, and maybe the manor house of the principal landowner of the region. Some agricultural communities were attached to monasteries and some were located near the walls of a town. Other manorial estates were remote and isolated. The level of prosperity varied from year to year and place to place. A village like Sennely in France outside of Orléans was constantly on the edge of poverty because it had poor soil, although it never faced an all-out famine. Other villages were not so lucky.

The peasants of Europe usually wore

A fourteenth-century manuscript page of *Ovide Moralise* by Chrétien Legouais. The miniature depicts a man obliged to work in order to live. Bibliotheque Municipale, Rouen, France. Photo courtesy of Giraudon/Art Resource.

simple, homespun clothes of sturdy fibers. Their underwear was usually made of wool with wool or linen outerwear. Many wore wooden shoes equivalent to modern clogs. Some well-off farmers had leather boots, whereas others went barefoot at times. Peasants tended to age rapidly and they were often bent over from frequent stooping in the fields. Some had yellowish skin, and others were deeply tanned in the summer from long hours in the sun. Almost every adult had poor teeth and fetid breath. Frequent bouts of ill health were a common occurrence for adults.

Coarse, dark bread was the staple of peasant diets throughout Europe, whether from grains of barley, rye, millet, wheat, or some combination of several grains. Corn or maize did not come into Europe until after Christopher Columbus's voyages to the so-called "New World" in the 1490s. Potatoes from Peru followed corn by two generations, first appearing in Spain in 1573 and then arriving in Italy by 1601. Even with the introduction of corn and potatoes, grains—whether baked as bread or mixed with water—remained the core of the European peasant diet.

When grain crops failed, starving peasants substituted acorns, tree bark, grass seeds, and even earth mixed with wheat flour. Fruit was usually too expensive for peasant households and green vegetables were rare. Dried beans, peas, and fish provided much needed protein and vitamins. Meat in any form was rare. King Henri IV, in the late sixteenth century, expressed the hope that every French rural family would be able to have "a chicken in its cooking pot every Sunday." Had this wish been fully realized in the Renaissance, it would have represented a considerable advance in the nutritional life of the French peasantry in many areas.

Such a dramatic change in the living standards of the peasantry did not occur during the Reformation, and their meager diets were reflected in the high levels of disease and malnutrition present throughout Europe and in the fact that some girls in northern Europe did not menstruate until the age of eighteen. Peasant girls in most of the rest of Europe typically had menarche between ages twelve and fourteen. Women in the northern parts of Europe married at about age twenty-three, usually to older

husbands. An estimated one third of all babies died in their first year. Couples aver-
aged three to four children with only about
45 percent reaching adulthood. Life spans
were about half of what they are now and
few peasant households had living grandparents.

improve.   In some senses, however, things were
slowly improving for Europe's peasantry
during the Renaissance. Most European
peasants were no longer "bound to the soil"
as serfs. Serfdom did linger on in parts of
eastern Europe and in Russia until well into
the nineteenth century, but many western
European peasants owned some land. Better-
off peasants might possess their own horses
for plowing and even their own wooden
plows. A prosperous peasant family in
France often had an estate worth about 2,000
livres. Those farmers just below them on the
social scale who did not own horses and
plows might be worth about 600 livres. They
often rented most of their land and were in
constant danger of falling into the status of
hired hands. Hired hands often owned
nothing other than a hut, a garden, and
maybe a pig.

Regardless of their relative wealth or
poverty, all peasants, including most children, worked exceedingly hard for most of
the year. Men worked the fields, gathered
wood, and repaired equipment. Children
assisted their parents in all farm activities as
soon as they were able. Peasant women usually helped the men with the plowing, manure spreading, weeding, reaping, and
threshing. Women were expected to do all
the internal household chores, as well as to
gather kindling, haul well water, garden,
tend animals, suckle infants, cook, sweep,
and tend the fires. In addition to doing laundry for themselves and sometimes others,
peasant women often sold cheese and but-
ter, cared for children, and made the family's clothes. As a nineteenth-century Sicil-

ian proverb put it, "If the father is dead, the
family suffers. If the mother dies, the family
cannot exist."[1]

The Continuities of Life for Men, Women, and Children

Other constants in the peasants' world be-
sides hard work included death and taxes.
Peasants who lived on manors had to pay
fees to use the lord's grain mill or to breed
livestock. They had to perform certain sea-
sonal duties for the lord, such as road and
fence repairs. A peasant son had to surrender his best animal to inherit his father's ten-
ancy. Normally a family had to pay about a
third of their harvests to landlords, priests,
and tax collectors. When the harvest was
bad, people starved to death and infants
were abandoned in larger numbers than
usual. Survival was always the central issue
for the peasantry in the culture of poverty
that was Renaissance Europe.

In parts of Europe such as the Mediterranean basin, northern England, Scotland,
Ireland, and Scandinavia, agricultural production was not as tightly organized as in
regions of richer soils, where the communal
farming of the manors predominated. Regardless of regional differences, the lives of
the rural working men, women, and children
of Renaissance Europe can be described as
difficult and only slightly improved over
that of their medieval ancestors. That superstitions still persisted, such as belief in the
magical powers of bull's blood, for example,
is hardly surprising for people who sought
help in a variety of ways.

Given the lives of drudgery that most
peasants experienced, it is little wonder that
church holidays, weddings, services, games
of all sorts, visits to market towns, and occasional fairs meant so much to them. These
were among the few occasions when a peas-

ant family did not have to labor from sunrise to sunset. Fairs allowed a peasant family to buy a few items, such as magical potions they could not make for themselves, and to dance, drink, and swap stories with friends. If peasant dancing was often frenetic, that is understandable, considering the hardships of their lives.

Even an occasional holiday, however, could not disguise the essential harshness of peasant life nor the contempt which they sometimes experienced from the more privileged estates. Crude jests about "dumb and illiterate" peasants abounded. To be a peasant was often to be looked down upon and taken for granted by those whom you fed and served. Sometimes the level of anger was so intense that peasants risked everything to rebel against their often absentee landlords. Major peasant revolts had broken out in Flanders between 1323 and 1328; in France in 1358; in 1381 in England; and in various places in Germany throughout the fifteenth century (called *Bundschuh* revolts for the cloglike shoes most peasants wore). Between 1524 to 1526 a major peasants' war was fought in southern Germany and spread to Austria. Since the peasantry was not generally trained in the use of arms and military leadership, all their revolts were brutally crushed by the authorities. These occasional, violent eruptions reflected the deep-seated desperation that often lay just below the surface calm of "those who work."

Town Dwellers

Although most Europeans lived in rural villages during the Reformation, the third estate of commoners also included those who lived in walled towns. As an old legal maxim confirmed: "Only a wall separates the burgher from the peasant." Even though the feudal nobility may have lumped the town dwellers with the peasants, the wealthiest members of an early modern urban community considered themselves to be more closely allied with Europe's noble families. Indeed, sometimes the leading citizens of a powerful and wealthy city might declare themselves to be noble, as did the wealthy merchant families of Venice in the fourteenth century. Other urban elites simply styled themselves as patricians, thereby forging a link with the aristocrats of ancient Rome.

The so-called patricians of the towns of Europe seldom numbered more than 5 to 6 percent of a community's populace, although they often had more than their share of political power. Ranking below the patriciate were the smaller merchants, skilled artisans, shop owners, lawyers, and teachers. The size of the clerical populations varied, but even a town without a resident bishop, such as sixteenth-century Nuremberg, might have had as many as 10 percent of its population in the ranks of the clergy. Since the clerical estate made up roughly 2 to 4 percent of the European population as a whole, the figure for Nuremberg shows how the clergy would often cluster around the protective walls of towns. Towns that were seats of bishops would have large clerical populations, whereas remote rural parishes often had difficulty in keeping enough priests.

Apprentices, journeymen, gardeners, servants, prostitutes, unskilled laborers, paupers, and peddlers comprised at least a third of a typical town's population. In times of economic difficulties, the ranks of a city's poor would swell. Nuremberg, for example, distributed free bread on a daily basis to 13,000 people in 1540 and 1541. Famine was always a possibility even inside a town with its grain storage warehouses, but usually cities seemed much more prosperous than the countryside. This could also be seen in the hordes of beggars who lined the roads leading to most urban centers. The upper echelon of urban society, in sharp contrast, ate the best the surrounding countryside could provide, including white bread made of the finest available grains, as well as fresh vegetables and meat on a regular basis.

Although Europe remained predominantly rural throughout the preindustrial age, towns had generally increased in size and wealth since the eleventh century. Even though urban populations may have fallen by as much as a third during the disasters associated with the widespread and lethal effects of the Black Death between 1347 and 1350, by the late fifteenth century trade and towns began to grow again. By 1500 modest increases had brought the European population up to 60 to 75 percent of what it had been before the mid-fourteenth century. Europe's population would continue to increase gradually over the course of the sixteenth century.

Most towns, however, numbered only a few thousand inhabitants. There were a few large communes such as Cologne in Germany and Marseilles in France, both of which had about 40,000 residents inside their walls in the beginning of the sixteenth century. Ghent in the Low Countries had around 50,000 inhabitants, as did London, Lyon, and Seville. Readers should be aware that all Reformation Era population figures are a matter of considerable debate. However, it appears that Florence, Milan, Rome, Venice, and Palermo in Sicily all had populations nearing 100,000, as did Lisbon in Portugal. Paris may have had almost 200,000 residents. Mighty Naples had perhaps as many as 230,000 people, thus rivaling Constantinople and the Aztec capital of Tenochtitlán in Mexico before its destruction in 1521 by Hernan Cortés and his allies.

All of these comparatively large cities had great ports or were near major land trade routes. Nuremberg, for example, was not a port city or on a navigable river, but it was located near twelve different trade routes in the heart of central Europe. Trade and financial centers such as Amsterdam, Antwerp, Lisbon, London, and Paris grew during the sixteenth and seventeenth centuries. There commercial life increased as the Atlantic Ocean and the North Sea gradually replaced the Mediterranean as the focal point of long-distance trade in the early modern world.

Most towns had surrounding clusters of peasant villages and sometimes smaller client towns as well. People liked the feeling of security that came from being near walled, fortified places. Some Renaissance towns bristled with armaments and fortifications, such as wealthy Nuremberg with its several rings of walls, large trenches, eighty-four towers on the inner wall and forty on the outer wall, and protected gates. York in northern England had fortifications going back to the Norman conquest; Chester's walls and gates dated to Roman times as did Trier's in Germany and Lyon's in France. Spanish towns such as Avila and Segovia bristled with barriers and defenses that had been used in the wars with the Muslims.

Inside even the largest of towns, people lived close together and their behavior was closely regulated by the community's leading male citizens. The majority of town dwellers lived in small, half-timbered cabins with some of the poor huddled in crude sheds clustered alongside town walls. Shopkeepers and their families and servants usually lived in a few rooms above their places of business. Only a few rich merchants and bankers such as the Medici of Florence or the Fuggers of Augsburg had imposing town houses with brick and stone facades and sometimes country homes as well. Goods were displayed for sale on the lower

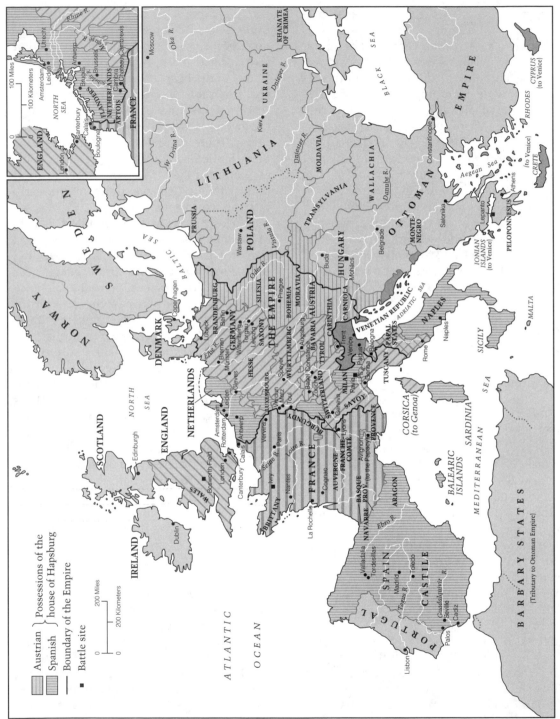

Europe in the Renaissance.

floor and sometimes sold on the streets and in the market square. Every town had its Weavers' Lane, its Butchers' Row, and its Fishmongers' Alley. The narrow streets were crowded with people, animals (scavenging pigs being a particular favorite), and various kinds of refuse including human excrement, often dumped from upper-floor windows. The practice of burying the dead within town walls did nothing to lower the threshold of disease.

DAILY LIFE

Church and town hall bells awoke the burghers and punctuated their days. Bells were also used to warn the inhabitants of the danger of approaching enemies. During the day, towns were filled with activity. Goods were made, bought, and sold as were the food products of the countryside. Inns and taverns were filled with travelers and locals. Religious processions, holy days, and civic festivals provided welcome distractions from the routine work activities. At sundown, gates were locked, vagrants were expelled, and curfews were enforced as darkness and quiet descended over the towns. City streets at night were places for honest citizens to avoid, even though crime was severely and publicly punished. Entrance gates to towns were often "decorated" with the severed, eyeless heads of executed criminals.

Despite the severity of punishment, Renaissance towns could often be dangerous places. The presence of unmarried journeymen away from the restraints of their hometowns posed a constant threat. Sexual assaults and drunken brawls were common. In sixteenth-century Venice, violence was ritualized to the point where several times each year, workers and artisans would gather on a Sunday or a holiday afternoon to battle with sticks and fists for the possession of a bridge. These prearranged, organized "wars" would be watched regularly by thousands of spectators. Violence, whether organized or not, was as much a part of urban life as barter in the marketplace or high-quality craft production in the workshops.

Maintaining law and order was the great preoccupation of most urban governments. Urban communities were usually governed by councils made up of the leading male merchants, who were sometimes joined by prosperous guildsmen. Crafts were still organized in the form of economic associations, called *guilds*, which regulated production and employment standards, set prices, and provided benefits for the widows and orphans of their members. The guilds also served as social and religious brotherhoods and typically sponsored floats in carnival parades and religious processions. Therefore, they were something like labor unions but with management functions and a firm commitment to religion as well.

URBAN WOMEN

Women were typically not allowed to be members of guilds and go through the full training course of being apprentices, journeymen, and finally masters. Girls might be apprenticed to makers of silk thread, to dressmakers, or to embroiderers. Often wives and daughters of a master craftsman learned the skills of the trade, and sometimes widows were allowed to take over their deceased husband's shop for a limited period of time. This was done chiefly to avoid having to provide financial support for widows and their children out of collective guild funds. As in the case of farm families, everyone was expected to work. Guild widows had to pay guild fees but had no voice in the running of the guilds. Although most urban women worked as housekeepers, others found additional employment primarily as shopkeepers, tavern maids, and servants. Female servants were in a particularly vulnerable position. Legal restrictions made it difficult for women to own much property or to conduct business.

Because women were denied economic power, they also had little political power in most towns. They were not eligible for public office and not allowed to make public policy decisions. The laws that bound them were made exclusively by males. Inside families, men ruled supreme and were able to enforce their power by brute force if necessary. Wife beating was common even though the church made efforts to limit it. Although theorists such as the architect Leon Battista Alberti (c. 1404–1472) urged husbands to treat their wives and children with kindness, there was no question where ultimate power resided.

Renaissance governments mirrored family and household structure in being not only patriarchal but also paternalistic. Tight social control was the supposedly divinely sanctioned order of the day and it was exerted by wealthy men over men of lower status, all women, and children. Households consisted of family members, relatives, and servants. City fathers took responsibility for regulating not only all aspects of market life but also the personal lives of their fellow citizens. For example, a typical town council spent time deliberating "how the extravagance of children in dressing during Holy Week might be prevented" or whether or not a woman "was too ardent in bed with her husband."[2] Nothing was considered beneath the notice of the paternalistic town rulers, whether they were bishops, dukes, or councils of merchants and guildsmen.

SOCIAL TENSIONS

Although animosities between men and women seldom erupted into public violence, many Renaissance towns experienced considerable tension between rich merchants, professionals, and the mostly illiterate masses who worked with their hands. The patriciate considered themselves to be "honorable men who earn their living in respectable business, not lowly manual work," as the lawyer Christoph Scheurl (1481–1542) put it.[3] Increasingly the business of government required more and more lawyers to transact. Towns kept lawyers on their payrolls as consultants and used men with legal training as bureaucrats despite the reputation of the legal profession for avarice, as Marinus van Reymerswaele's 1545 painting of a law office reveals. The artist was responding to a Dutch proverb: "If you go to a lawyer to get back your cow, you will have to bring the lawyer another to pay his fee." Despite the presence of those trained in the law and other public officials preoccupied with maintaining law and order, Renaissance towns were filled with festering jealousies and social grievances that often threatened to erupt into public violence.

Sometimes the struggles over employment, status, and representation on city councils, among other issues, boiled over into class warfare, as when the artisans of Nuremberg revolted in 1348 to 1349 or when the hungry cloth workers of Florence revolted in the summer of 1378. The unskilled Florentine cloth workers (called *Ciompi*) were crushed by their more prosperous brothers in the guilds. The Nuremberg craft workers were defeated by the patriciate allied with the Holy Roman Emperor Charles IV. In times of crisis, the privileged tended to stick together. The patricians of Nuremberg then used the artisans' revolt as an excuse to keep guildsmen off the city's elite

Marinus van Reymerswaele's, *The Lawyer's Office* (1545). Courtesy of the New Orleans Museum of Art, Ella West Freeman Foundation Matching Fund.

governing small council, whereas other German towns such as Augsburg and Strasbourg found means of accommodating the most powerful guildsmen.

At times public violence erupted between members of the same social class who lived in different neighborhoods with which they identified, as was the case of the famous bridge battlers of Venice. Factional violence could be almost as dangerous as class warfare. Further complicating the situation in many communes were family rivalries, such as that between the Albizzi and the Ricci families in fourteenth-century Florence. Often family and factional disputes were related to political matters, for example, the rivalry in Italy between the supporters of the German Holy Roman emperor and his frequent rival the pope (Ghibellines versus Guelfs) or factions within these larger groupings. Although life in many Renaissance towns was sometimes turbulent,

it was seldom dull. Urban centers were busy, colorful places of hard work and sometimes intense interactions.

The Rise of the Capitalists

The growth of towns in the late Middle Ages had accompanied the rise of capitalism. Capitalism involves private or corporate ownership of capital goods and investment decisions. Capitalists usually favor letting free markets determine prices, production, and distribution. During the Middle Ages, capitalists had struggled against the Old Testament injunction against "taking usury or increase" on loans. The highly influential theologian St. Thomas Aquinas (c. 1225–1274) and other leading church intellectuals agreed with Aristotle that "money is sterile" and that a good Christian should not take advantage of a neighbor in need.

Generally the Europeans lagged behind the Asians and Muslims as merchants and in technology and medicine during much of the medieval period. None of the European overland trade routes compared to the Asian "silk road" from Samarkand to Beijing in China. The Asians also had better ships and navigational instruments than the Europeans until the time of the Renaissance.

All of this began to change even before the fourteenth century. For example, the idea of usury became more and more acceptable as Christian bankers helped fund the Crusades and endowed chapels and hospitals at home and abroad. The medieval Crusades to the Holy Land (1096–1291) helped stimulate demand in Europe for luxury goods such as cottons, silks, muslin, dyestuffs, medicines, perfumes, spices, and much else. Once Europeans had sampled ginger and nutmeg, they were never going to be content again with just plain, but still expensive, salt as their main spice.

Italian merchants from port cities such as Genoa and Venice had long been active in trading with Byzantine and Arab merchants. Several members of the thirteenth-century Polo merchant family of Venice had spent decades in the Asia of Kublai Khan, grandson of the Mongol conqueror, Genghis Khan (c. 1160–1227). Marco Polo (c. 1254–1324) eventually published *Travels,* a widely read account of his time spent in the East the accuracy of which has been recently called into question. Be that as it may, by the thirteenth and fourteenth centuries, dozens of Italian cities were heavily involved in the growing trade in the Mediterranean.

That trade also included a lucrative traffic in human flesh as the thirteenth century witnessed a resurgence of the slave trade. Prisoners of war and children of desperate parents were sold in the markets of various towns such as bustling Genoa. Slaves came from Africa as well as the Balkans and the Black Sea region. Africans, Asians, and Ottomans were especially valued as house servants and for tasks in the expanding cloth industries of Italy. This shameful traffic in human beings also fueled the growth of capitalism.

To facilitate expanding and increasingly long-distance trade, banking operations had to be expanded and modernized. Bills of exchange and other written instruments of credit, together with more stable currencies such as the gold florin of Florence and the ducat of rich Venice, all helped increase long-distance trade. Florence became the banking capital of Europe as eighty banking houses were located there by 1338. Florentine trading houses such as the Bardi and Peruzzi used their banking operations to enhance trade and make easy profits on exchange rates. Pope Boniface VIII used Bardi banks for collecting papal taxes and transmitting money to Rome from all over Europe. Florentine bankers also loaned large sums of money to the crowned heads of Europe, sometimes to their financial peril.

JACOB FUGGER THE RICH (1459–1525)

What the Italians mastered, other Europeans emulated. Great financial centers such as Antwerp, Amsterdam, London, and Paris emerged in the north of Europe. In the Holy Roman Empire, the mighty banking empire of Jacob Fugger the Rich became the major bankroll behind Emperor Maximilian I. Fugger was a member of a prominent Augsburg banking family; his mother, Barbara (d. 1497) was one of the leading businesswomen of the period. Jacob had studied bookkeeping and business in Venice as a youth as families involved in international business typically sent their sons to work abroad. This allowed them to expand their horizons and learn foreign business tech-

Portrait engraving of Jacob Fugger. Bibliotheque Nationale, Paris, France. Giraudon/Art Resource.

niques, customs, currencies, and languages. Business was not studied in schools but learned on the job. In 1485 Jacob took charge of a Fugger branch bank in Innsbruck, Austria and made several successful ventures into the growing mining industry in the Tyrolian Alps. By 1502, after extending the family's mining interests into Hungary and Silesia, he became the virtual head of the Fugger family business. The Habsburgs, whose loans Fugger shrewdly secured by a claim against the royal salt mines, were among his most notable customers.

Amazingly successful, Jacob the Rich's motto was "I shall gain while I am able." To do that, Fugger not only loaned money to powerful princes at a high rate of interest, but he also involved his firm in the new East India spice trade opened up by the recent voyages of discovery. He also hired theologians such as Dr. Johann Eck of Ingolstadt to write defenses of usury. It was Jacob Fugger who loaned Albrecht of Brandenburg the 29,000 gulden necessary to secure the archbishopric of Mainz, which triggered Martin Luther's famous protests against the sale of indulgences. Fugger also helped secure Charles V's election as Holy Roman Emperor in 1519 by loaning him 544,000 gulden in bribe money. Jacob the Rich also used some of his wealth to found the Fuggerei in Augsburg, the world's first housing project for poor and retired workers. Towns all over Europe could only dream of having families like the Fuggers in their midst. Capitalists with or without consciences were here to stay.

MUSLIMS

Added to the social mix of some sixteenth-century communities were a small number of religious and ethnic minorities. It should be remembered that the overwhelming majority of Europe's people at the beginning of the sixteenth century were Roman Catholics. Orthodox Christians, who used either the Greek or the Slovonic rites, were a minority in the eastern parts of Europe. People thought of themselves not as Europeans but as part of the body of Christ (Christendom). Diversity in religion was not tolerated in very many parts of Christian Europe. Muslims predominated only in southern Spain until the fall of their last major stronghold, Granada, in 1492 to the armies of Isabella of Castile (1451–1504), the pious warrior-queen. By 1500 Spain was still unique in Europe, with a sizeable Muslim population of about one quarter of a million people.

After a period of initial toleration, Queen Isabella found herself under intense pressure to end religious pluralism. For many prominent Christians, those who kept other religious traditions were in danger of losing their immortal souls and infecting those around them. There was doubtless also a great deal of Christian jealousy about the sophisticated business and medical practices of a number of the Muslims. Therefore, the only allowed option for the thousands of Spanish Muslims was to convert to Christianity or leave the Iberian peninsula. Thousands converted but even more surrendered their property and fled to various places in Europe, Africa, and the Middle East often with dire consequences.

Although Islam was severely reduced in what became the Spanish kingdom, it grew apace on Europe's eastern flank after the Ottoman conquest of Constantinople, or Byzantium, in 1453. Sultan Mehmed II (r. 1451–1481) used cannons to breach the huge sea walls which protected the mighty city on the straits. Known to contemporaries for his intellectual curiosity, Mehmed then advanced to besiege Athens, which fell in 1456. His forces then moved on to conquer the rest of Greece and pushed on up the Balkans to take Serbia, Bosnia, Herzegovina, and Albania while spreading Islam in their wake.

After a period of consolidation and expansion to the east against the Persians, the Ottomans renewed their war of conquest against the Christian West under the leadership of the poetry-writing Sultan Süleyman I (r. 1520–1566), the Lawgiver. Süleyman's great armies took Belgrade in 1521, crushed the Hungarians in central Hungary in 1526, and threatened Vienna in 1529. Had well-fortified Vienna fallen, it is hard to imagine any force in Europe strong enough to resist the Ottomans. In fact, the Ottomans would have been an even greater threat had their feudal officers not found it necessary to return periodically to their home estates

Gentile Bellini, *Sultan Mehmed II Fahti, "The Conqueror"* (c. 1479–1481). National Gallery, London, Great Britain. Erich Lessing/Art Resource.

around Constantinople (now known as Istanbul). Such sudden departures by many members of the officer corps made sustaining lengthy sieges and campaigns difficult. Sultan Süleyman also worried about the effects of European winters on his beloved herds of cavalry horses. Nevertheless, his western campaigns permanently established Islam in the Balkans.

SLAVES FROM AFRICA AND THE LEVANT

In addition to Muslims, Europe's minority populations also included Africans of various religious and tribal backgrounds, who served primarily as domestic slaves in prosperous homes in Italy during the fifteenth century with the beginning of the Portuguese black slave trade in West Africa. Captured Africans as well as Tartars and Turks from the Levant were sold at the slave markets in Ancona, Genoa, Pisa, and Venice. It is difficult to determine how much cultural influence they exerted on their masters, but some cross-cultural stimulation was inevitable. Black faces fascinated a number of Renaissance artists including Albrecht Dürer. Merchants from Africa had appeared in England by the 1550s. William Shakespeare's play *Othello* uses black-white relations and racial prejudice as powerful themes.

   During the sixteenth century the supply of domestic slaves in Italy was sharply reduced by rising costs and the growing domination of the Ottomans, who fought to gain control of the slave markets. Slaves and prisoners continued to row galleys that plied the Mediterranean, although most rowers were free men. Domestic slavery did not develop in other parts of Europe in part because of the abundance of poorly paid workers, but became a major part of the growing slave trade to the "New World" of

Albrecht Dürer, *Head of a Black* (1508). Charcoal drawing, Graphisches Sammlung Albertina, Vienna, Austria. Foto Marburg/Art Resource.

the Americas. There slave labor came to be in great demand.

JEWS

Europe also had a small Jewish population in the sixteenth century despite periodic waves of expulsions, forced conversions, and judicial murder. Although often placed under the protection of a ruling prince, Jews were prohibited from owning land in most parts of Europe and barred from many other occupations. They worked for the most part as butchers, bookbinders, domestic workers, notaries, scribes, itinerant peddlers, money lenders, pawnbrokers, and physicians. Given the many restrictions under which Jews lived, they played only a minor part in the economy.

During the fourteenth century, Jewish communities were often blamed for such great disasters as the Black Death (1347–1350). Looking for scapegoats, some Christians accused their Jewish neighbors of poisoning wells and spreading the plague in other ways. Actually the Jews had nothing to do with the spread of the various epidemics that killed almost a third of the population of Europe in less than three years. As we shall see in the next chapter, the various epidemics that made up the Black Death were spread mostly by germs that lived on fleas, which were hosted by black Asian rats. This was, of course, not understood by people in the fourteenth century, most of whom thought God was punishing them for their sins. As a vulnerable minority, Jews were sometimes unjustly blamed for spreading the plague, allegedly by poisoning wells. Therefore, Europe's Jews in many places suffered waves of terror in the fourteenth century, which further reduced their population.

At the end of the fifteenth century, Jews in Castile and Aragon were forced to convert to Christianity or to leave. Thousands converted but continued to be treated with great suspicion and suffered waves of persecution as "New Christians." Others risked everything to migrate to Africa, the Middle East, and other parts of Europe, especially Italy. Many Jews and "New Christians" were the victims of the notorious Spanish Inquisition. Ritual public burnings of Jews in Spain continued until late in the seventeenth century with a particularly elaborate *auto de fé* held in Madrid's "Theater of Blood" in 1680. Portugal in 1496 under King Joao also forced its Jewish population to convert to Christianity or to flee. By 1517 Jews had been almost completely driven out of Spain and southern Italy.

During the sixteenth century, Jews had made something of a comeback in other parts of Europe, although they still made up less than 1 percent of the Continent's population. Even the largest known Jewish communities outside Italy, such as those in Prague and Vienna, did not number more than 500 to 700 members. Most others were considerably smaller. Some large towns such as Nuremberg had no Jewish citizens in the sixteenth century. Nuremberg had been given permission to expel its Jews in 1498 by Emperor Maximilian I (r. 1493–1519). Some of those driven from Nuremberg moved only a few miles away to the smaller town of Fürth, but their synagogue on the city's market square was torn down and replaced with a church dedicated to the Virgin Mary. Maximilian's grandson and successor, Charles V (r. 1519–1555), inspired by the Renaissance humanists, took a more benevolent attitude toward the empire's Jews. He was also impressed by the eloquence of Rabbi Joseph of Rosheim from Alsace. Emperor Charles did allow a few persecutions in the Holy Roman Empire, but conditions for Jews gradually improved throughout much of the empire and in Europe as a whole during the later part of the sixteenth century despite the scorn and neglect of the predominantly Christian society.

The Nobility

Although some rich city folk claimed to be noble, they were generally looked down upon by the remnants of the old feudal nobility or, as contemporaries viewed it, "those who fight." For the most part, the "nobles of the sword," who made up the second estate, were in relative decline for much of the later part of the Renaissance. Their landed estates did not produce as much wealth as could be secured from international trade by merchants and bankers. Some nobles tried to expand their incomes by changing the forms of peasant obligations, substituting cash for customary services, for example. These so-called commutations helped to free up peasant living conditions to a degree, but they failed to make some of the lesser nobility feel more economically secure.

Innovations in warfare had made the nobility as the major source of military strength largely obsolete even as early as the fourteenth century. Longbows and gunpowder made knights in shining armor a thing of the past, except for the tournaments, which continued to flourish until King Henri II of France died after receiving a fragment of a shattered lance in the eye during a joust in 1559. The premature death of this chivalrous king had a chilling effect on the noble sport of tournament jousting, which began to fall out of fashion in respectable circles.

MERCENARY AND ROBBER NOBLES

To meet rising expenses, some nobles were reduced to the role of mercenaries—hired paladins at the beck and call of the highest bidder. Although some such as Federigo da Montefeltro (1422–1482) of Urbino were honest, pious, and highly cultivated, others lapsed into thuggery or worse. Sigismondo Malatesta (c. 1417–1468), ruler of Rimini, was convicted of murder, rape, wife beating, sacrilege, perjury, incest, and adultery. Yet he was also an important patron of art and scholarship. Trained to kill from their early youth, it is not surprising that some nobles resorted to crime and robbery. Gangs of noble thugs and their armed retainers attacked merchant caravans moving from town to town.

One such robber knight was Götz von Berlichingen (c. 1480–1562). Götz was born to a German noble family and took service at the court of the margrave of Brandenburg-Ansbach. In 1504 he lost his right hand in combat in the War of the Bavarian Succession. Berlichingen hired a craftsperson to make him an iron hand, which he used to strike terror into the hearts of his enemies. Those enemies came to include the prosperous citizens of towns such as Bamberg, Mainz, and Nuremberg, whose merchant caravans he plundered for many years. In 1519 he fought as a mercenary for Duke Ulrich of Württemberg. Six years later, Berlichingen lowered himself socially by fighting for cash on the side of rebellious peasants, but deserted them in time to avoid being destroyed by their defeat in the summer of 1525.

Although placed under imperial ban as an outlaw on four occasions and jailed twice, Berlichingen fought for Emperor Charles V against the Ottomans in 1542 and against the French in 1544. Robber knights like Berlichingen often had family and friends in high places and were difficult to suppress. As much as princes might decry robber barony, they still needed skilled warriors to make up their officer corps.

THE REFINEMENT OF MANNERS

Those nobles of the higher strata who stayed out of trouble and had sufficient revenues saw their lifestyles improve in the course of the Renaissance. Castles became better heated and more luxuriously furnished and much better designed. Country estates came to be surrounded by lovely gardens, stocked fishponds, and ample facilities for leisure. During the sixteenth century, the nobility of Europe withdrew more and more from their contact with the lower orders. They stopped eating with their retainers in great halls and withdrew into separate dining rooms. Nobles in Lombardy stopped wrestling with their peasants and stopped killing bulls in public in Spain.

To further set themselves apart, nobles learned to talk and behave in a more formal and self-conscious style. Manners improved and became more refined as more was expected of the nobility than just skill in combat. Baldassare Castiglione's 1527 *Book of the Courtier* set new standards for noble behavior. To succeed at court, noblemen were expected by the humanist and former diplomat Castiglione (1478–1529) to be able to dance, play games, ride, recite and understand poetry, speak clearly, and give good advice. As for the noblewomen of the court, according to Castiglione:

> I wish this Lady to have knowledge of letters, of music, of painting, and know how to dance and how to be festive, adding a discrete modesty and the giving of a good impression of herself to those other things that have required of the Courtier.[4]

Noblewomen of all ranks were responsible for producing meals, supervising servants, and doing all sorts of needlework.

Although the nobility of Renaissance Europe may have been in a state of relative and gradual decline, overall it was a most privileged elite. Its male members especially had an enviable existence. After all, the nobility was still at the top of the social heap. Those at the top of the top were part of the extended family of the crowned heads of Europe. They held vast amounts of lands and had many privileges. Nobles had virtual monopolies on the best offices in the royal governments and in the military. Some received generous pensions from the crown. Noble sons and daughters received preferential treatment in the church and, like the clergy, the nobility in many places enjoyed widespread exemption from direct taxes. While revenues from lands may have failed

to keep pace with inflation in the sixteenth century, it is still important to remember that the nobility, which made up only about 2 percent of the population of Europe, controlled as much as half of the best land in many areas. So even though their incomes in many cases may have been falling during the period, they were still among the wealthiest people in Europe, and many rich commoners were eager to marry their daughters into the ranks of the nobility or to be made "noble" by royal favor.

Although it was difficult even for a rich commoner to secure a patent of nobility, many prosperous merchants attempted to imitate noble lifestyles. The sons of the merchant elite as well as the nobility enjoyed hunting, dancing, jousting, and feasting. Merchants also emulated the social pretensions of the nobility. Indeed, with their sumptuous meals of meat soup, boiled beef, roasted mutton, capons fattened on oats, pigeon, fresh or salted fish, white bread, jams, juices, gravies, fruits, vegetables, and cheeses, all washed down by beer or watered wine, there was a great deal in a typical noble's gastronomic life to be envied.

Noblewomen, while hardly creatures of total leisure, still had much better lives than those below them, especially if their fathers and husbands were kind, something that could never be taken for granted. As with the women of other social groups, noble females were brought up to expect a far different destiny from noble males. Their lives would revolve around family and domestic life. Some would go into the church as "brides of Christ." All women were taught that they held lower status than the males, for as the popular saying expressed it, "He is the sun and she is the moon."

Everyone in the nobility and the upper ranks of the merchant elite seemed to dress very sumptuously indeed when compared to the peasantry. Furs and fine fabrics, even-

Limbourg, *Month of March, Ploughing the Field*. Manuscript illumination from the *Trés Riches Heures du Duc de Berry*. Musée Conde, Chantilly, France. Giraudon/Art Resource.

tually including silk, made the "men in tights" (actually hose) of the era and their sumptuously clad and bejeweled ladies of lace and brocade appear to be figures worlds apart from the woolen-clad poor people who surrounded them and even the armies of servants who cooked for them and waited upon them. Clearly, the nobility of Europe were a privileged elite who often loved to display their power, status, and wealth in increasingly conspicuous consumption. Their "honor" demanded no less of them.

The Clergy

Also set apart from the roughly clad hordes of poor working people were the members of the first estate—the clergy—"those who pray." They were first, theoretically, in the medieval social hierarchy because they were considered to be closest to God. They were to pray, dispense charity, do good works, and sacrifice worldly pleasures for the sake of everyone's salvation. Therefore, they, like some in the second estate, were exempted from taxation by the state. They had their own legal code (canon law) and court system, which punished clerics less severely than secular courts punished the laity for similar crimes. Only the celebrant could receive both the cup and the bread during the Eucharist, among other signs of God's favor. The clergy made up 2 to 4 percent of the population at the beginning of the sixteenth century. This made them a relatively large group of privileged people in a culture where most people had little except hard work and deprivation. Like the laity, the clergy were divided along class lines. While those at the higher levels had large incomes, many priests, especially those in rural parishes, were paid very poorly.

The clergy were made up of two main groups: the secular clergy, or those who were in the world, and the regular clergy, who followed a religious rule and were either cloistered monks or worked among the laity as friars. The clergy was technically a male monopoly; women were not candidates for ordination. Even cloistered nuns had to receive the sacraments from males. The higher ranks of the secular clergy administered the church's elaborate sacramental system: baptism, confirmation, penance, the eucharist, ordination (for the clergy only), marriage (for the laity only), and final rites. The seven sacraments were considered outward signs of God's favor and were essential in order to achieve salvation. They helped instill a feeling of God's presence in the world and bound people of all stations into a sacred community of believers throughout the European world. They provided important rites of passage for all stages of a Christian's life on earth. The Latin of the Roman church and the Greek and Slovonic of the Orthodox church exposed Christians to common religious languages and rituals, which further enhanced the feeling of community for the majority who accepted the tradition. There were also those who secretly rejected many aspects of the church's tradition, but they were usually in the minority and ran great risks.

The secular clergy consisted of two groups: an upper and a lower clergy. The upper clergy was made up of priests and bishops. By the Renaissance, deacons and subdeacons were considered steps toward the priesthood. The lower clergy, or those in minor orders, consisted of doorkeepers, acolytes, lectors, and exorcists. The lower clergy were not often scrutinized carefully upon entrance and not bound by a permanent commitment to celibacy. Many in fact were married. They were set off from the world by their haircut (tonsure), which was short with a bald spot at the back of their heads. Members of the lower clergy could leave minor orders simply by growing their hair out. If they stayed in the service of the church, they shared in many of the clergy's privileges such as the right to be tried for crimes in church rather than in secular courts.

Much more was expected of the higher grades of the secular clergy than from those in the lower ranks. They were to be recognized by their tonsure and sober clothing. Since the eleventh century the church frowned upon sexual activity carried out by members of the higher clergy. Candidates for the priesthood were to be at least twenty-five years old, unmarried, of good moral character, educated, and have a reliable means of support. Those who lacked a church job of sufficient income could earn additional revenue in an "honorable profession" such as that of teacher or chaplain. All these requirements could be waived or ignored by securing a papal dispensation. Married priests or priests with concubines could still be found, especially in rural parishes.

The regular clergy followed such monastic rules as poverty, chastity, obedience, and humility. Some lived in cloistered religious communities behind walls away from the hustle and bustle of the workaday world. There they could experience lives of quiet devotion with usually seven occasions for prayer throughout the day from early in the morning to sunset. There was also time for study and manual work. This life was open to both men and women, although male houses always outnumbered female, and convents required male clerics to say

Mass. Monks and friars were tonsured and wore distinctive clothing from the black robes of the Augustinian friars to the white robes of the Cistercian monks. Nuns also had short hair and wore distinctive habits and head coverings, which visibly separated them from their lay sisters. Convents were the only places where European women in significant numbers could utilize fully their intellectual and administrative gifts. Intellectually inclined male clerics not only had their monasteries but also the universities, which excluded women with only a few rare exceptions.

Although membership in the religious orders was theoretically open to all, men and women from rich families dominated their ranks. Most monastic houses for women required a form of dowry or deposit. In fifteenth-century Florence, the average deposit for future nuns was 435 florins (more than sixteen times what the average journeyman made in a year). While it was still usually less expensive to become "a bride of Christ" than to marry a mortal man, convents were havens for the daughters of the privileged. Male clergy also came predominantly from the ranks of the nobility and the patriciate. Some came by choice, whereas others were sent into the church in order to avoid dividing inheritances or straining family resources.

Most clerics seemed to have kept their vows despite the popularity of stories of lascivious monks, friars, nuns, and priests written by writers such as Giovanni Boccaccio (1313–1375) in his *Decameron Tales,* Geoffrey Chaucer (c. 1340–1400) in his *Canterbury Tales,* and Marguerite of Navarre (1492–1549) in her *Heptameron.* Regional studies have indicated that 80 to 90 percent of the clergy in 1500 remained continent. The lifestyles of the clergy varied enormously from begging friars and monastic houses that practiced severe discipline and where food was modest, to Chaucer's drawn-from-life "regal" prioress, who ate "so primly and so well." Those at the top of the clerical hierarchy such as bishops, cardinals, and popes lived in splendor comparable to the great secular lords whose refined manners they emulated. The princes of the church were also waited upon by hosts of servants. Although the church had its share of problems, as we shall see, the surviving records indicate that the overwhelming majority of the sixteenth-century clergy lived lives of relative holiness despite the envy of some laity, who were all too willing to believe the worst of the first estate.

Further Reading

GENERAL SOCIAL HISTORY

Peter Burke, *Popular Culture in Early Modern Europe* (1978).

Roger Chartier, ed., *Passions of the Renaissance* (1989).

Natalie Davis, *Society and Culture in Early Modern France* (1975). A collection of her essays.

Lucien Febvre, *Life in Renaissance France.* Ed. and trans. by Marian Rothstein (1977).

Carlo Ginzburg, *The Cheese and the Worms: The Cosmos of a Sixteenth-Century Miller.* Trans. by John and Anne Tedeschi (1982).

George Huppert, *After the Black Death: A Social History of Early Modern Europe* (1986). An extremely valuable synthesis.

Henry Kamen, *The Iron Century: Social Change in Europe, 1550–1660* (1971). Still a valuable survey.

THE PEASANTRY

Wilhelm Abel, *Agricultural Fluctuations in Europe: From the Thirteenth to the Twentieth Centuries* (1980).

Andrew Appleby, *Famine in Tudor and Stuart England* (1978).

Natalie Davis, *The Return of Martin Guerre* (1983). A fascinating true story of a peasant imposter.

Jan de Vries, *The Dutch Rural Economy in the Golden Age, 1500–1700* (1974).

Emmanuel Le Roy Ladurie, *Montaillou: The Promised Land of Error* (1978). An intriguing account of life and heresy in a fourteenth-century French village.

———, *The French Peasantry, 1450–1660* (1987).

———, *The Peasants of Languedoc* (1969).

Thomas Robisheaux, *Rural Society and the Search for Order in Early Modern Germany* (1989).

David Warren Sabean, *Power in the Blood: Popular Culture and Village Discourse in Early Modern Germany* (1984).

Richard Wunderli, *Peasant Fires: The Drummer of Niklashausen* (1991).

WOMEN AND GENDER

Bonnie Anderson and Judith Zinsser, *A History of Their Own: Women in Europe from Prehistory to the Present.* 2 vols. (1988). Although a general survey, it has a great deal to say about women in the Renaissance period.

Natalie Zemon Davis and Arlette Farge, eds., *A History of Women in the West*, vol. 3, *Renaissance and Enlightenment Paradoxes* (1993). Seventeen very important essays.

Barbara Hanawalt, ed., *Women and Work in Preindustrial Europe* (1986). Ten significant essays.

Constance Jordan, *Renaissance Feminism: Literary Texts and Political Models* (1990).

Margaret King, *The Death of the Child Valerio Marcello* (1994).

———, *Women of the Renaissance* (1991). A very important overview with particular attention given to women in Italy.

Thomas Kuehn, *Law, Family, and Women: Toward a Legal Anthropology of Renaissance Italy* (1991).

Gerda Lerner, *The Creation of Feminist Consciousness* (1993).

Ian MacLean, *The Renaissance Notion of Woman* (1980).

Marilyn Migiel and Julianna Schiesa, eds., *Refiguring Woman: Perspectives on Gender and the Italian Renaissance* (1991). A collection of diverse essays.

Merry Wiesner, *Women and Gender in Early Modern Europe* (1993). A fine survey.

———, *Women in the Sixteenth Century: A Bibliography* (1983).

———, *Working Women in Renaissance Germany* (1986).

JEWS

Salo Baron, *A Social and Religious History of the Jews*, 2nd ed. 14 vols. (1952–1969).

Robert Bonfil, *Jewish Life in Renaissance Italy* (1994).

R. Po-chia Hsia, *The Myth of Ritual Murder: Jews and Magic in Reformation Germany* (1988).

———, *Trent 1475: Stories of a Ritual Murder Trial* (1992).

R. Po-chia Hsia and Hartmut Lehman, *In and Out of the Ghetto: Jewish-Gentile Relations in Late Medieval and Early Modern Germany* (1994).

Jonathan Israel, *European Jewry in the Age of Mercantilism, 1550–1750* (1985).

Heiko Oberman, *The Roots of Anti-Semitism* (1981).

Brian Pullan, *The Jews of Europe and the Inquisition of Venice, 1550–1670* (1983).

Raymond Waddington and Arthur Williamson, eds., *The Expulsion of the Jews: 1492 and After* (1994). Important essays.

AFRICANS AND OTTOMANS

Franz Babinger, *Mehmed the Conqueror and His Time* (1992).

Stanford Shaw, *Empire of the Gazis: The Rise and Decline of the Ottoman Empire, 1280–1808* (1976).

John Thornton, *Africa and Africans in the Making of the Atlantic World, 1400–1680* (1992).

Andrew Wheatcroft, *The Ottomans* (1994).

URBAN LIFE

Robin Briggs, *Communities of Belief: Cultural and Social Tensions in Early Modern France* (1989).

James Farr, *Hands of Honor: Artisans and Their World in Dijon, 1550–1650* (1988).

Barbara Hanawalt, *Growing Up in Medieval London: The Experience of Childhood in History* (1993).

Lewis Mumford, *The City in History* (1961).

Gerald Strauss, *Nuremberg in the Sixteenth Century* (1976).

Lee Palmer Wandel, *Always Among Us: Images of the Poor in Zwingli's Zurich* (1990).

THE CAPITALISTS

Janet Abu-Lughad, *Before European Hegemony: The World System 1250–1350* (1989).

Felix Gilbert, *The Pope, His Banker, and Venice* (1980).

Harry Miskimim, *The Economy of Early Renaissance Europe, 1300–1460* (1975).

Raymond De Roover, *The Rise and Decline of the Medici Bank, 1397–1494* (1966).

THE NOBILITY

Davis Bitton, *The French Nobility in Crisis, 1560–1640* (1969).

Jonathan Dewald, *The European Nobility, 1400–1800* (1996).

Kristin Neuschal, *Word of Honor: Interpreting Noble Culture in Sixteenth-Century France* (1989).

Ellery Schalk, *From Valor to Pedigree: Ideas of Nobility in France in the Sixteenth and Seventeenth Centuries* (1986).

Lawrence Stone, *The Crisis of the Aristocracy, 1558–1641* (1965).

THE CLERGY

John Bossy, *Christianity in the West: 1400–1700* (1985).

K. J. P. Lowe, *Church and Politics in Renaissance Italy: The Life and Career of Cardinal Francesco Soderini (1453–1524)* (1993).

Joseph Lynch, *The Medieval Church: A Brief History* (1992).

Francis Oakley, *The Western Church in the Late Middle Ages* (1979).

Paolo Prodi, *The Papal Prince. One Body and Two Souls: The Papal Monarchy in Early Modern Europe* (1982).

R. W. Swanson, *Religion and Devotion in Europe, c. 1215–c. 1515* (1995).

Larissa Taylor, *Soldiers of Christ: Preaching in Late Medieval and Reformation France* (1992).

Thomas Tentler, *Sin and Confession on the Eve of the Reformation* (1977).

John Thomson, *Politics and Princes 1417–1517: Politics and Polity in the Late Medieval Church* (1980).

Notes

1. Cited in Bonnie Anderson and Judith Zinsser, *A History of Their Own: Women in Europe from Prehistory to the Present*, 2 vols. (New York: Harper, 1988), vol. 1, p. 88.
2. Cited in Jonathan W. Zophy, *Patriarchal Politics and Christoph Kress (1484–1535) of Nuremberg* (Lewiston, N.Y.: Edwin Mellen Press, 1992), p. 41.
3. Ibid., p. 39.
4. Castiglione, *The Book of the Courtier.* Trans. by George Bull (Baltimore, Md.: Penguin, 1967), p. 216.

3

An Age of Disasters

The Renaissance was born against the background of one of the most catastrophic periods in all of human history. It was an age of almost incessant warfare, most notably the so-called Hundred Years' War between the English and French kingdoms, which actually dragged on for 116 years (1337–1453). That frequently horrific conflict was followed for the English by a civil war—the so-called War of the Roses (1455–1485). As if these wars were not enough tragedy, Europe also witnessed the even greater catastrophe of the Black Death (1347–1350). For nearly three years highly contagious and often fatal plagues ravaged the entire continent and killed almost a third of the European people. Although bubonic and pneumonic plagues would continue to afflict the Europeans until well into the eighteenth century, the worst of them hit the Europeans in the fourteenth century. Warfare and plague were accompanied by widespread outbreaks of famine and large-scale peasant rebellions in Flanders (1323–1328), France (1358), and England (1381).

Some viewed the plagues as God's judgment on a sinful world; others, however, were more concerned with the troubles in the Western church, particularly those involving what the early humanist Francesco Petrarca dubbed the "Babylonian Captivity of the Church of God" (1305–1376). This was the period when the headquarters of the Roman Catholic Church were moved from Rome to Avignon, a smaller town near the French kingdom. The Captivity was followed by the Great Western Schism (1378–1417) in which the Catholic Church had two and sometimes three popes: usually one pope sat in Rome and another sat in Avignon. These difficulties helped fuel an increase in questioning of church doctrine and practice and led to what some viewed as *heresy* (the denial of accepted doctrine, which was considered a form of treason against God). The ideas and lives of such fourteenth-century thinkers as John Wycliffe in England, Jan Hus in Bohemia, and Marsilius of Padua presented a serious challenge to the authorities of the Western church. The beginnings of the Renaissance as a cultural movement, indeed, took place during one of the most difficult periods in Western history.

The Black Death, 1347–1350

Of all the disasters to afflict Europe in the fourteenth century, the most lethal was the widespread outbreak of plague in Europe between 1347 and 1350. Called the Black Death by later historians, the era of plague epidemics began in the winter of 1347 and 1348 with the arrival of rat-infested merchant ships from the East. Those ships appear to have carried infected black rats, which in turn hosted parasitic fleas. The newly arrived rats mixed with local rodent

Congested urban centers such as Florence were particularly vulnerable, especially if they were involved in the rat-infested grain trade. Some areas were completely bypassed by the plagues, whereas others lost as much as half of their populations in less than three years. All told, the population of Europe declined by a third during the peak period of the Black Death.

Young children, the elderly, the sickly, and the undernourished were the hardest hit, but even some among the rich and powerful fell victim to the plagues that ravaged Europe. Those courageous priests who administered last rites to plague victims and medical personnel were also at special risk. Towns and families were ripped apart by the plague. The chronicler Agnolo di Tura described the horrors of the plague, which ravaged his hometown in 1348 as follows:

> . . . the victims died almost immediately. They would swell beneath their armpits and in their groins, and fall over while talking. Father abandoned child, wife husband, one brother another. . . . And none could be found to bury the dead for money or friendship. . . . And in many places in Siena great pits were dug and piled deep with the multitude of the dead. . . . I buried my five children with my own hands.[1]

Europeans were overwhelmed by the magnitude of the disaster. Many attributed the plagues to the anger of God, who was punishing his children for their sins. Some went around in bands flagellating themselves and each other. Others used such traditional scapegoats as the Jews, who were thought to have spread the plague by poisoning wells. Still others blamed cats, dogs, and pigs and ordered their destruction. Ironically, these creatures were enemies of the real culprits, the flea-infested black rats.

Gradually more and more surviving Europeans built up their immunities to the

Albrecht Dürer, *Knight, Death, and the Devil* (1513). Engraving. Foto Marburg / Art Resource.

populations. Fleas would then jump onto humans and animals and infect them with *bubonic plague*. When persons with respiratory infections contracted bubonic plague, they often became ill with a form of *pneumonic plague* as well. Recently some scholars have argued that anthrax, a highly contagious and lethal disease caused by spore-forming bacteria, was a major contributor to the Black Death. Anthrax can easily be transmitted from warm-blooded animals such as rats to humans.

Although no exact diagnosis is possible, it is quite clear that the various forms of plague spread rapidly from the Mediterranean ports throughout much of Europe. A series of mild, damp winters also helped keep the fleas and their host animals active.

plague germs and instances of the plague died out by 1350, but returned from 1361 to 1362, hitting children born after the first wave of plague especially hard. The plague struck again in 1369, 1374 to 1375, 1379, 1390, 1407, and throughout much of the remainder of the Renaissance period. Although later outbreaks were never as lethal as the first waves of the plague in 1348 and 1349, Europe would not be free of the plague until the introduction of brown rats into Europe in the eighteenth century. Short nosed, short tailed, and ferocious, the brown rats waged war on the black rats and virtually wiped them out. Because brown rats do not provide suitable hosts for the plague-bearing fleas and lice, the contagion lost its chief means of spreading. In addition, over time immunities had been built up in the human population; therefore, plague stopped being a widespread problem in Europe after the eighteenth century.

During the Renaissance, however, the repeated bouts of plague left indelible scars on the minds of Europeans. Their grief at losing so many people and expensive farm animals in so short a time was overwhelming. Instead of having a surplus of laborers, many villages were deserted; parts of cities were abandoned for almost a century. Some peasants attempted to take advantage of the situation to claim abandoned lands and to have their wages increased. Landlords attempted to artificially hold down wages. In England, for example, the Statute of Laborers of 1351 tried to freeze wages to pre-plague levels. Such measures angered peasants and were not always effective because some landlords were willing to pay wages above those dictated by law. Some of the landlords were proceeded against by the newly created chancellor's court, designed to close loopholes in the common law and compel obedience by the lower orders. The upper classes banded together to protect their privileges in the great crisis produced by the Black Death in England.

Some English landowners also decided to convert their fields to sheep runs and enter the lucrative wool trade. Because sheep farming is not as labor intensive as farming, such enclosures resulted in many peasant families in England being driven off the land, a situation that worsened during the late Renaissance. Enclosures only added to the unrest of people in the English countryside who were still trying to recover from the ravages of the Black Death. In other parts of Europe, some rural workers were displaced because of an increased shift to cash crops such as honey and wine production.

Peasant and Artisan Revolts

The Black Death also contributed to the rise of rural and urban violence. Ravaged by plague, depression, and mercenary marauders unleashed by the Hundred Years' War between France and England, elements of the French peasantry rebelled in 1358. Since so many peasant males were named Jacques, the insurrection in northern France was dubbed the "Jacquerie." For two weeks French peasants struck at the ruling elite. During one particularly savage episode, a noblewoman was forced to eat her roasted husband before being raped and killed. The nobility and urban elites then crushed the uprising with ferocious brutality.

Similar peasant rebellions also took place in parts of the Holy Roman Empire, Flanders, Italy, the Iberian peninsula, the Netherlands, and England. During the English Peasants' Revolt of 1381, an attempt was made to cast aside the last vestiges of serfdom. Some blamed the Oxford professor and church reformer John Wycliffe for contributing to the unrest by challenging the authority and wealth of the church. Some of his followers, called Lollards, insisted on using Wycliffe's English translation of the Bible and questioning injustices in both the church and the state. At one point in the 1381 rebellion, rebels paraded around London with the severed head of the archbishop of Canterbury. This rebellion, called the Wat Tyler Revolt after one of its leaders, was also put down with great savagery.

The plagues added to the considerable social tensions already present in some towns. People from plague-ravaged villages drifted into towns but were not always able to find work. Because the Black Death disrupted trade in many parts of Europe, unemployment levels were higher than usual. Guilds often overreacted to the crisis by making even greater than normal restrictions on employment and more jealously guarding their monopolies. Many guilds now made inheritance the only avenue to shop ownership. Recession, unemployment, poverty, tensions between factions, guild rivalries, struggles for power, and sometimes petty jealousies all contributed to outbreaks of urban violence in places such as Nuremberg (1348–1349), Lucca (1369), Siena (1371), Perugia (1370–1371, 1375), Florence (1378), and Bologna (1411).

Troubles in the Church

No segment of European society or institution was safe from unrest in the fourteenth century, not even the great papal monarchy that was the Roman Catholic Church. In the course of the Middle Ages the Western church had become one of the grandest monarchies in Europe. Talented canon-lawyer popes such as Gregory VII (r. 1073–1085) and Innocent III (r. 1198–1216) had developed a doctrine known as the "fullness of power" (*plenitudo potestatis*) ac-

cording to which the bishop of Rome had absolute authority over the church. The pope was not only the successor to Christ's great disciple St. Peter as the supreme spiritual head of the church and the representative (vicar) of Christ on earth but also the supreme administrator, lawgiver, and judge. These pretensions had, of course, been challenged by Holy Roman emperors among others during the reigns of Pope Gregory VII and Pope Innocent III. Still, aggressive popes had come to be recognized as formidable monarchs, who, in some cases, could overawe secular kings and emperors.

THE BABYLONIAN CAPTIVITY, 1305–1376

In 1294 the sacred college of cardinals found itself deadlocked between rival candidates for the papacy from the influential Roman families of the Colonna and the Orsini. Indeed, the cardinals had been deadlocked for eighteen months since the death of Pope Nicholas IV in 1292. Neither faction would agree to support the opposition's candidate. A division of the church (schism) seemed imminent. Peter Morone, a well-known Benedictine hermit in his eighties, sent the cardinals a stern letter warning them that divine vengeance would soon fall upon them if they did not elect a pope soon. In desperation the ailing and aged dean of the college of cardinals, Latino Malabranca, cried out, "In the name of the Father, the Son, and the Holy Ghost, I elect brother Peter of Morone!"[2]

The exhausted cardinals ratified Malabranca's inspired decision, and the venerable hermit became Pope Celestine V. Unfortunately, Celestine soon found that life as pope was not conducive to the quiet, spiritual life he craved. Even though he refused to move to congested Rome, Celestine ordered a special wooden cell to be built at the papal castle in Naples, so he could attempt to hide from the worldly cardinals, papal officials, and hordes of office seekers who made up the papal court. Miserable as pope, Celestine turned for advice to Benedict Gaetani, an accomplished canonist at the papal court and one of the cardinals who had elected him. The ambitious and oily Gaetani suggested that Celestine resign, which he agreed to do a mere fifteen weeks after his coronation.

Ten days after Celestine's abdication of December 13, the college of cardinals met again in Naples and elected Benedict Gaetani as pope. He took the name of Boniface VIII (r. 1294–1303), moved the papacy back to Rome, tried to increase papal revenues, and attempted to further develop the doctrine of the "fullness of power." In 1296 he found himself in a quarrel with King Philip IV, "the Handsome," of France (r. 1285–1314) and King Edward I (r. 1272–1307) of England. Philip and Edward had begun to tax their clergy without papal consent in order to pay for a war against each other. Incensed, Pope Boniface issued the bull *Clericis laicos*, which forbade taxation of the clergy without papal approval and threatened both kings with excommunication. To be excommunicated was to be deprived of the sacraments and guaranteed eternal damnation. It was a threat that his heroes Gregory VII and Innocent III had used to force several medieval monarchs to change their policies.

However, since the heyday of papal power in the high Middle Ages (eleventh through thirteenth centuries), things had changed most notably in the rise of power of the early Renaissance state. Both Philip and Edward refused to submit to Boniface's threats and were supported in that refusal by their nobles. Efforts to mediate the situation failed and Boniface was forced to back

down when King Philip stopped all papal revenues gathered in France from leaving the kingdom for Rome. Bolstered by the enormous success of a church jubilee for the year 1300, which brought hordes of pilgrims to Rome and swelled the papal coffers, Boniface in 1302 issued the papal bull *Unam Sanctam* in which he asserted "that all human creation be subject to the pope of Rome."[3]

The iron-willed and wily Philip the Handsome now summoned his estates and accused Boniface of such crimes as practicing black magic, sodomy, murder, and keeping a demon as a pet. Philip's agents had been spreading similar stories about Boniface for years so it was not surprising that the representatives of the French estates should have agreed to support their king in his struggle with the "evil pope." Philip dispatched armed men to Italy to confront Boniface at his villa at Anagni. Philip's troops pillaged the papal residence of "utensils, and clothing, fixtures, gold and silver, and everything" they found.[4] They also tried to force the aging pontiff to return with them to France to stand trial. Although Boniface was rescued from French hands three days later, he died a few weeks later in a state of shock and humiliation. The vicar of Christ was not used to such rude treatment.

What grief the wily Philip IV may have felt at the unexpected death of his papal rival was soon assuaged by the election of a Frenchman, Clement V (r. 1305–1314). Two years later Clement V moved the papal headquarters from faction-ridden Rome to Avignon, a papal town on the Rhone River, where his holiness could gaze out at the border of his native France. Needless to say, the French pope and his successors got along quite nicely for the most part with the French monarchy and they stayed in Avignon for the next seventy years. Since Avignon did not have a sufficient set of palaces and churches to accommodate the transplanted papal court, an enormous building boom commenced. At the same time, the papacy had to find funds for armies in order to reassert its control over central Italy and compensate for lost revenues in the Papal States. This put enormous pressure on the Avignon popes to raise money and contributed to such long-standing church problems as *simony* (the selling of offices). One Avignon pope, the prodigal Clement VI (r. 1342–1352), bellowed, "I would sell a bishopric to a donkey if the donkey had enough money."[5]

Some of the other popes at Avignon such as John XXII (r. 1313–1334) showed great skills in administration and as fund raisers, but they had lost some of that spiritual authority and an aura of impartiality which had gone with being located in Rome, the city where St. Peter, the first "pope," had allegedly been crucified upside down. With the papacy in Avignon, it was too easy to think of it as captive to the interests of the nearby French monarchy.

For the poet and cleric Francesco Petrarca, who had grown up in Avignon and returned there in 1326, it was the "Babylon of the West," where "instead of soberness, licentious banquets; instead of pious pilgrimages, unnatural and foul sloth."[6] Although we must make allowances for Petrarca's rhetoric and recognize that other critics have said much the same thing about the late medieval papacy when it was still at Rome, it was clear from the widespread circulation of his diatribe in intellectual circles that many prominent Catholics had real concerns about the papacy's presence at Avignon, its lifestyle, and some of its fund-raising methods. As King Edward III of England (1327–1377) observed: "The successors of the Apostles

were ordered to lead the Lord's sheep to pasture; not to fleece them."[7]

Despite these criticisms, many of the popes who ruled at Avignon were among the most talented in the long history of the church and were not always subservient to the interests of the French crown. There were several efforts during the Captivity to return the papacy to Rome, but factional violence in the city on the Tiber frustrated attempts to make the return.

Finally, in 1376 Pope Gregory XI (r. 1370–1378) returned the papacy to Rome. By so doing he was responding to growing public pressure including the urging of the visionary Catherine of Siena (c. 1347–1380), who was later canonized for her holiness and her many contributions to the welfare of the poor. As for Pope Gregory, he was soon appalled by the turbulent conditions in Rome, "the holy City," and made plans for a return to Avignon. His death in 1378 prevented him from carrying out those plans. Under severe pressure from Roman mobs, the college of cardinals elected an Italian to serve as pope. Pope Urban VI (r. 1378–1389), a previously colorless bureaucrat, surprised everyone by turning into a zealous reformer who sought to curb the power and wealth of the cardinals.

THE WESTERN SCHISM OF 1378–1417

Alarmed by Urban's efforts at reform, the homesick French cardinals ruled his election invalid because of mob duress and elected Robert, cardinal of French-speaking Geneva, as pope and returned with him to Avignon. Urban VI refused to recognize the validity of the new election, excommunicated the rebel cardinals and their new pope, and appointed new cardinals to replace those who had fled to Avignon. For the next thirty-seven years, the Catholic Church was torn between a succession of rival popes each claiming to be the lawful successor to St. Peter while damning his rival as the anti-Christ. Excommunications were hurled back and forth between Rome and Avignon for decades.

Such unseemly behavior only added to the confusion of many prominent Europeans. Choices had to be made about which pope to support. France backed the French popes of Avignon, as did Castile, Aragon, Navarre, Naples, Sicily, Portugal, and Scotland. Since England was still fighting France in the Hundred Years' War, it stayed loyal to the popes in Rome, as did parts of the Holy Roman Empire, Ireland, Flanders, and northern and central Italy. Some states shifted from one side to another as it suited their particular interests. Individual Christians wondered if their immortal souls were in danger should the sacraments be performed by a false priest ordained by a false bishop loyal to a false pope.

As the schism dragged on, thoughtful Christians began to suggest that the only solution was for a general council of the church's leaders to meet and settle the matter. Neither the pope in Avignon nor the one in Rome would agree to be judged by their "inferiors," even when in convocation. The situation got worse in 1409 when 500 prelates meeting in council at Pisa decided to depose both popes and elect a new one. Both the Roman pontiff and the one in Avignon refused to accept their deposition so for a while Europe had three living popes, each claiming to be the true supreme head of the church on earth. Three such popes, obviously, were not three times better than one.

Finally, the Holy Roman Emperor Sigismund of Luxembourg (r. 1411–1437) decided to break the impasse by playing the role that the Roman Emperor Constantine (r. 306–337) had played in calling the Council of Nicaea in 325 in order to settle a quarrel over the nature of Jesus, which threatened to rip apart the Christian community. Sigismund was well aware of the arguments made seventy years earlier by a physician and philosopher immersed in Roman legal traditions, Marsilius of Padua (1270–1342). Marsilius argued in his *Defender of the Peace* (1324) that the church must be subject to the state, which had the greater responsibility for maintaining law and order. He also asserted that a general church council, rather than the pope, should govern the church because councils represented the body of the faithful better than a single man. Since these ideas were considered by leading papal supporters to be subversive, Marsilius was forced to flee from his university position in Paris and ended his days in the service of Holy Roman Emperor Lewis IV (r. 1314–1347), who was pleased to have such a prominent intellectual tell him that he was superior to the pope.

Emperor Sigismund had no intention of asserting his own authority over the church on a lasting basis, but he did think he could use his power to help settle the crisis if supported by a sufficient number of powerful prelates, some of whom were sympathetic to the notions of sharing governance between pope and council. In 1414 Sigismund summoned important churchmen from all across Europe to come to the Swiss town of Constance for a great council that lasted until 1418. At Constance, the churchmen voted to depose all of the existing popes and elect a new pope, Martin V (r. 1417–1431). Although the three deposed popes were not eager to step down, none of them had the support necessary to stay in power. The Western Schism had at last ended, but what should be the nature of the governance of the church in the future? Should papal monarchs rule with the guidance of regular meetings of male church leaders meeting in council?

THE BURNING OF JAN HUS (C. 1372–1415)

Similar questions had occurred to a forty-three-year-old Czech cleric named Jan Hus, who was also at the Council of Constance. He had been invited to the council by Emperor Sigismund to answer charges of heresy. The emperor had promised Hus he would not be harmed, but shortly after his arrival at Constance in October 1414 he was imprisoned. He languished there until June 1415 when he was finally brought before the council meeting in the great cathedral at Constance and allowed to defend himself. When he tried to explain his views about the nature of the church, outraged churchmen shouted him down. Hus complained to no avail, "In such a council as this, I had expected to find more propriety, piety, and order."[8]

For the next four weeks, enormous pressure was placed on the condemned Czech to recant or deny his teachings. Brought to the cathedral of Constance for a final time on July 15, 1415, Hus was given one last chance to save his life if he would recant. Refusing, he was stripped of his clerical vestments and a paper crown with three demons painted on it was put on his head with the words "We commit thy soul to the devil." Hus was then led to the town market square and burned alive. Fire was thought of as a cleansing element and to burn an unrepentant heretic like Hus was the only way to clean his soul and stop the spread of his contagious "infection." Shortly before his death, Hus was heard to say, "In the truth of that Gospel which I have written about, taught, and preached, I now die."[9] The churchmen at Constance had literally cooked the goose, which is what Hus means in Czech.

What had Hus done to deserve such a death? Why were the assembled churchmen and the emperor at Constance so determined to see him die? The search for answers goes back to Hus's youth as a poor peasant lad encouraged by his mother and a local priest to escape from a life of rural poverty in southern Bohemia by entering the service of the church. The boy had excelled in school; his intelligence was obvious. In 1390 he enrolled in the recently founded Charles University in Prague, the capital of Bohemia. There he again proved a superior student, earning his B.A. three years later and an appointment to the faculty, where the handsome Hus became an exceptionally eloquent and popular lecturer.

Partly in order to advance his career, Hus had become a priest in 1400. In studying for the priesthood, he had become a serious student of the Bible. "When the Lord gave me knowledge of the Scriptures, I discarded from my mind all foolish fun-making," he wrote.[10] Already well known as an eloquent university lecturer, Hus now gained additional fame as a preacher. In 1401 he became the confessor of Queen Sophia of Bohemia. She also came to hear him preach at the new Bethlehem Chapel in the heart of Prague.

His talent, fame, and influential patrons should have made him eventually a great man in the church, but Hus's mind became increasingly troubled by the anticlerical ideas of an English theologian from Oxford University, John Wycliffe, especially the idea that all church doctrine should be based on the Bible. He said of the controversial Wycliffe:

> I am attracted by his writings, in which he makes every effort to lead all men back to the law of Christ, and especially the clergy, inviting them to abandon pomp and dominion of the world, and live, like the apostles, according to the law of Christ.[11]

However, many of Hus's German colleagues on the faculty were appalled by

Wycliffe's call for church reform. The dispute over reform threatened to tear apart the university, particularly as it also began to touch on the subject of who was to control the university and the church in Bohemia. Hus was the most prominent spokesperson for the cause of the Czech-speaking students.

Finally, in January 1409 King Wenceslaus IV, Emperor Sigismund's brother and a supporter of Hus and moderate reform, issued a decree that gave the Czech-speaking student "nation" at the university three votes for every German one, a complete reversal of the previous situation. Several thousand students and professors, mostly Germans, left Prague and founded a new university 150 miles away at Leipzig. On October 17, 1409, the new Czech national hero, Jan Hus, was elected rector of the university, its highest administrative office.

Despite his new honors Hus still had his enemies among the local clergy, and they urged Archbishop Zbynek to proceed against him as a dangerous heretic in the Wycliffite mold. Hus had spoken and written in favor of Wycliffe's notion of the universal priesthood of all believers, the idea that each person has a direct, spiritual relationship with Christ, the sole head of the church. This threatened the power of the priests as intercessors between the laity and God and made the hierarchy of church office holders seem unnecessary.

Hus also preached against the sale of *indulgences,* which were relaxations for some of the penalties in purgatory for sin. The church taught that most people are not ready for heaven but are not sinful enough for hell when they die. Instead, a truly penitent sinner goes to a cleansing place known as purgatory to have the soul purified in preparation for admission to heaven. Indulgences were being sold to finance a crusade against the Christian king of Naples, a po-

litical rival of one of the schismatic popes. Hus's preaching against indulgences not only threatened one of the papal pocketbooks, but also that of King Wenceslaus, who had been assured a percentage of the profits for the indulgences sold in Bohemia. The king's support of Hus evaporated rapidly. In July 1410, Zbynek ordered Wycliffe's books burned and excommunicated Hus.

Hus continued to preach his call for reform. Zbynek retaliated by placing the whole city under an interdict on June 20, 1411. The interdict was a general excommunication which closed all churches, and stopped all baptisms, marriages, and burials. Everyone in Prague was threatened with eternal damnation. Not wishing to cause such great harm to Prague, Hus left the city in October 1412 at the suggestion of King Wenceslaus. For the next year and a half, he preached and wrote in his homeland of southern Bohemia, winning many new friends and followers to the cause of church reform.

Then Hus was summoned to the great reform council at Constance by his king's brother. After his trial and execution of 1415, 452 Bohemian nobles sent an indignant protest to the council and the emperor. Sigismund angrily and foolishly replied that he would very soon "drown all Wycliffites and Hussites." This was the final insult from an emperor who was seen as responsible for the death of a Czech national hero. Rebellion soon spread throughout Bohemia, and King Wenceslaus was powerless to calm the storm.

THE HUSSITE REVOLT

Emperor Sigismund and Pope Martin V proclaimed a crusade against the Hussites, who found excellent military leadership in the person of Jan Zizka (1376–1424). Amazingly bold and resourceful, Zizka continued to direct artillery in battle even after being blinded. With such valiant officers and soldiers, the Hussite rebels managed to repel three successive waves of invasion led by an emperor increasingly obsessed with maintaining his imperial authority over Bohemia and encouraged by a papacy in Rome fearful that heresy might spread. Despite ferocious fighting and theological divisions among the Hussites, Sigismund could not crush Zizka's fighters. The Hussites had divided into two major groups: the *Utraquists*, a moderate group who believed in communion in both kinds (bread and wine), and the *Taborites*, who took their name from the town of Tabor, which became their capital. The Taborites recognized only the two biblically based sacraments of baptism and the Eucharist and wanted simple, early church style ceremonies. Zizka was a Taborite and less willing to compromise with Sigismund and the church than the Utraquists. A civil war between the Hussite factions raged on until the Utraquists scored a decisive victory over the Taborites at the battle of Lipan in 1434, ten years after the death of Zizka.

After gaining control of Bohemia and having beaten the forces of Sigismund on four major occasions, the Utraquists moved to achieve peace and official recognition from the church. In 1436 the Council of Basel wisely allowed the Utraquists to continue their unique practice of celebrating the Eucharist with the laity receiving both the bread and the wine. Having been unable to enforce uniformity of practice by the sword, the leadership of the church shrewdly knew that keeping Bohemia nominally Catholic was better than losing the Hussites altogether. Even Emperor Sigismund was forgiven by the Czechs and allowed to visit Prague for the first time in sixteen years.

The Council of Basel (1431–1449) in Switzerland, which achieved a measure of reconciliation with the Hussites, proved to be the last of the important late medieval councils. Enthusiasm was waning for the theories of the conciliarists. Even though the Council of Constance had decreed that a general church council derived its authority directly from Christ and, therefore, the entire church was bound by its decisions, the pope (Martin V) elected by that council believed in papal supremacy and did his best to undermine the theories of Marsilius of Padua and other conciliar thinkers. The Council of Constance had also declared in 1417 that the general council should meet frequently (*Frequens*), but popes stopped calling councils for the most part after Basel. They also ignored most of the reform measures advocated at Constance and elsewhere. Councils met at Florence (1439–1442) and at the Lateran (1503–1513), but not until the Council of Trent from 1545 to 1563 would a major church council succeed in making fundamental and lasting reforms.

The Hundred Years' War

The Latin church was not the only segment of society in deep trouble during the fourteenth and fifteenth centuries. The monarchies of England and France fought a terrible war in 1337, a conflict that was waged on and off for the next 116 years. The Hundred Years' War began in a sense with the Norman French conquest of England in 1066. Since the time of William the Conqueror, the affairs of France and England were thoroughly intertwined. Things had become even more entangled when the former wife of the French king Louis VII, Eleanor of Aquitaine (1122–1204), married the red-haired Henry of Anjou, who became King Henry II of England (r. 1154–1189). Henry had title to land in France and Eleanor had

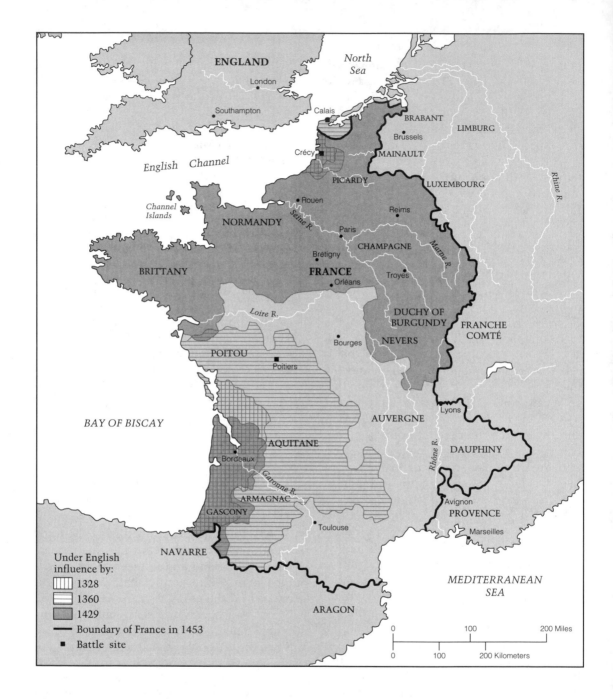

England

North Sea

London

Southampton

Calais

BRABANT

Brussels

LIMBURG

Crécy

MAINAULT

LUXEMBOURG

PICARDY

Rhine R.

English Channel

Rouen

Reims

Channel Islands

NORMANDY

Seine R.

Paris

CHAMPAGNE

Marne R.

BRITTANY

Brétigny

FRANCE

Troyes

Orléans

DUCHY OF BURGUNDY

Loire R.

FRANCHE COMTÉ

Bourges

NEVERS

POITOU

Poitiers

AUVERGNE

Lyons

BAY OF BISCAY

AQUITANE

Rhône R.

DAUPHINY

Bordeaux

Garonne R.

ARMAGNAC

GASCONY

Avignon

PROVENCE

Toulouse

Marseilles

NAVARRE

Under English influence by:

1328

1360

1429

Boundary of France in 1453

Battle site

MEDITERRANEAN SEA

ARAGON

0   100   200 Miles

0   100   200 Kilometers

The Hundred Years' War

control of even more French land than did the French monarchy.

During the course of the thirteenth century and early fourteenth century, French monarchs such as Philip II (r. 1180–1223) and Philip IV, the Handsome, had been working assiduously to recover land from the English and had clashed with their English rivals on a number of occasions. France and England also quarreled over Flanders, which the French claimed and with which England was intimately connected in the wool trade. Tensions between England and France escalated in 1328 when the last Capetian king of France died without sons. King Edward III of England decided to "pick the French lily" or claim the French crown. His mother was a daughter of Philip the Handsome. Philip of Valois challenged Edward's claim. He was the son of Philip IV's younger brother. Deeply disturbed by the possibility of an

English king sitting on the throne of France, the French nobility argued unhistorically that the right to inherit in France cannot pass through a woman (Salic law), even though no such impediment existed among the English. They then declared Philip of Valois to be their sovereign. His Valois dynasty would rule France until 1589, but not without a challenge from England, where the Salic law traditions did not apply.

In 1337 Edward III decided to press his claim to the French throne. Both Edward and Philip VI (r. 1328–1350) had romantic, chivalrous notions of warfare and neither was willing to make the necessary concessions to avoid war. They almost gleefully dragged their kingdoms into a conflict that went on for five generations and devastated many parts of France. The French learned at Crécy (1346) and at Poitiers (1356) that mounted knights on horseback were no

Battle of Crécy, Chronicles of Froissart (second half of the fourteenth century). Folio with illumination miniature. Bibliotheque Nationale, Paris, France. Snark/Art Resource.

match for longbowmen, whose arrows could pierce armor. Although England won the major battles of the war, subduing the much larger France proved impossible, especially when the English were distracted by the removal of Richard II, Edward III's successor, in 1399. Later King Henry V (r. 1413–1422) renewed hostilities and won a major victory for England in the mud at Agincourt in 1415. France seemed destined to lose the war despite the premature death of the seemingly robust Henry V in 1422.

JOAN OF ARC (1412–1431)

At this critical juncture, a sixteen-year-old peasant girl named Joan of Arc appeared in the spring of 1428 and claimed that God had called her to join the French army, lift the English siege of the town of Orléans, and see the dauphin (the Valois heir) crowned as king at Rheims. Joan (Jeanne d'Arc in French) claimed that since the age of thirteen she had been hearing the voices of Saints Michael, Catherine, and Margaret. The church had a long history of special, mystical people who claimed to receive direct communications from God or His angels. Mystics such as St. Francis of Assisi (c. 1182–1226) or Hildegard of Bingen (1098–1179) had achieved great fame and even papal recognition.

There were, of course, also those who claimed direct communication with God only to be eventually shown to be more concerned with self-aggrandizement than spiritual growth. Was Joan one of those fake mystics? Her voices had not spoken about a life of contemplation, which seemed to be the usual message given to mystics. Rather Joan's divine voices called her to a life of action, action considered impossible for a woman in the fifteenth century where military armor was officially defined as "male

clothing." This tradition obviously helped men maintain a virtual monopoly on military power. Initially Joan's efforts to be recognized were rejected by her local lord, Robert de Baudricourt, but eventually he relented and sent her with six of his men-at-arms to the court of the Dauphin Charles at Chinon.

There the seventeen-year-old, dressed in men's clothing, managed to convince the religious and secular elite of France that she was God's chosen instrument of their salvation. The dauphin authorized "the maid" to go with 4,000 troops to Orléans, which was besieged by the English. Her very presence inspired the French soldiers and alarmed the English. The French lifted the siege of Orléans in May 1429. Although twice wounded, Joan fought bravely in at least seven military engagements and advised the French military commanders on a number of occasions. Her presence changed the course of the war and in July 1429, the dauphin was crowned as King Charles VII of France (r. 1422–1461).

As for Joan, she continued to fight and was captured at Compiegne by the Burgundians, who sold her to the English. Joan was forced to endure a harsh imprisonment and a grueling series of cross-examinations by unsympathetic clergy with vested interests in discrediting her. Chained to a block of wood at night, she was questioned several times a day from January 9 to May 30, 1431. Unable to make her deny her visions or give up her wearing of men's clothes, French churchmen in the service of the English tried Joan as a heretic and a witch. Joan was accused of having been trained by some "old women" in "the use of sorcery, divination, and other superstitious works or magic arts." Faced with death, she recanted briefly before changing her mind. Joan of Arc was then convicted of being "a relapsed heretic" and burned at the stake on May 30, 1431.

Henri Scheffer, *Entry of Joan of Arc into Orléans, 8 May 1429*. Chateau Versailles, France. Giraudon/Art Resource.

King Charles VII and his government made no effort to rescue her. The brave young woman had served her purpose. The French were revitalized; her king saw no reason to allow her to become an even greater heroine, whose fame might outstrip his own. She was best forgotten. Others such as the courtier and writer Christine de Pizan disagreed. In her last known poem, Pizan hailed Joan as a heroine in the tradition of such biblical heroines as Esther, Judith, and Deborah:

Ah, what honor to the feminine sex!
Which God so loved that he showed
A way to this great people
By which the kingdom once lost,
Was recovered by a woman,
A thing men could not do.[12]

Following the death of Joan, French armies went from victory to victory. By 1453, the English were completely driven out of France with the exception of the well-fortified port city of Calais on the channel, twenty-six miles across from the English port of Dover. Large sections of France had been devastated by the war, plague, famine, and a ferocious peasant revolt in 1358. King Charles VII was able to devote himself to the rebuilding of his ravished country. During the war he had gained a standing army, secure tax revenues, and an expanded royal administrative structure. Charles used these tools to strengthen the monarchy as did his successors, most notably the "Spider King" Louis XI (r. 1461–1483). The crafty Louis loved plotting and removed several of his rivals by treachery and murder. In 1477 he confiscated the duchy of Burgundy when its last duke died fighting against Louis's allies, the Swiss. France, now disentangled from England, was well on the road to becoming an even greater power in Europe.

The War of the Roses, 1455–1485

The English, though humbled by their defeat in the Hundred Years' War, soon found themselves in a nasty struggle for the throne between the rival houses of York and Lancaster. Hostilities began in 1455 when Richard, the duke of York, attempted to overthrow the inept and mentally troubled Lancastrian King Henry VI (1422–1461), who was blamed for the humiliating defeat in France by many among the English nobility. King Henry's able and assertive wife, Margaret of Anjou (1429–1482), rallied those loyal to the house of Lancaster, whose emblem was the red rose. Although Richard of York was defeated and killed at Wakefield in 1460, the Yorkist (white rose) cause was ably championed by Richard's son, Edward IV (r. 1461–1483), whom the English Parliament declared king in 1461 after his great victory at Mortimer's Cross. The deposed King Henry and Queen Margaret fled to Scotland, where she continued to struggle against Edward.

Unknown, *Edward IV*. Courtesy of the National Portrait Gallery, London, United Kingdom.

King Edward IV was a brilliant military leader but could at times be lazy and cruel. He also had autocratic tendencies and called Parliament as seldom as possible. Things took an ugly turn when Edward's ally, the earl of Warwick, and his royal brother, Clarence, switched allegiances and sided with the Lancastrians. Supported by the Spider King, Louis XI of France, in 1470 they succeeded for a time in restoring Henry VI and Margaret to the throne. Six months later, however, Edward IV killed Warwick in battle at Barnet and then crushed Margaret and her army at Tewkesbury. Margaret was exiled to France; her husband and the treacherous Clarence ended their days in the Tower of London. Edward IV ruled England for the next twelve years before his sudden death in May 1483. The elder of his two infant sons was declared to be his successor as King Edward V (b. 1470).

Edward IV's younger brother, Richard, duke of Gloucester, who was the king's lieutenant in the north and protector of the child king, outfoxed his rivals and in less than three months mounted the throne as Richard III. The deposed young king was declared illegitimate and placed in the Tower of London along with his brother. Opposition leaders were executed and the king was widely suspected of murdering the two young princes in the tower. Henry Tudor, earl of Richmond, now appeared as the champion of all those who considered Richard an evil usurper. In 1485 during a showdown battle at Bosworth Field, Henry's forces overwhelmed those of Richard, who died in the battle. The able Henry, now King Henry VII (r. 1485–1509) of Lancastrian descent, married Elizabeth of York, ended the War of the Roses, and established the remarkable Tudor dynasty.

Chronology

1294	Election of hermit Pope Celestine V; replacement of Celestine with Boniface VIII.		1378	Cloth workers revolt in Florence; the Great Western Schism begins.
1302	Boniface VIII issues *Unam Sanctam*.		1381	Wat Tyler Peasants' Revolt in England.
1303	Humiliation and death of Boniface VIII at the hands of agents of Philip the Handsome.		1384	Death of John Wycliffe.
			1409	Council of Pisa (three popes).
			1414–1418	Council of Constance.
1304–1374	Life of Petrarca.		1415	Death of Jan Hus at Constance; English under Henry V win the battle of Agincourt.
1305	Beginning of the Babylonian Captivity (popes at Avignon).			
1324	Marsilius of Padua publishes *The Defender of the Peace*.		1417	End of the Great Western Schism.
1337	Hundred Years' War begins.		1429	French lift the siege of Orleans.
1340–1400	Life of Geoffrey Chaucer.		1431	Death of Joan of Arc.
1346	English win the battle of Crécy.		1432–1442	Council of Florence.
1347	Beginning of the Black Death.		1436	Council of Basel and the end of the Hussite Wars.
1348–1349	Artisans' Revolt in Nuremberg.		1453	End of the Hundred Years' War.
1356	The Jacquerie Peasant Revolt in France.		1455–1485	The War of the Roses in England.
			1461–1483	Reign of Louis XI (Spider King) in France.
1364–1430	Life of Christine de Pizan.		1485–1509	Reign of Henry VII (Tudor) in England.
1376	Papacy returns to Rome.			

Further Reading

GENERAL WORKS

C. Warren Hollister, *Medieval Europe: A Short History*, 8th ed. (1998). A highly readable textbook.

Johan Huizinga, *The Waning of the Middle Ages* (1954).

Robert Lerner, *The Age of Adversity: The Fourteenth Century* (1968).

Barbara Tuchman, *A Distant Mirror: The Calamitous 14th Century* (1968). To be used with care since she was not a medievalist, but very well written and lively.

Daniel Waley, *Later Medieval Europe*, 2nd ed. (1985).

THE BLACK DEATH

Robert Gottfried, *The Black Death: Natural Human Disaster in Medieval Europe* (1983).

Rosemary Horrox, ed. and trans., *The Black Death* (1994). A useful collection of documents.

William McNeill, *Plagues and Peoples* (1978).

Colin Platt, *King Death: The Black Death and Its Aftermath in Late Medieval England* (1996).

Paul Slack, *The Impact of the Plague in Tudor and Stuart England* (1991).

Philip Ziegler, *The Black Death* (1969).

POPULAR REVOLTS

R. H. Hilton and Trevor Aston, eds., *The English Rising of 1381* (1984). This collection also has materials on the Ciompi Revolt and the Jacquerie.

Michel Mollat and Philippe Wolff, *The Popular Revolutions of the Late Middle Ages* (1973).

William TeBrake, *A Plague of Insurrection: Popular Politics and Peasant Revolts in Flanders, 1323–1328* (1993).

TROUBLES IN THE CHURCH

Anthony Black, *Council and Commune: The Conciliar Movement and the Fifteenth-Century Heritage* (1979).

C. M. D. Crowder, ed., *Unity, Heresy, and Reform, 1378–1460* (1977). Valuable collection of sources.

Denys Hay, *The Church in Italy in the Fifteenth Century* (1977).

Howard Kaminsky, *A History of the Hussite Revolution* (1967).

Anthony Kenny, *Wyclif* (1985).

Richard Kieckhefer, *Unquiet Souls: Fourteenth-Century Saints and Their Religious Milieu* (1984).

Gordon Leff, *Heresy in the Later Middle Ages: The Relation of Heterodoxy to Dissent, c. 1250–1450* (1967).

Louise Ropes Loomis, *The Council of Constance* (1961).

Francis Oakley, *The Western Church in the Later Middle Ages.* (1979).

Yves Renouard, *The Avignon Papacy, 1305–1403* (1970).

Matthew Spinka, *Jan Hus* (1968).

Joachim Stieber, *Pope Eugenius IV, the Council of Basel, and the Secular and Ecclesiastical Authorities of the Empire* (1978).

Phillip Stump, *The Reforms of the Council of Constance, 1414–1418* (1994).

J. F. A. Thompson, *Popes and Princes, 1417–1517* (1980).

Brian Tierney, *Foundations of the Conciliar Theory* (1955).

Donald Weinstein and Rudolf Bell, *Saints and Society: The Two Worlds of Western Christendom, 1000–1700* (1986).

THE HUNDRED YEARS' WAR

Christopher Allmand, *Henry V* (1992).

———, *The Hundred Years' War* (1988).

Anne Curry, *The Hundred Years' War* (1993).

Marina Warner, *Joan of Arc: The Image of Female Heroism* (1981).

THE WAR OF THE ROSES

Michael Bennett, *The Battle of Bosworth* (1985).

S. B. Chrimes, *Henry VII* (1973).

John Gillingham, *The War of the Roses* (1981).

E. F. Jacob, *The Fifteenth Century, 1399–1485* (1993).

Charles Ross, *Edward IV* (1974).

Notes

1. Cited in William Bowsky, ed., *The Black Death: A Turning Point?* (New York: Holt, Rinehart, and Winston, 1971), p. 13.
2. Cited in E. R. Chamberlin, *The Bad Popes* (New York: Dial Press, 1969), p. 80.
3. Cited in C. Warren Hollister, et al., eds., *Medieval Europe: A Short Sourcebook,* 2nd ed. (New York: McGraw-Hill, 1992), p. 216.
4. Ibid., p. 217.
5. See Joseph Lynch, *The Medieval Church: A Brief History* (New York: Longman, 1992), p. 176.
6. Cited in Hollister, *Sourcebook,* p. 240.
7. Cited in John Harrison and Richard Sullivan, *A Short History of Western Civilization* (New York: Alfred Knopf, 1961), p. 127.
8. Cited in J. W. Zophy, "Hus," in his *The Holy Roman*

Empire: A Dictionary Handbook (Westport, Conn.: Greenwood Press, 1980), p. 228.

9. Ibid.

10. Cited in Theodore Rabb, *Renaissance Lives: Portraits of an Age* (New York: Pantheon Books, 1993), p. 20.

11. Ibid., p. 22.

12. Cited in Bonnie Anderson and Judith Zinsser, *A History of Their Own: Women in Europe from Prehistory to the Present*, 2 vols. (New York: Harper and Row, 1988), vol. 1, p. 161. Copyright © by Bonnie Anderson and Judith Zinsser. Reprinted by permission of HarperCollins Publishers, Inc.

4

Italy: Home of the Renaissance

Despite the great series of disasters that afflicted Europe beginning in the fourteenth century, Renaissance culture developed and took root in Italy and then eventually spread to the rest of Europe and the world. Why did the cultural movement known as the Renaissance first begin in the Italian peninsula? What was so special about Italy? What kind of places and people made up Italy during the Renaissance?

The nineteenth-century Swiss historian Jacob Burckhardt argued that "Italy began to teem with personalities; the interdict which had lain on personalities was here completely broken . . . the rest of Europe still lay under the spell of the community."[1] Although modern historians may be less inclined to view the Renaissance as the "triumph of individualism" as did Burckhardt, there is much to be said for his admiration of the great heroes of Renaissance culture. But what other factors help to account for the spectacular accomplishments of outstanding Renaissance individuals such as Cosimo de' Medici, Isabella d'Este, Lorenzo Valla, Machiavelli, Michelangelo, Titian, and Artemisia Gentileschi? What did their Italian world have to do with shaping them and the larger cultural movement of which they were a part? To find partial answers to these questions, let us begin by looking at the setting of the Renaissance.

In the fourteenth and fifteenth centuries, Italy was just a geographical expression for an enchanting land of lovely hills and valleys, dotted with remains of an ancient past. The Italian peninsula was made up of a series of independent city-states and principalities of varying size and power. Economically, Italy had taken advantage of its location between the well-developed markets of the eastern Mediterranean and the underdeveloped principalities of Europe north of the Alps. Italians had forged ahead of other Europeans in banking, trade, and cloth manufacturing to become the most urbanized and prosperous people of Europe even during the long depression of the fifteenth century. The wealth of the Italian elites would help stimulate a Renaissance in the arts.

Culturally, Italy was still the leading heir to the grandeur of the Roman Empire in the West, even though most of that grandeur had long since faded. Italy was the home and headquarters of the Roman Catholic Church once again after the Avignon papacy ended in 1417. As such it occupied a special place in the minds of many Europeans. Italy's stature as a cultural center would grow because of the intellectual and artistic creations of several generations of highly talented producers of art, literature, and scholarship.

Italy in the Fifteenth Century

Rome and the Papal States

Renaissance Rome, filled with the crumbled remains of ancient buildings, was no longer the center of a vast world empire nor was it even one of Italy's great trade centers. Ancient Rome had been home to over a million people in the third century; only about a tenth of that number lived in Renaissance Rome. Cows now grazed amidst the ruins of the ancient Roman forum, where Julius Caesar and Cicero once debated. Except for the difficult period from 1305 to 1376 when the

headquarters of the church was in Avignon, Renaissance Rome's economy was mostly sustained by the presence of the huge bureaucracy of the Roman Catholic Church and tourism (pilgrimages). Rome was also the largest market town in the Papal States. Wealthy patrician families such as the Colonna, Gaetane, Frangipani, Orsini, Santa Croce, and others struggled with each other and the popes to control Rome's municipal government and to win favors from the papacy. These families also struggled repeatedly to gain control of the papacy itself.

COLA DI RIENZO (1313–1354)

In 1347 and again in 1354, Cola di Rienzo took advantage of the absent papacy to attempt to win Rome's independence from papal and feudal control. The son of a tavern keeper and a laundress, Rienzo was a student of Roman history and archaeology. An eloquent speaker, he managed to convince some of his followers that he was the illegitimate son of the Holy Roman Emperor Heinrich VII (r. 1308–1313) and as such could be the new Roman "tribune of the people," who would restore Rome to its lost glory. Wearing a toga, Rienzo urged his supporters to "die in freedom so that posterity may be born in freedom."[2] They managed to gain control of the city for seven months before being toppled from power by the combined forces of the major Roman families and the papacy, who were appalled at the pretensions of this upstart.

In 1350 Rienzo traveled to Prague to gain the support of the Holy Roman Emperor Charles IV (r. 1347–1378). The wily Charles found him interesting but unstable. The emperor declined to support Rienzo's bid for power in Rome. Instead Charles had Rienzo imprisoned until Pope Innocent VI (r. 1352–1362) secured his release. The pope hoped that the still influential Rienzo might help pave the way for the return of the papacy from Avignon. In 1354 Rienzo led a second successful revolt in Rome and took over the city. Despite his pretensions of planning to restore the glories of the ancient Roman republic, Rienzo soon showed himself to be a petty tyrant and was killed less than a year later during a revolt of the common people, who felt betrayed by their erstwhile champion.

RENAISSANCE POPES

The papacy reasserted its full control over the impoverished and strife-torn city and its surrounding communities in the late 1350s. Then came the difficult period when the papacy moved back to Rome in 1376, only to be followed by the Great Western Schism with one pope in Rome and another in Avignon. Finally, with the reign of Pope Martin V (r. 1417–1431), the papacy was back in Rome for good. It faced a considerable rebuilding task, but papal leadership during the Renaissance became dedicated to restoring the grandeur of Rome. Pope Nicholas V (r. 1447–1455) resumed the massive cleanup campaign begun by Martin V. He constructed a new Vatican palace, rebuilt the Trevi fountain, and began rebuilding St. Peter's Basilica. A true friend of learning, he brought in the renowned humanist Lorenzo Valla to help him create the superb Vatican Library.

Three years later, Aeneas Silvius Piccolimini, one of the leading humanists in Italy and poet-laureate of the empire, succeeded to the throne of St. Peter. As Pope Pius II (r. 1458–1464), he supported artists and writers and tried to launch a crusade against the Ottomans. The next major pope, Sixtus IV (r. 1471–1484), initiated an ambitious program to establish the political power and prestige of the papacy. Completely ruthless, he plotted the death of his enemies in central Italy and Florence (the Pazzi Plot of 1478). As a patron, he was responsible for the building of the Sistine Chapel in St. Peter's.

Political corruption and immorality in the Vatican reached their all-time peak during the reign of Rodrigo Borgia as Alexander VI (r. 1492–1503). Borgia was the nephew of Pope Calixtus III (r. 1455–1458) and as such rose rapidly in church preferment. Even as an up-and-coming young churchman, he gave signs of things to come. In June 1460, Pope Pius II wrote a letter of reproach to the young cardinal and vice-chancellor in which he admonished Borgia for indulging in "licentious dances" and an "orgy" in Siena with several married women. Despite this reprimand, the Spaniard, who was also a skilled administrator, managed to bribe and cajole his way onto St. Peter's throne.

As pope, Borgia continued to indulge both his political and sensual appetites. He continued to live an extravagant lifestyle that included lavish parties, weddings, receptions, and even bullfights. Gangsterism flourished in Alexander's Rome and according to his master of ceremonies, Johannes Burchardus, the pope had "full knowledge" of more than 250 murders.[3] Although little was done to improve the plight of the Roman poor, Pope Alexander used the power and wealth of the papacy to foster the careers of his four children by his beloved mistress, the inn-keeper Vanozza Catanei, who lived like a queen.

The worst of the papal brood was the ambitious, handsome, and vicious Cesare (1476–1507), who was made a cardinal of the church at age fourteen. Cesare fascinated the diplomat and political theorist Niccolò Machiavelli and others by his ruthlessness, which extended to murdering his older brother as well as the second husband of his sister, Lucretia. With the support of his father, he attempted to carve out a large state for himself in the Romagna of central Italy. In 1498 an alliance with the French king Louis XII brought him a French bride and the title of Duke of Valentinois. Taking advantage of the French invasions, Cesare made progress in creating his new state until his father's death in 1503 seriously reduced his revenues. Alexander VI's successor was his bitter enemy Giuliano della Rovere, Pope Julius II (r. 1503–1513), who wanted to expand the papal state in central Italy. Cesare's empire quickly collapsed around him and he was imprisoned in a castle at Ischia. He died three years later in Spain.

Unknown, *Portrait of Cesare Borgia*. Accademia Carra, Bergamo, Italy. Alinari/Art Resource.

Julius II became known as "Papa Terrible" because of his relentless energy, love of war, and the fear and awe he inspired. Contemporaries said that he "loved the smell of smoke and the blood of battle."[4] Papa Terrible attempted to strengthen the papacy by expanding papal land holdings in central Italy. In 1505 he marched through the Romagna and Emilia, territories formerly ruled by Cesare Borgia. In November 1506 the warrior-pope forced the proud city of Bologna to surrender. He also masterminded a coalition of forces determined to weaken the French and drive them out of Italy. In between diplomatic negotiations and military campaigns, the energetic pope found time to commission spectacular works of art by the great Michelangelo, Bramante, and others before dying of fever.

It was the Renaissance papacy, through its patronage of artists, that managed to rekindle some of the greatness of the city on the Tiber. Rome endured even after being horribly sacked by rebellious troops of the Holy Roman Emperor Charles V in the summer of 1527. The popes of the Catholic reform continued their interests in the arts while seriously raising the spiritual tone of the papacy. In fact, Rome became one of the fastest growing cities in Europe in the second half of the sixteenth century. The papacy helped encourage the development of such important Roman artists as Bernini, Caravaggio, and Artemisia Gentileschi, plus many others who were attracted to the city for its abundant patronage and stimulating cultural and religious life. The eternal city would live on through its rich artistic and spiritual heritage.

Naples and Sicily

South of the Papal States lay the kingdoms of Naples and Sicily, both of which were surrounded by a mountainous countryside with relatively poor soil. Like the Papal States, power was concentrated at the top. How much power was shared with chancellors and other officials depended to a large extent on the whim of the sovereigns. Naples was one of the great port cities in Europe at the beginning of the Renaissance and would become one of the largest cities in Europe in the course of the sixteenth century. Ships from all over the Mediterranean, including Sicily, which had been the major granary of the ancient Roman Empire in the West, used the deep harbor of Naples. Palermo on Sicily was another major economic and cultural center early in the period. While surrounded by feuding nobles, other coastal towns in south Italy also flourished as market centers.

Unfortunately, the region suffered from a turbulent political history caused in part by its vulnerability to outside invasion. Southern Italy had been overrun by Muslim and then Norman invaders in the Middle Ages. The Holy Roman Emperor Frederick II (1197–1250) attempted to rule his vast empire north of the Alps from his base in Sicily. After his death, ties to the Holy Roman Empire gradually weakened until Charles of Anjou, third son of King Louis IX of France, seized the thrones of Naples and Sicily in 1266. Cruel, glum, and reckless, Charles of Anjou managed to hang onto power until a bloody uprising against the French broke out on Easter of 1282.

The Sicilian revolt began when a French soldier molested a young married woman on her way to evening Vesper services in Palermo. Outraged Sicilians struck down the Frenchman and raised the cry, "Death to the French!" A long, indecisive struggle ensued between the French monarchy supported by the papacy against the Sicilians and the kings of Aragon from Spain, who saw this as a good time to gain a toehold in southern Italy. This twenty-year conflict, known as the War of the Sicilian Vespers, separated Naples from Sicily, which came to be ruled by the house of Aragon for the remainder of the fourteenth century and into the fifteenth century.

Naples was dominated by the French house of Anjou, whose brightest light was Duke Robert (1309–1343), a friend and admirer of Petrarca. He had given the city on the bay a short period of cultural splendor. His granddaughter, the beautiful Joanna I (1343–1382), brought Naples into great disrepute. She had been married at age five to her seventeen-year-old cousin, Andrew of Hungary. Andrew was a dull, lumpish fellow whom the intellectually inclined Joanna grew to despise. One of her lovers murdered him and Joanna had to journey to Avignon to plead her innocence before the pope. Although judged innocent, a cloud of suspicion hung over Joanna and finally in the summer of 1381 another relative, Charles of Durazzo (r. 1382–1384) led a campaign with the support of the Roman pope to overthrow the sensual Joanna. Charles succeeded in capturing Joanna and had her strangled with a silken cord and her body exposed in the marketplace. His power over Naples was challenged by Louis of Anjou, brother of the king of France.

THE REIGNS OF JOANNA II (1414–1435), ALFONSO V (1416–1458), AND FERRANTE I (1458–1494)

At the start of the fifteenth century, Naples was ruled by the aggressive Ladislaus (r. 1386–1414). He occupied Rome in 1408 and then threatened Florence. Naples and Florence finally agreed to peace in 1411. Ladislaus was succeeded by the cultivated but dissolute Joanna II, who was corrupted by her power and wealth and fully indulged all her appetites. Joanna's reign was marked by a series of adulteries, intrigues, and assassinations. In July 1421 one of her lovers, King Alfonso V, agreed to support her against the French in return for being named her heir.

Because Alfonso was already king of Aragon and Sicily, when he finally drove out the French in 1442 he was able to unite all three crowns and provide a measure of stability for war-torn southern Italy. King Alfonso was also a major patron of the arts. A friend of learning, Alfonso the Magnanimous founded a university at Catania and helped support important scholars such as Lorenzo Valla.

His son, Ferrante I (r. 1458–1494), reverted back to the old ways of cruelty and caprice. In 1479 he had joined Pope Sixtus IV (r. 1471–1484) and the duchy of Milan in making war against the republic of Florence led by Lorenzo de' Medici (1449–1492). He

so alienated his subjects that many preferred Muslim invaders to him. Ferrante, in vivid contrast with his father, did little to stimulate the arts and learning. His death in 1494 gave King Charles VIII of France (r. 1483–1498) an opportunity to invade Italy and assert old French claims to the crowns of Naples and Sicily. Following the defeat of the French, Naples reverted to the control of the Spanish and underwent a period of growth, becoming one of the most populous cities in Europe by the end of the sixteenth century and a major center of cloth manufacture and trade. Nobles crowded into squalid but beautiful Naples to escape an increasingly impoverished countryside.

The Power of Milan

To the north of the Papal States in the center of the rich Po River Valley lay the bustling city of Milan, whose rulers exerted a great deal of power in Italy. Milan was dominated by the house of Visconti. Holy Roman Emperor Heinrich VII, whose ancestors had long claimed "overlordship" of Milan, designated Matteo Visconti imperial vicar in 1311. After a series of bloody family feuds including the murder of his coruler and uncle, Giangaleazzo Visconti (1352–1402) took supreme power in 1385. Ten years later he purchased the title of Duke of Milan from Emperor Wenceslaus (r. 1378–1400). Not only did Duke Giangaleazzo start the construction of the gigantic, white, many-spired Gothic cathedral of Milan, he dreamed of making himself king of Italy. Toward that end, he conquered the city-states of Bologna, Perugia, Pisa, Siena, and Verona. All this was a prelude to his assault on the republic of Florence, which was encircled by Milanese power. It was a classic confrontation between a principality and a republic, where governance was shared at least among an elite.

Then in September 1402, as Florence seemed ready to fall to the Goliath of the north, Giangaleazzo died of the plague. His kingdom of northern Italy dissolved as his two dissipated young sons, Giovanni Maria (r. 1402–1412) and Filippo Maria (r. 1412–1447), failed to hold what their father had conquered. Giovanni was a vicious psychopath who kept a menagerie of leopards, English hounds, and falcons, which cost a fortune to maintain. His reign ended with assassination. His younger, more able brother, Filippo, succeeded in restoring Milan and expanding its territory into Lombardy before degenerating into a self-indulgent recluse. His aggression provoked a war with Florence and Venice, which lasted, on and off, until Filippo's death in 1447.

THE RISE AND FALL OF THE SFORZA, 1450–1499

During the last stages of this war, Filippo gave his only child, an illegitimate daughter, Bianca Maria, in marriage to the ambitious mercenary general (*condottiere*) Francesco Sforza (r. 1450–1466). The son of a peasant, Sforza had risen to power as a skillful military man and leader of soldiers of fortune. A sometimes unscrupulous opportunist, he was capable of taking money from both sides in the same conflict, as he did when he offered his services to Venice in 1446 while still in the pay of its enemy Milan. In 1450, claiming that Milan had not adequately compensated him for his military services, Francesco Sforza overthrew the republic that had been established following the death of Filippo Visconti and declared himself duke and Bianca Maria duchess of Milan.

Four years after taking power, Sforza succeeded through clever diplomacy in securing peace with Venice and making a new alliance with Florence, Milan's old rival.

Francesco and Bianca Sforza ruled Milan from a massive redbrick fortress they had reconstructed in the heart of the city, and which still stands today. A symbol of princely power, the Sforza Castle housed several thousand of Francesco's best soldiers. It was quite clear on what his power as duke was based.

The Sforza dynasty continued through the coldly efficient reign of their son, Galeazzo (r. 1466–1476), and grandson, Giangaleazzo II (1476–1494), whose dark-skinned uncle Ludovico il Moro (the Moor) usurped the throne as regent for his seventeen-year-old nephew. In 1491 the ambitious Ludovico married Beatrice d' Este (b. 1475), the fifteen-year-old daughter of the duke of Ferrara. Despite her youth, the fashionable and cultivated Beatrice had a profound influence on the Milanese court during her six years there as duchess. She died shortly after giving birth to a stillborn son in January 1497. The Sforza court had attracted the services of marvelous artists such as Leonardo da Vinci, who had come to Milan as a military engineer and court painter in 1481, and the architect and painter Bramante.

Beatrice's life had been complicated by her husband's infidelities, extravagances, and political intrigues. In 1494 Ludovico il Moro encouraged the twenty-four-year-old French king, Charles VIII, to claim the throne of Naples as a prelude to a crusade against the Ottomans. Ludovico wanted French help against Duke Louis of Orléans, Pope Alexander VI, and the Florentine republic, who were determined to remove Ludovico from power. Sforza calculated that the French king could save him from his enemies. He and Beatrice greeted the young French king with open arms at Pavia in October 1494. Delighted by Beatrice's charms, King Charles headed south on his way to an easy conquest of Naples with 30,000 troops, the largest army anyone had ever seen in

Italy since the time of the ancient Romans. The French force also included the largest artillery train ever in Europe, about seventy large guns.

While the French were moving through the peninsula in what became a virtual military parade, the ailing Giangaleazzo II finally succumbed to tuberculosis. Ludovico had himself proclaimed master of Milan by his fellow citizens and persuaded Holy Roman Emperor Maximilian I (r. 1493–1519) to declare him and his heirs dukes of Milan, disregarding a surviving son of Giangaleazzo II. Duke Ludovico and his duchess, Beatrice, celebrated their new titles with a sumptuous coronation, including imaginative displays and fireworks designed by the ingenuity of Leonardo da Vinci.

As news of Charles VIII's easy conquest of Naples reached Milan, Ludovico began to worry that the successful French might make good on their own claim to his duchy. He soon joined an anti-French "Holy League" with Venice, Mantua, the papacy, Emperor Maximilian, and the king of Aragon. The French had taken Naples without fighting a single battle, but holding the prize proved more difficult than anyone could have imagined. The arrogance and corruption of the conquerors soon alienated the people of Naples, who found the French as bothersome as the Aragonese. An epidemic of syphilis, brought to Europe by returning sailors from Christopher Columbus's first voyage to the Americas, soon decimated the ranks of the French army.

Realizing he was overextended, King Charles soon led a hasty retreat toward France. On July 6, 1495, he fought a brief and bitter battle at Fornova with the forces of the Holy League, led by Ludovico's brother-in-law, Francesco Gonzaga of Mantua. Both sides claimed victory, but Charles was able to withdraw to France with most of his surviving army. He died three years later still

dreaming of glory and adventure. His successor King Louis XII (r. 1498–1515), the former duke of Orléans, invaded Italy in 1499 and claimed both Milan and Naples. The spendthrift Ludovico, who had made an elaborate display at the death of his wife, Beatrice, in 1497 by burning thousands of candles in her honor and wrapping her corpse in gold, was soon driven from Milan. Although he managed to hire Swiss mercenaries in the Tyrol, he was captured by the French in 1500 and died imprisoned in a French castle in 1508. Milan remained relatively prosperous, although dominated by the French until 1535 and then by the Spanish until 1714.

The Mantua of Isabella d'Este

Although Beatrice d'Este was unfortunate in her parents' choice of a husband, her older sister, Isabella (b. 1474), married the leader of the Italian forces at the battle of Fornova against the retreating French army of Charles VIII. She became the wife of Francesco Gonzaga, marquis of Mantua (r. 1494–1519) in 1490 after a ten-year engagement. At first it seemed Isabella had married below her younger sister, who had gained the hand of Ludovico il Moro, the real power of the great duchy of Milan. Mantua, which bordered Beatrice's family duchy of Ferrara, was a much smaller principality. Both Ferrara and Mantua, however, were major centers of Renaissance learning, thanks in part to the establishment of humanistic court schools by Guarino da Verona and Vittorino de Feltre, two of the leading lights in Renaissance education.

Both d'Este daughters received an excellent classical and linguistic education in Ferrara and at their grandmother's court in Naples, where they spent eight years. The lovely Isabella was especially adept and while still a teenager had mastered Greek and Latin grammar, could quote large sections of Vergil and other Roman poets from memory, played the lute well, danced skillfully, embroidered faultlessly, and could converse with great political sophistication with anybody. She became the model of the intellectually well-rounded, politically astute Renaissance woman. Her soldier-husband shared her interests in the arts and learning and their court soon became a great center of literary and artistic life, attracting important talent from all over Italy.

Isabella not only became a focal point of the intellectual life of the court, she also worked to gather one of the finest libraries in Italy and was a demanding patron of the arts who knew exactly what she wanted. For example, in one of her letters to the artist Perugino, she wrote:

> Our poetic invention, which we greatly want to see painted by you, is a battle of Chastity against Lasciviousness, that is to say, Pallas and Diana fighting vigorously against Venus and Cupid. And Pallas should seem almost to have vanquished Cupid, having broken his golden arrow and cast his silver bow underfoot; with one hand she is holding him by the bandage which the blind boy has before his eyes, with the other she is lifting her lance and about to kill him.[5]

The marchioness also carried on an extensive correspondence with family, friends, nobles, artists, merchants, and intellectuals all over Europe.

Relations with her sister, Beatrice, became strained when she aided and abetted her husband's scheme to bring the French into Italy in 1494. Isabella's husband, in contrast, became the hero of Italy's liberation. Mantua's security was enhanced not only by Francesco's skills as a soldier, but also by Isabella's talents as a diplomat. When, for example, her brother, Duke Alfonso d'Este of Ferrara, married the cultivated Lucretia Borgia (1480–1519) of the unsavory papal family in 1501, Isabella secured her goodwill and that of her malevolent brother, Cesare, to keep him from attacking her small principality.

When her husband was captured in a war against Venice in 1509, she ruled so well in his absence that Francesco became jealous of her success as an administrator. He was also frustrated by the slowness of the process for obtaining his release, for which he blamed his wife. Francesco wrote her from prison in 1512: "We are ashamed that it is our fate to have as a wife a woman who is always ruled by her head." Isabella responded with firmness and pride, "Your excellency is indebted to me as never a husband was to a wife."[6]

After Francesco's release from captivity, relations between the two were frosty until his death in 1519. Isabella then governed six years for her nineteen-year-old son, Federigo, who was in awe of her abilities. Her skills as a diplomat secured him the title of duke from Holy Roman Emperor Charles V (r. 1519–1556) and a cardinalate for her second son, Ercole. She died on February 13, 1539, honored by her contemporaries as "the first lady of the world."

Duke Federigo's Urbino

Located in central Italy, southeast of Florence in the northern Marches, lay the small hill town of Urbino. During the Renaissance, this principality also became a leading center of art and culture under the leadership of the great *condottieri* Duke Federigo da Montefeltro (1422–1482). As a boy he had studied under Vittorino de Feltre in Mantua, where he learned "all human excellence."[7] Although he made his career as a mercenary soldier, Federigo never lost his taste for art, learning, and piety. In 1444 he succeeded his assassinated half brother as ruler of Urbino. Duke Federigo continued to sell his services as one of Italy's most successful soldiers, winning a great reputation for honesty and benevolence.

Federigo da Montefeltro's greatest legacy was his contribution to Renaissance patronage. A competent Latinist, he attempted to create in Urbino the greatest library since antiquity. Virtually the whole corpus of known classics was in his library, as well as important works by the great Muslim scholars Avicenna and Averroës. The duke also had a great taste in architecture and his palace was considered one of the most tasteful in Italy. His cultural activities were supplemented by those of his second wife, Battista Sforza, who was celebrated for her Greek, Latin, and remarkable memory. The duke praised her as "the delight of my public and private hours."[8] She ruled Urbino for him during his frequent absences while campaigning.

Their son Guidobaldo (1472–1508) continued to promote culture after he became duke in 1482. Less skilled than his father as a soldier, he was overshadowed by his remarkable wife, Elisabetta Gonzaga (1471–1526). She was the daughter of Federigo Gonzaga, marquis of Mantua, whose court was another lively center of art and learning. Elisabetta married Guidobaldo in 1488 and earned a great reputation during twenty years of childless married life for her fortitude and virtue. She set the tone for the court life in Urbino and is immortalized in Castiglione's *Book of the Courtier.*

Venice: The Queen of the Adriatic

As important as princely patronage was to the development of Renaissance culture, city-states such as Venice and Florence played crucial roles in stimulating and supporting the arts and learning. Venice, known as the queen of the Adriatic and the hinge of Europe, was the busiest of all the Italian maritime ports. Its share of Mediterranean commerce surpassed even Naples and the bustling sometimes republic of Genoa on the northwest coast of Italy. Venice was also a major producer of books, glass, saddles, soap, metalwork, and other luxury goods. Added to Venice's strategic location and well-defended port was the stability of its government. From 1297 to 1797, an oligarchy of wealthy merchant families controlled the beautiful city of bridges, canals, and islands situated on a lagoon. Venice was in an ideal spot to dominate the trade of the Adriatic Sea and the eastern Mediterranean.

VENETIAN POLITICS AND SOCIETY

As a republic, Venice had a more complex form of government than many of its neighboring principalities. The Venetian state was headed ceremonially by an official, the *doge,* who was elected for life by the male members of the richest families. The doge, with his six councilors and three chief judicial magistrates, made up the ducal council. It set the agenda for the Great Council and presided over the Venetian Senate of 300 men. The doge was the head of state for ceremonial purposes and was also responsible for watching over the functioning of government. The Senate was the real center of power; it had the responsibility for making laws, directing foreign policy, and managing the finances of the state.

In times of emergency, actual authority rested with the Council of Ten, chosen from among the wealthiest and most influential patrician families. Meeting in secret, the Ten dealt with urgent matters of state security

Giovanni Bellini, *Portrait of the Doge Leonardo Loredano,* National Gallery, London, Great Britain. Alinari/Art Resource.

for power; gangs of artisans fought mock battles on bridges with fists and sticks; and incidental violence sometimes broke out during Venice's famous and licentious carnival season. Yet compared to the often stormy political life of Florence or Naples, Venice seemed specially blessed by fortune despite her frequent involvement in wars to protect the commune's robust commercial life and expanding territory.

Venice's closed oligarchy wanted to maintain not only a vast trading empire but also to hold a great deal of the territory surrounding the city for security and economic reasons. In order to survive as a great commercial power, Venice had fought rival maritime power Genoa for much of the fourteenth century. Venice finally emerged victorious from that long struggle. During the fifteenth century, Venice reached its peak of military strength, defeating the Turks at Gallipoli in 1414. The Venetians went on to secure the Morea, Cyprus, and Crete between 1414 and

and could exercise judicial power. Underneath all of the Venetian organs of government was the Great Council, which served as an electoral body. Since 1297 its ranks had been closed to all except males twenty-five years of age or older who came from 200 elite families. The various organs of Venetian government tended to work well together, for the most part, and the interests of the rich merchant families were well protected.

Because its internal history and lifestyle seemed relatively calm compared to many of the less affluent city-states in Italy, Venice was also known in the Renaissance as the "most serene one." Beneath the sometimes placid surface lurked social and political tensions, but they were seldom as disruptive as in other Italian communes. Aristocratic families vied with each other

Andrea del Verrocchio, *Monument to Bartolommeo Colleoni* (c. 1481–1496). Campo SS Giovanni e Paolo, Venice, Italy. Alinari/Art Resource.

1428. In Italy they captured Verona, Vicenza, Padua, Udine, Brescia, and Bergamo. For much of the second half of the fifteenth century, Venice dueled the Ottomans for control of the Adriatic Sea. In the sixteenth century, as trade shifted to the Atlantic, Venice gradually declined as an economic and military force. Its role in helping to defeat the Ottomans at the major naval battle of Lepanto in 1571 in some ways marked the republic's "last hurrah" as a great political power.

VENICE AND THE ARTS

Even in gradual decline, Venice's enormous commercial prosperity helped to support a host of celebrated Renaissance artists, including Jacopo Bellini and his sons Gentile and Giovanni, Giorgione, Tintoretto, Titian, and Veronese. The gifted Florentine sculptor Andrea del Verrocchio created his last and greatest sculpture, the giant equestrian statue of the mercenary general Colleoni, in Venice. Pietro Aretino, famous for his satirical *Lewd Sonnets,* and Veronica Franco, a courtesan and one of Italy's leading female poets, were established residents of Venice and drew inspiration from its vibrant and cosmopolitan economic and social life. Cardinal Pietro Bembo (1470–1547), a native Venetian noble, was a great arbiter of literary taste and a skilled historian, poet, and humanist.

Venice's churches and stately mansions were filled with art and craft goods. Their construction also afforded Renaissance architects and builders with a great deal of employment. Venice was renowned throughout Europe for the glories of its architecture both domestic and public. Even skilled Jewish persons were welcomed to cosmopolitan Venice as the city prized their talents. Only Sicily had a larger Jewish population in Italy. Venice's public pageantry at

civic and religious festivals was remarkable. Such was its prosperity that the government in 1512 felt compelled to limit the size of banquets. Renaissance Venice was, indeed, a place of marvels, which continued to inspire great art long after its political eclipse.

Florence: "The Most Beautiful of Cities"

The perceptive English poet Elizabeth Barret Browning (b. 1806), who spent fifteen years living in Italy, hailed Florence as the "most beautiful of cities." Given the stunning beauty of places like Pisa, Siena, and Venice, this was quite a compliment, but one which Florence deserves. The trade and cloth manufacturing town on the Arno River became known as "queen city of the Renaissance." Artists of the stature of Giotto, Masaccio, Brunelleschi, Donatello, Fra Angelico, Botticelli, Fra Filippo Lippi, Leonardo da Vinci, Michelangelo, Cellini, and a host of others flourished. The city on the Arno was also the home of the poets Dante, Petrarca, and Boccaccio, who helped to make their Tuscan dialect into a superb literary vehicle. Historians such as Machiavelli and Guicciardini were native Florentines, as was the philosopher Marsilio Ficino. Florentine humanism was graced by the likes of Poggio Bracciolini, Leonardo Bruni, Francesco Filelfo, Niccolò Niccoli, and Coluccio Salutati.

Arts and letters thrived there almost in spite of the city's troubled political history. In the twelfth and thirteenth centuries, the commune was torn between rival factions loyal to the Holy Roman emperors (Ghibellines) or the popes (Guelfs). In 1283 the wealthy merchants of Florence initiated constitutional changes that would give them supremacy over the often unruly Florentine nobility. Only male members of the

Arnolfo di Cambio, Palazzo Vecchio (Town Hall), Florence, Italy. Alinari/Art Resource.

seven great guilds of cloth importers, dealers in wool, silk manufacturers, furriers, bankers, judges and notaries, and doctors and apothecaries were allowed to hold public office. That monopoly was challenged by members of some of the less powerful guilds (blacksmiths, shoemakers, butchers, carpenters, bakers, cloth sellers, etc.), who were given a minority share in the government. Noblemen were specifically excluded from public office.

The patriarchal government of Florence was headed by a board of nine guildsmen (the *Signoria*), one of whom was known as the "Standard Bearer of Justice" and was responsible for maintaining law and order throughout the town. The members of the *Signoria* were chosen by lot and served a two-month term. They met daily and lived in the great fortress-like town hall in the heart of the city during their two months in office. Any legislation proposed by the *Signoria* had to be approved by two other bodies with rotating membership—the Twelve Good Men and the Sixteen Standard Bearers. Major laws had to gain the additional approval of the 300-member Council of the People and the 200-member Council of the Commune. On rare occasions, an assembly of all male citizens could be convened by the *Signoria* for the purpose of altering the governmental structure.

The political wisdom of the elite Florentine guildsmen was severely challenged during the calamitous fourteenth century. Its greatest banking houses—the Bardi and the Perruzi—had loaned too much money to King Edward III of England and others at the start of the Hundred Years' War. In 1339 King Edward suspended payment on his loans to the Florentines and then in 1346 repudiated them altogether. Already overextended, the Bardi and Peruzzi banks collapsed and never recovered fully from this blow. Three years later the Black Death hit Florence and killed almost half of its citizens. Periodic famines in the countryside also troubled the Florentines as did a series of wars with Lucca, Milan, Pisa, and the Papal States. In 1378 the unskilled cloth workers known as *Ciompi* revolted, demanding a more popular form of government and burning some of the houses of the rich. Not

until 1382 was order restored after the lesser guilds were granted political representation in the *Signoria*.

At the start of the fifteenth century, Florence was almost conquered by Duke Giangaleazzo of Milan before his premature death in July 1402. The republic had triumphed over the principality. Florence now identified itself as the biblical hero David having defeated the mighty Goliath of the north with the aid of God as many Florentines believed. Having escaped conquest by Milan, the Florentines now assumed the offensive and captured Pisa in 1406. The city now had a port fifty miles away on the west

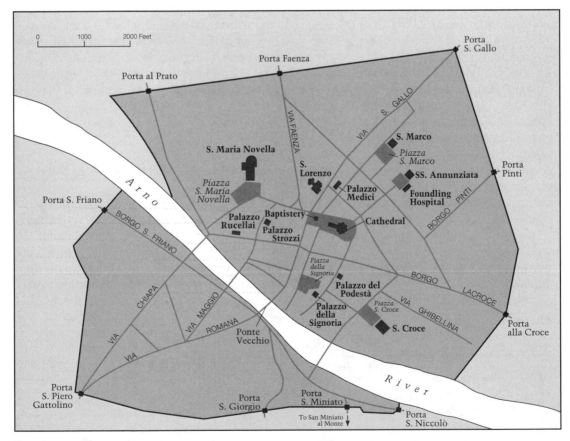

Renaissance Florence

coast of Italy at the mouth of the Arno River, which flowed through the heart of Florence. The Florentines had to fight off Naples between 1409 and 1411, Milan again in 1421, and Lucca in 1429 to 1433. The fight with the nearby silk-producing republic of Lucca eventually drew in Milan as well and almost resulted in disaster for the Florentines.

THE MEDICI IN FLORENCE

Although Florence had many prominent families striving for economic and political power, one family—the Medici—came to dominate the city for 300 years. The rise of the Medici to political prominence began with Cosimo de' Medici's (1389–1464) opposition to the war with Milan and Lucca, which was championed by the politically dominant Albizzi family. The Medici were a well-established banking and cloth manufacturing family. Cosimo de' Medici was married to Contissena Bardi, the daughter of one of his father's old banking partners. The Bardi were no longer rich, but they were still respected, as were the Medici, who had shown sympathy to the working people during the crisis of the Ciompi Revolt. The public criticisms of the war and tax policies of the ruling oligarchy by this popular member of a prominent family threatened the Albizzi hold on power in Florence. Under some pressure Cosimo moved to the relative safety of Verona.

Much to the consternation of the Albizzi, a new *Signoria* favorable to the Medici was chosen in the fall of 1434, and Cosimo was recalled from exile. An Albizzi plot to overthrow the government failed, and they and their mostly aristocratic followers were sent into exile. For the next 300 years, the house of Medici dominated the political history of Florence. They had a wide circle of business and political friends and married into many other prominent families who identified their business and political interests with that of the Medici.

Cosimo de' Medici consulted often with his political support groups and remained accessible to a wide range of people during his thirty years in power. He respected the forms of republican government, only serving as Standard Bearer of Justice for a total of six months, and always supported moderate policies. The newly created executive council (*balia*), which had broad powers to scrutinize voter lists, pass tax bills, and appoint ministers, often met in his palace. Working to keep taxes low, Cosimo made huge personal loans to the city in times of crisis. He also loaned money to other prominent Florentines, making them personally obligated to him. As the owner of three textile factories and a leading banker, Cosimo de' Medici was one of Florence's major employers, something he seldom let his employees forget. He was often present when wages were paid to Medici workers.

THE RISE OF THE MEDICI BANKING EMPIRE

Cosimo de' Medici knew that ultimately his political power rested upon the financial success of his business empire. His father, Giovanni (d. 1429), had carefully studied the example of the Bardi when he set up his own banking network. To avoid becoming overly centralized and overextended, the Medici shared risks with their local partners. Local managers were allowed to make independent decisions, but they had to make considerable investments of their own capital to ensure their caution. If need be, the Medici in Florence could exercise control over their subsidiaries because they always held at least 50 percent of the branch bank's stock.

Better guarantees for loans were also

Michelozzo, Palazzo Medici Riccardi, Florence, Italy. Alinari/Art Resource.

demanded from royal creditors than those obtained by the Bardi and the Peruzzi. Even when banking for the papacy, the Medici demanded and received a controlling interest in the lucrative papal alum mines at Tolfa in northeastern Italy. Cosimo's father had established branch banks in Naples, Rome, Venice, and Geneva in Switzerland. Cosimo added branches in Avignon, Bruges, London, Milan, and Pisa. They dealt in all forms of credit and loans. Money deposited in the Medici banks was then invested in a wide variety of business activities, further extending the family's influence.

Cosimo de' Medici as a Patron

Many of the early capitalists of the Renaissance made a great deal of money. Why did the Medici give so much more back to their community in the form of cultural patronage? Why did they worship the florin less than some of their business rivals? The answers lie partly in the background and wide-ranging interests of Cosimo himself. Educated at a monastic school and "grave in temperament," Cosimo had learned German, French, Latin, and some Hebrew, Greek, and Arabic. His active mind found business and politics to be insufficiently stimulating to absorb all his considerable mental energies and to enrich his spirit. Therefore, he continued to attend humanist discussion groups throughout his life as he found philosophy challenged him as nothing else did in the world of affairs. Cosimo even "adopted" the Neoplatonic philosopher Marsilio Ficino (1433–1499), the son of his physician, and helped establish the Platonic Academy, a group of scholars dedicated to the thought of the Greek philosopher.

Cosimo also developed an interest in art and architecture, which he found could be used to enhance his family's "honor" as well as that of his city. A good friend to the sculptor Donatello, Cosimo was supportive of many artists and architects. The fortress-like Medici Palace, which Cosimo had built in the heart of the city, provided his family and friends with comfort, aesthetically pleasing surroundings, privacy, and security. Although the Medici Palace made an impressive show of power and wealth, it was not as excessive as the Pitti Palace. Influenced as well by the Ciceronian notion that the rich must give something back to their communities, Cosimo was directly or indirectly responsible for erecting many other structures in Florence, including the church of San Lorenzo, the monastery of San Marco, and several villas in the countryside. Given the title "father of the state," Cosimo growled, "in a few years, they will remember me only for my buildings."[9]

The Medici dynasty in Florence was continued by Cosimo's son, Piero "the Gouty." A skilled financier, Piero did not have his father's political sophistication and was limited by his poor health. He did continue Cosimo's alliances with Milan and the papacy and kept the Venetians at bay. Piero's position was enhanced by the abilities of his poet-wife, Lucretia, who came from a prosperous, venerable Florentine family. She helped her husband dispense abundant patronage to artists and produced five well-educated children. Their children were all married into prominent families. Piero's five years of dominance ended in 1469, but he was able to pass a great deal of power to his more talented sons, Lorenzo and Giuliano.

THE MAGNIFICENT LORENZO (1449–1492)

Lorenzo de' Medici was a talented and complex individual who became renowned for his generous support of the arts. Many talented artists, musicians, and philosophers were directly supported or encouraged by the sensual Lorenzo, known as "the Magnificent." Filippo Lippi, Domenico Ghirlandaio, Sandro Botticelli, Verrocchio, Michelangelo, and others received commissions from Lorenzo. The Medici library expanded under his patronage and he continued to support the Platonic Academy of Marsilio Ficino, his intimate friend. A sensual man of many interests and abilities, Lorenzo also wrote provocative and often ribald poetry and staged elaborate annual festivals.

As the political leader of Florence, Lorenzo de' Medici attempted to defend aggressively the financial interests of the city. Unfortunately for him, his family's friend Pope Paul II (r. 1464–1471) was succeeded

Andrea del Verrocchio, *Lorenzo de' Medici*. Photo courtesy of the National Gallery of Art, Samuel H. Kress Collection, Washington, D.C.

by Francesco della Rovere as Pope Sixtus IV. Sixtus IV distrusted and disliked Lorenzo, who had attacked Volterra in 1472 for its rich alum mines. Alum, a very valuable sulfate, was absolutely essential in the dyeing of textiles. Both the pope and the banker wanted to control this important asset. Sixtus also had his own family ambitions and wanted to bestow strategic Imola in the Romagna on one of his nephews. Lorenzo opposed this and also the appointment of Francesco Salviati as archbishop of Pisa.

THE PAZZI PLOT OF 1478

As relations with the papacy cooled, enemies of the Medici flocked to Rome and found a sympathetic papal ear. Foremost among them were members of a rival Florentine banking family, the Pazzi, who replaced the Medici as papal bankers. With the blessing of the pope, Francesco de Pazzi, Archbishop Francesco Salviati, and others attempted to assassinate Lorenzo and Giuliano de' Medici during the celebration of High Mass at the cathedral of Florence on April 26, 1478. Giuliano was stabbed to death, but Lorenzo escaped with only a shoulder wound.

The Pazzi conspirators also failed to seize the town hall or to rally the people against the Medici. Instead the people of Florence joined Lorenzo in severely punishing the conspirators. Francesco de Pazzi and Archbishop Salviati were hanged from the windows of the Florentine town hall. Other plotters were brutally murdered by angry mobs. Pope Sixtus retaliated by excommunicating Lorenzo de' Medici, imposing an interdict on Florence, and then invading Tuscany with his ally Naples. Abandoned by its ally Venice, Florence struggled for two desperate years to hold off its enemies.

During the course of the war, Lorenzo de' Medici risked his life on a secret diplomatic mission to the court of the capricious and often cruel Ferrante I of Naples. He finally managed to persuade Ferrante that it would not be in Naples's interest to increase the power of the Papal States at the expense of Florence. Without the support of Naples, Sixtus IV had to agree to a separate peace with Florence.

The Fall of the Medici

Having survived the great crisis of the Pazzi Plot, Lorenzo de' Medici continued to dominate Florentine politics for the rest of his life. He helped to create a new executive committee, the Council of Seventy, which controlled most of the executive powers of government through its subcommittees. Lorenzo was a permanent member of the Seventy and had his representatives serve on the other important organs of power. He also fused his personal fortune with that of the state, probably to his own advantage.

His generous expenditures continued throughout his life, although not to the same extent as in an earlier time. Between 1434 and 1471, the Medici spent 663,755 gold florins on architectural and artistic commissions, charity, and taxes. Lorenzo said of this astounding sum: "I think it casts a brilliant light on our estate, and it seems to me that the monies were well spent and I am very well pleased with this."[10] Indeed, Medici's preoccupation with artistic and political matters caused him to neglect his family's business affairs. Ignoring one of the key lessons of the Bardi experience, he made an overly generous loan to a fellow art collector, Charles the Bold, duke of Burgundy, which was never repaid. Medici banks were already closing before Lorenzo's death in 1492 and the invasion of the French two years later.

The French invasion caused the Medici to close the Rome branch and finally the home bank in Florence itself. There was still enough wealth left to secure the futures of Lorenzo's children if competently managed. His second son, Giovanni, had become a cardinal at age thirteen and later became Pope Leo X (r. 1513–1521). Lorenzo de' Medici was succeeded in Florence by his oldest son, the wastrel Piero. The incompetent Piero was blamed for losing territory to the invading French and was exiled from Florence for life in November 1494. The unthinkable had happened: The Medici of Florence had fallen.

Chronology

1254	Coining of the first florin.	1458–1464	Reign of Pope Pius II (Aeneas Silvius).
1282–1302	War of the Sicilian Vespers.	1458–1494	Reign of Ferrante I in Naples.
1295	Marco Polo returns to Venice from Asia.	1471–1484	Reign of Pope Sixtus IV.
1297	Founding of the Venetian republic.	1474	Birth of Isabella d'Este.
1346	Collapse of the Bardi and Peruzzi banks.	1476	Ludovico il Moro takes power in Milan as regent; birth of Cesare Borgia.
1347	Outbreak of the Black Death; Cola di Rienzo seizes control of Rome.	1478	Pazzi Plot in Florence.
1354	Fall of Cola di Rienzo.	1492	Reign of Pope Alexander VI (Borgia).
1376	Papacy returns to Rome.	1494	Invasion of King Charles VIII of France; closing of Medici banks in Rome and Florence.
1378	Cloth workers revolt in Florence.	1495	Battle of Fornova.
1385–1402	Reign of Giangaleazzo I in Milan.	1496	Burning of the vanities in Florence.
1389–1464	Life of Cosimo de' Medici.	1498	Death of Savonarola.
1414–1435	Reign of Joanna II in Naples.	1499	Invasion of King Louis XII of France.
1416–1458	Reign of Alfonso V of Aragon and South Italy.	1503–1513	Reign of Pope Julius II (Papa Terrible).
1417–1431	Reign of Pope Nicholas V; rebuilding of Rome.	1507	Death of Cesare Borgia.
1444–1482	Reign of Federigo da Montefeltro in Urbino.	1508	Death of Ludovico il Moro.
1449–1492	Life of Lorenzo de' Medici.	1527	Sack of Rome.
1450–1466	Reign of Francesco and Bianca Sforza in Milan.	1535	Death of Isabella d'Este.

Further Reading

THE ITALIAN RENAISSANCE:
GENERAL STUDIES

Peter Burke, *The Historical Anthropology of Early Modern Italy* (1987).

Denys Hay and John Law, *Italy in the Age of the Renaissance* (1989).

Michael Mallett, *Mercenaries and Their Masters: Warfare in Renaissance Italy* (1984).

Lauro Martines, *Power and Imagination: City-States in Renaissance Italy* (1979).

Garrett Mattingly, *Renaissance Diplomacy* (1955).

John Stephens, *The Italian Renaissance: The Origins of Intellectual and Artistic Change Before the Reformation* (1990).

Giovanni Tabacco, *The Struggle for Power in Medieval Italy* (1990).

David Waley, *The Italian City Republics*, 3rd ed. (1988).

PAPAL ROME

Anthony Grafton, ed., *Rome Reborn: The Vatican Library and Renaissance Culture* (1993). Important collection of essays by various scholars.

Egmont Lee, *Sixtus IV and Men of Letters* (1978).

Michael Mallett, *The Borgias* (1969).

Rosamond Mitchell, *The Laurels and the Tiara: Pope Pius II* (1962).

Laurie Nussdorfer, *Civic Politics in the Rome of Urban VIII* (1992).

Peter Partner, *The Pope's Men: The Papal Civil Service in the Renaissance* (1990).

Kenneth Setton, *The Papacy and the Levant, 1204–1571*, 4 vols. (1976–1984).

Christine Shaw, *Julius II, The Warrior Pope* (1993).

Charles Stinger, *The Renaissance in Rome* (1985).

VENICE

David Chambers, *The Imperial Age of Venice, 1380–1580* (1970).

David Chambers and Brian Pullan, eds., *Venice: A Documentary History, 1450–1630* (1993). 250 wide-ranging documents.

Robert Davis, *The War of the Fists: Popular Culture and Public Violence in Late Renaissance Venice* (1994).

Robert Finlay, *Politics in Renaissance Venice* (1980).

Paul Grendler, *The Roman Inquisition and the Venetian Press, 1540- 1605* (1977).

Margaret King, *Venetian Humanism in an Age of Patrician Dominance* (1986).

Frederic Lane, *Venice, A Maritime Republic* (1973).

Richard Mackenney, *Tradesmen and Traders: The World of Guilds in Venice and Europe* (1987).

John Martin, *Venice's Hidden Enemies: Italian Heretics in a Renaissance City* (1994).

Ruth Martin, *Witchcraft and the Inquisition in Venice* (1989).

Edward Muir, *Civic Ritual in Renaissance Venice* (1981).

John Norwich, *A History of Venice* (1989).

Brian Pullan, *Rich and Poor in Renaissance Venice* (1971).

Donald Queller, *The Venetian Patriciate: Myth vs. Reality* (1986).

Dennis Romano, *Housecraft and Statecraft: Domestic Service in Renaissance Venice, 1400–1600* (1996).

———, *Patricians and Popolani: The Social Foundations of the Venetian Renaissance State* (1987).

Guido Ruggiero, *Binding Passions: Tales of Magic, Marriage, and Power at the End of the Renaissance* (1993).

FLORENCE

Marvin Becker, *Florence in Transition*, 2 vols. (1967–1968).

Gene Brucker, *The Civic World of Early Renaissance Florence*, 2nd ed. (1985).

———, *Renaissance Florence* (1969).

Samuel Cohn, *The Laboring Poor in Renaissance Florence* (1980).

Christopher Hibbert, *Florence* (1990).

Dale and F. W. Kent, *Neighbors and Neighborhoods in Renaissance Florence* (1982).

Carol Lansing, *The Florentine Magnates: Lineage and Factions in a Medieval Commune* (1991).

Anthony Molho, *Marriage Alliance in Late Medieval Florence* (1994).

John Najemy, *Corporation and Consensus in Florentine Electoral Politics* (1982).

Ferdinand Schevill, *A History of Florence* (1936).

Laura Stern, *The Criminal Law System of Medieval and Renaissance Florence* (1994).

Richard Trexler, *Public Life in Renaissance Florence* (1980).

Ronald Weissman, *Ritual Brotherhood in Renaissance Florence* (1982).

THE MEDICI

C. M. Ady, *Lorenzo de' Medici and Renaissance Italy* (1955).

Frances Ames-Lewis, ed., *Cosimo "il Vecchio" de' Medici, 1389–1464* (1992).

Alison Brown, *The Medici in Florence: The Exercise of Language and Power* (1992).

Melissa Bullard, *Lorenzo il Magnifico: Image and Anxiety, Politics and Finance* (1994).

J. R. Hale, *Florence and the Medici* (1977).

Dale Kent, *The Rise of the Medici: Faction in Florence* (1978).

Nicolai Rubenstein, *The Government of Florence Under the Medici (1434–1494)* (1966).

OTHER STATES

Jerry Bentley, *Politics and Culture in Renaissance Naples* (1987).

William Bowsky, *A Medieval Italian Commune: Siena* (1981).

M. E. Bratchel, *Lucca: The Reconstruction of an Italian City-Republic, 1430–1494* (1995).

Judith Brown, *In the Shadow of Renaissance Florence: Pescia* (1982).

Trevor Dean, *Land and Power in Late Medieval Ferrara: The Rule of the Este* (1988).

Joanne Ferraro, *Family and Public Life in Brescia, 1580–1650: The Foundations of Power in the Venetian State* (1993).

James Grubb, *Firstborn of Venice: Vicenza in the Early Renaissance State* (1988).

Werner Gundersheimer, *Ferrara: The Style of a Renaissance Despotism* (1973).

David Herlihy, *Medieval and Renaissance Pistoia* (1967).

———, *Pisa in the Early Renaissance* (1958).

P. J. Jones, *The Malatesta of Rimini and the Papal State* (1972).

John Larner, *The Lords of the Romagna* (1965).

Gregory Lubkin, *A Renaissance Court: Milan under Galezzo Maria Sforza* (1994).

Edward Muir, *Mad Blood Stirring: Vendetta and Factions in Friuli during the Renaissance* (1993).

Alan Ryder, *Alfonso the Magnanimous, King of Aragon, Naples, and Sicily, 1396–1458* (1990).

Kate Simon, *A Renaissance Tapestry: The Gonzaga of Mantua* (1988).

Nicholas Terpstra, *Confraternities and Civic Religion in Renaissance Bologna* (1993).

Thomas Tuohy, *Herculean Ferrara: Ercole d'Este (1471–1505) and the Invention of a Ducal Capital* (1996).

Notes

1. Cited in G. R. Elton, ed., *Renaissance and Reformation 1300–1600,* 3rd ed. (New York: Macmillan, 1976), p. 94.
2. Cited in Lewis Spitz, *The Renaissance and Reformation Movements* (Chicago: Rand McNally, 1971), p. 94.
3. Cited in Kenneth Bartlett, ed., *The Civilization of the Italian Renaissance: A Sourcebook* (Lexington, Mass.; D. C. Heath, 1992), p. 316.
4. Cited in De Lamar Jensen, *Renaissance Europe: Age of Recovery and Reconciliation,* 2nd ed. (Lexington, Mass.: D. C. Heath, 1992), p. 305.
5. Cited in D. S. Chambers, ed., *Patrons and Artists in the Italian Renaissance* (Columbia, S.C.: University of South Carolina Press, 1971), p. 136.
6. Cited in Maria Bellonci, "Beatrice and Isabella d'Este," in *Renaissance Profiles,* J. H. Plumb, ed. (New York: Harper and Row, 1961), p. 151.
7. Cited in Denis Mack Smith, "Federigo da Montefeltro," in ibid., p. 125.
8. Cited in Jensen, *Renaissance,* p. 71.
9. Cited in Spitz, *Renaissance and Reformation,* p. 108.
10. Cited in Lauro Martines, *Power and Imagination: City States in Renaissance Italy* (New York: Alfred Knopf, 1979), p. 243.

5

The Culture of Renaissance Humanism in Italy

The city-states and principalities of Renaissance Italy produced artistic masterpieces in abundance throughout the period. Seldom has so much talent appeared at one time and place and achieved such comparatively high levels of sophisticated public and private support. Underlying the achievements of the Renaissance artists was the culture of Renaissance humanism. Humanism can be defined as a movement that encouraged the study of the form and content of classical learning. Renaissance humanists were obsessed with the recovery, study, interpretation, and transmission of the intellectual heritage of ancient Greece and Rome. They were particularly interested in what the Roman philosopher and statesman Cicero (106–43 B.C.) defined as "humane studies" or the liberal arts. Cicero favored those subjects such as grammar, rhetoric, poetry, literature, and moral philosophy (ethics), which help us to become more eloquent, thoughtful, and virtuous human beings. The fundamental agenda of the humanists was to use what they called the study of humanity (humanitas) to make people more civilized and more humane.

The humanists of the Renaissance, whether businessmen such as Cosimo de' Medici, politicians such as Isabella d'Este, or professional scholars such as Lorenzo Valla, had a tremendous faith in the power of language. They urged the study of classical languages such as Greek and Roman and the return to the original source materials whenever possible. Some of the humanists also hoped to transform the use of Latin in their own day, to purge it of what they thought were barbarisms and return it to the glories of Cicero's day. Inspired by classical models, Renaissance humanists made rich contributions to the development of history and philosophy. In literature, many of the humanists contributed to the flowering of Italian vernacular drama and poetry.

Setting the Agenda: Early Renaissance Humanists

Much of the agenda of early Renaissance humanism came from the lives and thoughts of Francesco Petrarca and Giovanni Boccaccio. Both were men of formidable literary talents, whose Italian writings along with those of Dante helped to shape the development of that language as a literary vehicle. They became good friends and came to share a passion for the ancient Greek and Latin classics that greatly influenced the development of Renaissance humanism in Italy and elsewhere.

FRANCESCO PETRARCA (1304–1374)

Petrarca was born in Arezzo near Florence in 1304. His notary father had been exiled from Florence for his involvement in a long-standing political dispute between different factions of the Guelph (papal) movement. When Francesco was seven years old, his family moved to Pisa and then a year later to a small village near Avignon, where the papacy had moved during the period of what he would later call the "Babylonian Captivity of the church of God." His father, Pietro, worked in the papal bureaucracy. Young Francesco picked up his interest in the classics from his father, who was fond of reading Cicero's letters aloud at home.

At age twelve Petrarca was sent fifty miles away to the University of Montpellier in France to begin the study of law, which he hated. Instead of concentrating on his legal studies, he immersed himself in the Latin classics. His mother died while he was away from home at Montpellier. At age sixteen, he was dispatched by his father to the University of Bologna, the foremost law school in Europe. When his father died in 1326, the handsome and vain Petrarca returned to Avignon and lived the life of a young dandy. As he wrote later, "I could not face making a merchandise of my mind."[1] Indeed, he seemed more worried about his reddish-brown hair, which had turned prematurely gray. To support himself and his growing interest in poetry, he took minor orders in the church but was never ordained.

His career as a poet was bolstered after he first laid eyes on the lovely "Laura" at a church in Avignon on April 6, 1326. She was married to someone else and they had no significant, personal contact. Nevertheless, Petrarca immortalized her charms in his increasingly popular Italian sonnets. He called her "the candid rose, thorn-compassed and shy, and yet our age's glory and despair."[2]

In 1330 he became a chaplain in the house of a cardinal but insisted on having ample time for his writing and scholarship. Francesco Petrarca was quickly recognized as the greatest Italian poet since Dante. Occasional diplomatic missions, church benefices, gifts, prizes, and his writings gave him sufficient income for a life of travel, a bit of art patronage, and retirement to a modest villa. Petrarca made it all the way to the Netherlands traveling through the forested lands of the Holy Roman Empire in central Europe. Back in Italy he was crowned "Poet Laureate" by the Roman senate in a magnificent ceremony in Rome in April 1341.

Italy's incessant wars almost did him in as he traveled about seeking inspiration and hospitality. Petrarca was nearly killed in 1344 during a siege of Parma. He survived the Black Death, but many of his friends perished, as did the inspiration of his sonnets, Laura. The poet was also a friend of Cola di Rienzo, who shared his love for the ancient Romans. After Cola's second effort to restore the grandeur of Rome ended in petty tyranny in 1354, the disappointed Petrarca made the long journey from Milan to Prague in order to beg Holy Roman Emperor Charles IV to bring peace to troubled Italy. Petrarca spent the last years of life in quiet solitude tended by his illegitimate daughter, Francesca, at his retirement villa near Venice.

Before his death, Petrarca had done a great deal to help revive the study of antiquity. He had even imitated the Roman poet Vergil by producing his own epic poem, *Africa*, in honor of Scipio Africanus, who defeated the Carthaginian Hannibal in 202 B.C. The modern historian Lewis Spitz, Jr. has called it an "epic bore." Petrarca also edited a version of the writings of the Roman historian Livy. He even published a collection of *Letters to the Ancient Dead* in which he informed the ancients Cicero, Seneca, Horace, Vergil, Homer, and others of how bad things were in his own day and how much he wished he was living with them. To get to know the ancients better, Petrarca tried to learn classical Greek and began searching for ancient manuscripts.

Increasingly religious as he grew older, Petrarca also found great solace in the writings of St. Augustine of Hippo in Africa (d. 430). His own love of the classics never diminished and he continued to urge others to make their own discovery of the rich heritage of ancient Greece and Rome. <u>He passed on to later humanists the idea of the active and contemplative lives, the Stoic notion of virtue as "greatness of soul," a hostility to speculative knowledge, and a strong faith in human rationality.</u> Petrarca developed many of the fundamental ideas of Renaissance humanism and influenced generations of thinkers, both men and women. As the later humanist Leonardo Bruni wrote of him, "Francesco Petrarca was the first who had such grace of talent and who recognized and restored to light the ancient elegance of style which was lost and dead by recovering the works of Cicero."[3]

GIOVANNI BOCCACCIO (1313–1375)

In his own lifetime, Petrarca had a profound impact on one of the most gifted literary men of the early Renaissance, Giovanni Boccaccio. Boccaccio was born the illegitimate son of a Florentine merchant and a French woman. His father intended him to pursue a career in business and sent him to Naples to learn the profession. He worked for a branch of the Bardi bank and also tried his hand at studying canon law. The collapse of the Bardi bank and the disorders connected with the Black Death forced his return to Florence to assist his father.

In the stimulating atmosphere of disaster-plagued Florence, Giovanni Boccaccio found time to pursue his literary interests and wrote some of the most important works of the Renaissance. Out of the catastrophe of the Black Death came Boccaccio's finest literary accomplishment, the *Decameron*, 100 folk tales, some of them irreverent and lascivious, but told with great elegance of style. Written in Italian, the *Decameron* also contains the best surviving derivative account we have of the Black Death. The tales, written in an essentially medieval style, became extremely popular and established Boccaccio's literary fame. They provided a world still stunned by grief with some badly needed comic relief of high quality. Few have matched his gifts as a storyteller.

Under the influence of Francesco Petrarca, whom he called his "illustrious teacher," Boccaccio began to write more in Latin and to devote more attention to classi-

Andrea del Castagno, *Portrait of Giovanni Boccaccio*. S. Apollonia, Florence, Italy. Alinari/Art Resource.

cal and religious subjects. Like his mentor, he tried to learn Greek and was instrumental in having a chair in that language established at the University of Florence. Boccaccio also loved collecting ancient manuscripts and managed to find texts of the Roman satirist Martial, the poet Ovid, and the historian Tacitus. His classical studies also resulted in a *Genealogy of the Gods,* a manual of ancient geography, and a collection of essays on famous men and women from antiquity. Boccaccio's *Concerning Famous Women* treats 106 women from the Old Testament through medieval times. Although filled with misogynistic assumptions, it did a great deal to make his readers aware of a gender normally forgotten in a period of male-dominated letters and scholarship. His legacy includes a biography of the great Florentine poet Dante and a commentary on his *Divine Comedy.*

Civic Humanists

Although Francesco Petrarca and his associate Giovanni Boccaccio pursued their classical studies for their own sake and that of their souls, some later humanists chose to become more involved in the affairs of their communities. They chose to live more active and public lives as had their hero Cicero, the ancient Roman lawyer-statesman-philosopher. Coluccio Salutati and Leonardo Bruni were two of the many civic humanists who chose to put their knowledge of the classics to practical use in the service of their communities. Once again, a grounding in the humanities proved to be the best training for careers as well as life.

COLUCCIO SALUTATI (1331–1406)

Coluccio Salutati was yet another Florentine humanist who was influenced by Petrarca. Salutati studied law at Bologna and became a notary. He held bureaucratic positions in Rome and at various places in Tuscany before becoming chancellor of the republic of Lucca. In 1375 he became chancellor of the Florentine government, a position he held for the rest of his life. Salutati used his position to promote the growth of humanism and was an elegant Latin stylist. Giangaleazzo I of Milan said that a letter from Salutati was "worth a contingent of cavalry."[4]

Salutati helped guide Florence through the great crisis of the Cloth Workers (*Ciompi*) Revolt of 1378 and counseled the ruling elite to avoid harsh reprisals against the rebels. During outbreaks of plague, he refused to leave his post or to allow his family to leave. His reading of the Roman Stoics had convinced him that no one could die before his appointed time. When the Milanese threatened Florence, Salutati's rally of its defenders so infuriated Giangaleazzo that he sent assassins to kill him; when that failed he sent forged letters implicating the chancellor in treason. Giangaleazzo had used a similar ruse to get the marquis of Mantua to behead his own wife. Fortunately for Salutati, the Florentine *Signoria* did not fall for the trick.

In addition to his numerous civic duties, Salutati found time to write on the classics and religion and to locate lost manuscripts, including Cicero's *Familiar Letters.* Devoted to ancient learning, the chancellor also brought Manuel Chrysoloras (c. 1350–1415), a leading Greek scholar, from Constantinople to Florence in 1396. Chrysoloras became a municipally paid public lecturer and helped further spread classical learning among the Florentine elite, including Leonardo Bruni, Salutati's civic humanist successor as chancellor.

LEONARDO BRUNI (1370–1444)

Bruni was born in Arezzo near Florence to a family of modest means. An obviously gifted and determined youth, he was helped by Salutati and taught Greek by Manuel Chrysoloras. He became a language tutor in the Medici household. His celebrated skill as a Latinist won him a position in 1405 as a secretary in the papal chancery in Rome. Bruni returned to Florence for good in 1427 as a member of the Florentine bureaucracy, rising to the position of chancellor in 1427, an office he held to his death in 1444.

Leonardo Bruni continued Salutati's tradition of civic humanism, using his intellectual skills for the good of his community. He urged others to "read authors who can help you not only by their subject matter, but also by the splendor of their style and their skill in writing; that is to say, the works of Cicero and of any who may possibly approach his level." On the other hand, Bruni found nothing except boredom in the study of law, which he called "the yawning science" and found no honor in "the mercenary traffic in law-suits."[5]

His own writings were extremely important to the development of the discipline of history. He is best known for his influential *History of the Florentine People,* on which he labored for three decades. Bruni's *History* was modeled after the classic work of the Roman historian Livy. Bruni argued that events were the result of human rather than divine activity and that even recent history was a worthwhile enterprise because of the moral lessons it taught. He also translated Aristotle's *Ethics* and *Politics* and much of Plato into Latin. His attitudes toward women seemed more in keeping with the spirit of Aristotle, who viewed women as "defective men," than Plato who had to concede that women could be admitted to the highest (guardian) class in his ideal *Republic* because in essence equal potential for reasoning is found in both sexes. A great Florentine patriot, the Florentine chancellor also wrote *In Praise of the City of Florence*, a book which lauded the freedom of the republican form of government, its capitalistic business practices, and praised the beauty of the city. In his life and in his work, Leonardo Bruni affords us a significant example of the humanist in the service of his community.

The Illustrious Lorenzo Valla (c. 1407–1457)

Fifteenth-century Renaissance humanism hit its peak in the life and work of Lorenzo Valla. Valla was arguably the most brilliant of the humanists of the Italian Renaissance. A native of Rome, he studied under Vittorino da Feltre (1378–1447), the foremost schoolmaster of the Italian Renaissance. Excelling in Latin and Greek, Valla served as a professor of eloquence at the University of Pavia beginning in 1429. In 1433 he was forced to flee Pavia after a controversy over his spirited attacks on the legal theories of the popular Bartolus of Sassoferato. He then resumed his life as a wandering scholar with stops in Milan, Genoa, and Mantua, among other places. He made the acquaintance of most of the leading humanists in Italy, including Leonardo Bruni and Poggio Bracciolini. In 1437 Valla took a position as secretary to King Alfonso the Magnanimous of Naples, whom he advised on cultural matters.

Lorenzo Valla parted company with other humanists in preferring the Latin style of Quintillian to Cicero and Epicureanism to Stoicism. In his *On Pleasure*, he argued that while the ethical doctrines of Christianity were superior to those of the Epicureans, it was better to pursue happiness than pain. His own pleasure was found chiefly in scholarship despite the attacks of his critics. Undaunted by his foes, Valla wrote:

I have published many books, a great many, in almost every branch of learning. Inasmuch as there are those who are shocked that in these I disagree with certain great writers already approved by long usage, and charge me with rashness and sacrilege, what must we suppose some of them will do now![6]

More controversy followed with his *On the False Donation of Constantine* of 1440 in which Valla demonstrated through historical, linguistic, and logical analysis that the first Christian emperor could not possibly have been the author of the document which allegedly transferred the territorial sovereignty over the Western Roman Empire to the papacy. Valla showed that a number of terms used in the *Donation* were not in use until at least a century after the time of Constantine. He wondered: Would Constantine "give up the best part of his empire?" If the emperor did so, why is there "no proof that it was received?"[7] Although summoned to Rome in 1444 by Pope Felix V (r. 1439–1449), Valla stayed in Naples under the protection of the pope's enemy, King Alfonso.

His *On the Elegances of the Latin Language* (1444) became the standard textbook throughout Europe for all those interested in philological precision and a graceful writing style. Applying his critical methods to the Bible, Valla produced his highly influential *Annotations on the New Testament*, which demonstrated many errors in the Vulgate translation of the Bible, the official Bible of the medieval Roman Catholic Church. This work was known only in manuscript form to a limited circle until published by the northern humanist Erasmus in 1505. Erasmus then used Valla's work in producing his own remarkable translation of the New Testament in 1516.

Valla also entered into some of the other great intellectual debates of the age. In his treatise *On Free Will*, he argued that predestination was not necessarily incompatible with free will, even if faith and love must be emphasized. Valla also rendered a great service to history by his translations of the classical Greek historians Herodotus and Thucydides as well as writing his own history of the reign of King Ferrante I of Naples. In 1448 he became secretary to Pope Nicholas V (r. 1447–1455) and a professor at the University of Rome. In Rome, Valla spent the last years of his life helping the humanist pope collect rare Greek editions and establishing the papal library. It was a fine ending to a life of controversy and scholarship.

Women Humanists

Scholarship, like most public activities, was considered a man's field during the Renaissance and the centuries that had preceded it. With only a few rare exceptions, women were not admitted to the universities or allowed to practice the learned professions. Opportunities for learning were severely restricted for women outside the walls of convents and elite courts. Indeed, only 186 European laywomen have been identified as book owners during the fourteenth and fifteenth centuries. Those who tried to enter the world of the male humanists found mostly ridicule and suspicion. Despite all this discouragement, several women did manage to make contributions to the humanist movement. Following are brief sketches of two of these female Renaissance humanists, whose lives reveal many of the challenges intellectual women faced in the period.

Isotta Nogarola (1418–1466)

One of the most talented of the women humanists was Isotta Nogarola of Verona. She was born to a noble family with a tradition of learning that included her aunt, Angela. Isotta's widowed mother insisted that both her daughters have the finest education possible for girls in the Renaissance, which was not a typical attitude for mothers in an age that assumed females to be lesser creatures than males. Isotta and her talented sister, Ginevra, were tutored by Martino Rizzoni, a student of the great humanist pedagogue Guarino da Verona.

The Nogarola sisters became quite well known for their learning in northern Italian humanist circles. Even among the humanists, however, learned women were considered threatening. The usual mode of attack was to impugn their character. Anonymous letters were circulated accusing Isotta of making "her body generally available for promiscuous intercourse." Snubbed by Guarino da Verona, Isotta lamented, "Why then was I born a woman, to be scorned by men in words and deeds?" When Guarino finally replied, he praised her learning. He then told her that she should set her gender aside and create "a man within the woman." That is, if she were going to enter into what he considered "masculine pursuits," she must become like a man in her mind.[8]

In 1438 Ginevra married a Brescian nobleman and was forced to give up her studies completely, as so often happened to the few young, educated women of the period. Duties as a wife and mother were expected to take almost all the time of even a noblewoman. Most Renaissance wives did not have parents or husbands who encouraged them to use their minds. Few could defy the society's insistence on submission to the absolute authority of husbands.

Distressed by the loss of her sister to marriage and the scorn she received from some of her humanist correspondents, Isotta moved to more cosmopolitan Venice

but returned to Verona in 1441. She vowed never to marry and instead retreated to her "book-lined cell" in her mother's house to pursue religious rather than classical studies. In the 1450s she drew close to the civic humanist and diplomat, Ludovico Foscarini, whom she had known earlier when he was the Venetian governor of Verona. Out of their correspondence grew her two most important writings, *Dialogue on Adam and Eve* and *Oration on the Life of St. Jerome,* both of which revealed a sophisticated understanding of theological issues. The Venetian scholar, Lauro Quirini, praised her for overcoming her "own nature. For that true virtue, which is essentially male, you have sought with singular zeal."[9]

LAURA CERETA (1469–1499)

Like Isotta Nogarola, Laura Cereta was a talented scholar, who also found it difficult to find acceptance from male humanists. She began life as the daughter of a noble in Brescia and received some of her early education in a convent. At the age of nine, Laura returned home to be tutored by her supportive father in Latin, Greek, and mathematics. Inspired by the example of Petrarca, she began an active correspondence and showed a fine Latin style. Cereta was married to a Brescian merchant at age fifteen but was widowed eighteen months later when he died of the plague. In little more than a year, she had been "a girl, bride, widow, and pauper."

Her humanist studies helped her recover from the death of her beloved and supportive husband. She plunged more deeply than ever into mathematics, philosophy, and theology, where she found knowledge not "shadowy and vaporous," but "perpetually secure and perfect." "I care more for letters than for flashy clothes," she wrote. "Moreover, I have committed myself absolutely to that cultivation of virtue which can profit me not only when alive but also after death." Cereta was attacked for her learning and outspoken opinions. A prominent Dominican, Thomas of Milan, advised her to "blunt your pen and temper it with the file of modesty" and give up classical studies as "things unworthy of her."[10] Before lapsing into obscurity, Laura Cereta wrote a wide range of Latin works, including her letters to fellow humanists and an important defense of humanist learning for women. She died at age thirty and is only now being rediscovered as an important Renaissance thinker, whose full potential was never realized.

Humanists as Philosophers, Historians, and Social Theorists

Although women of intellect such as Isotta Nogarola and Laura Cereta were seldom allowed to develop fully their interests in subjects such as philosophy, bright young men had opportunities to pursue lives of learning and to make valuable contributions to many areas of inquiry during the Renaissance. While Greek philosophers such as Aristotle continued to be important, especially for medieval theologians such as Thomas Aquinas, the Renaissance witnessed a renewed interest in the Macedonian as well as a revival of interest in his great rival and teacher, Plato. Ancient historical models also inspired a new interest in history and political theory. Renaissance humanists made lasting additions to the subjects of education, manners, and social theory. In what follows, we will examine briefly the lives and thoughts of four important male Renaissance theorists: Giovanni Pico della Mirandola, Niccolò Machiavelli,

Francesco Guicciardini, and Baldassare Castiglione.

Giovanni Pico della Mirandola (1463–1494)

Giovanni Pico was one of the most attractive personalities and intellects of the Italian Renaissance. He was the son of the count of Mirandola and Concordia, a small principality just west of Ferrara in the Po Valley. At age fourteen, Giovanni began the study of canon law at the University of Bologna and then moved to Padua and Florence. In Florence, he became a close friend and pupil of the influential Neoplatonic philosopher Marsilio Ficino, who had a profound influence on the development of his thought.

Moving on to Paris, Giovanni Pico della Mirandola became engrossed with scholastic theology and languages. Blessed with a hunger for learning and a gift for languages, Pico mastered Greek, Latin, and Hebrew. He also studied Arabic and other Near Eastern languages. His Hebrew studies led him into the mystical texts of Jewish theology known as the *Cabala*. Believing that all knowledge could be reconciled, Pico also ventured into Arabic philosophy, mathematics, music, and physics. In defense of this thesis, the twenty-four-year-old Pico traveled to Rome in 1486 and attempted to publish his 900 *Conclusions,* a summary of his vast erudition. He dared any learned person to come to Rome to debate him in public and offered to pay their expenses if necessary.

Officials of Pope Innocent VIII's court forbade Pico's debate after having found thirteen of his theses to be heretical and prohibited his book's distribution. He wrote a hasty defense of his *Conclusions,* which got him in more trouble with some church authorities fearful of his fascination with Jewish and Arabic materials. The tall and handsome Giovanni Pico fled to France but was arrested by the order of a papal legate and imprisoned in a castle at Vincennes outside Paris. Friends arranged his escape and he returned to Florence in Italy. Lorenzo de' Medici used his influence to have Pico forgiven by the new pope, Alexander VI. In Florence he came under the hypnotic spell of the preacher Savonarola and gave up his mistresses, renounced his love poetry, and distributed his wealth to the poor. Shortly before he could take up the life of a Dominican friar, Pico died of a fever at age thirty-one just as King Charles VIII of France was entering the city.

Although his love poetry, written in both Latin and Italian, was quite well thought of, Pico's reputation rests primarily on his life and philosophical writings. His most famous work was his "Oration on the Dignity of Man," which was originally composed as a preface to his *Conclusions*. Pico argued that humans, created specially by God, are "the most fortunate of creatures," not merely a link in the "universal chain of Being." Humans have the ability to rise upward toward the angels by the use of reason or to sink downward to the level of beasts by indulging in their sensual appetites. In support of his argument, he quoted from a vast array of sources, ranging from the Koran to the Persian prophet Zoroaster to the Pythagoreans.

Similar syncretistic tendencies are found in his other works such as his *Of Being and Unity* in which he discusses God and creation. Unlike many of his contemporary humanists, Pico made use of Plato, Aristotle, and many other thinkers from a diversity of backgrounds and religious traditions. Like Ficino, he was interested in the occult Hermetic writings, but went beyond his master in his explorations of Jewish mystical writings found in the *Cabala*. As Pico

declared, "And surely it is the part of a narrow mind to have confined itself with single Porch or Academy. Nor can one rightly choose what suits oneself from all of them who has not first come to be familiar with them all."[11] Although he continued to be fascinated by the occult, later in his life Giovanni Pico della Mirandola became one of the few Renaissance intellectuals to challenge the widely held beliefs in astrology. He had observed that astrological weather predictions were usually wrong and that astrology was not supported by Aristotle or Plato. That bold treatise, however, did not appear until after his death.

LIONS AND FOXES: NICCOLÒ MACHIAVELLI (1469–1527)

Of all the great thinkers of the Italian Renaissance, few have spoken more clearly to our time than Niccolò Machiavelli. Machiavelli came from a minor Florentine noble family. His father was a lawyer who practiced little law and mostly lived off farm and rental properties. As a boy, Niccolò received an excellent humanist grounding in Latin and Italian literature and a smattering of Roman law. He started as a clerk in the Florentine government in the period following the exile of the Medici, and by 1498 he was appointed chancellor of the Second Chancery concerned with foreign affairs and secretary to the Council of Ten, the department of war.

In the tradition of civic humanists such as Bruni and Salutati, Machiavelli loved being able to use his classical education in the service of the state. He was heavily involved in the voluminous foreign correspondence of Florence, inspected fortifications, helped organize militia units, and went on numerous diplomatic missions. A great deal of the art and institutions of diplomacy were developed during the Renaissance, including the use of resident ambassadors. As a diplomat, Machiavelli traveled to the courts of King Louis XII of France, Emperor Maximilian I, and to various states in Italy. He met with the dissolute Cesare Borgia three times between 1502 and 1503. Borgia's boldness, cunning, ruthlessness, and handsome—if cruelly scarred—features fascinated him. Machiavelli was also with the warrior-pope Julius II during his campaign of 1506 in the Romagna. Thus, the Florentine diplomat had first-hand experience with many of the leading political figures of his day.

With the sudden return of the Medici to power in 1512, Machiavelli lost his job, as he was unfairly viewed as an enemy of the recently restored Medicis. After a period of torture and imprisonment, he was allowed to retire to a small farm outside Florence as a gesture of goodwill when Lorenzo de' Medici's son, Giovanni, was elected Pope Leo X in 1513. While Machiavelli missed the political life terribly, he spent the next fifteen years of his life as a successful man of letters and gentleman farmer. After a day of farm business, tavern games, and gossip, he retired to his study in the evening dressed in the "regal and courtly garments" he once proudly wore as a public official. There he did his reading and writing.

MACHIAVELLI'S WRITINGS

As a literary man, Machiavelli produced a well-received book of Italian poetry, several satires, a short story, and three plays. His most successful comedy, *The Mandrake Root*, is a lascivious bedroom farce that is traditionally considered the best dramatic work of the Italian Renaissance. It played to large, enthusiastic audiences in both Florence and rival Venice. His literary works reveal him as a deft satirist who always had a political agenda.

Santi di Tito, *Portrait of Niccolò Machiavelli*, Palazzo Vecchio, Florence, Italy. Alinari/Art Resource.

As talented as Machiavelli was as an artist, his ultimate reputation was made by his political writings, particularly *The Prince* (1513), written in an effort to curry favor with the Medici. Convinced that Italy needed a strong ruler to protect it from its enemies and instability, Machiavelli instructs a despot in the art of gaining and holding power. Machiavelli argued that a prince must imitate the lion and the fox. The prince must have the strength of a lion to frighten enemies and the cunning of a fox to avoid traps. If necessary to maintain power, a prince must be prepared to "lie, dissemble, and even murder while appearing to seem merciful, faithful, humane, sincere, and religious."[12]

Most medieval political theorists such as Dante had agreed with Aristotle that politics is a branch of ethics. In his *On Monarchy*

(c. 1313), Dante had argued that Christian princes must be people of peace and justice who draw their power from God.

Now here was Machiavelli arguing that because people are basically bad, rulers may have to behave in ways totally inappropriate for private citizens. In *The Prince*, Machiavelli boldly asserted that the realities of power politics may have to take precedence over normal standards of good and evil.

Much the same assumptions about human nature are reflected in another of his influential writings, *Discourses on the First Ten Books of Livy*. While much of this work is a perceptive commentary on the thought of the pro-republican Roman historian, Machiavelli repeats his assertion that "all men are bad and ever ready to display their vicious nature." Therefore, he argues for a strong form of government that combines the best elements of a "principality, an aristocracy, and a democracy, one form keeps watch over the other." Although Machiavelli asserted that "all forms of government are defective," he thought that for Florence a republic was preferable to a monarchy if it maintained law and order and protected the state from its enemies.[13]

Machiavelli's admiration for Florence was also shown in his last major work, *The History of Florence*, which traced the city's history from its origins until the death of Lorenzo de' Medici in 1492. He dedicated this history to Lorenzo's nephew, the second Medici pope, Clement VII. Influenced by Roman historians such as Sallust and Tacitus, Machiavelli was concerned with demonstrating the importance of "good laws and institutions," which could be established by strong and enlightened leaders. Perhaps the worldly Machiavelli was not as Machiavellian as his notorious reputation would suggest?

FRANCESCO GUICCIARDINI (1483–1540)

Machiavelli's sometimes pessimistic outlook and admiration for Tacitus was shared by his fellow historian Francesco Guicciardini. From a venerable Florentine family, Guicciardini had been educated in the humanities and civil law at Florence, Ferrara, Padua, and Pisa. For a number of years he served the Medicis in Florence as a diplomat and then entered the service of the Medici popes, Leo X and Clement VII. In 1534 he returned to Florence to again serve the Medicis before being retired to his villa three years later.

While in retirement, Guicciardini wrote a *History of Florence*, which covers the period from 1378 to 1509, a celebrated *History of Italy*, which begins with the death of Lorenzo de' Medici, and a collection of *Maxims and Reflections*. In the *Maxims* he argued that historians "should write so that someone born in a far distant age would have those things as much before his eyes as did those who were then present. That is indeed the aim of history."[14] In his own historical writings, Guicciardini produced models of scholarship and analysis of political and diplomatic events and motivations. He was particularly concerned about the moral choices that individuals make as well as the role of necessity in determining events. In some respects, Guicciardini's histories still have not been surpassed and remain some of the finest scholarly work produced during the Renaissance.

BALDASSARE CASTIGLIONE (1478–1529)

Another of the most influential prose writers of the Renaissance was the courtier Baldassare Castiglione. Born near Mantua to a noble family, he was well educated in Greek and Latin at Mantua and Milan. In 1500 Castiglione entered into the service of the Gonzaga family at Mantua as a soldier-diplomat. From 1504 to 1516 he served at the court of Urbino before returning to Mantua. In 1524 he became papal representative in Spain and then bishop of Avila. By then he had already written his most famous Neoplatonic work, *The Book of the Courtier* (1516).

In *The Courtier* Castiglione imaginatively reconstructed a series of discussions held at the brilliant court of Urbino in 1507 about the characteristics of the perfect court ladies and gentleman. Urbino had become one of the greatest centers of Renaissance artistic and intellectual life under a series of cultivated dukes and duchesses, including the remarkably refined Elisabetta Gonzaga (1471–1526). Duchess Elisabetta presided over the circle of luminaries in Castiglione's famous guide to etiquette.

According to the sensitive and thoughtful Castiglione, male courtiers were to be handsome and graceful, loyal to their princes, skilled in games and swordsmanship, conversant in Latin and Greek, well read in literature, appreciative of music, and able to draw and paint. They should be honest, but tactful, as well as "genial and discreet" with women. Castiglione demanded a great deal of court women, who were expected to be paragons of virtue. Ladies of the court should be able to show a "certain pleasing affability," a "quick vivacity of spirit," and be able "to entertain graciously every kind of man with agreeable and comely conversation."[15] While many of the courtiers of the Renaissance fell far short of Castiglione's ideals, it is clear from the influence of his book that the humanists' notion of educating the whole person had taken deep roots in Renaissance culture.

The Flowering of Italian Literature

Many of the humanists discussed previously also made important contributions to literature. Indeed, Petrarca and Boccaccio joined Dante in shaping Italian as a respected literary vehicle. Giovanni Pico della Mirandola and Machiavelli also made important contributions to the development of Italian poetry, and the latter also achieved fame as a dramatist. The Renaissance in Italy also featured many other new voices, such as Ludovico Ariosto, Pietro Aretino, Veronica Franco, and Vittoria Colonna.

LUDOVICO ARIOSTO (1474–1533)

Italian poets such as Ludovico Ariosto became well known for their romantic epics, which combined the style of classic epics by Homer and Vergil with the tradition of medieval romance. After a career in military and government service, Ariosto retired to Ferrara, where he ran the state theater of the ruling Este dynasty.

In 1516 Ariosto published his romantic epic, *Orlando Furioso* (Mad Roland), which expounded on the legends of Charlemagne and Roland (Orlando) and their wars with the Muslims. Although intended to glorify his patrons, the Este family, *Orlando* treats many of the conventions of chivalry in a satirical fashion and takes a wry, bemused look at life. Ariosto also wrote comedies, odes, Latin poems, satires, and sonnets. While his theatrical works were well appreciated, his poetry was never popular in his own lifetime. Only later was his genius as a poet fully appreciated. Ariosto's *Orlando Furioso* remains one of the greatest epics produced during the Renaissance, rivaled only by Torquato Tasso's *Jerusalem Delivered* (1575).

THE POET AS BLACKMAILER: PIETRO ARETINO (1492–1556)

Pietro Aretino was one of the most colorful and controversial poets who lived during the late Renaissance. Born to a poor family, Pietro spent much of his hardscrabble youth on the streets of his native Arezzo, where he had little formal education. Friends of his mother helped him gain employment with a rich Roman banker, Agostino Chigi, and Pope Leo X. However, his penchant for writing pornography and his scandalous lifestyle soon cost him his Roman patronage and led to a life of adventuring throughout Italy and France. He became known as "The Scourge of Princes" for his merciless satires of the rich and famous. Aretino made enough money through blackmail and his writings that he was able to live "with all the pleasure there is in life" in a fine house on the Grand Canal in Venice from 1527 until his death. Some people paid him to write scurrilous attacks on their enemies; others paid him not to write about themselves.

When Aretino did write, it was usually in superb Italian—witty, sensual, and compelling. In addition to his controversial *Lewd Sonnets,* he composed several successful comedies and one outstanding drama, the *Orazia* (Horatius), based on Livy's story of the struggle between love and honor in ancient Rome. It was considered the best tragedy of the sixteenth century written in Italian. Aretino also composed dialogues, letters, satires, and, most surprisingly, some sensitive devotional literature. He claimed in one of his letters that "all that I have written has been in honor of genius, whose glory was usurped and blackened by the avarice of powerful lords . . . true men should always cherish me, because I have always fought for genius with my life's blood."[16]

THE HONEST COURTESAN: VERONICA FRANCO (1546–1591)

Veronica Franco was the daughter of a prostitute who became one of the most successful courtesans in Venice. She also became a highly talented poet who wrote movingly of her own difficult life. Franco began as a poorly paid sex worker listed in the 1565 Venetian traveler's guide as available for two scudi. By the time she reached her twenties, the beautiful Veronica's clients included members of some of Venice's wealthiest families. In July 1574 she was selected by King Henri III of France (r. 1574–1589) for his entertainment. Since the king was a practicing homosexual, it is more likely that he was attracted to Veronica's gift as a conversationalist and musician rather than her sexual abilities. She wrote of her artistry as a courtesan: "So sweet and appetizing do I become when I find myself in bed with he who loves me and welcomes me that our pleasure surpasses all delight."[17]

A number of Franco's clients and friends were men of literary ability, and they recognized similar talents in her. After all, courtesan-poets were not unknown in sensual Venetian society. Earlier in the century, Gaspara Stampa (c. 1520–1554) had composed lyric poetry of a high quality. In 1575 Franco's friends published a collection of her verses that showed what an accomplished poet she had become. Her lyrical love poetry also added to her fame as an accomplished prostitute. Although she made a good deal of money as a courtesan, Franco was fully aware of the evils of the profession. As she wrote to a friend who was thinking of training her own daughter as a prostitute, "I tell you, you can do nothing worse in this life . . . than to force the body into such servitude . . . to give oneself in prey to so many, to risk being despoiled, robbed, or killed."[18] So that so many others in Venice would not have to endure the life of prostitution, Veronica Franco opened a refuge center for prostitutes shortly before her death in 1591.

VITTORIA COLONNA

Other more conventional women emerged as poets during the Renaissance. Perhaps the best known and most talented was Vittoria Colonna. A member of one of Rome's leading families, the bright, devout, and beautiful Vittoria was married to the marquis of Pescara as a young woman but was widowed when she was thirty-three. She returned to Rome and was active in church reform circles, including the Oratory of Divine Love. A Neoplatonist in the tradition of Marsilio Ficino and Giovanni Pico, Colonna was a close friend of the great artist Michelangelo, with whom she shared many interests. Much of her love poetry was written to eulogize her deceased husband. Later in life she wrote mostly religious poetry focusing on Christ, the Virgin Mary, and Mary Magdalene, the former prostitute who was so devoted to Jesus. From the bawdy Aretino to the pious Vittoria Colonna, the Renaissance produced literature to satisfy all tastes.

Chronology

1265–1321	Life of Dante.	**1433–1499**	Life of Marsilio Ficino.
1304–1374	Life of Petrarca.	**1463–1494**	Life of Giovanni Pico della Mirandola.
1313–1375	Life of Boccaccio.		
1331–1400	Life of Coluccio Salutati.	**1469–1499**	Life of Laura Cereta.
1370–1444	Life of Leonardo Bruni.	**1469–1529**	Life of Niccolò Machiavelli.
1396	Manuel Chrysoloras (1350–1415) comes to Florence to teach Greek.	**1474–1533**	Life of Ariosto.
		1478–1529	Life of Castiglione.
		1483–1540	Life of Guicciardini.
c. 1407–1457	Life of Lorenzo Valla.	**1492–1556**	Life of Pietro Aretino.
1418–1466	Life of Isotta Nogarola.	**1546–1591**	Life of Veronica Franco.

Further Reading

RENAISSANCE HUMANISM IN ITALY

Hans Baron, *The Crisis of the Early Italian Renaissance*, 2nd ed. (1966).

Eric Cochrane, *Historians and Historiography in the Italian Renaissance* (1981).

E. B. Fryde, *Humanism and Renaissance Historiography* (1993).

Victoria Kahn, *Rhetoric, Prudence, and Skepticism in the Renaissance* (1980).

Donald Kelley, *Renaissance Humanism* (1993).

Margaret King and Albert Rabil, eds., *Her Immaculate Hand: Selected Works by and about the Women Humanists of 1400 Italy* (1983). An invaluable source collection.

Paul Oscar Kristeller, *Renaissance Thought and Its Sources* (1979).

———, *Renaissance Thought and the Arts* (1980). Important essays by a leading authority.

George McClure, *Sorrow and Consolation in Italian Humanism* (1992).

Albert Rabil, ed., *Renaissance Humanism*, 3 vols. (1988). A major collection of essays by modern scholars.

Jerrold Siegel, *Rhetoric and Philosophy in Renaissance Humanism* (1968).

Charles Trinkaus, *In His Image and Likeness: Italian Humanists on God and Human Dignity*, 2 vols. (1971).

———, *The Scope of Renaissance Humanism* (1983).

Roberto Weiss, *The Renaissance Discovery of Classical Antiquity*, 2nd ed. (1988).

Donald Wilcox, *In Search of God and Self: Renaissance and Reformation Thought* (1975). A very readable survey.

RENAISSANCE EDUCATION AND PHILOSOPHY

Brian Copenhaven and Charles Schmitt, *Renaissance Philosophy* (1992).

Arthur Field, *The Origins of the Platonic Academy of Florence* (1988).

Anthony Grafton and Lisa Jardine, *From Humanism to the Humanities: Education and the Liberal Arts in Fifteenth- and Sixteenth-Century Europe* (1988).

Paul Grendler, *Schooling in Renaissance Italy: Literacy and Learning, 1300–1600* (1989).

Charles Schmitt, *The Cambridge History of Renaissance Philosophy* (1988). Important survey by an outstanding authority.

ITALIAN RENAISSANCE LITERATURE

David Quint, *Origin and Originality in Renaissance Literature* (1984).

Richard Waswo, *Language and Meaning in the Renaissance* (1987).

Katharina Wilson, ed., *Women Writers of the Renaissance and Reformation* (1987). An important collection of writings by women authors.

INDIVIDUAL AUTHORS

Albert Ascoli, *Ariosto's Bitter Enemy: Crisis and Evasion in the Italian Renaissance* (1987).

Flora Bassanese, *Gaspara Stampa* (1982).

Thomas Bergin, *Boccaccio* (1981).

Morris Bishop, *Petrarch and His World* (1963).

Vittore Branca, *Boccaccio: The Man and His Works* (1976).

William Craven, *Giovanni Pico della Mirandola: Symbol of His Age* (1981).

Nicholas Mann, *Petrarch* (1984).

Albert Rabil, *Laura Cereta, Quattrocento Humanist* (1981).

Margaret Rosenthal, *The Honest Courtesan, Veronica Franco* (1992).

Ronald Witt, *Hercules at the Crossroads: The Life, Works, and Thought of Coluccio Salutati* (1983).

MACHIAVELLI

Peter Bondanella, *Machiavelli and the Art of Renaissance History* (1973).

Sebastian de Grazia, *Machiavelli in Hell* (1989). A striking, imaginative biography.

Victoria Kahn, *Machiavellian Rhetoric: From the Counter-Reformation to Milton* (1994).

J. G. A. Pocock, *The Machiavellian Moment: Florentine Political Thought and the Atlantic Republican Tradition* (1975).

Notes

1. Cited in Morris Bishop, "Petrarch," in *Renaissance Profiles*, J. H. Plumb, ed. (New York: Harper and Row, 1961), p. 3.
2. Ibid., p. 11.
3. Cited in James Bruce Ross and Mary Martin McLaughlin, eds., *The Portable Renaissance Reader* (New York: Viking Press, 1970), p. 128.
4. Ibid., p. 73.

5. Cited in Elton, *Renaissance and Reformation,* p. 57.
6. Cited in Werner Gundersheimer, ed., *The Italian Renaissance* (Englewood Cliffs, N.J.: Prentice Hall, 1965), p. 56.
7. Ibid.
8. Cited in Margaret King, *Women of the Renaissance* (Chicago: University of Chicago Press, 1991), p. 196.
9. Ibid., p. 197.
10. Cited in Margaret King and Albert Rabil, eds., *Her Immaculate Hand: Selected Works by and about the Women Humanists of 1400 Italy* (Binghamton, N.Y.: Medieval and Renaissance Texts and Studies, 1983), p. 79.
11. Cited in Gundersheimer, *Italian Renaissance,* pp. 110–111.

12. Machiavelli, *The Prince,* trans. and ed. Robert Adams (New York: Norton, 1977), p. 50.
13. Peter Bondanella and Mark Musa, eds., *The Portable Machiavelli* (Baltimore, Md.: Penguin, 1979), p. 179.
14. Cited in Bartlett, *Italian Renaissance,* p. 392.
15. Baldassare Castiglione, *The Book of the Courtier* (Baltimore, Md.: Penguin, 1967), p. 212.
16. Cited in Bartlett, *Italian Renaissance,* p. 392.
17. Cited in Bonnie Anderson and Judith Zinsser, *A History of Their Own: Women in Europe from Prehistory to the Present,* vol. 2 (New York: Harper and Row, 1988), p. 71.
18. Ibid., p. 77.

6

Painting in Renaissance Italy

The Renaissance in Italy was one of the most exciting periods in the history of the fine arts. It was an incredibly fortunate melding of artistic talent, patronage, and demand. The elite of Italy provided a lively market for both religious and secular art. The dramatic increase in the numbers of churches and confraternities (lay religious brotherhoods) in the period and the expansion and remodeling of existing facilities helped provide abundant opportunities for architects, artists, and craftspersons. Religious organizations increased their use of art to tell biblical stories to a largely illiterate public. Discriminating patrons such as Isabella d'Este, Lorenzo de' Medici, and many others filled their palaces with great works of art. They also supported art that was visible to the public in churches and town squares. Even city governments commissioned public art in an effort to beautify their communities and to display their wealth and power. The result is a rich legacy of artistic masterpieces that still inspires us and influences our sense of what is beautiful.

Renaissance architects, painters, sculptors, and musicians made striking departures from the conventions and styles of medieval artists. Influenced by the culture of humanism, painters began to seek a window into nature and made a concerted effort to capture what the human eye actually saw. Sculptors, inspired by classical models, also sought greater naturalism. Although religious subject matter continued to dominate the art of the Renaissance, it was supplemented by greater use of classical themes and was presented in strikingly new ways. Architects also used and modified classical models but felt free to make striking innovations. The Renaissance was also a great period of creativity in music. All in all, it was an age of extraordinary achievement in the arts.

Early Renaissance Painting: Giotto

Giotto (c. 1266–1337) was one of the first great artists of the Italian Renaissance. He was born the son of a laborer in a little town fourteen miles from Florence. Even as a young boy Giotto showed a talent for drawing and may have studied with one of the greatest Florentine painters of his day, Giovanni Cimabue (c. 1240–1302). Like many artists of the time, Giotto was broadly trained as an architect, sculptor, and painter. However, it was as a painter that he achieved his greatest fame. In contrast to the flat, elongated, unnatural figures of "Greek or Byzantine art," Giotto attempted to draw every figure from nature. He was among the very first Western painters to capture actual human emotions in scenes of compelling realism and to add a third dimension—depth—to painting.

An example of Giotto's ability to capture emotion is his famous fresco painting

Giotto, *The Lamentation*. Scrovengni Chapel, Padua. Photo courtesy of Alinari/Art Resource.

for the Arena Chapel in Padua, *The Lamentation*. The dead Christ is stretched across the lap of Mary while Mary Magdalene gazes down at his feet. Mary stares intently at the face of her dead son as the apostles share her grief and anguish. The angels above twist and turn discordantly and all nature seems lost in deepest mourning. Giotto's concern for an organic whole is reflected in the geometric clustering of the figures.

Giotto's art was greatly influenced by the tradition of St. Francis of Assisi and his reverence for nature. Like Francis, Giotto recognized the intimate connections between all living things and the importance of living in harmony with all God's creations. The Franciscans in Giotto's day kept alive the tradition of their founder's interest in nature. They, like the rival order of the Dominicans, wanted to use art for religious instruction. Increasingly, artists such as Giotto were hired to paint murals on the walls of their churches and chapels.

Artists painted on moist plaster with pigments ground in water so that the paint was absorbed by the plaster and became part of the wall itself. Giotto became a master of this *fresco* (fresh) technique and was hired to paint the walls of numerous churches and chapels. He had a particular affinity for Saint Francis of Assisi, and his admiration for the legendary saint is readily apparent in the numerous depictions of various scenes from the life of Francis painted for his church in Assisi and for the Bardi and Peruzzi banking families' chapels in the church of Santa Croce in Florence. In wall paintings such as *St. Francis Receiving the Stigmata*, one of twenty-eight scenes from the life of Francis that Giotto and his associates painted for the church built above the saint's tomb, the artist captures the moment when the saint learns that he is to receive wounds (stigmata) identical to those of Christ. Francis can now fully identify with the Son of God.

Giotto and associates, *St. Francis Receiving the Stigmata.* S. Francesco, Assisi, Italy. Alinari / Art Resource.

Pronounced the greatest painter of his day by Dante, Boccaccio, and Petrarca, Giotto received commissions from patrons in Assisi, Florence, Milan, Padua, Naples, and Rimini primarily for church frescoes. Toward the end of his life, he was appointed master of public works and building supervisor of the Florentine cathedral, for which he designed a graceful bell tower. His efforts at greater naturalism in painting attracted a vast number of imitators, but no one was able to rival his skill and technique until the time of Masaccio seventy-five years later.

MASACCIO (1401–1428)

Masaccio (Tommaso Guidi) was born the son of a notary in a small town outside Florence.

He joined the artists' guild of Florence in January 1422 and worked there except for part of 1426 when he accepted a commission in Pisa. In the summer of 1428, Masaccio moved to Rome, where he died a virtually penniless young man of twenty-eight. Before his death, Masaccio achieved great fame as the greatest master of naturalism since Giotto. His painting had an influence on the work of his sculptor friends Brunelleschi and Donatello. Obsessed with "the things of art," he was known for his indifference to money, clothes, and even food. His nickname, Masaccio, means literally "the messy one."

Masaccio's reputation as an artist rests primarily upon a celebrated series of frescoes of the life of St. Peter painted for the Brancacci Chapel in the church of Santa

Maria del Carmine in Florence. His *The Trib-ute Money* dominates the chapel and depicts a group of disciples clustered around Jesus waiting to hear his answer to the question: "Is it lawful to pay tribute to Caesar?" Masaccio's depiction of this scene is unique and came at a time when Florence was introducing a new system of taxation (the *cas-tato*). The artist appears to be celebrating God's sanctioning of taxation. To underscore contemporary application, it should be noted that the setting of *The Tribute Money* is the banks of the Arno; the apostles are depicted as Florentine men of the street.

On the left side of the painting, the artist shows Peter finding a fish in shallow water. Jesus told Peter that he would find the tax gatherer's money in the mouth of a fish. On the right side of the painting, Peter is paying off the tax collector. The center of the painting is dominated by Christ instructing his apostles on how to handle the tax gatherer. It is a confrontation between secular and spiritual power, and the faces of the apostles clearly reveal their surprise and concern. All the figures in the fresco are shown as uniquely individual rather than as medieval archetypes. *The Tribute Money* reveals that, like Giotto, Masaccio could capture great moments of psychological truth, as do his vivid depictions of *The Crucifixion of St. Peter and the Martyrdom of St. John the Baptist*. In the left panel Peter is shown, according to tradition, being nailed to a cross and hung upside down in a scene of great poignancy and power. Humanism with its emphasis on individuality had already begun to shape Renaissance art.

Luminaries of the High Renaissance such as Leonardo da Vinci, Michelangelo, and Raphael studied the works of Masaccio for their use of perspective, skill in composition, psychological insight, and use of *chiaroscuro* (the contrast of light and shade to enhance modeling). His work in the Brancacci Chapel also had a profound influence on the Umbrian painter Piero della Francesca (c. 1416–1492). Masaccio may have learned about linear perspective from his friend Filippo Brunelleschi. Brunelleschi discovered that by making figures in the background of a painting smaller than those in the fore-

Masaccio, *The Tribute Money*. S. Maria del Carmine, Florence, Italy. Alinari/Art Resource.

Masaccio, *The Crucifixion of St. Peter and Martyrdom of St. John the Baptist*. Gemäldegalerie, Staatliche Museen, Berlin, Germany. Foto Marburg/Art Resource.

ground, the artist was able to give his or her painting an illusion of depth. Mathematical proportions and rationalized geometric patterns further enhanced the effect of three dimensionality. Masaccio also achieved the feeling of depth in his paintings by creating a physical quality of atmosphere, hence his attention to landscapes and backgrounds.

A Distinctive Style: Sandro Botticelli (c. 1444–1510)

Renaissance art continued to develop in the decades following the death of Masaccio as a host of artists mastered the techniques of perspective and naturalism. Oil painting, imported from the Netherlands, also began to influence Italian painters. Among the greatest of them was the Florentine Sandro Botticelli. Sandro was raised by his brother, a successful broker, and received much of his artistic training from the Carmelite monk Fra Filippo Lippi (1406–1469), a protégé of Cosimo de' Medici. He worked with Lippi and they became so close that when Lippi died he entrusted Botticelli with the care of his son, Filippino (1458–1504). Filippino became a master painter and com-

pleted Masaccio's frescoes in the Brancacci Chapel, among other works.

Botticelli also worked along with the young Leonardo da Vinci in the workshop of Andrea del Verrocchio. Although immersed in all the great traditions of Florentine art, Botticelli developed his own highly individualized and uniquely poetic style and did not always adhere to the growing tradition of scientific naturalism which followed from Giotto and Masaccio. Botticelli became the favorite painter of the circle of humanists and poets that surrounded Lorenzo de' Medici. For this circle, he produced his two most famous paintings: *The Birth of Spring* (*La Primavera*) and *The Birth of Venus*.

In *The Birth of Spring* Botticelli painted a mysterious, dreamlike allegory that has long fascinated viewers. It was painted for a cousin of Lorenzo de' Medici on the occasion of his marriage. Perhaps the artist was also celebrating the reign of Lorenzo the Magnificent as a new beginning for Florence. The painting is set in a grove of dark orange trees, thickly massed. On the right side is Zephyr, the west wind god, who is pursuing the virgin nymph, Chloris, whose mouth is filled with flowers. He will rape

Botticelli, *La Primavera*. Uffizi Gallery, Florence, Italy. Alinari/Art Resource.

and then marry her. She will then be transformed into the eerily placid Flora, the goddess of spring, shown strewing flowers from her flower-embroidered garment.

On the left side of the painting, the messenger god, Mercury, pokes his staff up among storm clouds that are trying to gather. Next to him, Three Graces dance provocatively in transparent garments in a ring. Above, the blindfolded Cupid is ready to shoot a golden arrow in their direction. In the center is a chaste and demure Venus, the goddess of love and marriage. For Marsilio Ficino, Botticelli's Venus represented "Temperance and Honesty, Comeliness, and Modesty."[1] In depicting so many changeable aspects of spring and marriage (sudden, violent changes of weather and emotion), Botticelli reminds us that both nature and love can be dangerous as well as beautiful.

Painted on canvas with oil, Botticelli's *The Birth of Venus* is another work of allegory and mystery. It depicts a nude but modest golden-haired goddess of love, standing on a seashell while Zephyr and a nymph waft her to shore. On the right a waiting Grace stands ready to cover Venus with a flowing cloak. Contemporaries thought Botticelli was showing them the birth of studies of humanity, a Neoplatonic triumph of the spirit (mind) of Venus over her body.

Later in life Botticelli also came under the influence of the preacher Savonarola and was quite affected by his overthrow and death. Always a deeply religious man, some of his best work uses religious subject mat-

Botticelli, *The Birth of Venus*. Uffizi, Florence, Italy. Alinari/Art Resource.

ter. As he grew older, he withdrew more and more from the world. Botticelli seems to have painted little in the last decade of his life. Commissions went to the new stylists of the High Renaissance, artists such as Leonardo, Michelangelo, and Raphael. According to Giorgio Vasari, Botticelli "became old and useless and fell to walking with two canes."[2] If true, this is a sad ending for one of the most original and poetic painters of the Renaissance.

The High Renaissance

Building on the work of great talents such as Giotto, Masaccio, Fra Angelico, Fra Filippo Lippi, and Botticelli, the next generations of Renaissance artists were able to go even further in creating windows into nature. Inventive minds such as Leonardo da Vinci utilized oil painting techniques imported from the Netherlands, new ways of modeling figures and treating light and shade, and his own scientific studies to produce masterpieces of scientific realism. Talented as Leonardo was, Michelangelo, Raphael, and Titian vied with him for commissions and for a reputation as Italy's greatest artist. The High Renaissance also witnessed the emergence of extraordinarily accomplished women painters such as Sofonisba Anguissola and Artemisia Gentileschi, the first female plastic artists in the West to be given public recognition for their artistic brilliance.

Leonardo da Vinci (1452–1519)

Of all the multitalented men and women of the Renaissance, no one could match Leonardo da Vinci's accomplishments in so many fields. Not only was he a great painter, sculptor, and architect, but he also made valuable contributions to art theory, engineering, military science, anatomy, botany, geology, geography, hydraulics, aerodynamics, and optics. This incredible polymath began life as the son of a notary and a servant near the fortified village of Vinci, west of Florence. Leonardo's father had seduced his mother, Caterina, a family servant, but refused to marry her. Leonardo was raised by a stepmother at his father's home. His father married four times in all and had eleven children.

When he was fourteen, the left-handed Leonardo was apprenticed to the renowned Florentine artist Andrea del Verrocchio, with whom he studied from 1470 to 1477. Verrocchio recognized his pupil's precocious talent and employed him on a number of major projects. Young Leonardo also learned from his painter friends Botticelli and Perugino (the latter eventually became the teacher of another artistic legend, Raphael). At age twenty, Leonardo da Vinci was admitted to the painters' guild and began receiving commissions from Lorenzo de' Medici and religious institutions.

A keen student of nature with unusually excellent eyesight, Leonardo sought to learn the causes of things. He filled his *Notebooks* with observations of many things including human anatomy, birds in flight, rock formations, rare plants, and the motion and power of water. A congenial, handsome, young, homosexual man, Leonardo was also a skilled horseman and musician. He had a wide circle of friends and seemingly sufficient patronage. Then suddenly at age thirty, he left Florence for the Milanese

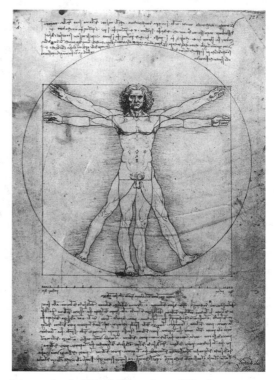

Leonardo da Vinci, "Drawing of Ideal Proportions of the Human Figure." Accademia, Venice, Italy. Alinari/Art Resource.

court of Ludovico il Moro, to whom he offered his services primarily as a military engineer.

In addition to military and scientific projects, Ludovico also commissioned Leonardo to sculpt a giant equestrian statue of his father to honor his own marriage to Beatrice d'Este in 1491. Although Leonardo finished dozens of drawings for a project that was to be even larger than the equestrian statutes of Donatello and Verrocchio, the work was never completed in what became a familiar theme in Leonardo's life as his interests shifted from project to project. As da Vinci wrote over and over again in his notebooks: "Who will tell me if anything was ever finished?"[3]

During his first Milanese period, Leonardo did manage to complete a number of stunning paintings including his first *Virgin of the Rocks*, which was painted for the chapel of the Confraternity of the Immaculate Conception. Here Leonardo showed his mastery of oil painting that had been introduced in the fifteenth century and allowed artists to work in much greater detail than ever before and freed paintings from their earlier dependence on architectural settings as parts of altarpieces or walls. Oil paintings were also less expensive than frescoes or panel paintings and made art more affordable. Leonardo also demonstrated a new technique, *sfumato* ("smoky"), which he developed for modeling figures by virtually imperceptible gradations from light to dark.

In the altar painting *The Virgin of the Rocks*, Leonardo portrayed the youthful Madonna kneeling on the ground, her arm around the kneeling John the Baptist. Her left hand is extended protectively over the seated Christ child, who acknowledges the worship of John by blessing him. A kneeling angel steadies the Christ child and completes the third side of a compositional triangle. The painting is filled with a full array of scientifically identifiable rocks and plants. The shadowy caves stand in contrast to the brilliant light coming from behind the Virgin, which gives "a grace to faces" as the artist wrote. Leonardo showed a mastery of *chiaroscuro, sfumato,* and the portrayal of nature that few others have ever been able to rival.

A dozen years later, da Vinci completed *The Last Supper* for a wall of the refectory of St. Mary's of Grace in Milan. Unhappy with the limitations of traditional fresco techniques, Leonardo experimented with an oil-tempera medium that did not adhere properly to the wall. By 1517 the painting began to deteriorate but still earned great critical praise and several efforts at restoration. *The Last Supper* is a brilliant, psychological study of the reactions of Christ's disciples to his charge that "one of you shall betray me." In dark profile and grasping a money bag, Judas is to the right of Christ with his hand defiantly stretched toward the bread on the table. In most traditional renderings of the scene, Judas is shown on the opposite side of the table from the disciples. Placing him with the other disciples emphasizes to a degree his common humanity with the other disciples, all of whom are asking "Lord, is it I?" Leonardo's *Last Supper* reveals his great skill in geometric and psychological composition. The disciples are clustered in four groups of three each with the eyes of most of them focused on Christ in the exact center of the

Leonardo da Vinci, *The Virgin of the Rocks*. Louvre, Paris, France. Alinari/Art Resource.

Leonardo da Vinci, *The Last Supper*. S. Maria delle Grazie, Milan, Italy. Alinari/Art Resource.

painting. Even the architectural lines of the room direct our eyes first to Christ and then out again to reveal the reactions of each of the disciples. Judas's shadowy profile contrasts with the lighted faces of the other disciples. He is one of them; yet he is different and certainly not worthy of the sacrament of the Eucharist.

With the fall of Milan to the French in 1499, Leonardo was forced to leave the employ of the Sforzas. After brief stays in Mantua and Venice, he returned to Florence, where he worked chiefly as an engineer and a surveyor. Even master artists like Leonardo, who "lived like a gentleman," had to worry about finances. Although socially slightly above the ranks of the artisans, masters like Leonardo were considered inferior to the nobles, rich merchants, and bankers who dominated the economic and political scene. After a brief stint as a military engineer for Cesare Borgia, he returned to Florence to finish the great portrait

of a young married woman, known to us as the *Mona Lisa*.

Leonardo worked for three years on this portrait, which has become famous for its mysterious expression. *Mona Lisa* appears to be a very self-confident young woman whose lips betray a hint of a smile. She dares to look directly at the viewer, in contrast to the advice of Renaissance etiquette books, which stressed that a woman must never look directly at a man. Her hands are gracefully poised and further reinforce the sense of calm that she exudes. Behind her is a harsh, possibly violent landscape of rocks and water, a striking contrast to this relaxed young woman of quiet resolve in the foreground. Is this a representation of the clash between *fortuna* (the background representing the forces of nature) and *virtú* (her face as a symbol of her qualities as a person)? Whatever the painting's real meaning, it is clear that da Vinci's contemporaries were shocked by this bold departure from of sixty-seven. As the great polymath wrote in his *Notebooks*, "While I thought I was learning how to live, I have been learning how to die."[4]

Leonardo da Vinci left behind less than a dozen completed paintings, but his *Notebooks* are filled with wonderful philosophical musings and intriguing studies of anatomy, mathematics, and nature. "Let no one read me who is not a mathematician in my beginnings," he wrote.[5] His notes are also filled with designs of airplanes, parachutes, helicopters, screw propellers, machine guns, canal locks, and many other inventions that anticipated the modern world. His self-portrait reveals a man frustrated that he had not done more.

Leonardo da Vinci, *La Giaconda* (*Mona Lisa*). Louvre, Paris, France. Giraudon/Art Resource.

Leonardo da Vinci, *Self-Portrait*. Biblioteca Reale, Turin, Italy. Alinari/Art Resource.

traditional depictions of women and that moderns continue to be enthralled by the beauty and mystery of the painting.

In Florence Leonardo also competed with a younger rival, Michelangelo, for a commission to paint a mammoth battle-scene fresco for the government. This work and several others were never completed because Leonardo returned to Milan in 1506 to work for the French king, Louis XII. He occupied himself mostly in scientific and anatomical studies until 1513 when he went to Rome to secure the support of Pope Leo X. In 1517 Leonardo accepted the invitation of King François I of France to live at the little chateau of Cloux near Amboise, where his only required duty was to talk to the king. He died there two years later at the age

Michelangelo Buonarroti (1475–1564) as a Painter

Like his great rival Leonardo da Vinci, Michelangelo was also talented in many areas. Although his primary reputation is as a sculptor, Michelangelo was a fine painter, poet, engineer, and architect. He began life in Florence as the son of a minor shopkeeper and merchant, who claimed ancestors among the lesser nobility. His father had a would-be aristocrat's contempt for manual labor and was terribly disappointed when young Michelangelo showed nothing but a passion for art. Because Michelangelo was a sickly infant, his nineteen-year-old mother turned him over to a wet-nurse who was the wife of a stonecutter. He later claimed he had sucked in a love for art with this mother's milk in the fresh air "among the chisels and hammers of stonecutters."[6]

Despite the reluctance of his father and uncle, Michelangelo was apprenticed at age thirteen to the well-known Florentine artist Domenico Ghirlandaio (1449–1494). Already exhibiting a remarkable talent for drawing, Michelangelo was paid a salary by his teacher, which was most unusual for an apprentice. Ghirlandaio modestly confessed that "this youth understands more than I do myself."[7] After barely a year with Ghirlandaio, Michelangelo was invited into the house of Lorenzo de' Medici and worked in an art school setting with other artists and humanist intellectuals. In the Medici circle, Michelangelo learned a great

Michelangelo, *Creation of Adam.* Sistine Chapel, Vatican Palace, Vatican State.

Michelangelo, *The Last Judgment*. Sistine Chapel, Vatican Palace, Vatican State. Alinari/ Art Resource.

deal about art, humanism, and Neoplatonic theory, all of which had a profound effect upon his subsequent career.

With the death of Lorenzo the Magnificent in 1492, Michelangelo was forced to return to the house of his father. He later found work in Venice and Bologna before moving to Rome in June 1496, where he had a spectacular career as a sculptor, working in his favorite medium. In 1508, he was ordered by his powerful patron, Pope Julius II, to stop work on the pope's monumental but incredibly expensive tomb and instead to paint frescoes on the ceiling of the Sistine

Chapel of St. Peter's Basilica. Michelangelo objected that he was a sculptor and not a painter, but the pope insisted.

For the next four years, Michelangelo labored to cover the 6,300-square-foot, barrel-vaulted ceiling with nine huge panels depicting scenes from Genesis. Arranged out of chronological order, Michelangelo took his viewers on a Neoplatonic, allegorical journey from the *Drunkenness of Noah* to *The Creation of the World*. Working by himself on a high scaffold, he was assisted only by paint mixers and plaster grinders. As the recent restoration efforts have shown us,

Michelangelo used bright colors to paint over 300 figures in sumptuous detail. He portrayed the ascent of humans from the spiritual abyss of the drunkenness of Noah and the shameful nakedness of Adam and Eve through the purge of the flood upward to the final reunion with God. In his depiction of the *Creation of Adam*, Michelangelo shows the cosmic moment when God reaches out his powerful, naked arm to touch a reclining Adam and give him life. This is a magnificent rendering of the greatness of God and the potential nobility of individual humans as God's special creations.

Completing the Sistine Chapel ceiling in spite of enormous discomfort, fatigue, illness, and fierce quarrels with his patron left Michelangelo partially crippled for life, but he managed to continue his career as a sculptor, architect, and poet in both Rome and Florence. In 1534, however, Pope Clement VII commissioned him to paint the altar wall of the Sistine Chapel. His *Last Judgment*, completed in 1541, is one of the monumental achievements of Renaissance painting. Medieval depictions of the last judgment generally showed figures dressed according to their social rank with Christ, the Virgin, and the apostles enthroned in heaven.

Breaking sharply with medieval custom, Michelangelo's painting depicts a unified scene with 300 mostly undressed figures grouped around the central figure of a standing, muscular Christ as judge. The figures that surround Christ are part of an enormous wheel of fortune, where some rise from their graves, others gather round Christ, and still others sink downward toward Hell. The angels are shown without wings or halos. Christ is shown larger than any of the apostles who surround him, including an agonized self-portrait of Michelangelo as St. Bartholomew, who was flayed alive (to the lower right of Christ).

The Virgin Mary is at Christ's side as he damns some and blesses others. Although influenced greatly by Dante's poetic visions, Michelangelo created his own special vision of the day when Christ comes again. It was an extraordinary achievement for a man in his fifties who was such a reluctant painter.

RAPHAEL SANZIO (1483–1520)

The sociable and calm Raphael stands in sharp contrast to the solitary and stormy genius of Michelangelo and the frustrated and aged Leonardo. He was born in the lively cultural center of Urbino in Umbria. His father was a mediocre painter and poet, who gave his son his earliest lessons before dying when Raphael was only eleven. In 1500 he moved to Perugia to study with the master artist Pietro Perugino (1446–1524), whose frescoes Michelangelo would later paint over for his rendering of *The Last Judgment*. Perugino was one of the favorite artists of Is-

Raphael, *Madonna della Seggiola* (*Madonna of the Chair*). Galleria Palatina, Palazzo Pitti, Florence, Italy. Alinari/Art Resource.

Raphael, *The School of Athens*. Stanza della Segnatura, Vatican Palace, Vatican State. Alinari/Art Resource.

abella d' Este, who commissioned a number of works from him. Raphael quickly absorbed the nuances of Perugino's graceful style and soon became the outstanding member of a busy workshop.

In 1504 he journeyed to Florence to find work and to learn from the brilliance of Leonardo da Vinci, Michelangelo, and others. The sister of the duke of Urbino recommended him as "a modest young man of distinguished manners."[8] While learning the techniques of the Florentine masters, Raphael soon created his own mature idea of beauty in a stunning series of Madonnas.

One of the best is his striking *Madonna of the Chair,* painted in 1516. Raphael's Madonnas are real flesh-and-blood women in the tradition of Fra Filippo Lippi, some of whom were modeled for by his beloved mistress, Margherita. Raphael's fleshy baby Jesus was also a figure drawn from life. The artist has skillfully captured the special bond between mother and child as the infant John the Baptist looks on.

Raphael's fame as a painter attracted the attention of Pope Julius II, who invited him to Rome in 1508 at the same time Michelangelo was at work on the Sistine

Chapel ceiling. He remained there until his early death at age thirty-seven. One of his most stunning accomplishments during this period in Rome was *The School of Athens*. In this fresco, Raphael paid a glorious, humanist tribute to many of the legendary sages of antiquity including Plato and Aristotle, who are featured in the painting's center. The old man sprawled on the steps is Diogenes, the Greek philosopher who searched for an honest man. Below him, isolated in the foreground, is a mysterious figure whose features are doubtlessly Michelangelo's, one of Raphael's heroes from whom he had learned so much.

In contrast to the moody and often tortured Michelangelo, the handsome Raphael seemed to float serenely through life. He was able to create almost effortlessly and his congenial disposition and gentle manners won him a host of friends. Deeply loved and admired by his contemporaries, Raphael's early death from fever in 1520 set off waves of grief in Rome. He was buried in the Pantheon, that marvelous temple to all the gods redesigned by the Stoic Roman emperor Hadrian in 120.

THE PROLIFIC TITIAN (C. 1488–1576)

The fine arts flourished throughout Italy during the Renaissance. Of the many fine artists working in Venice, Titian was clearly one of the greatest painters of the Venetian School during the Renaissance. He was born in the town of Cadore, high in the Dolomite Mountains. Little is known of his youth until 1508 when he assisted the talented Venetian artist Giorgione in painting exterior frescoes on the German commercial headquarters in Venice. He also learned from the great Giovanni Bellini. Titian became the first known painter to use the brush as a way of converting the direct per-

ception of light through color into an unimpeded expression of feeling. He also used many layers of glazes to tone down the brilliant colors that were part of his unique style.

His artistic talent, abundant energy, and shrewd investments made him rich and famous. After the death of Raphael, Titian became the most widely sought-out portraitist in Europe. Prominent individuals wanted to have themselves immortalized in painting and sculpture by renowned artists, something few of the rich had dared to even think of in the Middle Ages, when humility and self-effacement were stressed. To com-

Titian, *Portrait of Emperor Charles V*. Alte Pinakothek, Munich, Germany. Foto Marburg/Art Resource.

mission a portrait of oneself was considered a sign of immodesty, pride, and vanity. This changed with the Renaissance, a time when many prominent people even paid artists to place them in group paintings of biblical scenes or with the saints.

As one of the greatest portraitists of the age, by 1531 Titian had secured so many commissions from the affluent that he was able to buy a mansion in Venice with a fine view. Later he was made a count by Holy Roman Emperor Charles V, for whom he served several times as a court painter. Titian's superb portrait of the mature, seated emperor captured much of his dignity, earnestness, and somber piety. This was a prince who, because of his strong sense of duty and his enormous responsibility as Holy Roman emperor and king of Spain and its colonial empire, had the weight of the world on his shoulders. Charles was a devout Catholic who had to endure what for him was the embarrassment of the first phases of the Lutheran Reformation. Titian's portrait seems to reveal all this and more.

In addition to painting insightful portraits, Titian was attracted to religious scenes and themes from classical Greek and Roman mythology such as his marvelous rendering of the *Venus of Urbino*. In this painting, finished in 1538 for the duke of Camerino, Titian's sensual goddess of love has just been awakened and looks at us with a calculating stare. She lies upon her couch with her little dog asleep at her feet. With one hand she holds a nosegay while her rich and silky golden-brown hair floods over one of her delicate shoulders. In the background a servant looks for something in a clothes chest while another splendidly dressed woman looks on. Little wonder that Titian's work dazzled many of his contemporaries, despite Michelangelo's snide comment that while "he liked his coloring and style, it was a pity that good design was not taught at Venice from the first."[9] Titian's long and successful career spanned the High Renaissance through the religious tensions of Mannerism and into the period known as the Baroque.

Titian, *Venus of Urbino*. Uffizi, Florence, Italy. Giraudon/Art Resource.

Sofonisba Anguissola (c. 1532–1625)

As Titian's career illustrates the rise in status and wealth of some widely recognized artists, the career of Sofonisba Anguissola reveals a greater public recognition of women artists at the end of the Renaissance. Rich and powerful women such as Isabella d'Este played a great role as patrons during the Renaissance even if their contributions to art were seldom acknowledged. The situation was worse for those females who actually produced art. Daughters and wives of male painters labored in the workshops of Renaissance Italy, but they were not formally apprenticed or allowed to become members of art guilds. No woman artist was profiled by Giorgio Vasari. Their contributions, therefore, remain anonymous. All this changed with the career of Sofonisba Anguissola, followed by that of Artemisia Gentileschi.

The eldest of six daughters, Sofonisba was born into an aristocratic family in the northern Italian town of Cremona. Following the kind of advice found in Castiglione's *The Courtier,* her parents made sure she and her two elder sisters became accomplished in painting and music. Because she and her sister Elena showed signs of major talent as painters, they were able to study formally with an important local painter, Bernardino Campi. Elena eventually gave up her painting to become a nun, but Sofonisba continued to develop her talent as an artist and was encouraged to do so by her father, Amilcare. In 1557 he asked Michelangelo in Rome to send his daughter several of his drawings to be copied in oil paint and returned for his criticism. Michelangelo was so impressed that he allowed Sofonisba to study with him informally for two years in Rome.

During this period she painted such a splendid portrait of the duke of Alba that he recommended her to his liege lord, King

Sofonisba Anguissola, *Portrait of a Couple.* Galleria Doria Pamphilj, Rome, Italy. Alinari/Art Resource.

Philip II. For nearly twenty years, Anguissola worked as court painter and friend of the royal family in Spain. In 1569 she married the Sicilian nobleman Fabrizio de Moncada with a dowry which the late Queen Isabella had provided. King Philip gave her in marriage and presented her with numerous, costly gifts. When her husband died, she returned to Genoa by ship, where she had a whirlwind romance with a merchant who became her second husband. In that prosperous maritime city, Sofonisba continued her prolific career as a painter, painting portraits of the nobility as well as religious subjects to great acclaim.

Over fifty of her works have survived including the *Portrait of a Couple* shown in the accompanying photograph. In this portrait, Sofonisba revealed her distinctive style with the husband and wife gazing mysteriously at the viewer. He holds her with a combination of tenderness and control, which suggests all sorts of possibilities in their relationship. The brilliant Flemish painter Anthony van Dyck (1599–1641) made a pilgrimage to visit her as one of the last remaining giants of the Renaissance. Sofonisba Anguissola's life and work inspired a host of other artists including Lavinia Fontana (1552–1614) and Artemisia Gentileschi.

ARTEMISIA GENTILESCHI (1593–C. 1632)

Born in Rome, Artemisia was the eldest child and sole daughter of the painter Orazio Gentileschi and his wife, Prudentia Malone, who died when Artemisia was twelve. None of her three brothers showed any aptitude as artists, so her father trained Artemisia as a painter. Orazio may have also used her as the model for his striking *Portrait of a Young Woman as a Sibyl*, which

Caravaggio, *David with the Head of Goliath*. Galleria Borghese, Rome, Italy. Alinari/ Art Resource.

Orazio Gentileschi, *Portrait of a Young Woman as a Sibyl*. Samuel H. Kress Collection. Photo courtesy of The Museum of Fine Arts, Houston, Texas.

shows a strong sense of color and reveals the emotional complexity of its subject. If Artemisia was indeed the model, the sometimes strained relationship between artist father and daughter is strongly suggested in the mysterious look and expression of the sibyl.

Artemisia Gentileschi received additional instruction in the painter's art from the renowned master Caravaggio (1569–1610), a friend of her father. Orazio recognized that his own talents were limited and that the great Caravaggio had even more to teach his talented daughter. Caravaggio's powerful biblical scenes, such as his *David with the Head of Goliath*, had a profound impact on her developing style and choice of subject matter. She also seems to have been influenced by his dramatic use of light and shade

Artemisia Gentileschi, *Judith Slaying Holofernes*. Uffizi, Florence, Italy. Alinari/Art Resource.

to heighten emotions and his strong sense of composition.

In the year of Caravaggio's death, when Artemisia was only seventeen, she completed her first known painting, *Susanna and the Elders*. Based on the biblical story of a vulnerable young woman in a dangerous world of men, *Susanna* would prove tragically prophetic. In May 1611, Agostino Tassi, a painter friend of her father and one of her teachers, raped Artemisia. Her father sued him eight months later. During the ordeal of a seven-month trial, Artemisia, despite being tortured with thumbscrews, testified that Tassi had been trying to seduce her and became infuriated when she preferred her painting to his advances. She actively resisted him and at one

point wounded him with a knife. After raping her, Tassi promised to marry her. Finding that he had other prospects, she consented to sexual relations with him in the hope that he would marry her. "What I was doing with him, I did only so that as he had dishonored me, he would marry me."[10]

Tassi, a veteran seducer, denied having assaulted Artemisia. He had been previously charged with having murdered his wife and had already been imprisoned for incest with his sister-in-law by whom he had three children. Following the usual custom of the day, Tassi assumed the court would find him more believable than a teenage girl and brought in phony witnesses to attempt to disparage Artemisia's character. One of them, Pietro Stiattesi, later broke ranks and supported Artemisia's version of the events in question. The court finally concluded that Artemisia was the one telling the truth. Tassi was found guilty but was released from prison after he had served only eight months. Since women were not valued fully as humans, the all-male courts of the period did not always consider the rape of a nonnoblewoman to be a particularly serious offense.

For Artemisia it was a devastating experience from beginning to end and she could not remain in Rome with its painful memories of her public humiliation. Although relations with her father had become strained, he used his contacts in Florence with the Grand Duchess Christina de' Medici, mother of Duke Cosimo II. Assured of Medici patronage, she moved to Florence with her new husband, the painter Pietro Stiattesi, the former friend of Tassi's who had testified on her behalf at the rape trial. She married him a month after the trial ended "to restore her honor."

They both worked as painters in Florence and had two daughters. Despite the responsibilities of a family, Artemisia's art flourished and in 1616 she became the first woman admitted to the prestigious Florentine Academy of Art. Among her supporters were Duke Cosimo II, the scientist Galileo, and the grandnephew of Michelangelo. It was during her Florentine period that she painted her powerful masterpiece, *Judith Slaying Holofernes*. Gentileschi was fascinated by the biblical heroine Judith and painted at least six different versions of the story. According to the Old Testament, as an act of war Judith had supper with the Assyrian tyrant, Holofernes, murdered him, cut off his head, and brought it back to the Hebrews.

Commissioned by the Grand Duke Cosimo II, Artemisia's rendering of the scene was extremely vivid and dramatic. A fiercely determined Judith, assisted by a maidservant, cuts off the head of the tyrant with grim determination. Blood spurts from the head of Holofernes onto white bedding in a depiction that is much more graphic than a similar work by Caravaggio, her mentor, in 1598. As a victim of sexual assault, Artemisia may have felt herself to be avenging in a sense all the wrongs she had suffered. Judith is a strong heroine with whom the artist clearly identified. The painting reveals not only her passion for justice but also her incredible talent and such technical abilities as the mastery of dramatic composition, *chiaroscuro*, modeling, and bold use of color.

In 1621 Gentileschi separated from her husband, whose career she threatened to

Artemisia Gentileschi, *Self-Portrait as the Allegory of Painting*. Kensington Palace, London, United Kingdom. Collection of Her Majesty the Queen.

eclipse, and left Florence shortly after the death of her patron, the grand duke. Reunited with her father, she went on to undertake commissions in Genoa, Venice, Rome, and Naples. Between 1638 and 1641 Artemisia painted at the court of King Charles I and Queen Henrietta Maria of England. The ravages of the English Civil War forced her to return to Naples, where she lived her remaining years. Most of her subject matter was biblical, including a tender *Madonna and Child* of 1609, but Artemisia Gentileschi had a special interest in strong women and painted spectacular portraits of Cleopatra, Lucretia, Minerva, and Mary Magdalene.

She was also courageous enough to paint herself as the living embodiment of painting. In *Self-Portrait as the Allegory of Painting* (1630), Artemisia depicted herself bearing the widely recognized attributes that identify the allegorical figure "Painting." The artist's unkempt, dark hair shows her obsession with painting over appearance. On her gold neck chain is a mask that represents imitation. She holds a paintbrush in one hand and a palette in the other, as light floods in on her face from an unknown source. Artemisia Gentileschi's stunning self-portrait and the career of Sofonisba Anguisola help mark the beginning of a new era for women artists. No longer would all women artists continue to labor in obscurity. Painting had become a woman's art as well as a man's, and all the world should be able to see and know that.

Chronology

c. 1266–1337	Life of Giotto.		*Supper* in Milan.
1401–1428	Life of Masaccio.	1508	Michelangelo begins the Sistine Chapel ceiling.
c. 1406–1469	Life of Fra Filippo Lippi.		
1444–1510	Life of Botticelli.	1511–1574	Life of Giorgio Vasari.
1446–1524	Life of Perugino.	c. 1532–1625	Life of Sofonisba Anguissola.
1452–1519	Life of Leonardo da Vinci.		
1475–1564	Life of Michelangelo.	1534	Michelangelo begins *The Last Judgment*.
1482–1520	Life of Raphael.	1569–1610	Life of Caravaggio.
c. 1488–1576	Life of Titian.	1593–c. 1632	Life of Artemisia Gentileschi.
1495	Leonardo begins *The Last*		

Further Reading

GENERAL WORKS

Paul Barolsky, *The Faun in the Garden: Michelangelo and the Poetic Origins of Italian Art* (1994).

Michael Baxandall, *Painting and Experience in Fifteenth-Century Italy* (1972).

Lorne Campbell, *Renaissance Portraits: European Portrait-Painting in the Fourteenth, Fifteenth, and Sixteenth Centuries* (1990).

Kenneth Clark, *The Art of Humanism* (1983).

Bruce Cole, *The Renaissance Artist at Work* (1983).

Samuel Edgerton, *The Heritage of Giotto's Geometry: Art and Science on the Eve of the Scientific Revolution* (1992).

John Hale, *Italian Renaissance Painting from Masaccio to Titian* (1976).

Marcia Hall, *Color and Meaning: Practice and Theory in Renaissance Painting* (1992).

Frederick Hartt and David Wilkins, *History of Italian Renaissance Art*, 4th ed. (1994). The sumptuously illustrated, widely used textbook.

Paul Hills, *The Light of Early Italian Painting* (1987).

George Holmes, *Art and Politics in Renaissance Italy* (1994). A collection of his essays.

———, *The Florentine Enlightenment, 1400–50* (1969).

Peter Humfrey, *Painting in Renaissance Venice* (1995).

Norbert Huse and Wolfgang Walters, *The Art of Renaissance Venice* (1990).

Norman Land, *The Viewer as Poet: The Renaissance Response to Art* (1994).

David Landau and Peter Parshall, *The Renaissance Print 1470–1550* (1994).

E. Ann Matter and John Coakley, eds., *Creative Women in Medieval and Early Modern Italy* (1994).

Linda Murray, *The High Renaissance* (1967).

Patricia Lee Rubin, *Giorgio Vasari: Art and History* (1994).

James Saslow, *Ganymede in the Renaissance: Homosexuality in Art and Society* (1986).

Laurence Schmeckebier, *A New Handbook of Italian Renaissance Painting* (1981).

Alistair Smart, *The Dawn of Italian Painting, 1250–1400* (1978).

Giorgio Vasari, *Lives of the Painters, Sculptors and Architects*, ed. by Edmund Fuller (1968). Written by a Renaissance artist but must be used with caution because of his fondness for legends. See the discussions in Paul Barolsky and Patricia Rubin.

Martin Wackernagel, *The World of the Florentine Renaissance Artist* (1981).

John White, *Art and Architecture in Italy, 1250–1400*, 3rd ed. (1993).

PATRONAGE

Clifford Brown, *Our Accustomed Discourse on the Antique: Cesare Gonza and Gerolamo Garimberto: Two Renaissance Collectors of Greco-Roman Art* (1994).

Rona Goffen, *Piety and Patronage in Renaissance Venice* (1986).

Mary Hollingsworth, *Patronage in Renaissance Italy from 1400 to the Early Sixteenth Century* (1996).

INDIVIDUAL ARTISTS

Mosche Barash, *Giotto and the Language of Gesture* (1987).

Carlo Bertelli, *Piero della Francesca* (1992).

George Bull, *Michelangelo: A Biography* (1995).

Bruce Cole, *Masaccio and the Art of Early Renaissance Florence* (1980).

Charles Dempsey, *The Portrayal of Love: Botticelli's Primavera and Humanist Culture at the Time of Lorenzo the Magnificent* (1992).

Luba Freedman, *Titian's Portraits through Aretino's Lens* (1995).

Mary Garrard, *Artemisia Gentileschi* (1989).

Gail Geiger, *Filippino Lippi's Carafa Chapel* (1986).

Rona Goffen, *Giovanni Bellini* (1989).

Howard Hibbard, *Michelangelo* (1986).

Roger Jones and Nicholas Penny, *Raphael* (1983).

Ronald Lightbrown, *Botticelli*, 2 vols. (1978).

Ilya Sandra Perlingiere, *Sofonisba Anguissola* (1993).

LEONARDO DA VINCI

James Beck, *Leonardo's Rules of Painting* (1979).

Serge Bramly, *Leonardo, the Artist and the Man* (1995).

Kenneth Clark, *Leonardo da Vinci* (1975).

Martin Kemp, *Leonardo da Vinci* (1981).

Martin Kemp, Jane Roberts with Philip Steadman, *Leonardo da Vinci* (1989).

Jane Roberts, *Leonardo da Vinci* (1989).

Notes

1. Cited in Frederick Hartt, *History of Italian Renaissance Art*, 4th ed. (New York: Abrams and Prentice Hall, 1994), p. 335.
2. Giorgio Vasari, *Lives of the Painters, Sculptors, and Architects*, trans. A. B. Hinds, ed. Edmund Fuller (New York: Dell, 1968), p. 182.
3. Cited in Kenneth Clark, *Leonardo da Vinci: An Account of His Development as an Artist* (Baltimore, Md.: Penguin, 1959), p. 147.
4. Vasari, *Lives*, p. 348.
5. Cited in Kenneth Bartlett, ed., *The Civilization of the Italian Renaissance: A Sourcebook* (Lexington, Ma.: D.C. Heath, 1992), p. 243.
6. Vasari, *Lives*, p. 349.
7. Ibid.
8. Cited in Lewis Spitz, *The Renaissance and Reformation Movements* (Chicago: Rand McNally, 1971), p. 216.
9. Vasari, *Lives*, p. 436.
10. Cited in Mary Garrard, *Artemisia Gentileschi: The Image of the Female Hero in Italian Baroque Art* (Princeton, N.J.: Princeton University Press, 1989), p. 22.

7

Renaissance Sculpture, Architecture, and Music

The Fatiguing Art: Sculpture

The achievements of Renaissance painters were complemented by stunning creations by sculptors, architects, and musicians. Many of the great artists of the period excelled in a variety of mediums. Others chose to specialize in a particular art and were not above disparaging the arts of their colleagues. Leonardo da Vinci, jealous of the growing fame of his younger rival Michelangelo, wrote:

> I do not find any difference between painting and sculpture except that the sculptor pursues his work with greater physical fatigue than the painter, and the painter pursues his with greater mental fatigue. This is proved to be true, for the sculptor in producing his work does so by the force of his arm, striking the marble or some other stone to remove the covering beyond the figure enclosed within it. This is a most mechanical exercise accompanied many times with a great deal of sweat, which combines with dust and turns to mud.[1]

Unlike painting, of which few classical examples had survived, Renaissance Italy was filled with surviving models of ancient sculpture. However, Renaissance sculptors did more than just imitate classical models; they also made their own unique contributions to the art of sculpture. The ingenuity of sculptors such as Ghiberti, Donatello, and Michelangelo showed that Leonardo was wrong. Great sculpture required both brains and brawn.

LORENZO GHIBERTI (C. 1381–1455)

Lorenzo Ghiberti of Florence was one of the first to imitate and adapt classical models. He first achieved prominence by winning the famous competition of 1401 and getting the commission to cast a complete set of doors for the Baptistery of St. John adjacent to the Florentine Cathedral. The competition was sponsored by the Wool Merchants Guild in thanks to God for saving the commune from the plague of 1400.

Seven important Tuscan sculptors competed for the commission including Ghiberti and the multitalented Filippo Brunelleschi. Each competitor was to sculpt a bronze panel depicting how the faith of the biblical patriarch Abraham was tested when God asked him to sacrifice his only son, Isaac. Although trained as a painter and still not a graduate of any guild, the young Ghiberti's panel was declared the winner. Brunelleschi was so angry at losing to his younger rival that he left Florence to study ancient architecture in Rome. If he could not be Florence's best sculptor, he would become its greatest architect.

Ghiberti's winning panel showed the first truly Renaissance nude figure in direct imitation of ancient Roman models. The nude figure of Isaac is kneeling on the right side of the panel while his father, Abraham, is poised with his knife pointed toward his son. With a single gesture, the angel floating directly above them stops the sacrifice. On the left is a ram resting quietly in a thicket while servants converse below. Ghiberti's panel revealed a clarity of composition, which combined classical and natural elements. His figures were also hollow and less expensive to produce, a fact that was probably not lost on the practical-minded among the judges.

Ghiberti spent the next twenty-three years of his life designing, modeling, and

Lorenzo Ghiberti, *Sacrifice of Isaac*. Bargello, Florence, Italy. Alinari/Art Resource.

sculpting the full bronze doors, whose subject matter was changed to scenes from the New Testament. After their completion in 1424, he was awarded a commission for a second set of bronze doors showing episodes from the Old Testament. When completed in 1447, the second set of doors was considered an even greater success than the first. Michelangelo later declared that the second set of baptistery doors was worthy to serve as "the gates of paradise." Ghiberti also sculpted monumental, heroic statues of *St. John* and *St. Matthew* for the banking guild's niches at the Orsanmichele, a public structure in Florence that served as a shrine, wheat exchange, and granary.

DONATELLO (1386–1466)

Although Ghiberti serenely confessed in his autobiography that "few things of importance were made in our country [Florence] that were not designed and planned by me," his student Donatello surpassed him as a sculptor and continued the wonderful tradition of art as part of the civic revival of Florence after the political crisis at the beginning of the century.[2] He was a member of the stone and wood workers' guild but also studied goldsmithing and worked for a long time in Ghiberti's busy studio. He became a close, lifelong friend of Brunelleschi and studied classical monuments and statues in Rome. However, Donatello was not interested in either Brunelleschi's concern for strict proportions nor Ghiberti's interest in graceful line. Instead, he chose to depict the inner life of his subjects in dramatic force and power.

Much of Donatello's early sculpture in Florence was done in relation to architectural settings; however, he is famous for having sculpted the first freestanding nude statue in the round since antiquity. Dona-

Lorenzo Ghiberti, *Gates of Paradise.*
Baptistery, Florence, Italy. Alinari/Art
Resource.

tello's revolutionary *David* of 1425 to 1430 was sculpted for the Medici palace gardens, where viewers could see it from all angles. In contrast to other heroic Davids, including one of his own done earlier in his career in marble, this bronze David is a slight boy of twelve or thirteen, clothed only in leather boots and a shepherd's hat. He holds a sword in his right hand, while his left hand relaxes at his hip. His right foot rests upon a wreath, but his left foot toys idly with the severed head of the giant Goliath. David (Florence) has triumphed over Goliath (Milan) with the help of God and is utterly relaxed in victory.

In the early 1440s Donatello departed for Padua and remained there for over a decade. There he sculpted a colossal equestrian statue in bronze of Erasmo da Narni, the Venetian mercenary general known as Gattamelata (the "Honeyed Cat"). The dead general's family paid an enormous sum for this tribute as stipulated in his will. Donatello's models included the great ancient equestrian statue of the Stoic Roman Emperor Marcus Aurelius, which he had studied in Rome. When finished in 1453, the statue was placed in the square in front of the Basilica of St. Anthony, where it still stands today as a monument to Donatello's genius.

Gattamelata shows the artist's mastery of equine, as well as human, anatomy. The powerful horse with his swelling veins, open jaws, and flaring eyes and nostrils is firmly under the general's command. His rider, dressed in fifteenth-century armor with Roman details, holds a general's baton and is armed with a huge broadsword. *Gattamelata*'s face, with its firmly set jaw, arched eyebrows, and widespread eyes, reveals the force and confident personality of this accomplished general. It is a masterful portrayal of the power of command.

Growing weary of the adulation he received in Padua, the bachelor Donatello returned to the more critical atmosphere of Florence where he spent his last years

Donatello, *Monument to General Gattamelata*. Piazza del Santo, Padua, Italy. Alinari/Art Resource.

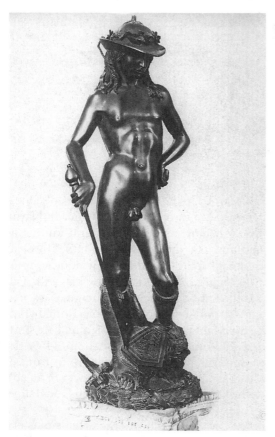

Donatello, *David*. Bargello, Florence, Italy. Alinari/Art Resource.

sculpting and arguing with clients over fees. The temperamental Donatello is reputed to have destroyed some of his own compositions when he failed to receive the proper compensation. Fortunately, enough of his work survives to assure his reputation as the greatest sculptor of the Renaissance before Michelangelo. His dramatic depictions also had a profound influence on painters such as Botticelli and many others.

MICHELANGELO AS A SCULPTOR

The young Michelangelo had long been impressed by the sculptural mastery of Ghiberti, Donatello, and other Florentines. He had also studied available classical models and made his own intensive studies of human anatomy. Immersed in Neoplatonic idealism from his time with the Medici and an associate of Marsilio Ficino and the Platonic Academy, he was interested as an artist was in the life of the human soul as expressed in the structure and movement of the human body. For Michelangelo, the body was the "mortal veil" of divine intention. Only by creating bodies could he dare do something analogous to God's creation of body and soul.

In June 1496 Michelangelo left Florence for Rome. An art agent had payed him thirty ducats for a sleeping cupid done in Roman style. The agent then buried it in the earth to give it the appearance of age and sold it for 200 ducats to a Roman cardinal as an antique. When Michelangelo learned of the fraud, he quickly dashed off to Rome to correct the problem. He stayed for five years and received a number of excellent commissions, including one from a French cardinal for a *Pietà*.

Images of the dead Christ on his mother's lap were common in France and the Holy Roman Empire but were virtually unknown in Italy. Michelangelo made his first trip to Carrara to find marble of the highest quality for this statue. In the Vatican *Pietà*, the twenty-five-year-old artist showed his deep religiosity and a technical virtuosity that surpassed even the mature Donatello. Never had anyone sculpted with the refinement and delicacy of touch as shown in the torso and limbs of the dead Christ and the complex arrangement of the drapery. Michelangelo's tender Mary is years younger than her son, whose wounds have virtually disappeared. Their purity of soul has removed all traces of injury and age. Typical of Renaissance self-promotion, the artist sculpted his name across the chest of Mary.

In 1501 the government of Florence commissioned the now famous sculptor to

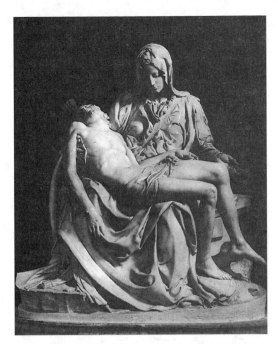

Michelangelo, *The Pietà*. St. Peter's Basilica, Vatican State. Alinari/Art Resource.

create a David out of a block of Carrara marble that other sculptors had rejected as cut too narrowly for a fully rounded, freestanding statue. Michelangelo went into seclusion with the marble for two years and emerged with a giant *David* that defiantly glorified the naked human body. David is shown before his battle with Goliath, his sling over his shoulder and a stone resting in his right hand. His muscles are taut, but his face is confident and defiant. Gone is the young Hebrew boy in desperate need of God's help; instead Michelangelo has sculpted a godlike classical hero. The sculptor has pushed beyond the limits of classical realism to create a colossal superhuman, who belongs to the world of the mannerists. The Florentine government placed Michelangelo's *David* in front of the town hall as a valued symbol of the city, but they also prud-

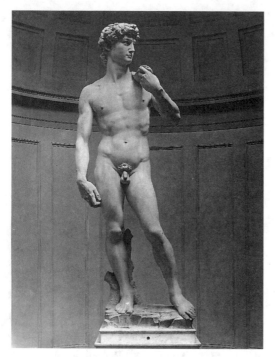

Michelangelo, *David*. Accademia, Florence, Italy. Alinari/Art Resource.

ishly insisted on placing a brass girdle with twenty-eight copper leaves around the defiant hero's waist!

In 1506 Michelangelo returned to Rome, where he spent the three most productive decades of his life in the service of four Renaissance popes, beginning with the crusty warrior-pope Julius II (Papa Terrible). Julius commissioned Michelangelo to create a gigantic tomb for him to stand three stories high and to be filled with dozens of statues of saints, apostles, cherubs, and sibyls. "Let it cost any amount and you shall have it," bragged Papa Terrible. The reality was that Michelangelo frequently had a difficult time collecting his money despite assurances from church officials that he was "our most dear friend."[3]

The pope also interrupted Michelan-

gelo's work on the tomb to force him to paint the ceiling of the Sistine Chapel as discussed in the previous chapter. Even this work was interrupted by the restless pope, whose inner demons almost matched Michelangelo's and who inspired so much dread among his enemies. For years Julius had been attempting to expand the papal state in central Italy. When he had finally cleared the Romagna of foes and entered Bologna in triumph, he ordered Michelangelo to sculpt a huge bronze, seated figure of the pope with the keys of the kingdom in one hand and a gesture of benediction in the other. The Bolognese hated it as a symbol of their humiliation and later melted it down to make cannonballs during an attempt to throw off papal rule.

Despite these interruptions, Michelangelo worked with great speed to advance the tomb, although only three of the statues were ever brought even close to completion. One of the finished works was a heroic and heavily muscled *Moses*. In this work Michelangelo depicts Moses as the man who saw and talked to God on Mount Sinai. There the biblical hero received the Tablets of the Law, which he holds under his right arm. He is shown with "horns," as was traditional, based on a deliberate mistranslation of the Hebrew word for "rays" by St. Jerome. When Moses came down from Mount Sinai for the second time, rays of light shone from his face. St. Jerome, the translator of the Vulgate Bible, refused to attribute light to anyone who preceded Christ.

Michelangelo's rendering of Moses was not traditional in most of its details including the unusually spectacular beard that tumbles down his chest. Meant to be viewed from below because it was intended for the second level of Pope Julius's tomb, Michelangelo's *Moses* reveals the artist's fascination with the male human body and his ability to create superhuman figures. In an effort to illustrate how Neoplatonic notions permeated his art, he once claimed that he could envision the completed figure inside the marble slab and what he had to do was to chip away the exterior. Few others have ever been able to release such incredible sculpted figures upon the world.

Michelangelo received patronage from Julius's successors but later returned to Florence to work on the facade for San Lorenzo. When that project was canceled, he began work on the Medici Chapel. For the chapel he sculpted not only giant portrait sculptures of dukes Lorenzo (d. 1519) and Giuliano de' Medici (d. 1516) and their more famous predecessors of the same names, but he also added the mysterious, allegorical figures of *Day*, *Night*, *Dawn*, and *Twilight*.

Michelangelo, *Moses*. S. Pietro in Vincoli, Rome, Italy. Alinari/Art Resource.

The full, gigantic project was never completed because he was called to Rome by the reformer Pope Paul III (r. 1534–1549) for the painting of *The Last Judgement* on the altar wall of the Sistine Chapel. Michelangelo spent the last thirty years of his life in Rome, turning down invitations from all over Europe and even one from the ruler of the Ottoman Empire, Süleyman the Magnificent, who had received some training as a goldsmith and valued great art and architecture.

Because sculpture was too physically demanding for a man in his sixties who had suffered so much from years of inner turmoil and bad eating habits, Michelangelo turned most of his attention to the less exhausting work of drawing architectural plans and composing lyrical and metaphysical love poems. He fell deeply in love with a handsome young Roman aristocrat, Tommaso dei Cavalieri, for whom he wrote passionate sonnets. Michelangelo also had a close, platonic friendship with the religious poet Vittorina Colonna. He died in his ninetieth year still working on a dome of St. Peter's Basilica, one of his greatest architectural efforts.

Architecture

In addition to the glories of Italian painting and sculpture, the Renaissance was also an incredible time for architecture. The highly influential architect, artist, musician, and theorist Leon Battista Alberti (c. 1402–1472) had called for the building of beautiful cities worthy of humanistically inclined men and women of virtue. In his seminal book, *On Building* (c. 1452), Alberti praised architecture as a social art, concerned with the health and welfare of people. No structure should be designed as an isolated unit; each building should be planned in relation to its social functions and setting. According to

Alberti, a disciple of the first century A.D. Roman architect Vitruvius, creative design should utilize classical forms because their principles had been proven to work over time.

FILIPPO BRUNELLESCHI (1377–1446)

Alberti applied these ideas in his own designs, as did his supremely gifted contemporary Filippo Brunelleschi. The son of a notary, Brunelleschi had served an apprenticeship as a goldsmith but departed from Florence upon losing the baptistery sculpture competition to Lorenzo Ghiberti in 1401. In Rome in the company of Donatello, he studied the great designs and monuments of classical architecture. With his mind filled with ideas, Brunelleschi returned to Florence in 1407 at the very time the city government had decided to complete the construction of the dome of the cathedral of Santa Maria del Fiore (St. Mary of the Flowers). The Florentines were still in the throes of their struggles with Milan and wanted to use public art to express their thanks to God for delivering them from the Milanese and to express their confidence in the future.

After lengthy wrangling, Brunelleschi's design for the dome was accepted and construction was finally begun in 1420 and was

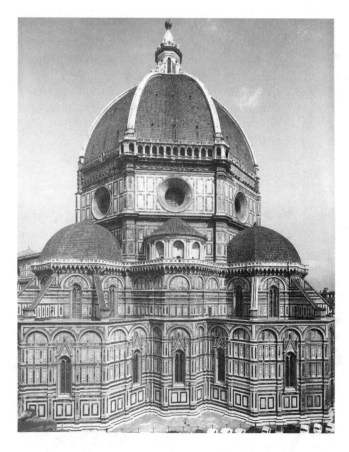

Brunelleschi, Dome of the Cathedral of Santa Maria del Fiore. Florence, Italy. Alinari/Art Resource.

Brunelleschi, Interior view down the nave toward the apse, San Lorenzo. Florence, Italy. Alinari/Art Resource.

completed in 1436. His dome was the largest ever built since the time of the Roman Pantheon, towering nearly 180 feet. Brunelleschi was able to displace some of the ceiling weight of the dome by making it higher than a fully rounded dome. He also used such innovative features as an inner and outer shell, ribbed vaulting, smaller support domes, and a thick drum at the roof base. Brunelleschi's dome for the cathedral was so successful that he soon became the most celebrated architect in Florence.

Brunelleschi's architectural legacy included the graceful Pazzi Chapel, a strikingly original Hospital of the Innocents, and several revolutionary churches, including the Medici's San Lorenzo. In contrast to Gothic architecture with its emphasis on verticality, Brunelleschi's design with its flat ceilings and horizontal lines emphasized the control of space. He was intrigued with the simple three-aisle system of early Christian basilicas that he had observed so carefully in Rome. In addition to his work as an architect, Brunelleschi made invaluable contributions to painting with his explanations of the working of linear perspective. He also came up with several clever mechanical devices and advised his fellow inventors not "to share your inventions with many, share them only with a few who understand and love the sciences."[4]

MICHELOZZO MICHELOZZI (1396–1472)

Brunelleschi submitted plans for a sumptuous new Medici palace to Cosimo de' Medici, who rejected them as too grand. Instead the commission went to Michelozzo Michelozzi, who also supervised the completion of San Lorenzo. Michelozzi, the son of a tailor, began his artistic career as a sculptor, working in bronze, silver, and marble with Donatello and Ghiberti. His skill, moderation, and good taste won the admiration of Cosimo de' Medici, who commissioned him to design his family palace. Michelozzi's modest and graceful design is much less grandiose than Brunelleschi's larger Pitti Palace, which was built partly with slave labor, and more in keeping with

Michelozzo, Palazzo Medici-Riccardi. Florence, Italy. Alinari/Art Resource.

Cosimo's determination not to flaunt his wealth beyond the bounds of good taste and civic virtue. The rough-cut stones of the ground floor suggest an urban fortress. The Medici coat-of-arms is prominently displayed on the building's corner. The finished building was so successful that it became a model of Renaissance domestic architecture. Michelozzi went on to become one of Italy's most important architects.

BRAMANTE (1444–1514)

Donato d'Agnolo Bramante was the leading architect of the second half of the fifteenth century. A native of Urbino, he was trained as a painter in Mantua and Milan. Bramante made his first appearance as an architect in 1485 when he undertook the rebuilding of the church of Santa Maria Presso San Satiro in Milan. His design was so well received that he soon became the leading church architect of the Sforzas. With Ludovico il Moro's fall in 1499, Bramante left for Rome hoping for better luck and new patrons in the papal city. One of his greatest masterpieces is the circular Tempietto (little temple) commissioned by Ferdinand and Isabella of Spain in 1502. Bramante based his design on ancient round temples he had observed in Rome and Tivoli. His Tempietto has no single elevation; it exists in space like a work of sculpture and has come to be regarded as a paragon of Renaissance architecture.

The success of the Tempietto helped bring Bramante to the attention of the papal court. He soon became the leading papal architect and reached the climax of his architectural career with his designs for the new St. Peter's Basilica and a grand renovation of the Vatican Palace. When completed later in the century using mostly the plans of others, St. Peter's became one of the greatest monuments to the genius of a host of Renaissance architects, artists, and patrons. As the largest and most expensive house of worship in western Europe, the cost of its construction helped to spark the Protestant Reformation.

WOMEN IN SCULPTURE AND ARCHITECTURE

What contributions women made to Renaissance sculpture and architecture are not as yet fully known. Even the exact role of noblewomen in architectural patronage is unclear. Architecture and sculpture were considered male monopolies and because those arts were even more public than painting, it was impossible for females to gain commissions to sculpt or design buildings. Most Renaissance men assumed that women were

Bramante and others, Exterior of St. Peter's. Vatican State. Alinari/Art Resource.

not to be trusted with the expenditure of large sums of money and the supervision of male construction workers. Not until the nineteenth century do we hear of female architects.

Potential women sculptors were barred from the field by the fifteenth-century requirement that all sculptors be familiar with human anatomy, especially the nude male. Sweaty sculptors' workshops were considered even less suitable for females than workshops that focused on other arts such as glassmaking or painting. Young women in the Renaissance found it impossible to receive training as sculptors even from the most supportive of males. Therefore,

Michelangelo could offer Sofonisba Anguissola training in drawing and painting but not in architecture and sculpture.

The Sounds of the Universe: Music

Renaissance humanists also had a passion for music. Had not the revered Greek philosopher Pythagoras (sixth century B.C.) shown that harmony was the essential component of the universe? Music was a critical ingredient of medieval worship from the Gregorian chants onward. The Renaissance Neoplatonist Marsilio Ficino had argued that music was a way to approach God and heal disease. Renaissance courts relied heavily on musicians for entertainment and enrichment. Progressive humanist schools such as that of Vittorino da Feltre included music as part of the experience. Musical instruments such as the lute, viol, flute, and harp were used primarily as accompaniment for songs or dances. Eventually, instrumental music also became popular, especially at civic festivals and public events, where trumpets, trombones, and oboes were used with great effect.

Francesco Landino (1325–1397), the blind organist of the church of San Lorenzo in Florence, was one of the greatest musicians of the early Renaissance. He was a skilled performer with the lute, recorder, and organ and also wrote hundreds of madrigals (a complex, unaccompanied vocal piece), ballads, and other mostly secular music. Landino also won fame as a humanist, philosopher, and mathematician. The cadential formula, *Landino sixth*, is named after him.

Building on the growing reputation of Florence as a center for music, Lorenzo de' Medici founded a "School of Harmony," which attracted musicians from all over Italy. Isabella d'Este brought many singers to her court at Mantua. She had learned to sing and play instruments and appreciate music growing up at the court of her father, Duke Ercole, in Ferrara. He was an avid musical enthusiast. Ferrara's reputation as a leading musical center continued into the late sixteenth century when the duke organized a group of "lady singers" in 1580, who proved to be the first professional female court musicians. One of them, the virtuoso singer and instrumentalist Tarquinia Molza (1524–1617), wrote arrangements for voice, lute, viol, and harp. Tragically, her compositions have all been lost, but the fashion for "lady singers" spread to Mantua, Rome, and elsewhere.

GIOVANNI PALESTRINA (C. 1525–1594)

Giovanni Palestrina was arguably the most talented composer of the sixteenth century. Influenced by Flemish as well as Italian traditions, he spent most of his life at various churches in Rome, eventually becoming the papal organist and director of the papal choir. There Palestrina composed masses, motets (choral compositions on a sacred text), madrigals, and settings for the biblical *Song of Solomon*. Not an innovator, he brought to a head the century-and-a-half development of polyphonic (vocal counterpoint) music. Inspired by the Catholic Reformation and the Council of Trent, Palestrina later sought to purge his music of all secular elements. His later compositions are not nearly as sensuous or as complex as his earlier ones, but they are still powerful expressions of the growing power of music. Papal Rome continued to be a great source of patronage for musicians long after the death of Palestrina in 1594.

CLAUDIO MONTEVERDI (1567–1643)

Claudio Monteverdi was the seminal figure in the dramatic development of opera. Born in Cremona, he was attached to the sophisticated court of the Gonzagas in Mantua for many years. There Monteverdi came up with the idea of combining singing, acting, dancing, and instrumental music with elaborate stage designs and costumes. His first opera, *Orfeo* (*Orpheus*), was performed at Mantua in 1607. It created a sensation and was followed by other grandiose open-air productions. In 1613 Monteverdi moved to St. Mark's Cathedral in Venice to serve as its master of music. He remained in Venice for the rest of his life, composing sacred music, operas, madrigals, and motets in his harmonic style. His legacy continues to enrich us today.

Chronology

c. 1325–1397	Life of Francesco Landino.	**1420**	Brunelleschi begins work on the Florentine dome.
1377–1446	Life of Brunelleschi.	**1444–1514**	Life of Bramante.
c. 1381–1455	Life of Ghiberti.	**1475–1564**	Life of Michelangelo.
1386–1466	Life of Donatello.	**1500–1571**	Life of Benvenuto Cellini.
1396–1472	Life of Michelozzo Michelozzi.	**c. 1525–1594**	Life of Giovanni Palestrina.
1402	Competition for the doors of the Baptistery of St. John in Florence.	**1542–1617**	Life of Tarquinia Molza.
		1567–1643	Life of Claudio Monteverdi.
c. 1402–1472	Life of Leon Battista Alberti.	**1568**	Cellini begins composing his *Autobiography*.

Further Reading

SCULPTURE

Bonnie Bennett and David Wilkins, *Donatello* (1985).

Bruce Boucher, *The Sculpture of Jacopo Sansovino* (1991).

Charles de Tolnay, *Michelangelo* (1975). By the leading authority.

Michael Hirst and Jill Dunkerton, *The Young Michelangelo: Making and Meaning, The Artist in Rome, 1496–1501* (1994).

Richard Krautheimer, *Lorenzo Ghiberti* (1970).

Anita Moskowitz, *The Sculpture of Andrea and Nono Pisano* (1986).

Roberta Olson, *Italian Renaissance Sculpture* (1992).

John Pope-Hennessy, *The Study and Criticism of Italian Sculpture* (1980).

Charles Seymour, Jr., *Sculpture in Italy, 1400–1500* (1994).

William Wallace, *Michelangelo at San Lorenzo: The Genius as Entrepreneur* (1994).

Sarah Blake Wilk, *Fifteenth-Century Italian Sculpture* (1986).

Diane Zervas, *The Parte Guelfa, Brunelleschi and Donatello* (1988).

ARCHITECTURE

James Ackerman, *The Architecture of Michelangelo* (1986).

Eugenio Battisti, *Filippo Brunelleschi* (1981).

Joan Gadol, *Leon Battista Alberti: Universal Man of the Early Renaissance* (1969).

Richard Goldthwaite, *The Building of Renaissance Florence* (1986).

Deborah Howard, *The Architectural History of Venice* (1980).

Frances Kent, *A Florentine Patrician and His Palace* (1981). A study of the Rucellai Palace in Florence.

Peter Murray, *The Architecture of the Italian Renaissance* (1986).

Howard Saalman, *Filippo Brunelleschi: The Buildings* (1993).

Christine Smith, *Architecture in the Culture of Early Humanism: Ethics, Aesthetics and Eloquence, 1400–1470* (1992).

David Thomson, *Renaissance Architecture: Patrons, Critics, and Luxury* (1993).

MUSIC

Allan Atlas, *Music of the Aragonese Court of Naples* (1985).

Paolo Fabri, *Monteverdi* (1994).

Iain Fenlon, *Music and Patronage in Sixteenth Century Mantua*, 2 vols. (1981).

Frederick Hammond, *Music and Spectacle in Baroque Rome: Barberini Patronage under Urban VIII* (1994).

Barbara Hanning, *Of Poetry and Music's Power: Humanism and the Creation of Opera* (1980).

Lewis Lockwood, *Music in Renaissance Ferrara, 1400–1505* (1985).

Nino Pirrotta, *Music and Culture in Italy from the Middle Ages to the Baroque* (1984).

Reinhard Strohm, *The Rise of European Music, 1380–1500* (1994).

Gary Tomlinson, *Monteverdi and the End of the Renaissance* (1987).

Notes

1. Cited in G. R. Elton, ed., *Renaissance and Reformation, 1300–1648,* 3rd ed. (New York: Macmillan, 1976), p. 67.
2. Cited in De Lamar Jensen, *Renaissance Europe: Age of Recovery and Reconciliation,* 2nd ed. (Lexington, Mass.: D. C. Heath, 1992), p. 166.
3. Cited in D. S. Chambers, ed., *Patrons and Artists in the Italian Renaissance* (Columbia, S.C.: University of South Carolina Press, 1971), p. 35.
4. Cited in Kenneth Bartlett, ed., *The Civilization of the Italian Renaissance: A Sourcebook* (Lexington, Mass.: D. C. Heath, 1992), p. 211.

8

The Northern Monarchies
and Their Expansion

Although the north of Europe was not as economically advanced or as urbanized as Italy at the beginning of the fourteenth century, it too participated in and made valuable contributions to the Renaissance. Oil painting, for example, was first developed in the Low Countries and spread to Italy in the fifteenth century. Italian humanists and artists came north as diplomatic envoys, secretaries, and university lecturers. Northerners went to Italy as university students and admirers of Italian culture. The Nuremberg artist Albrecht Dürer was typical of many northern artists who found it necessary to travel to Italy to learn from the work of the Italian masters. Businesspeople went in both directions and helped spread Renaissance humanist ideas throughout Europe. As the north of Europe became wealthier and more urban, it too immersed itself in Renaissance culture.

The Economic Background

Northern Europe was a land of small farming villages, hundreds of small towns, a few large cities, and various territorial states. As in Italy, most people still worked the land, but commercial life grew apace during the fifteenth and sixteenth centuries. Northern cities grew in size, primarily along water trade routes in the Low Countries, on the Baltic coast, and along the Rhine and Danube Rivers. Great capitalist families such as the Fuggers and Welsers of Augsburg or the Kresses and Tuchers of Nuremberg emulated the methods of their colleagues in Italy and amassed considerable fortunes. South German towns banded together in the Swabian League to protect their trade caravans from robber knights. Elsewhere individual entrepreneurs like Jacques Coeur (1395–1456) in France made and lost great sums loaning money to the French king and supplying Eastern luxury goods to the court. Coeur had also been arrested for coin clipping and later for poisoning a royal mistress and intriguing with the Ottomans.

Trade in the Baltic and North Sea regions was facilitated by a loose federation of about 200 far-flung towns known as the Hanseatic League, whose members included Bremen, Breslau, Bruges, Brunswick, Cologne, Cracow (Krakow), Danzig, Deventer, Dortmund, Hamburg, Königsberg, London, Lüneberg, Magdeburg, Münster, Novgorod, Osnabrück, Reval, Riga, Stockholm, Thorn, and Visby. The German town of Lübeck served as its capital because of its strategic

Renaissance Europe

location on the Holstein isthmus that connected the North and Baltic Seas. The league concentrated on trade in consumer goods of western and northern Europe for the furs, timbers, ores, and grains of northeastern Europe and Russia.

Like Italy, northern Europe suffered the ravages of the Black Death in the fourteenth century and saw its population gradually increase back to preplague levels by the end of the sixteenth century. Europe north of the Alps also endured a long depression throughout much of the fifteenth century. As its population grew and trade increased, northern and central Europe was poised to make its own substantial contributions to the movements known as the Renaissance and the Reformation. However, those movements took place against a background of increasing social and religious tensions, political instability, and ferocious struggles for power between emerging national monarchies.

The Political World

In contrast to the small states of the Italian world, the drama of the Renaissance in northern Europe was acted out against a political background of large monarchies that had emerged from the decentralized, highly feudalized states of the Middle Ages. Northern monarchs were developing greater control over their mighty subjects by relying more on mercenary armies and less on feudal levies. Royal bureaucracies and court systems had also expanded. As national monarchies became stronger, they sought to extend their influence and often their borders as well. This contributed to the fall of the duchy of Burgundy, which could not compete with the rising power of the French monarchy.

THE DISAPPEARANCE OF BURGUNDY

The duchy of Burgundy was made up of the free county of Burgundy (Franche-Comté), Luxembourg, upper Alsace, and much of the Netherlands. Although scattered, Burgundy had rich farm land, prosperous cities such as Bruges, and a strategic location. During the half-century following the Hundred Years' War, the dukes of Burgundy were among the richest and most powerful princes in Europe. Philip the Good (r. 1419–1467) was a leading patron of the arts. Talented artists flocked to his court, including Guillaume Dufay (1400–1475), the leading composer of the fifteenth century.

Philip's son, Charles the Bold (r. 1467–1477), sought to realize his father's dream of an independent middle kingdom between France and the Holy Roman Empire. Toward that end, he conquered the duchy of Lorraine in 1475 and secured claims to Guelders and Zutphen in the Netherlands. However, King Louis XI of France soon organized a coalition with Rhineland and Swiss towns against the Burgundians. During the fall of 1476, the Burgundians were defeated in a series of battles against the French and their allies. Finally, in January 1477, at the battle of Nancy, Charles the Bold was killed. Since he had no male heir, his French territories reverted to the French. Only the marriage of his daughter to Maximilian of Habsburg, son of Emperor Frederick III, prevented Franche-Comté and Flanders from also being gobbled up by France. Power politics in the Renaissance could be a very dangerous game.

FRANCE UNDER FRANÇOIS I (r. 1515–1547)

The French kingdom emerged from the Hundred Years' War as one of the strongest monarchies in Europe and twice launched major invasions of Italy in the late fifteenth century. With the absorption of much of Burgundy in 1477, France was well on its way to becoming the largest kingdom in Europe with a population between 12 and 15 million persons. Although an unattractive personality, Louis XI (r. 1461–1483), known as "the spider king," succeeded not only in taking large sections of Burgundy, but he also reduced the power of the French nobility. Ruthless, energetic, and able, he laid many of the foundations for making France a successful Renaissance monarchy. His son, Charles VIII (r. 1483–1498), was only thirteen when Louis XI died. Weak in mind and body, his capable older sister, Anne of Beaujeau, took control of the government for seven years as regent. When barely literate Charles did finally take the reins of power from his sister, his major accomplishment was the ill-fated invasion of Italy in 1494.

With his premature death at age twenty-eight, the French throne passed to his cousin and rival, Louis of Orléans. Despite the failure of his Italian invasion, Louis XII managed to enact a number of reforms inside France. He saw himself as a benevolent "father of his people" and pursued state-building policies, which increased the power of the crown at the expense of the nobility. Since Louis died without a son, the throne passed to his son-in-law François, duke of Angoulême, who launched an even more grandiose era of French history in 1515. He was an energetic young prince, who loved sensual pleasures, the hunt, and the joust. Determined to drive the Swiss out of Milan, François I made an alliance with the Venetians and crushed the Swiss at the battle of Marignano in September 1515. Milan was returned to French control, although François gave up all claims to Naples to avoid a continuation of the Italian wars and a confrontation with the Holy Roman Emperor Maximilian a year later.

In addition to his aggressive efforts in foreign policy, the king was also an avid builder of well-designed palaces and a great patron of the arts. King François not only served as Leonardo da Vinci's last patron, he also supported French men and women of letters. His sister, Marguerite, queen of Navarre, was the author of the *Heptameron* and an important leader of humanists. Guillaume Budé (1468–1540), a leading French humanist and legal scholar, was made secretary to the king and master of the rapidly growing royal library. Trained as a lawyer, Budé provided useful studies of Roman law and coinage. His most important work, *Commentaries on the Greek Language,* was published in 1529. He also persuaded the king to establish the College of France.

François I ruled France with a strong hand, even reducing the power of the

Jean Clouet, *François I of France.* Louvre, Paris, France. Giraudon/Art Resource.

French church early in his reign. Although sympathetic to some of the religious reformers, he stayed loyal to the Roman Catholic Church and strengthened his ties with the papacy. In foreign policy, the king continued his dynasty's rivalry with England and the Habsburgs. A shrewd pragmatist, he was willing to make alliances even with the feared and reviled Ottomans to avoid being boxed in by his rivals in the west. For most Christian rulers of Europe, to ally themselves with an Islamic state even for commercial and political reasons was equivalent to a pact with the devil. François was quite likely to put practical economic and dynastic considerations ahead of ethnic and religious prejudices.

ENGLAND UNDER THE EARLY TUDORS

Although defeated by France in the Hundred Years' War and then racked by the civil war known as the War of the Roses, England made a considerable comeback during the reign of Henry VII (1485–1509). A determined monarch with a clear focus, Henry Tudor used the Court of Star Chamber to attack the feudal privileges of the nobility. Levying stiff fines and confiscating the property of recalcitrant nobles, the frugal Henry worked to build up the crown revenues. He encouraged foreign commerce and demanded from foreign merchants who enjoyed privileges in England reciprocal privileges for English merchants. Henry also saw to it that a heavy duty was placed on the export of raw wool in order to promote the English manufacture and export of woolen textiles. The Navigation Act of 1485 gave further encouragement to the development of the English merchant fleet. The act stipulated that wines from Bordeaux in France must be carried in English ships with English, Welsh, or Irish crews.

King Henry VII worked well with Parliament, which had gained the right to vote on personal property taxes, customs, and levies for war. Henry also made favorable marriages with the royal house of Spain and Scotland. His oldest son, Arthur, was married to Catherine of Aragon (1485–1536), the daughter of Queen Isabella of Castile and King Ferdinand of Aragon. In 1499, Henry arranged to have his daughter Margaret (1489–1541) marry King James VI (r. 1488–1513) of Scotland. Although this marriage led to only a temporary improvement in Anglo-Scottish relations, it did lay the foundations for the eventual union of the English and Scottish crowns.

Henry VII's son, the talented and aggressive Henry VIII (r. 1509–1547), inherited a relatively stable and prosperous kingdom, whose international status was on the rise. Henry's older brother Arthur had died of consumption in 1502. Henry VII then arranged for his second son, Henry, to marry Arthur's widow. As king, Henry VIII's extravagance and military buildup soon dissipated much of that hard-won wealth. Eager for military glory, young Henry VIII in 1511 joined his father-in-law, Ferdinand of Spain, and Pope Julius II in the Holy League to drive the French out of Italy. In 1512 he allied with Spain and the Holy Roman Emperor Maximilian I against the French. Leading an English army into France, Henry VIII won the battle of Spurs and seized Tournai. Having been forsaken by his allies, the English king made peace in 1514 with France, who agreed to pay an annual subsidy.

The new French king, François I, renewed French aggression in Italy, taking rich Milan in 1515 as we have seen. England supported Spain in the ensuing struggles between the Habsburgs and the Valois. In 1522, England went to war with France. English campaigns in France in 1522 and 1523 accomplished little but proved exceedingly costly. Worried about the power of Charles V, Henry VIII made peace with François I in 1526. His new pro-French policy proved unpopular, and the king was unable to secure the finances from Parliament necessary to launch an attack on Charles V. By the end of the decade, the king had become enmeshed in domestic affairs, including his struggles to set aside Catherine of Aragon and secure a male heir. That led to the crisis of the English Reformation.

Spain under Isabella and Ferdinand

During much of the Middle Ages, the Iberian peninsula had been under Muslim control. As the Christians gradually pushed the Muslims into the single kingdom of Granada in the south, they had forged a number of separate kingdoms. In 1469 the royal houses of two of the largest Spanish kingdoms were brought together by the marriage of Isabella of Castile (1451–1504) with Ferdinand of Aragon (1452–1516). Both were highly intelligent, energetic, and determined to strengthen royal power. They took steps shortly after their accession to curb the powers of the feudal magnates. Instead of appointing nobles to administrative offices, Isabella and Ferdinand began to rely more on clerics and lawyers. The queen had her husband appointed to head three prominent Castilian military orders. This added to his prestige in Aragon and brought in badly needed revenues.

When the Parliament (*Cortes*) of Castile was summoned, the noble members were frequently not invited to attend and that body became increasingly subservient to the royal couple's wishes. The *Cortes* of Aragon, which was dominated by the nobility, was frequently ignored. Isabella and Ferdinand made greater use of separate administrative councils for Castile and Aragon, which were controlled by crown-appointed officials, most of them jurists.

To further increase the power of the crown and promote religious uniformity, the monarchs petitioned Pope Sixtus IV to establish the Holy Office of the Inquisition in 1478 for Castile. Five years later, it was extended into Aragon. The Inquisition had been used in the Middle Ages as a tribunal to examine the faith and morals of suspected heretics. The Spanish lands had large populations of Muslims and Jews. Isabella was strongly pressured by her advisors to eliminate religious diversity as other European monarchies had tried to do from time to time. Jews were required to wear distinctive insignia and were forbidden to live in certain areas. In March 1492, a royal edict ordered all Jews to convert to Christianity or leave. Thousands, many of them skilled artisans and professionals, emigrated. The Jews who converted and remained in Spain were supervised closely by the Inquisition.

Even before the expulsion of the Jews, Isabella and Ferdinand had launched a crusade against the last Muslim stronghold, the kingdom of Granada. Isabella herself donned armor and participated in some of the campaigns against the Muslims. By 1490 the Christians had virtually surrounded the city of Granada. In January 1492, the Muslim king surrendered the keys of the city to Isabella and Ferdinand. The terms of the surrender permitted Granada to maintain its Islamic faith, but soon overzealous church officials instigated a policy of forced conversion. Many Muslims left, but those who converted and remained were often treated with great suspicion and hostility, just as they were in most parts of Europe. Tragically, Spain was not the only European monarchy to expel whole populations. England, France, and parts of the Holy Roman Empire also engaged in expulsions. In those

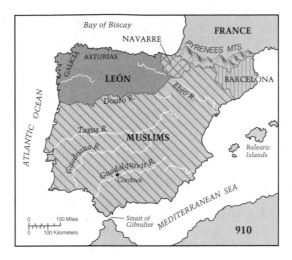

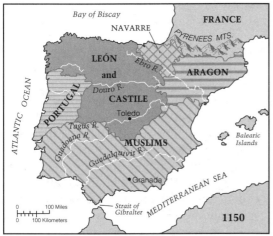

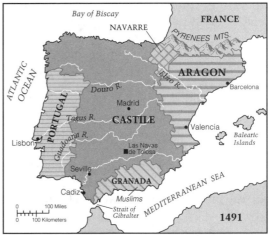

Unification of Spain

cases, the victims were almost exclusively Jews.

Queen Isabella was so pleased with her victory over the Muslims and her expulsions of religious minorities that she gave the Genoese mariner Christopher Columbus permission to sail and some help toward purchasing three small ships for his voyage of discovery and conquest. Spain's conquests in the Americas brought in enormous wealth. The Machiavellian Ferdinand also extended Spanish influence from Sicily and Naples into other parts of Italy and added the kingdom of Navarre to the Spanish crown.

Isabella sought to make Spain more of a Christian intellectual center. She assembled a large royal library of spiritual and secular books and commissioned the first Castilian grammar. The female scholar, Beatriz de Galindo (1473–1535), was brought from Italy to teach the queen Latin. Isabella personally supervised the education of her children, who like the Tudor children in England were well trained in foreign languages.

THE HOLY ROMAN EMPIRE

The Holy Roman Empire was the largest state in Europe, encompassing most of central Europe. Its roughly 15 million inhabitants spoke a variety of languages and dialects, though various forms of German predominated. In contrast to the hereditary monarchs of England, France, and Spain, the Holy Roman emperors were formally elected by a powerful group of seven electors. The electoral process had become fixed in 1356 when the Emperor Charles IV of Luxembourg-Bohemia (r. 1347–1378) issued a written constitution for the empire known as the Golden Bull. By the terms of the Golden Bull, the archbishops of Mainz, Trier, and Cologne, the king of Bohemia, the duke of Saxony, the margrave of Brandenburg, and the count palatine of the Rhine were to serve as imperial electors and make up the first house of the Imperial Parliament (Diet).

The electoral princes were virtually sovereign in their own lands and could mint their own coins, among other privileges. These privileges were reconfirmed in Frankfurt on the Main River at the election of each new emperor. Because the empire was a complete patriarchy, only males could be elected as emperor or serve as one of the seven electors. The second house of the Imperial Diet was made up of the nonelectoral princes. The third house was made up of representatives from the towns, who in 1489 finally got a vote in imperial affairs. Although Holy Roman emperors had a great deal of prestige as descendants of such legendary monarchs as Charlemagne and Otto

I, they were, in fact, dependent on their mighty subjects for special revenues and troops. There was no imperial tax or standing army.

In reality the Holy Roman Empire was a loose confederation of over 300 virtually autonomous principalities and towns. During the Renaissance, the Austrian house of Habsburg succeeded in getting its sons elected as Holy Roman emperors. Since 1273 nearly every emperor was a Habsburg, a dynasty that made their influence felt throughout Europe by their extraordinary success in marrying well. The Habsburgs followed the old motto: "Others may fight and die, thou happy Austria marry!" Among the many able Habsburg dynasts, few were as successful in playing the marriage game as Maximilian I (r. 1493–1519), "an odd little man, whose chin stuck out like a shelf."[1]

In 1491 Emperor Maximilian began negotiating a double marriage treaty with Isabella and Ferdinand of Spain. His daughter, Margaret, married the Spanish heir, Juan, while his son, Philip, married Juan's unstable sister, Juana. Although Juan died shortly thereafter, Philip and Juana (later called the Mad) produced a son, Charles, who inherited Spain, Austria, and the inside track on his grandfather's imperial title. A second grandson, Ferdinand, was engaged to King Vladislav of Hungary's daughter Anna, thus adding Habsburg claims to both Hungary and Bohemia.

As Holy Roman emperor, Maximilian attempted to strengthen the power of the crown, a move strongly resisted by the German princes. He also opposed French advances in Italy and warded off French attempts to seize the Low Countries. The Swiss Confederation won its independence from imperial control in 1499 and Maximilian also failed to mount a crusade against the Ottoman Turks. He was more successful as a patron of the arts, supporting such well-respected artists as Albrecht Dürer and Hans Burgkmair and such humanists as Johann Cuspinian and Conrad Peutinger. His own writings were mostly autobiographical in nature, such as his *Theuerdank*, which tells of his journey to claim Mary of Burgundy as his first wife. Few of his predecessors had written much more than their names on royal documents, although Frederick II (r. 1211–1250) did write a handbook on falconry. His political achievements would be overshadowed by the reign of his grandson Charles in the Holy Roman Empire and Spain.

SCANDINAVIA AND MARGARET OF DENMARK

The Scandinavian countries of Denmark, Norway, and Sweden were not as populous as the monarchies to the south, but they did achieve a degree of political power during the reign of Margaret of Denmark (1353–1412). Margaret was one of the two surviving daughters of Waldemar IV (1340–1375), the aggressive Danish king. She was betrothed at age seven to King Haakon of Norway as part of an alliance. When Margaret was seventeen, she had a son, Olaf (1370–1387). After her father's death in 1375, the leading nobles chose her as regent for her son because they were impressed with her intelligence, commanding presence, and the need for stability. The choice was also approved by the Hanseatic League, the powerful trading association that linked 200 towns throughout the Baltic and North Sea regions and the north of Germany. League officials figured the unification of the Norwegian and Danish thrones would be good for business and they were right.

Queen Margaret proved an able and assertive ruler; when her husband and then her son died, both the Danish and Norwegian kingdoms named her their sovereign for life. In 1389 she added Sweden to her realm and created the Union of Kalmar, which provided for separate institutions in all three kingdoms but unified them under Margaret's authority. Styled "the lady king" by her subjects, Margaret succeeded in curbing the power of her fractious nobility and ushering in an era of relative peace and prosperity. While the Union of Kalmar never functioned as well under her successors, it did last until 1523 and gave the rugged Scandinavian lands a degree of stability and prosperity.

EASTERN EUROPE

Eastern Europe was dominated by the threat of the Mongols, followed by that of the Ottomans. In the second half of the fifteenth century, Hungary was ruled by the able Matthias I Corvinus (r. 1458–1490). Matthias broke the power of the feudal magnates, held the Ottomans at bay, and supported humanism and the arts. His capital at Buda became one of the most brilliant courts in Europe outside of Italy. Much of his work was undone by his weak successor, Vladislav II of Bohemia, who resided in Prague.

The Polish monarchy also struggled in the fifteenth century despite the considerable talents of King Casimir IV (r. 1447–1492). Casimir did succeed in gaining a port on the Baltic and reducing some of the power of the feudal barons. Wars with both the Russians and the Ottomans, however, led to a breakdown of royal authority. The noble-dominated national diet became the supreme legislative organ of government and had a hard time coming up with sensible policies. Incessant wrangling among the elite resulted in continued misery for the Polish peasantry, who were bound to the soil by an act of the Polish Diet in 1511. This was at a time when serfdom had almost completely vanished in the West.

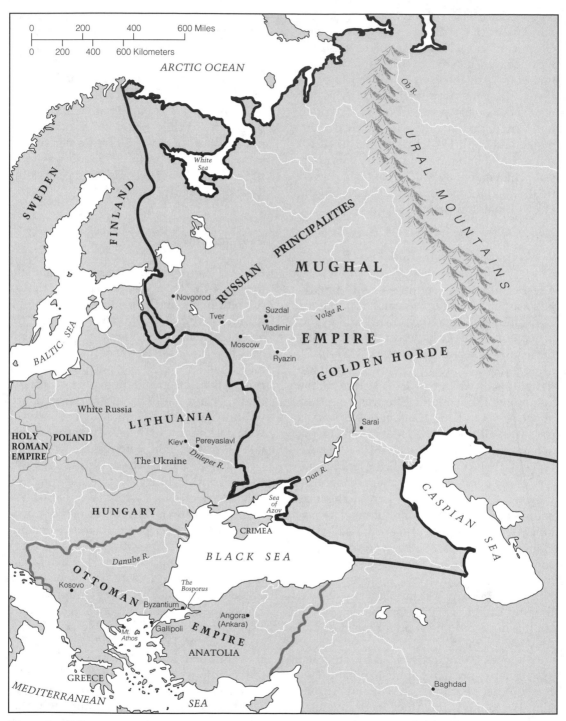

Mongol and Ottoman Invasions

RUSSIA

The Expansion of Europe

As for Poland's neighbors to the east, the Grand Princes of Moscow had been forced to pay heavy tribute to the descendants of Ghengis Khan (1160–1227) until 1480 when Ivan III, the Great (1462–1505), threw off the Mongol yoke and abolished tribute. Ivan then annexed Novgorod in the north and parts of Poland and Lithuania. Preferring diplomacy and intrigue to war, the tall and awe-inspiring Ivan achieved a great deal with a minimum of bloodshed. Not only did he ward off the pretensions of his four brothers, Ivan also married his son to the niece of the last Byzantine emperor. This marriage allowed him to claim the vacant Byzantine throne for his dynasty. Ivan also reduced the powers of his nobility and strengthened the institutions of his government. Despite the improved organization and expansion of the Muscovite state, the Russians were still not strong enough to become major players in the ruthless world of European power politics.

The Mongol position as the great eastern threat was replaced by the Ottomans, who had conquered most of the Balkan peninsula late in the fourteenth century. In 1453, Mehmed the Conqueror took Constantinople, the last bastion of the old Roman Empire in the East and one of the largest city's in the world. After that the Islamic Ottomans conquered Greece, then Serbia, Bosnia, Herzegovina, and Albania. Venice fought the Ottomans for control of the Adriatic Sea and its trade empire. Sultan Selim I (1512–1520) overran Syria, Palestine, and Egypt. In full control of the eastern Mediterranean, the powerful Ottomans were ready and able to exert renewed pressure on the quarreling monarchies of western Europe, which had been unable to achieve sufficient cooperation to mount a successful crusade against them.

The expanding Ottoman empire also threatened the growth of European commerce. By the end of the fifteenth century, the Ottomans controlled much of the luxury and spice trade from Asia. Added to the duties imposed by the Ottomans upon Arab overland traders was the profit demanded by the Venetians, who in turn sold their cargoes from the eastern Mediterranean to northern merchants in Venice. Price markups of as much as 2,000 percent were not unusual for valued spices such as pepper and nutmeg. Some spices were literally worth more than their weight in silver. All this led to a feverish desire to bypass the Mediterranean and reach the markets of Asia directly by sea.

HENRY THE NAVIGATOR AND PORTUGUESE EXPLORATION

Although small in size and population, Portugal took the lead in the European race to the Orient. After fighting the Moors in North Africa, Prince Henry the Navigator (1394–1460), the third son of the king of Portugal, became obsessed with finding a new route around Africa to Asia. He established a school for mariners at Sagres Castle, near the southwest tip of Portugal. From there Henry sent out annual expeditions southward along the west African coast. His mariners returned with observations about the winds, currents, peoples, geography, and astronomical readings they had made on their voyages. This information was evaluated by Henry's staff and passed on to succeeding generations of cartographers, navigators, and ocean pilots. Those who studied at Henry's school included Vasco da Gama and Ferdinand Magellan. Henry's mariners also benefited from better ships, the invention of the magnetic compass, and the ability to sail against the wind (tacking).

By the time of Prince Henry's death in 1460, his mariners had reached the westernmost bulge of West Africa at Cape Verde. In 1488 Bartholomew Dias rounded the southern tip of Africa, soon to be christened the Cape of Good Hope by the jubilant Portuguese king. Using information from Dias's voyage, thirty-seven-year-old Vasco da Gama succeeded in 1498 in reaching Calcutta, on the west coast of India, with a fleet of four ships. Da Gama's fleet was out of sight of land for almost ninety days, nearly three times as long as Columbus on his first voyage. Although only two ships returned to Lisbon with a handful of very sick mariners, da Gama's return cargo of pepper and gems was sold for nearly sixty times the cost of the expedition.

Six months after da Gama's return to Lisbon, Pedro Alvarez Cabral set sail for India with a fleet of thirteen heavily armed ships and more than 1,200 soldiers and sailors. Despite being blown by a hurricane so far to the west that they touched the eastern bulge of South America (Brazil), Cabral's fleet made it to India in six months, less than a third of the time it had taken da Gama. However, his encounters with Arab warships and Indian warriors were even bloodier than da Gama's. Cabral's voyage was considered a great success by the Portuguese because he had returned with rich cargoes of spices, drugs, woods, and jewels.

Arab and Muslim merchants were alarmed at the European incursion into their trading empire. In February 1509, a Portuguese fleet of twenty vessels defeated a combined Egyptian-Turkish-Arab fleet of 100 vessels off the island of Diu on the northwest coast of India. The Portuguese had boldly struck into the center of the enemy fleet and nullified the Muslim advantage in numbers. Most of the Muslim fleet was destroyed and the Europeans were never seriously challenged on the sea road to India

Sixteenth-century sailing ship. Woodcut. Giraudon/Art Resource.

again. European ships had become three-masted and larger than ever before (400 to 1,000 tons), and were better armed than most of their opponents by the beginning of the sixteenth century. Advances in ship-rigging, naval architecture and construction, and bronze cannons would give Europeans a large advantage over the rest of the world for the remainder of the Renaissance.

CHRISTOPHER COLUMBUS (1451–1506)

The initial financial success of the Portuguese in opening trade with India, and by 1513 with a small part of China through the mouth of the Canton River, led other European monarchs to become interested in sponsoring their own voyages of discovery. In 1492 Queen Isabella of Castile helped the mariner Christopher Columbus (Colon) obtain three small ships and ninety men for his own voyage of discovery. The son of a wool worker in the port city of Genoa, Columbus had left weaving to become an itinerant mariner, working on ships that plied the

Mediterranean and the coast of West Africa. After he was shipwrecked off the coast of Lagos, Portugal when he was twenty-five he found his way to Lisbon, where one of his brothers had a map-making business. Columbus then married Dona Filipa de Perestrelo, the daughter of a prominent ship owner. This fortunate marriage helped make his career by providing him with valuable connections and a dowry.

After years of sailing, interviews with veteran navigators, and an intensive study of the existing travel and geographical literature, Columbus became convinced that Asia was far closer than most people believed and that it could be reached by sailing due west. Influenced as well by his immersion in mystical literature, the mariner came to believe that he was a special man of destiny who had been touched by God. After failing to interest the Portuguese king in his plans in 1484, Columbus next approached the rulers of Castile and Aragon with his "small world theory." His proposals were studied seriously, but as Isabella and Ferdinand were preoccupied by their war with the Muslims of Granada, they avoided making a financial commitment. The kings of France and England also turned him down. Finally, in the throes of exultation after the fall of Granada, Queen Isabella of Castile agreed to sponsor his voyage, partly as an act of piety. Columbus's religious zeal had made a favorable impression upon the queen.

On August 3, 1492 Columbus's small fleet of three caravels set sail from Palos. Thirty-three days later he made landfall somewhere in the Bahamas. He encountered a gentle people with "handsome bodies and good faces," whom he attempted to convert to Christianity. After exploring some of the coastline of Cuba and Haiti, Columbus established a small settlement with thirty-nine of his crew and sailed back to

Francesco Salviati, *Portrait of Christopher Columbus*. Palazzo Comunale. Alinari/Art Resource.

Spain. There he was given a warm welcome, but the Portuguese asserted that what Columbus had found was theirs because of their earlier efforts at exploration. Queen Isabella appealed to Pope Alexander VI. The worldly Borgia pope issued several papal bulls that confirmed that whatever discoveries Columbus had made belonged to the crown of Castile and drew an imaginary line of demarcation between the competing claims, which became the basis of later negotiations between Spain and Portugal.

The triumphant Columbus returned to the "Indies" with a fleet of seventeen ships and over 1,500 sailors, soldiers, churchmen, and officials. Even some Spanish gentlemen were eager to make their fortunes and serve God in the New World. On November 27, 1493, they reached Haiti only to discover that the European outpost had been destroyed by disease and by attacks from some of the native peoples, who had grown hostile in response to the violence of the Spanish and their demands for gold. A second settlement was established while Admiral Columbus went off on a search for the Asian mainland. While Columbus never did find Asia, he did explore many of the West Indian islands. In 1498 Columbus made his third voyage of discovery to find his colony on Haiti in turmoil. He was arrested by the royal commissioner and returned to Spain in chains with his two brothers. Queen Isabella freed him and allowed him to make a fourth voyage to the New World in 1502. He spent two years along the coast of Central America trying desperately to find a route to the Asian mainland.

Having survived mutinies, wars with the natives, and shipwreck, a disappointed Christopher Columbus returned to Spain, where he died at Valladolid a year and a half later. Among his mixed legacy was the beginnings of the slave trade. Columbus had brought back several Amerindians with him after his first voyage to impress the Spanish court. He later thought to use the native population as slave laborers in the newly discovered territories. His royal patron Queen Isabella disagreed and soon forbade the sale of native inhabitants and declared them to be direct subjects of the crown of Castile. She ordered her colonial governors to protect and Christianize the "Indians." The queen also allowed the Spaniards the right to collect tributes from the indigenous people and use them as laborers. Estate holders, chartered by the crown, were to care for the Amerindians' spiritual and physical needs. However, even this paternalistic policy proved impossible to enforce on settlers over 3,000 miles from Spain, especially after the queen's death in 1504. The actual treatment of the Native Americans by most of the Spanish colonizers was often extremely brutal even after their replacement

as plantation workers by imported slaves from Africa.

Although Columbus was not the first European to come to the Americas, little had come from the early eleventh-century voyages to Greenland and North America by the Norse led by Eric the Red and Leif Ericson. Other Europeans followed in Columbus's wake, bringing wide-scale plagues and destruction to the Native Americans and forever changing the world. Among the Renaissance European explorers was the Florentine geographer and cartographer Amerigo Vespucci (1451–1512), who sailed to the New World in 1497, 1499, 1501, and 1503 for Spain. Vespucci realized that what Columbus had found was distinct from Asia. The cartographer Martin Waldseemüller used Vespucci's writings in drawing his influential map of 1507, which named the New World "America" in honor of the Florentine.

Other European Explorers

In 1497 and 1498, Giovanni Caboto (John Cabot) of Venice, chartered by King Henry VII of England, explored the coastline of North America from Labrador to Maryland. These voyages became the basis for England's claim to North America, as European monarchies greedily vied with each other to lay claim to the lands long since settled by Native Americans. In 1513 Vasco Nunez de Balboa crossed the Isthmus of Panama and gazed upon the Pacific Ocean. In September 1519 the brave but arrogant Portuguese captain Ferdinand Magellan (c. 1480–1521) headed west with five ships in the service of Spain. Sailing through the straits that now bear his name at the tip of South America, Magellan's surviving ships and crew endured endless hardships in crossing the Pacific Ocean. They reached the island of

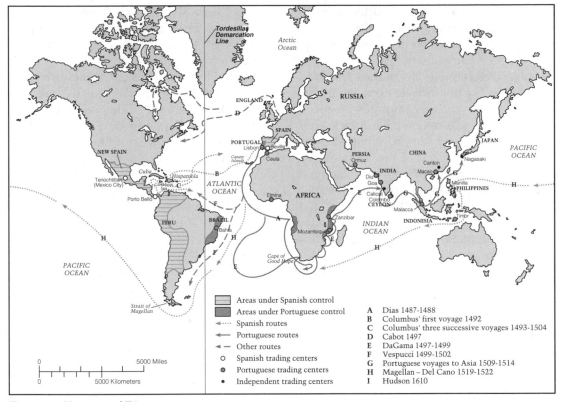

European Voyages of Discovery

Guam in March 1521 and later the Philippines. Unwisely intervening militarily in a local civil war, Magellan was killed, but one of his ships managed to circumnavigate the globe and returned to Seville with eighteen surviving crew members.

The Spanish Conquest of the Americas: Cortés

In the same year that Magellan's crew began its monumental journey around the world, the Spanish adventurer, Hernan Cortés (1485–1547) left Cuba with 530 armed men and one women, fourteen pieces of artillery,

sixteen horses, and eleven ships for the eastern coast of Mexico. Cortés came from modest origins in Medellin, Castile and had sailed to Santo Domingo in 1504 to seek his fortune after working for a number of years as a notary. He joined Diego Velázquez in the conquest of Cuba and then worked as his secretary when Velázquez was appointed governor. Given land in Cuba, Cortés left the employ of the governor while planning for even better things to come. He was determined to conquer the vast Aztec (Mexica) Empire, which sprawled over 250,000 square miles. After fighting several battles, he established a base in the summer of 1519 at what became the important port of Vera Cruz on the eastern coast. Cortés then journeyed inland toward the heart of the Aztec Empire in central Mexico, fighting several battles along the way and attempting to force Christianity upon the native peoples. Determined "to conquer this land or die," the Castilians were appalled by the ritual human sacrifices commonly practiced in Mexico. They tore down skull racks and toppled statues of gods and replaced them with altars and images of the Virgin Mary.

Cortés was militarily successful against superior numbers of Amerindians because his opponents usually fought to wound not kill. In addition, the artillery, gunpowder and steel weapons, horses, and ruthlessness of the Castilians gave them a great advantage over the tribes of Mexico, who fought largely with obsidian-edged weapons and bows and arrows. They had never seen horses, guns, or even beards before and some thought Cortés was a returning god or at the least a great human lord. Cortés's efforts at diplomacy and conversion were greatly aided by a war captive, called Marina, who spoke one of the Aztec dialects. She also became his mistress and was completely loyal to him.

His force of 300 Castilians was joined by over a thousand Tlaxcalans and other former subjects of the Aztecs who had grown tired of paying tribute. Cortés made a peaceful entry into the huge island city of Tenochtitlán, which he described as the most beautiful city on earth. It was also one of the largest with a population of over 200,000 people. Tenochtitlán was filled with elaborate palace complexes and several massive pyramids. Like the Mayans before them, the Aztecs were also accomplished architects, engineers, mathematicians, and astronomers.

Although he had been welcomed into Tenochtitlán as was the custom of a region that stressed hospitality to all visitors no matter how threatening, Cortés treacherously took Emperor Montezuma II captive. Montezuma was a gifted diplomat, religious leader, and warrior, but he was ill-prepared to deal with such ruthless invaders whose customs differed so greatly from any he had experienced. Highly religious, Montezuma was also done in by his belief that Cortés had come in fulfillment of ancient prophecy of doom for the Aztecs. While Cortés had to leave Tenochtitlán to intercept a rival Castilian army, his remaining men, fearing an attack, massacred large numbers of Aztecs during a major religious ceremony and inflicted heavy casualties. When Cortés returned, having defeated his rivals, he found himself and his Indian allies under siege. Montezuma was killed trying to restore order and Cortés and his followers were forced to flee the city on July 1, 1520. His local allies stayed loyal and the expedition received reinforcements from Cuba, which allowed them to retake the Aztec capital in the summer of 1521 after ferocious fighting, almost completely destroying the wondrous terraced city in the process. The Aztecs had been severely weakened by an outbreak of smallpox brought by the Spanish.

With the fall of its capital, the rest of the Aztec Empire soon fell to its Spanish and Native American conquerors. Cortés sent out other expeditions to conquer the remains of Mexico as far south as Panama. His lieutenant, Pedro de Alvarado (c. 1485–1541), was especially brutal. A Dominican friar from Seville, Bartolomé de Las Casas (1476–1566), the first priest to be ordained in the New World, reported that Alvarado and his troops "advanced killing, ravaging, burning, robbing, and destroying the country."[2] The sophisticated Mayas and others were thus subdued with great violence and most of their written books destroyed as "seed of the devil." Alvarado, the ruthless conqueror of Ecuador and Guatemala, became the latter's governor from 1530 to 1534.

In direct contrast to Alvarado's systematic cruelty, Las Casas attempted to improve the condition of the Native Americans. He took up their cause in a series of books, pamphlets, and sermons, including his highly influential *History of the Indies*. While some of his statistics and accounts are exaggerated, Las Casas, because of his friendship with Emperor Charles V, had a significant impact on trying to ameliorate some of the features of colonialization. Although he advocated the importation of African slaves to replace the Amerindians as laborers, Las Casas came to repent even that notion. Like almost all of his generation, he assumed that Christianity was "the one, true religion," which all Americans should accept and that Spain had a right to colonize the New World.

As for Hernan Cortés, he was eventually recalled to Spain in 1528 after rounds of incessant quarreling among various Spanish colonial officials. He later died in obscurity in Spain seeking redress of various grievances against the crown officials who had replaced him in Mexico. Cortés would later be eulogized by the Franciscan missionary Girolamo Mendieta as a "Moses" who had led the "Indians" from idolatry to the blessings of Christianity, just as the biblical Moses had led his people out of Egypt to the promised land. For Mendieta, Cortés helped to counterbalance the "evil work" of Martin Luther, who had caused thousands of souls to perish by his splintering of the church. Cortés, as a true Christian soldier, had aided the Franciscans in their mass conversions of Native Americans. According to Mendieta, these gains in the New World would hopefully outweigh the losses to Protestantism in the Old World.

FRANCISCO PIZARRO (C. 1475–1541)

The treasure stolen from Mexico was supplemented by that gained by the adventurer Francisco Pizarro's attacks against the Inca Empire of Peru. The illegitimate and illiterate son of an infantry colonel, Pizarro had not been part of Cortés's expedition to Mexico but had later joined Balboa when he journeyed to the Pacific. In 1525 Francisco Pizarro led an expedition down the west coast of South America, only to be nearly wiped out by native peoples. Two years later, he attempted to conquer the powerful Incas but failed when a majority of his men deserted him at the island of Gallo near the equator. He successfully petitioned Emperor Charles V for permission to launch yet another assault on Peru.

In 1533 Pizarro and his small force of 100 infantry and 60 cavalry reached the encampment of the Inca ruler Atahualpa, who was locked in a bitter struggle for the throne with his half brother. Imitating the more sophisticated Cortés, Pizarro kidnapped and ransomed the Inca king and used him to control his people. The Spanish conqueror informed the Inca leader:

> Do not take it as an insult that you have been defeated and taken prisoner. . . . I have conquered greater kingdoms than yours, and have defeated other more powerful lords than you, imposing upon them the dominion of the Emperor, whose vassal I am. . . . We come to conquer this land by his command, that all may come to a knowledge of God and His Holy Catholic Faith . . . in order that you may know him, and come out from the bestial and diabolical life you lead.[3]

Later the Spanish ruthlessly executed Atahualpa.

By November the conquerors were in control of the sophisticated and well-planned Inca capital of Cuzco, a city of 150,000 inhabitants located 12,000 feet high in the Andes Mountains. The Incas had been greatly weakened by smallpox. Pizarro sent his lieutenants out exploring, south into Chile, and north to New Granada. Fierce struggles over the spoils eventually broke out and Pizarro and hundreds of his followers died in the fighting. Greed had triumphed over other motivations.

The conquest of Mexico and Peru helped spark a boom in the European economy that lasted throughout the sixteenth century. Commodities such as sugar, dyes, vanilla, cacao, cotton, potatoes, spices, tea, and silver poured into Europe in much greater amounts than ever before. New products from the Americas such as corn, potatoes, chocolate, coffee, tomatoes, pineapple, and tobacco were introduced into Europe for the first time. The Europeans brought sugarcane, chickpeas, wheat, cows, sheep, and horses to the Americas, which completely changed the lifestyles of many groups of Native Americans.

Tragically, lethal diseases were also exchanged. Syphilis became widespread in Europe following the return of Columbus and smallpox, measles, and typhus decimated millions of Amerindians. The brutal African slave trade resulted in the deaths of millions more. Even those who survived the dislocations and deaths brought by the wars of conquest, colonization, and the trafficking in human flesh suffered enormously. The world would never be the same or as large again. European arms had triumphed, but at a horrible human cost.

Chronology

1340–1384	Reign of Margaret of Denmark.
1356	Golden Bull of Nuremberg issued by Emperor Charles IV.
1394–1460	Life of Henry the Navigator.
1447–1492	Reign of Casimir IV of Poland.
1451–1506	Life of Christopher Columbus.
1453	Fall of Constantinople to Mehmed the Conqueror.
1458–1490	Reign of Matthias Corvinus in Hungary.
1467–1477	Reign of Duke Charles the Bold of Burgundy.
1469	Marriage of Isabella of Castile to Ferdinand of Aragon.
1485–1509	Reign of Henry VII in England.
1485–1542	Life of Hernan Cortés.
1492	Fall of Granada; Columbus's first voyage to the Americas.
1493–1519	Reign of Emperor Maximilian I.
1499	Da Gama returns from India.
1500	Cabral discovers Brazil.
1504	Death of Isabella of Spain.
1509–1547	Reign of Henry VIII in England.
1515–1547	Reign of François I in France.
1515	Battle of Marignano; Francis I takes Milan.
1516–1556	Reign of Charles of Habsburg as king of Spain.
1519	Charles of Habsburg becomes Holy Roman Emperor; Magellan begins his voyage; Cortés leaves Cuba for Mexico.
1522	Fall of the Aztecs to Cortés.
1533	Fall of the Incas to Pizarro.

Further Reading

THE ECONOMY

Douglas Bisson, *The Merchant Adventurers of England: The Company and the Crown, 1474–1564* (1993).

Philippe Dollinger, *The German Hansa* (1970).

Hermann Kellenbrenz, *The Rise of the European Economy, 1500–1750* (1976).

Peter Kriedte, *Peasants, Landlords, and Merchant Capitalists. Europe and the World Economy, 1500–1800* (1983).

Immanuel Wallerstein, *The Modern World-System, Capitalist Agriculture and the Origins of the European World-Economy in the Sixteenth Century,* 2 vols. (1974).

THE NORTHERN MONARCHIES AND PRINCIPALITIES

BURGUNDY

Walter Prevenier and William Blockmans, *The Burgundian Netherlands* (1986).

Richard Vaughan, *Charles the Bold, the Last Valois Duke of Burgundy* (1973). Vaughan has a series of fine books on the dukes of Burgundy.

FRANCE

Frederic Baumgartner, *Louis XII* (1994).

Richard Jackson, *Vive Le Roi!: A History of the French Coronation Ceremony from Charles V to Charles X* (1984).

Paul Murray Kendall, *Louis XI, the "Universal Spider"* (1971).

R. J. Knecht, *Renaissance Warrior and Patron: The Reign of Francis I,* 2nd ed. (1994).

ENGLAND

S. B. Chrimes, *Henry VII* (1973).

J. R. Lander, *Government and Community, 1450–1509* (1981).

J. J. Scarisbrick, *Henry VIII* (1968).

Neville Williams, *The Life and Times of Henry VII* (1973).

SPAIN

Felipe Fernández-Armesto, *Ferdinand and Isabella* (1975).

J. N. Hilgarth, *The Spanish Kingdoms,* 2 vols. (1978).

Peggy Liss, *Isabel the Queen: Life and Times* (1992).

Derek Lomax, *The Reconquest of Spain* (1978).

Marvin Lunenfeld, *Keepers of the City: The Corregidores of Isabella of Castile (1474–1504)* (1988).

B. Netanyahu, *The Origins of the Inquisition in Fifteenth-Century Spain* (1995).

Nancy Rubin, *Isabella of Castile: The First Renaissance Queen* (1991).

Teofilo Ruiz, *Crisis and Continuity: Land and Town in Late Medieval Castile* (1994).

THE HOLY ROMAN EMPIRE

Gerhard Benecke, *Maximilian I (1459–1519), An Analytical Biography* (1982).

F. R. H. Du Boulay, *Germany in the Later Middle Ages* (1983).

Michael Hughes, *Early Modern Germany, 1477–1806* (1992).

Joachim Leuschner, *Germany in the Late Middle Ages* (1980).

Jonathan Zophy, *An Annotated Bibliography of the Holy Roman Empire* (1986).

———, ed., *The Holy Roman Empire: A Dictionary Handbook* (1980).

OTHER STATES

John Fine, Jr., *The Late Medieval Balkans: A Critical Survey from the Late Twelfth Century to the Ottoman Conquest* (1994).

Paul Knoll, *The Rise of the Polish Monarchy* (1972).

Janet Martin, *Medieval Russia, 980–1584* (1995).

Birgit Sawyer and Peter Sawyer, *Medieval Scandinavia: From Conversion to Reformation, circa 800–1500* (1993).

Nancy Shields, *The Making of the Muscovite Political System, 1345–1547* (1987).

Dorothy Vaughan, *Europe and the Turk: A Pattern of Alliances, 1350–1700*, 2nd ed. (1970).

Exploration, Conquest, and Colonialization

Jerry Bentley, *Old World Encounters, Cross Cultural Contacts and Exchanges in Premodern Times* (1993).

Charles Boxer, *The Dutch Seabourne Empire, 1600–1800* (1965).

——, *The Portuguese Seabourne Empire, 1415–1825*, rpr. (1977).

Peter Hulme, *Colonial Encounters: Europe and the Native Caribbean, 1492–1797* (1986).

Bernard Lewis, *Cultures in Conflict: Christians, Muslims, and Jews in the Age of Discovery* (1994).

James Lockhart, *Spanish Peru, 1532–1560* (1964).

William Maltby, *The Black Legend in England* (1971). Fine study of the legends of Spanish cruelty.

Samuel Eliot Morison, *The European Discovery of America*, 2 vols. (1971–1973).

Anthony Pagden, *European Encounters with the New World* (1992).

J. H. Parry, *The Age of Reconnaissance*, 2nd ed. (1981).

Boise Penrose, *Travel and Discovery in the Renaissance* (1962).

G. V. Scammel, *The World Encompassed: The First European Maritime Empires* (1981).

Stuart Schwartz, ed., *Implicit Understandings: Observing, Reporting, and Reflecting on the Encounters Between Europeans and Other Peoples in the Early Modern Era* (1994). Important essays by a number of scholars.

Roger Smith, *Vanguard of Empire: Ships of Exploration in the Age of Columbus* (1993).

David Stannard, *American Holocaust: The Conquest of the New World* (1992). Impressive scholarship on a horrific subject.

Richard Trexler, *Sex and Conquest: Gendered Violence, Political Order, and the European Conquest of the Americas* (1995).

Columbus and His Impact

Alfred Crosby, Jr., *The Columbian Exchange: Biological and Cultural Consequences of 1492* (1972).

Zvi Dor-Ner with William Scheller, *Columbus and the Age of Discovery* (1991). Handsomely illustrated, coffee table book.

Cecil Jane, ed., *The Four Voyages of Columbus* (1988). A valuable anthology of sources.

Valerie Flint, *The Imaginative Landscape of Christopher Columbus* (1992).

Djelal Kadir, *Columbus and the Ends of the Earth: Europe's Prophetic Rhetoric and Conquering Ideology* (1992).

Marvin Lunenfeld, ed., *1492: Discovery, Invasion, Encounter: Sources and Interpretations* (1991). A first-rate collection of primary and secondary materials.

William Philips, Jr. and Carla Rahn Philips, *The Worlds of Christopher Columbus* (1992).

Irving Rouse, *The Tainos: The Rise and Decline of the People Who Greeted Columbus* (1992).

Kirkpatrick Sale, *The Conquest of Paradise: Christopher Columbus and the Columbian Legacy* (1991). Polemical but interesting.

Cortés and the Conquest of Mexico

Charles Gibson, *The Aztecs under Spanish Rule* (1964).

Serge Gruzinski, *The Conquest of Mexico: The Incorporation of Indian Societies into the Western World in the 16th-18th Centuries* (1994).

Richard Marks, *Cortés: The Great Adventurer and the Fate of the Aztec Mexico* (1993).

Hugh Thomas, *Montezuma, Cortes, and the Fall of Mexico* (1994).

Notes

1. Cited in Jonathan W. Zophy, *Patriarchal Politics and Christoph Kress (1484–1535) of Nuremberg* (Lewiston, N.Y.: Edwin Mellen Press, 1992), p. 28.

2. Cited in Marvin Lunenfeld, ed., *1492: Discovery, Invasion, Encounter: Sources and Interpretations* (Lexington, Mass.: D. C. Heath, 1991), p. 209.

3. Cited in G. R. Elton, ed., *Renaissance and Reformation 1300–1648*, 3rd ed. (New York: Macmillan, 1976), p. 306.

9

The Renaissance in the North

The Literary Culture of the North

Although the European conquest of much of the Americas changed the material and political life of Europe enormously, a more gradual change was occurring in the artistic and intellectual world of Europe north of the Alps. Courts, churches, and wealthy individuals expanded their patronage of artists and musicians. The Renaissance in northern Europe witnessed not only the revival of Greek, Latin, and Hebrew studies by the humanists, it also saw the development of vernacular languages such as English, French, Spanish, and German as literary vehicles. Even though it took the Renaissance longer to blossom north of the Alps, the achievements of the northerners were quite substantial.

CHRISTINE DE PIZAN (1365–c. 1429)

Many writers contributed to the rise of French as a literary language, but few have had such a significant impact on the modern world as Christine de Pizan. Pizan was the first woman to write professionally and the first published feminist. Born in Venice, she moved with her family to France when she was still a child. Her father, Thomas, who had achieved fame in Bologna and Venice as a physician and astrologer, had been hired to serve King Charles V of France (r.

1364–1380). Thomas de Pizan soon became a court favorite with the king, who made him one of his trusted advisors and court physician.

Despite the objections of her mother, who feared that too much education would dampen her matrimonial prospects, Christine was unusually well schooled by her remarkably progressive father. She learned to read French, Italian, and some Latin before her marriage at age fifteen to Etienne de Castel, a young nobleman and courtier from Picardy. Castel became the king's secretary and notary and proved to be a good husband for Christine. Her family flourished until the king's sudden death in September 1380. As Christine wrote later, "now the door to our misfortunes was open."[1]

Her father fell out of favor with the new king, who withdrew his pension and cut his salary. His health suffered and he died sometime between 1385 and 1390. Her husband, Etienne, became ill while traveling with King Charles VI to Beauvais and died in the autumn of 1390. At age twenty-five, Christine de Pizan found herself with a mother, three children, and a niece to support. She also had to ward off four lawsuits over debts incurred by her husband.

What was she to do? Few choices were available to fourteenth-century women. Most remarkably, Christine de Pizan took the unprecedented step for a woman of deciding to pursue a literary career. Petrarca and Boccaccio were among the few men able to sustain themselves in part through their writings, but Pizan was determined to succeed. She began intensive studies of history, poetry, and science to prepare herself intellectually for the task ahead. Armed with this added learning, Pizan began to write poetry, which fortunately met with some success beginning around 1393. She also supported her family by copying and producing books, doing illustrations, and possibly by working as a notary.

In addition to verse, Pizan wrote a history of King Charles V of France, written at the request of his brother, Duke Philip the Bold of Burgundy. She composed other biographical pieces upon commission, which were generally well received. Familiar with the world of court politics, her book of advice for princes, *The Body of Policy*, was remarkably respected, given the prejudices against women. *The Book of Feats of Arms and Chivalry* was considered so useful that King Henry VII of England later had it translated into English. Pizan's *Book of Peace* of 1413 stressed the importance of education. An early admirer of Joan of Arc, she wrote the only contemporary tribute to her in *Hymn to Joan of Arc*. Pizan saw Joan as a heroic woman and an example of the triumph of good over evil in politics.

Christine de Pizan also earned a major reputation as a defender of women by critiquing Jean de Meun's conclusion to the *Romance of the Rose*, a popular thirteenth-century allegory in the courtly love tradition. In her treatise of 1399, *The Letter to the God of Love*, she took Meun to task for his mockery of women and his blatant misogyny. This led to a heated literary exchange between Meun's admirers and those who agreed with Pizan, of whom there were many. These arguments set off a debate known as the *Querelle des Femmes* (quarrel over the nature of women), which lasted throughout the Renaissance.

Undaunted by the attacks on her reputation and ideas, Pizan continued her defense of women in her most important work, *The Book of the City of Ladies* (1405). In that revolutionary work, she imagined a world in which women could do all the jobs necessary to the running of a city. Pizan took on all the traditional arguments including those from the Bible that had been used to justify women's inferior status. She pointed out that woman "was created in the image of God. How can any mouth dare to slander the vessel which bears such a noble imprint? . . . God created the soul and placed wholly similar souls, equally good and noble, in the feminine and masculine bodies."[2] As for the alleged physical weaknesses of women's bodies, they were more than compensated for by determination and moral strength. Pizan urged women to rely on their own experience and not to be deterred by the "ignorant scribbles of men about what they can achieve."[3]

In 1405 she wrote *The Treasure of the City of Ladies or the Book of the Three Virtues*, a sequel to *The Book of the City of Ladies*. This work was a practical guide to etiquette and survival for women ranging from queens to servants and prostitutes. Pizan urged women to follow the three cardinal virtues of "Reason, Rectitude, and Justice," regardless of their social status. Pizan showed surprising insight into the real lives of women from rich to poor and her advice was consistently sensible. She urged women to always stick together, for their lives were never secure.

As her fame as a writer spread, Pizan began to receive offers of patronage from crowned heads all over Europe. Duke Giangaleazzo Visconti of Milan invited her to decorate his court but she refused as she did a similar invitation from King Henry IV of England. She did allow her son, Jean, to ac-

Early fifteenth-century manuscript miniature depicting Christine de Pizan presenting her manuscript to Isabella of Bavaria. British Museum, London, Great Britain. Snark/Art Resource.

cept an invitation from the earl of Salisbury to become a page at the English court and later to accept a place at the court of Burgundy. King Charles VI and his colorful queen, Isabella of Bavaria, became loyal patrons and presented her with generous gifts, as did other French nobles. Yet as the political scene in Paris deteriorated, Pizan left for life in a convent, perhaps the one at Poissy where her daughter was a nun. She died there leaving a remarkable legacy of accomplishment and her subsequent influence upon the raising of feminist consciousness has been enormous.

Later French Writers

FRANÇOIS VILLON (1431–C. 1464)

The greatest French lyric poet of the fifteenth century was the vagabond François Villon. Raised in the slums of Paris among beggars and thieves, Villon eventually became a student at the University of Paris. In 1455 he fatally stabbed a priest in a drunken quarrel but was pardoned for having acted in self-defense. The following year Villon and four others stole a substantial amount of money from the College of Navarre. He was later arrested and spent the summer of 1461 in the prison of the bishop of Orléans. In 1462 Villon was arrested for theft and brawling and was banished from Paris for ten years. Before his early death, Villon managed to write several long poems, and some forty *ballades* and *rondeaux* that revealed his innermost thoughts, yearnings, and fears more honestly than any previous poet had done.

LOUISE LABÉ (C. 1520–1566)

Louise Labé was another unconventional French literary figure. The daughter of a ropemaker from Lyon, she received a much better education than was typical of her class. Trained in music, letters, languages, art, needlework, weaponry, and ropemaking, the beautiful Labé urged other women to "raise their minds somewhat above their distaffs and spindles" and find pleasure in study.[4] To experience life more fully, Labé may have fought in a battle disguised as a man and worked as a courtesan before marrying a wealthy rope manufacturer. She composed several fine sonnets and elegies, as well as a prose dialogue, *The Debate Between Madness and Love* (1555). Despite her rather unusual life, Labé could be quite traditional in her treatment of subjects such as romantic love. In her "Poor Loving Soul," she extolled the delights of the "illusion of love":

> Him then I think fondly to kiss, to hold him
> Frankly then to my bosom; I that all day
> Have looked for him suffering, repining, yea
> many long days.[5]

MARGUERITE OF NAVARRE (1492–1549)

The most renowned female literary figure of the period was Marguerite of Navarre, sister of King François I. Her talented mother,

Queen Louise of Savoy (1476–1531), taught her French, Spanish, and enough Italian to read Dante and Petrarca's sonnets. She also learned Latin and some Greek. Known for her humanist learning and her physical beauty, Marguerite sometimes served as regent for her brother. After the death of her first husband, the duke of Alençon, she married Henri d'Albret, king of Navarre, and presided over a circle of artists, poets, humanists, and religious reformers. Her circle included the brilliant poet Clémont Marot (1496–1544), who helped bring together courtly French, the language of the streets, and classical Latin. Others in her sphere became leaders of the Reformation in France and elsewhere.

Marguerite's own literary output was remarkable given her many political responsibilities. She wrote intensely mystical poetry of great emotional power, including the well-known *The Mirror of a Sinful Soul*. At the time of her death, the queen was secretly composing her most famous prose work, the *Heptameron*. Influenced by Boccaccio, her seventy-two short stories are risqué and witty reflections of elite French society. The tales range from the bawdy to the spiritual. Resolute in her defense of women, Marguerite of Navarre also demonstrated her interest in reform by describing the abuses of the church and monasteries. She also used her influence to protect a reform-minded group of clerics and scholars at Meaux. Many of them shared her concern about friars who "can talk like angels, and are for the most part importunate as devils."[6]

FRANÇOIS RABELAIS (1483–1553)

Marguerite of Navarre's description of friars who "can talk like angels" but have a lot of the devil in them might well fit François Rabelais. An extraordinary bundle of contradictions, he was at times a licentious monk, a medical student, a classicist who preferred to write in the vernacular, and a mocker of religious beliefs who was at the same time a true believer. His father, a prosperous lawyer and landowner in central France, provided his son with a good basic education at a nearby Benedictine abbey. Later Rabelais joined the Franciscans at an early age. He found monastic life to be stifling as his studies of Greek were treated with suspicion. Rabelais then worked for a time as a secretary to a Benedictine abbot and bishop, to whose order he transferred. Taking up the life of a student, Rabelais earned his B.A. in 1530 at Montpellier. He studied the humanities as well as medicine, science, and mathematics.

By 1532 Rabelais was practicing medicine in Lyons, corresponding with humanists such as Erasmus, and publishing translations of medical treatises. At that time, he also wrote his first great satirical tale, *Gargantua*, and dedicated it to "most noble boozers and you, my very esteemed and poxy friends."[7] In 1534 *Pantagruel*, its sequel, appeared. These ribald satires were filled with tremendous displays of classical learning as well as an abundant scatological humor. Both were exceptionally popular and quickly condemned by the University of Paris as obscene. Fortunately for Rabelais, he had found a powerful protector in the person of Jean du Bellay, bishop of Paris, who took him to Rome on two occasions as his doctor.

Rabelais later returned to Montpellier, where he earned his doctorate in medicine in 1537. After brief stints at the court of King François I and in Turin, he went to Metz as city secretary. Finding his salary insufficient, Rabelais found additional patronage from du Bellay, now a cardinal, and continued to revise and enlarge his famous tales until his death in Paris. Controversy contin-

ues to swirl about Rabelais. He is viewed by many as the greatest comic and satirist of the Renaissance. For example, his Gargantua is a giant, who as a young man founds the Abbey of Thélème, the ideal monastic community for it welcomes members of both sexes and adopts the motto "Do what you wish." Rabelais's targets also included members of the church hierarchy, theologians, lawyers, and philosophers. French humanism had found its comic genius in Rabelais, a man who loved to play with words and ideas no matter how outrageous.

The Emergence of the Vernacular in England

Middle English flowered in the days of Geoffrey Chaucer (c. 1340–1400), whose superb *Canterbury Tales* has long been considered one of the greatest literary achievements of the late Middle Ages. Yet at a time when Italian and French had become relatively stable in the fifteenth century, English continued to change and develop. Not until the second half of the sixteenth century did English emerge as the primary literary language of England, despite the fine poetry of Sir Thomas Wyatt and others. Even such an important work as Thomas More's *Utopia* (1516) was not translated from Latin to English until 1541. All of this changed, however, during the life of William Shakespeare (1564–1616).

WILLIAM SHAKESPEARE: THE BARD OF AVON

Shakespeare was born in the town of Stratford-upon-Avon to a prosperous glove maker and trader who later became a civic official. His mother came from a substantial landowning family. In 1582 William married Anne Hathaway and they had several chil-

Engraved portrait of William Shakespeare.
SEF/Art Resource.

grounding in the works of Plutarch as well as historians closer to his own time such as Raphael Holinshed (c. 1525–c. 1580) and Thomas More. His historical plays range from dramas set in ancient Rome, such as *Julius Caesar* and *Antony and Cleopatra*, to some which are closer to his own era, such as *Richard III* and *Henry VIII*. In all his plays, the bard of Avon exhibited an unusually sophisticated understanding of the minds and speech of both men and women of a variety of social classes. He was as familiar with the world of Cheapside taverns as he was with the inner workings of power politics. William Shakespeare is usually considered to be the greatest English writer to date, and his work was of fundamental importance in establishing English as a literary vehicle.

OTHER WRITERS OF THE ELIZABETHAN RENAISSANCE

The England of Queen Elizabeth I (r. 1558–1603) also featured such remarkable literary talents as the bold dramatist Christopher Marlowe (1564–1593), the poet Edmund Spenser (c. 1552–1599), the poets Sir Philip Sidney (1554–1586) and his sister Mary, countess of Pembroke, among many others. Educated at Cambridge University, Marlowe translated the Roman poet Ovid and wrote seven plays plus a considerable body of poetry. His most notable included *Edward II, Doctor Faustus, The Jew of Malta,* and *Tamburlaine.* In a great era of playwrights, Marlowe ranked second only to Shakespeare among Elizabethan dramatists. His career was cut tragically short when he was stabbed to death in a tavern brawl in London.

dren. Ten years later he was established as an actor and playwright in London. In 1594 Shakespeare became a charter member of a theatrical company, the King's Men, with which he remained affiliated until his retirement to Stratford in 1611. The earl of Southampton became one of his most important patrons. Thirty-seven plays and a number of nondramatic poems are attributed to him. Few others have ever managed to produce masterpieces in both tragedy (*Hamlet, King Lear,* and *Macbeth*) and comedy (*A Midsummer Night's Dream, Much Ado About Nothing*). A number of Shakespeare's plays are set in Renaissance Italy (*Othello, Romeo and Juliet, The Merchant of Venice,* and *Two Gentlemen of Verona*). They show to what an extent the Italian world had captured the imagination of northerners.

Shakespeare was also keenly interested in history and showed an excellent

Sir Philip Sidney was the eldest son of Sir Henry Sidney (later lord deputy of Ireland) and Lady Mary Sidney (sister of the earls of Leicester and Warwick). Educated first at Shrewsbury School, he left Oxford in 1571 without taking a degree. For the next several years he traveled widely throughout Europe, sometimes assisting on diplomatic missions. After losing favor with the queen, he retired to his sister Mary's home and composed his long prose romance, the *Arcadia*. In 1581 Sidney became a member of Parliament and three years later was named governor of Flushing. He died from a wound suffered at the battle of Zutphen in 1586 against the Spanish. He left a considerable legacy of poetry and an important *Defense of Poetry*.

Mary Sidney (1561–1621) wrote religious poetry, translations of Petrarca, elegies, pastoral dialogues, and a metrical version of the Psalms. She joined the court when she was only fourteen and married the count of Pembroke two years later. Mary impressed the queen with her fluency in languages and her skills in music and embroidery. Like the queen, Mary Sidney dispensed patronage to other poets including several women. Her courtier-brother's friend, Edmund Spenser, considered the greatest English poet since Chaucer, used his major work, the *Faerie Queene,* to pay fulsome tribute to Elizabeth as "Gloriana." Although Spenser spent a number of years in Ireland away from the court, he shared much of the awe of his contemporaries for their brilliant queen. Her reign was, indeed, a glorious time for English letters.

The Golden Age of Spanish Literature

Spanish also emerged as a major literary language during the Renaissance. Miguel de Cervantes (1547–1616) has long been considered the greatest Spanish author of all time. Born at Alcalá de Henares, he was the son of an unsuccessful apothecary-surgeon who became something of a wanderer. Cervantes went to school in Madrid and made his debut as a poet. After having fought in a duel, he was forced to flee Spain for Rome, where he entered the service of a cardinal. In 1570 Cervantes joined the Spanish army and fought bravely in the battle of Lepanto against the Ottomans in October 1571. He later fought in the campaign for Tunis in North Africa. Sailing back to Spain in September 1575, his ship was captured by Moorish pirates, who sold him into slavery. Cervantes was finally ransomed in 1580 and returned to tell of his adventures in his *Pictures of Algiers*.

In December 1584 Cervantes married Catalina de Palacios Salazar y Vozmediano, daughter of a prosperous peasant of Esquivias. Her dowry was modest and Cervantes was forced to eke out a meager living in Seville by a variety of poorly paid jobs. Although they had no children, their household included two sisters, his illegitimate daughter Isabel, a niece, and a maidservant. Hoping for relief from the pecuniary liabilities under which he struggled, in 1588 Cervantes took a job as one of the many government procurement officers in charge of gathering supplies for the great armada sent against Protestant England in that same year. Having seized supplies belonging to the dean of the cathedral chapter at Seville, he was temporarily excommunicated. When discrepancies were discovered in his financial records, he was jailed and then dismissed from royal service. Cervantes spent the rest of his life in poverty but managed to write the masterpiece *Don Quixote de la Mancha*, which did not make him rich but did make him famous.

By 1610 many in Spain were laughing mightily at the mockingly heroic tales. Although intellectuals such as the playwright Lope da Vega dismissed *Don Quixote* as not worthy of literary praise, it found a vast audience in numerous editions. Cervantes did not benefit greatly financially from its success and a few years before his death he joined the Tertiary Order of St. Francis. After a life filled with difficulties, he died in Madrid on April 23, 1616, the same day on which Shakespeare died in England. His purpose in *Don Quixote* was to ridicule chivalric romances; however, his story created an incredible panorama of Spanish society and showed genuine affection for the knightly ideals of its hero, the knight Don Quixote, the man of La Mancha. Quixote is joined in his adventures by his earthy squire, the practical Sancho Panza. They have become two of the best-known figures in all literature. Cervantes used many of his life experiences in crafting his wondrous tale, including his familiarity with Spanish jails and the rich life found on the Andalusian plains.

Spanish drama also thrived during the Renaissance with significant contributions from Lope de Vega (1562–1635), Tirso de Molina (1571–1658), and Juan Ruiz de Alarcon (c. 1581–1639). Lope de Vega was a particularly prolific genius, who wrote over 500 comedies and other plays. While he failed to recognize the genius of Cervantes, his own work was enormously influential. Many of his plays are still being performed today. Molina established the character of the insatiable lover Don Juan, loosely based on the half brother of the king of Spain. Although Spanish like English theater was dominated by males (men played all the parts), the Renaissance was one of its greatest periods.

The Fine Arts in the North

The Northern Renaissance also witnessed impressive displays of creativity in architecture, the fine arts, and music. State-building princes such as François I of France proved great builders of palaces. Renaissance courts also attracted a galaxy of talented musicians. In painting the Flemish master Jan van Eyck (c. 1390–1441) was one of the most important contributors to Renaissance art. We know that Eyck worked in Holland from 1422 to 1424, in Lille from 1425 to 1429, and after that in Bruges, where he died. From time to time Duke Philip the Good of Burgundy employed him as a diplomat as well as a court painter. Some of his famous works were possibly done in collaboration with his older brother, Hubert.

JAN VAN EYCK

Jan van Eyck is most famous for using a form of oil painting. He built pictures up by applying layers of translucent oil over an opaque ground of tempera. This gave his work an unprecedented atmospheric depth and luminosity. The use of oil painting also allowed Eyck to rival manuscript illuminators in the minute detail he could put into his paintings, some of which were done on canvas. Jan van Eyck was able to paint traditional subject matter such as the Madonna and baby Jesus with an unprecedented degree of realism. In fact, Mary was one of his favorite subjects as her cult blossomed all over Europe. Many found the mature Jesus a figure to be frightened of, but Mary was always much more approachable and a good intercessor with her sometimes angry son. Her frequent depiction in annunciation scenes with a book in hand was an implied recognition of growing female literacy.

Eyck was also able to flatter contemporaries by placing them in scenes with biblical figures. Imagine how exciting it must have been for a contemporary figure like the chancellor to be portrayed so realistically in the same space with the mother of God and

Jan van Eyck, *Virgin Mary and Child*. Galleria Doria Pamphilj, Rome, Italy. Alinari/Art Resource.

the baby Jesus. Usually, Jan van Eyck's portraits feature motionless figures set against architectural and scenic backgrounds. His vivid use of color and high level of minute detail had an enormous impact on painting throughout the Low Countries, Germany, and Italy, where oil painting became all the rage in the fifteenth century.

LATER FLEMISH PAINTING

Flemish art continued to be among the finest in Europe in the generations following the deaths of the van Eycks. The Low Countries were one of the most prosperous parts of Europe and prosperous patrons could be found in many places. By the sixteenth cen-

tury, Italian influences were also being felt in the Low Countries as evidenced by the brilliant work of artists such as Quentin Massys (c. 1464–1530) of Antwerp, who used classical themes and Italian settings in a number of his works. He is also known for his biblical scenes and superb portraits, including a marvelous rendering of the humanist Erasmus, which rivals the Erasmus portrait of Hans Holbein. Both of his sons became painters.

Hieronymus Bosch (c. 1450–1516) and Pieter Brueghel the Elder (c. 1525–1569), two of Massys's fellow artists, represent striking new departures from tradition. Bosch's fantastic pictorial imagery is a precursor of Surrealism, while Brueghel dared to concentrate on sometimes bitter scenes of peasant life and landscapes. Bosch's work had a profound influence on Brueghel. Working-class men and women were obviously not going to provide an artist with much in the way of patronage. Fortunately, Brueghel made enough money from his more traditional depictions of biblical scenes for patrons such as Cardinal Grandvelle to indulge in his fondness for bucolic life. A master satirist, Brueghel also affords us a vivid record of some of the merciless activities of the Inquisition in the Low Countries. Yet he moved from Protestant-controlled Antwerp to Catholic Brussels.

Peter Paul Rubens (1577–1640) became the greatest figure of the Flemish school in the age of the Baroque. After spending eight years at the court of Mantua in Italy, he opened an enormous studio in Antwerp. Students flocked from all over Europe to learn from a master who made such a good living. He used his students and his assistants to complete the details of massive canvases that he designed, such as series of huge scenes of the life of Queen Marie de' Medici of France. Rubens became one of the most sought-after court painters in Europe

Jan van Eyck, *Madonna and Child with Chancellor Rolin*. Louvre, Paris, France. Giraudon/Art Resource.

and worked in Paris, London, and Madrid. He is remembered for his rich coloring and roseate, sensuous nudes. His subject matter ranged from portraits of royalty such as *King Philip IV* of Spain to biblical scenes such as his famous *Descent from the Cross*.

Renaissance Art in Germany

The German-speaking lands of the Holy Roman Empire also produced an abundance of outstanding artists during the Renaissance. Like the Italians and the Netherlanders, German craftspeople had a tradition of quality work. Renaissance artists built on those traditions of excellence with imagination and splendid technique. Patronage improved in Germany as the wealthy sought ways to express themselves by endowing

churches and private homes. Some of these German artists, such as Albrecht Dürer, were influenced by developments both in Italy and the Low Countries. Hans Holbein of Augsburg achieved his greatest fame at the Tudor court in England. Lucas Cranach the Elder, a friend of Martin Luther, captured some of the key personalities of the early Reformation movement in Saxony. Sculpture was well represented by Tilman Riemenschneider.

ALBRECHT DÜRER (1471–1528)

Albrecht Dürer of Nuremberg served as one of the most important links between Italian and northern art. He was also the greatest artist of the Renaissance in Germany, a master of an astonishing variety of techniques and styles. The son of a goldsmith, Dürer was at first apprenticed to his father. Having shown an early talent for drawing, he joined the workshop of Michael Wolgemut (1434–1519), a Nuremberg master painter and woodcut designer in November 1486. He remained with Wolgemut for four years before starting his travels about the Holy Roman Empire. In the spring of 1494 Dürer returned to his home town to marry Agnes Frey, an attractive and modest young woman.

Always eager for new knowledge, Dürer left for Italy in the fall of 1494, where he made a thorough study of some of the glories of Renaissance art. Back in Nuremberg in the spring of 1495, Dürer opened up his own workshop and began getting important commissions. In 1505 he made his second trip to Italy. The handsome Dürer earned a number of commissions from the Holy Roman Emperor Maximilian I. When Maximilian died in 1519, the Nuremberger journeyed to the Netherlands, hoping to secure a continuation of his imperial pension from the new sovereign, Charles V. Dürer stayed for almost a year, studying intensely the works of the Dutch and Flemish masters. He also contracted malaria while examining a beached whale in the swamps of Zeeland, which undermined his health for the rest of his life.

His last years were spent in Nuremberg, where he was an important member of the city's humanist movement and an early supporter of Martin Luther. Dürer thought that Luther had captured the essence of the New Testament message of God's love and forgiveness. After hearing the false news that Luther had been killed after the 1521 Diet of Worms, the artist exclaimed, "Oh God, if Luther is dead, who will expound the Holy Gospel to us with such clarity!"[8]

Success as an artist earned him a comfortable home near the Imperial Castle in the

Albrecht Dürer, *Self-Portrait*. Alte Pinakothek, Munich, Germany. Scala/Art Resource.

heart of the town and the admiration of his community. He left behind more than 70 paintings, more than 100 engravings, about 250 woodcuts, about 1,000 drawings, and three books on geometry, fortification, and human proportions. His media, style, and subject matter varied widely, ranging from realistic depictions of peasants to allegorical works such as *Knight, Death, and the Devil*. Like Leonardo da Vinci, Albrecht Dürer sought to discover the meaning of nature. He wrote, "For truly art is embedded in nature."[9] His own nature was exceedingly complicated. Prone to bouts of melancholy, Dürer also dared to portray himself looking remarkably Christ-like but prosperous in a fur-trimmed coat. This self-portrait was one of a series beginning with a self-study he finished while still a teenager. His mature self-confidence was surely merited by his achievements, some of which are illustrated in this book.

LUCAS CRANACH (1472–1553) AND HANS HOLBEIN (1497–1543)

Lucas Cranach the Elder and Hans Holbein the Younger, Dürer's contemporaries, also made great names for themselves even if their subject matter and style did not vary as much as the Nuremberger's. Cranach was a northern Franconian who learned the art of engraving from his father. Active in Vienna from 1500 to 1503, he became court painter to Duke Frederick the Wise of Saxony. There he became a member of the city council and a close friend of the reformers Martin Luther and Philip Melanchthon. His portraits of many of the major figures of the early Saxon Reformation and his striking rendition of many biblical themes helped establish his reputation. Although less refined than Dürer's, his art shows an abundance of psychological power and deeply felt religious sensitivity.

Hans Holbein of Augsburg was the son of a well-known artist, who sent him to Italy to further his skills. He spent most of the period from 1515 to 1526 in Basel, Switzerland, where he established excellent connections among leading northern humanists. Holbein did a number of book illustrations for Johann Froben, the publisher of Erasmus. He also received commissions for portraits from a number of wealthy merchants and nobles. His reputation as a brilliant portraitist brought him to England, where he painted a number of luminaries, including Erasmus, Thomas Cromwell, and Thomas More. His painting of Anne of Cleves was used to interest King Henry VIII in marrying the German princess. Holbein's mastery of oil painting and ability to convey shrewd psychological insights assure his enormous modern reputation. He was able to flatter his subjects while at the same time reveal the essences of their character.

THE SCULPTOR TILMAN RIEMENSCHNEIDER (C. 1460–1531)

The Renaissance in the north produced no sculptors of the reputation of Donatello or Michelangelo, but there was some first-rate work done, particularly in wood altar-pieces. Tilman Riemenschneider of Würzburg became famous as one of the greatest altar sculptors of the period. Born in Osterode near Hildesheim in the Harz Mountains in Saxony, he moved to Würzburg to join the guild of painters, sculptors, and glaziers. He became so successful as a sculptor that he was elected several times to the city council and later held other civic offices. Put on trial and tortured because of his expressed sympathies with rebellious peasants during their revolt of 1524 to 1526, Riemenschneider's last years have been described as dark and empty. Although the Reformation period created a great deal of uncertainty for sculptors in the north because of the feeling of some Protestants that statues were fearsome idols which should be destroyed, some artists found ways of adapting and surviving. Overall, however, the Reformation did not prove a boon to Renaissance art in the north.

Northern Renaissance Humanism

Europe north of the Alps also witnessed its own unique humanist movement. Although sharing many of the concerns of the Italian humanists with the revival of classical learning, northern humanism had its own special character. Northern humanists were able to build on the work of the great Italian scholars but also to add their own concerns as well. Some of the northerners were interested in promoting a sense of pride in their particular national identities. Religious ideals drove many northern humanists. In the north of Europe, humanism also came to be infused with a spiritual movement of great importance.

THE BROTHERS AND SISTERS OF THE COMMON LIFE

The Brothers and Sisters of the Common Life were concerned essentially with deepening inward religious faith and with cultivating practical Christian living. Education was seen as a tool for promoting these spiritual concerns. The Brothers and Sisters of the Common Life were founded by Gerard Groote (1340–1384), a well-educated lawyer who became a Carthusian monk. Not finding sufficient religious satisfaction inside monastic walls, Groote left the monastery in 1369 and spent the rest of his life trying to reform the clergy, encourage new forms of devotion, and teach the young at his school at Deventer in the Low Countries.

Groote's ministry attracted male and female followers, who eventually created a semimonastic order of laymen and women as well as members of the clergy. The Brothers and Sisters took no irrevocable vows but sought to live holy lives following the ethics of Christ's Sermon on the Mount. Perhaps their best-known member was Thomas à Kempis (1380–1471), who lived in the convent of St. Agnes in the Low Countries for more than seventy years. There he composed *The Imitation of Christ*, which records a personal search for God and shows others how to achieve a direct, personal relationship with God (mysticism). Enormously popular, it has been published in over 6,000

editions, including one translated into English by Margaret Beaufort, mother of King Henry VII.

The Brothers and Sisters established boarding schools, opened hostels for poor university students, and operated newly invented printing presses to make classics of devotional literature more widely available. Since they found the ethical treatises of ancients such as Cicero and Seneca to be of great value in teaching the young, they became instrumental in promoting a revival of classical studies in the north. Brethren houses spread from the Netherlands into Germany. The humanists Erasmus and Johann Reuchlin as well as the reformer Martin Luther were influenced by them as were thousands of less prominent Christians on the eve of the Reformation.

German Humanism

CONRAD CELTIS (1459–1508)

Every part of Europe produced its own brand of humanism. In the German-speaking lands, humanism became infused with incipient nationalism. Conrad Celtis was one of the most influential of the German humanists as well as a major lyric poet. Celtis began life in a peasant family near Würzburg. After running away from home, he managed to study at a number of schools and universities in Germany. On April 18, 1487, Holy Roman Emperor Frederick III crowned him Germany's first poet laureate. Armed with this recognition, Celtis wandered about the empire and made his way to Italy, where he was disgusted by the pretensions of the Italians to cultural superiority over the "barbarians" to the north. Later he studied mathematics and poetry at the University of Cracow in Poland. Eventually he became a professor of rhetoric at the University of Ingolstadt and later at Vienna at the behest of Emperor Maximilian I, where he wrote, taught, and died of syphilis at age forty-nine.

In his inaugural address at Ingolstadt, Celtis challenged his fellow Germans to a cultural rivalry with Italy. "Take up arms, O Germans. Rekindle that old spirit of yours with which so many times you terrorized the Romans."[10] He introduced the German world of letters to the writings of the Roman historian Tacitus, who had praised the Germans in his *Germania,* which Celtis published. He also launched an extensive search for the writings of the tenth-century nun and author Hrosvit of Gandersheim. Hrosvit wrote verse, history, and the only dramas we know of composed between the fourth and eleventh centuries. His published editions of her work were intended to demonstrate the antiquity and excellence of German culture. Celtis also wrote his own histories, including his *Germany Illustrated,* to demonstrate the greatness of the Germans.

CARITAS AND WILLIBALD PIRCKHEIMER

Like many humanists, Conrad Celtis enjoyed a rich circle of friends and correspondents. Among his more gifted humanist correspondents were Caritas (1467–1532) and Willibald Pirckheimer (1470–1530), the brother and sister humanists from Nuremberg. Caritas came from a prominent patrician family, which valued humanistic learning for both its sons and daughters. She won special permission to enter a convent of the Poor Clares in Nuremberg when she was only twelve by dazzling a Franciscan vicar general with her fluency in Latin. The Convent of St. Clare in Nuremberg had a substantial library, a community of literate nuns which came to include one of her own sisters, and a steady

supply of talented preachers and confessors assigned from a nearby Franciscan friary.

There she blossomed as a religious figure and as an intellectual. She provided editorial leadership in producing a *Chronicle* in German and Latin versions detailing the history of the Order of St. Clare and her own convent. She also began to correspond with leading humanists including Conrad Celtis, Johann Reuchlin, and through her brother, Willibald, with the great Erasmus of Rotterdam. Observing monastic modesty and characteristic self-effacement, she continued to downplay her intellectual gifts, writing Conrad Celtis in 1515, "You know that I am not learned, but merely a friend of learned men."[11]

Some of her self-disparagement may also have come from the fact that in 1503 when she became abbess of St. Clare's, one of her Franciscan superiors ordered her to stop writing in Latin. Many in the church were uncomfortable with the notion of learned women, who shared their passion for humanistic learning with others outside the cloisters. Although Caritas continued to do some writing in Latin, her output had become carefully circumscribed. Her *Memoirs* became an important source for the history of the early Reformation in Nuremberg. In 1525 Caritas led a spirited defense of her convent, which the Nuremberg City Council wanted to close as part of its adoption of Lutheranism. She used all her humanistic and theological skills to argue the case for her convent and succeeded in reaching a compromise with the city authorities, which allowed St. Clare's to stay in existence until 1590.

Caritas's younger brother, Willibald, became an even more famous humanist, but as a privileged male he had many more opportunities. He was allowed to travel with his father on diplomatic missions for the bishop of Eichstätt, whom his father served as a legal advisor. Willibald studied law at the universities of Padua and Pavia from 1488 to 1495. Along the way he mastered Greek and became fully immersed in humanistic studies. In 1496 Willibald was elected to the all-male Nuremberg City Council, where he remained until 1523. He also served Nuremberg as an occasional diplomat and military commander.

Willibald Pirckheimer was more than just a civic humanist; he was also a patron of the arts, especially the work of his close friend Albrecht Dürer. Willibald also produced major translations of various classical Greek and Latin authors, including Aristophanes, Aristotle, Galen, Plutarch, Ptolemy, Thucydides, and Xenophon. Deeply religious, he also translated the works of a number of important Greek theologians including his favorite, Gregory of Nazianzus. His own writings included a satire in praise of gout, a historical geography of Germany, a brief autobiography, and various treatises on theological and moral issues. His contemporaries placed him in the company of Erasmus, Reuchlin, and Jacob Wimpfeling (1450–1528) as a group from whom one might expect a "better and greater future for all Christendom."[12]

Johann Reuchlin (1455–1522)

The most celebrated of the German humanists was Johann Reuchlin. Like his role model Giovanni Pico della Mirandola, Reuchlin was interested in all aspects of knowledge. "Truth I worship as God," he once declared.[13] He was born in Germany at Pforzheim and educated by the Brethren of the Common Life and later at the universities of Basel, Freiburg, Orléans, Paris, and Tübingen, where he also taught Greek and served as a magistrate. He made three study trips to Italy and came to know the philoso-

phers Marsilio Ficino and Giovanni Pico. He was also a great admirer of the German humanist and Neoplatonic philosopher Nicholas of Cues (1401–1464).

A professional lawyer, Reuchlin worked for many years as chancellor to the duke of Württemberg, where he also served as head jurist of the Swabian League between 1502 and 1513. His last years were spent as a professor of Greek and Hebrew at the universities of Ingolstadt and Tübingen. From all his vast knowledge, Reuchlin became convinced that the study of Hebrew more than anything else brought him close to God. He claimed that "no one can understand the Old Testament unless they know the language it was written in."[14] Reuchlin concluded that Moses and the other Old Testament prophets had transmitted many divine truths orally through seventy wise men in an unbroken tradition until they were embodied by the medieval Jewish mystics in the *Cabala.* Because of the many references in the *Cabala* to the Messiah or chosen one, Reuchlin believed that the great Jewish mystical book supported Christian revelation.

In 1506 after more than a decade of work in Hebrew sources, the mild-mannered humanist published a Christian-Hebrew grammar. *The Rudiments of Hebrew* was the first reliable manual of Hebrew grammar to be written by a Christian scholar. He followed it with *On the Cabalistic Art* of 1517 in which he sought to demonstrate that Greek Pythagorean theories and Talmudic and Cabalistic works harmonize with Christian beliefs. His studies came to the attention of a recent convert from Judaism to Christianity, Johann Pfefferkorn, who was making a name for himself by attacking the new interest of humanists in Hebrew writings. In his book *A Mirror for Jews,* Pfefferkorn argued that all Hebrew books should be confiscated and received support for this notion from some of the Dominicans of Cologne, who feared that humanism was undermining traditional scholastic understandings of Christianity.

In 1519 Emperor Maximilian I ordered that all Hebrew books should be confiscated. In response to an inquiry from the archbishop of Mainz, Reuchlin offered the opinion that Hebrew books should not be taken away but instead should be studied more intensely by Christians. Pfefferkorn then attacked Reuchlin directly in a pamphlet accusing him of ignorance. Although he dreaded public controversy, Reuchlin felt compelled to defend his reputation and fired back a treatise aimed at his antagonist as well as a collection of testimonials on his behalf titled the *Letters of Famous Men*. Despite being overshadowed by Martin Luther's controversy with church authorities over indulgences, the Reuchlin affair dragged on until 1520 when Pope Leo X condemned the humanist to silence. Although broken hearted, Reuchlin accepted the church's judgment and died two years later still loyal to the Roman Catholic Church.

In defense of Reuchlin and humanistic studies, two of his most ardent admirers, Crotus Rubianus and Ulrich von Hutten, published one of the most famous popular satires of the period, *The Letters of Obscure Men*. The letters, ostensibly written in deliberately faulty Latin in support of the Dominican Orwin Grotius of Cologne, ridiculed the ignorance and foolishness of those who followed Pfefferkorn's lead. Yet they also contained anti-Semitic jibes such as the charge that Pfefferkorn "still stank like any other Jew."[15] It was also filled with many nasty jokes about women, as female bashing was still a favorite pastime among many male humanists.

A stern papal bull forbidding the reading of *The Letters* only brought more attention to the satire and further increased sales. One of the anonymous authors, the humanist-knight Hutten, went on to fire additional salvoes against the Catholic Church. He condemned hypocritical monks, superstitious priests, the luxury of the papal court, and challenged the pope to support the reformation of the church. Hutten also published an edition of Lorenzo Valla's exposure of the *False Donation of Constantine* and offered his sword and pen to the service of the dissident friar and university professor Martin Luther.

English Humanism

Humanism found a welcome reception in England. It not only infiltrated the universities, but it also reached into the heart of the Tudor court, where King Henry VIII hired humanist scholars to tutor his children. John Colet (1466–1519), the founder of St. Paul's School in London, was one of the most influential of the English humanists. He studied at the universities of Cambridge and Oxford, where he earned his doctorate in theology. Colet had spent two years in Italy in the 1490s and made the acquaintance of Ficino and other members of the Platonic Academy in Florence. In his lectures at Oxford and later at St. Paul's, Colet argued that the new learning would help people to better understand the Bible and strengthen their faith. He very much regretted that he had never learned Greek himself, "without which we can get nowhere."[16] Among the many English scholars influenced by Colet, none became more famous than Thomas More.

THE MAN FOR ALL SEASONS: THOMAS MORE (1478–1535)

Although some of the northern humanists evinced a high degree of dissatisfaction with the practices of the Renaissance church, many others stayed loyal to the papacy. Sir Thomas More, England's renowned humanist-lawyer, was one of best known of those who defended the teachings and practices of the old church. He began life in London as the son of a prosperous lawyer and developed a taste for the classics in a Latin grammar school. Young Thomas then served as a page in the household of Cardinal John Morton, archbishop of Canterbury. After studying at Oxford for two years, More turned to common law, which he read at Lincoln's Inn in London.

When More was about twenty, he experienced an acute spiritual crisis and gave serious thought to renouncing his father's dream of a legal career and becoming a Carthusian monk. More spent some time living in a monastery, wearing a hair shirt, sleeping with a block of wood for a pillow, and beating himself every Friday in remembrance of Christ's suffering at the hands of Roman soldiers. He later resumed his legal career, but from time to time he would retreat to the monastic world for brief stays.

In 1504, still only twenty-six, he was elected to Parliament. The next year More married Jane Colt, a woman from a good family, and he personally supervised the education of their children including a daughter, Margaret, who was known as a brilliant student of the classics. Beginning in September 1510 More served as undersheriff of London, representing the city's interest in court. More also entered the diplomatic service of King Henry VIII and undertook a number of missions to the Continent. In 1518 he became a member of the king's council, was named a treasury official in 1521, and was elected as Speaker of the House of Commons in 1523.

When Cardinal Thomas Wolsey lost favor because of his failure to secure an annulment of the king's marriage to Catherine of Aragon in 1529, the multitalented Thomas More was chosen to succeed him as lord chancellor of England. A staunch Roman Catholic, he later resigned when Henry rejected papal supremacy. In 1535 More was executed for having followed his conscience and defied the king. His strength of convictions has become the stuff of legends.

Despite his spectacular public career, More took the time to pursue his intellectual and spiritual interests. He was a very close friend of leading humanists such as John Colet and the witty Dutchman Erasmus. Erasmus in fact wrote his famous satire, *Praise of Folly*, at More's home. *Praise of Folly* (*Encomium Moriae*) can also be rendered as "Praise of More." More's humanist friends encouraged his continuing study of the classics and his writings, including an important *History of Richard III*, which served as one of the sources for Shakespeare's play.

The fantasy *Utopia* (Nowhere) of 1516 was Thomas More's most significant published work. In the first part of *Utopia*, he criticized the political and social abuses of his times such as the harsh punishments of the criminal code, the sufferings of the rural poor from the enclosing of land, the incessant wars between Christian states, and materialism. More wrote that "as long as there is any property and while money is the standard of all things, I cannot think that a nation can be governed either justly or happily."[17] In the second part, he described the social arrangements of an imaginary island called Utopia set in the New World.

More revolutionized Plato's *Republic* by describing his perfect republic in exact detail and stressing a greater degree of equality than had the Greek. In More's fantasy world, ordinary people work only a six-hour day and live in nice houses with glass windows, fireproof roofs, and gardens. The water supply is unpolluted and even marketplaces and hospitals are clean. Reason and righteousness rule the land. There is no private property and the goods in the shopping centers are free for the taking. Everyone is required to work. Even the lawgivers dress like everyone else except priests. Women are somewhat subordinated to men but receive military training. Wars of conquest are not allowed, except for the purpose of claiming unused land. Religion is flexible and undogmatic. The contrasts with More's England are obvious and even he failed to live up to the ideals of his Utopia. For example, as lord chancellor, More vigorously persecuted Lutherans. Nevertheless, *Utopia* remains as a fascinating vision of a humanist patriarch's dreamworld.

Erasmus (c. 1466–1536), Prince of the Humanists

Desiderius Erasmus was generally acknowledged as the most respected northern humanist of the sixteenth century. Popes, emperors, kings, princes, and rich merchants wished to be among his patrons, universities offered professorships, and scholars sought out his company. His manners and conversation were "polished, affable, and even charming."[18] No one could match his knowledge of the classics or the writings of the church fathers. His own writings were prodigious. All this was quite an accomplishment for a man who started life as the illegitimate son of a priest and a daughter of a physician. His mother placed him and his older brother at a school in Deventer, a major center of the Brothers and Sisters of the Common Life. Later Erasmus studied at a Brethren school at Bois-le-Duc for two years.

Shortly after both of his parents died from the plague, he entered an Augustinian monastery. Six years later Erasmus accepted ordination as a priest as a way out of the monastery. In 1494 he became secretary to the bishop of Cambrai and later enrolled at the College de Montaigu in Paris. Later he claimed to hate both its "stale eggs and stale [scholastic] theology."[19] The year 1499 found him in England as a tutor, where he heard the brilliant humanist John Colet lecture on Paul. Colet urged Erasmus to study Greek as preparation to a more serious study of theology. Erasmus also began a strong friendship with Thomas More.

Returning to the Continent, Erasmus settled first in Paris and then in Louvain, where he published 800 Latin *Adages* in 1500. This collection of wise sayings culled from the classics was enormously popular because it made some of the wit and wisdom of the classics available to the nonclassically trained elite. The *Adages* were followed by his *Handbook of the Christian Soldier* (1503), which stressed the importance of faith; editions of Cicero's and Saint Jerome's letters; and a critical edition of Valla's *Anno-*

Hans Holbein the Younger, *Erasmus Writing.* Louvre, Paris, France. Giraudon/Art Resource.

tations on the New Testament. In 1505 Erasmus was back in England to begin working on his own translation of the New Testament. From 1506 to 1509 he worked in Italy as a tutor and immersed himself deeply in classical studies while drawing inspiration from the work of Italian humanism.

Back in England in 1509 while resting from his Italian journey, Erasmus penned his most popular writing, *Praise of Folly*. In this work he attempted to criticize abuses in the church and society and to promote purer spirituality in religion. Erasmus lambasted "the cheat of pardons and indulgences" and those who worshiped the Virgin Mary "before the Son." Even the papacy failed to escape his censure: "Now as to the popes of Rome, who pretend themselves Christ's vicar, if they would but imitate his exemplary life," poverty, and contempt of the world.[20] *Praise of Folly* was tremendously popular despite being placed on the Index of Forbidden Books by the papacy in the 1560s.

For the next three years Erasmus taught theology and Greek at Cambridge University. Then he moved to Basel in Switzerland to be closer to his publisher as his nine-volume edition of the writings of St. Jerome rolled from the presses of Johann Froben, one of the great names in the history of publishing. Erasmus found the Swiss town to be a congenial environment: "I am extraordinarily happy. Every day I enjoy the company of learned men. . . . Nowhere have I found so delightfully instructive a society."[21] In 1516 his influential Greek New Testament issued from the presses, as did editions of the writings of Cato, Plutarch, and Seneca. Erasmus like other humanists thought the classics of Greece and Rome would prepare the mind for the reception of God. In addition, the classics were worth studying in their own right. Scholastics, who felt compelled to reconcile the classics

with Christian understandings, were ridiculed as people "extant in their own lifetimes," who were content with using faulty translations and missed the essence of Christianity's message in their preoccupation with complex reasoning.[22]

Although capable of ridiculing most women, Erasmus was one of the first prominent male humanists to recommend study at least for the daughters of the rich after having been impressed by the erudition of Thomas More's daughter, Margaret Roper (1504–1544). She had translated his treatise on the Lord's Supper. Study "is not only a weapon against idleness but also a means of impressing the best precepts upon a girl's mind and leading her to virtue" he wrote. In his "Dialogue between an Abbot and a Learned Lady," Erasmus has his learned housewife inform an ignorant abbot that "if men can't play their parts, they should get off the stage and let women assume their roles."[23]

Erasmus was also a pacifist who hoped Europe would bloom with flowers rather than continued strife. In his *The Complaint of Peace* of 1517, he rejected even the Augustinian notion of a just war. Erasmus argued that "war incessantly sows war, vengeance seethingly draws vengeance, kindness generously engenders kindness."[24] He was also appalled by the concept of crusades and holy war and the involvement of the church's leadership in alliances and military actions. Erasmus begged the papacy to follow the example of Christ and reign as princes of peace.

Erasmus is well known for his criticisms of a great deal in contemporary church practice. Yet what he criticized in the church, he criticized out of love and with a hope for peaceful reform. Although initially sympathetic with Martin Luther's concern about abuses in the church, Erasmus increasingly became alarmed at the Wittenberger's dogmatism, the violence of some of his followers, and the movement to separate from the church. Accused of being a "heretic Lutheran," Erasmus denied authorship of the 1517 satire *Julius Excluded from Heaven,* in which the swaggering warrior-pope is excluded from paradise (a draft was later found in Erasmus's own handwriting). In 1524 he also published against Luther's conception of predestination, arguing for *The Freedom of the Will.* When the Protestant Reformation came to Basel in 1529, the scholarly Erasmus fled to Freiburg, where he lived for six more years. In August 1535 he returned to Basel to edit the works of the third-century church father Origen. Still mourning the martyrdom of his friend Sir Thomas More, he died eleven months later.

The Printing Press and Its Impact

During the lifetime of Erasmus, the virtual religious unity of Europe was shattered for all time. Why did Martin Luther's quarrel with the papacy over indulgences lead such major religious upheavals throughout Europe when similar concerns expressed by Jan Hus a century earlier had not? It is true that by 1517 Europe as a whole was in a delicate state, with many continuing economic, political, social, and religious tensions; yet these tensions had been present throughout much of the previous centuries. In fact, things had often seemed worse in the fourteenth century and parts of the fifteenth, those ages of disasters. Europe was still a land of many poor and a few rich. Complaints about the clergy were a staple of European life. What was different about 1517?

While it is impossible to say with complete certainty why Europe exploded in the sixteenth century, one thing is certain—there would not have been as widespread a reaction to the writings of Martin Luther

and John Calvin without the printing press. The Chinese had used a form of printing from hand-carved blocks of wood since at least A.D. 800; the Europeans had been printing in that fashion only since the twelfth century. Improvements in paper and the invention of printer's ink were essential to the eventual development of moveable type sometime between 1445 and 1450 by Johann Gutenberg (c. 1398–1468) and his associates in Mainz, Germany.

Experimenting with metals, Gutenberg seemed to have discovered an alloy that could be poured into molds to form letters that would not shrink or twist upon cooling. These letter stamps could be assembled to form completely different pages. Moveable type could be used to print many copies of the same book or many copies of different books. Even more importantly, books could be printed for only a fraction of the cost of hand-copied manuscripts.

The demand for printed books was incredible. Printing presses mushroomed throughout the Holy Roman Empire and then spread to the rest of Europe by the end of the century. Printing became a major industry in Europe. By 1500 some 9 million copies of 40,000 different titles were in circulation. Over half of the newly printed books were religious: Bibles, commentaries, devotional works, sermons, and the like. Also popular were ancient classics, legal handbooks, philosophical treatises, stories of miracles, astrological predictions, encyclopedias, almanacs, and knightly romances.

Eventually most of the work of the great humanists and literary figures found their way into print, as did many ancient writings. Marguerite of Navarre's *Heptameron,* for example, was printed by 1554. Erasmus's *Praise of Folly* was eventually published in over 600 editions. The writings of Martin Luther were enormously popular, even when officially condemned. He was able to reach a much greater audience than had Hus, Wycliffe, Marsilius of Padua, or even his Catholic opponents such as the Franciscan Thomas Murner. The media revolution touched off by the invention of moveable type gave written ideas an impact without precedence in history. Without printing, the spread of Renaissance culture and the Reformation of the sixteenth century is inconceivable. The scientific revolution begun in the sixteenth century also benefited enormously from the rise of printing.

Chronology

1340–1384	Life of Gerard Groote.	1471–1528	Life of Albrecht Dürer.
1365–c. 1429	Life of Christine de Pizan.	1478–1538	Life of Thomas More.
1380–1471	Life of Thomas à Kempis.	1483–1553	Life of Rabelais.
c. 1390–1441	Life of Jan van Eyck.	1488–1523	Life of Ulrich von Hutten.
1431–c. 1464	Life of François Villon.	1492–1549	Life of Marguerite of Navarre.
1445–1450	Invention of moveable type.	1520–1566	Life of Louise Labé.
1455–1522	Life of Johann Reuchlin.	1547–1616	Life of Miguel de Cervantes.
1459–1508	Life of Conrad Celtis.	c. 1552–1594	Life of Edmund Spenser.
1459–1525	Life of Jacob Fugger, the Rich.	1561–1621	Life of Mary Sidney.
1466–1519	Life of John Colet.	1562–1621	Life of Lope de Vega.
c. 1466–1535	Life of Erasmus.	1564–1593	Life of Christopher Marlowe.
1467–1532	Life of Caritas Pirckheimer.	1564–1616	Life of William Shakespeare.
1470–1530	Life of Willibald Pirckheimer.	1577–1640	Life of Peter Paul Rubens.

Further Reading

RENAISSANCE LITERATURE: GENERAL WORKS

Ernest Grassi and Maristella Lorch, *Folly and Insanity in Renaissance Literature* (1986).

Thomas Greene, *The Light in Troy: Imitation and Discovery in Renaissance Poetry* (1986).

R. A. Houston, *Literacy in Early Modern Europe: Culture and Education 1500–1800* (1988).

David Quint, *Origin and Originality in Renaissance Literature* (1983).

FRENCH LITERATURE

Mikahil Bakhtin, *Rabelais and His World* (1968).

Lucien Febvre, *The Problem of Unbelief in the Sixteenth Century: The Religion of Rabelais* (1982).

Donald Frame, *François Rabelais: A Study* (1977).

Gertude Hanish, *Love Elegies of the Renaissance: Marot, Louise Labé and Ronsard* (1979).

George Joseph, *Clément Marot* (1985).

I. D. McFarlane, *A Literary History of France: Renaissance France, 1470–1589* (1974).

Zachary Schiffman, *On the Threshold of Modernity: Relativism in the French Renaissance* (1991).

M. A. Screech, *Rabelais* (1979).

Marcel Tetel, *Marguerite de Navarre's 'Heptameron': Themes, Language and Structure* (1973).

Charity Cannon Willard, *Christine de Pizan: Her Life and Works* (1984).

ENGLISH LITERATURE

Elaine Beilin, *Redeeming Eve: Women Writers of the English Renaissance* (1987).

Alan Bray, *Homosexuality in Renaissance England* (1982).

Stephen Greenblatt, *Renaissance Self-Fashioning: From More to Shakespeare* (1980).

Anthea Hume, *Edmund Spenser, Protestant Poet* (1984).

M. M. Resse, *Shakespeare: His World and His Work* (1980).

Murray Roston, *Sixteenth-Century English Literature* (1982).

Retha Warnicke, *Women of the English Renaissance and Reformation* (1983).

SPANISH LITERATURE

William Byron, *Cervantes: A Biography* (1978).

Stephen Gilman, *The Novel According to Cervantes* (1989).

Melveena McKendrick, *Theatre in Spain, 1490–1700* (1984).

Paul Smith, *Writing in the Margin: Spanish Literature in the Golden Age* (1988).

RENAISSANCE ART IN THE NORTH: PAINTING

Carl Christensen, *Art and the Reformation in Germany* (1979).

Walter Gibson, *Bruegel* (1977).

André Hayum, *The Isenheim Altarpiece: God's Medicine and the Painter's Vision* (1992).

Jane Campbell Hutchinson, *Albrecht Dürer: A Biography* (1990).

Joseph Koerner, *The Moment of Self-Portraiture in German Renaissance Art* (1993).

Carol Purtle, *The Marian Paintings of Jan van Eyck* (1982).

Larry Silver, *The Paintings of Quinten Massys* (1984).

Christopher White, *Peter Paul Rubens, Man and Artist* (1987).

Diane Wolfhal, *The Beginnings of Netherlandish Canvass Painting, 1400–1530* (1989).

NORTHERN SCULPTURE

Michael Baxandall, *The Limewood Sculptures of Renaissance Germany* (1982).

Jeffrey Chipps Smith, *German Sculpture of the Later Renaissance* (1994).

NORTHERN HUMANISM

Jerry Bentley, *Humanists and Holy Writ: New Testament Scholarship in the Renaissance* (1983).

Eckhart Bernstein, *German Humanism* (1983).

Maria Dowling, *Humanism in the Age of Henry VIII* (1986).

Donald Kelley, *The Foundations of Modern Historical Scholarship* (1970).

David O. MacNeil, *Guillaulme Budé and Humanism in the Reign of Francis I* (1975).

Robert Mandrou, *From Humanism to Science, 1480–1700* (1978).

Richard Marius, *Thomas More: A Biography* (1984).

Louis Martz, *Thomas More: The Search for the Inner Man* (1990).

Charles Nauert, Jr., *Humanism and the Culture of Renaissance Europe* (1995).

James Overfield, *Humanism and Scholasticism in Late Medieval Germany* (1985).

Eugene Rice, Jr., *Saint Jerome in the Renaissance* (1988).

Erika Rummel, *The Humanist-Scholastic Debate in the Renaissance and Reformation* (1995).

Franco Simone, *The French Renaissance: Medieval Tradition and Italian Influence in Shaping the Renaissance in France* (1970).

Lewis Spitz, Jr., *The Religious Renaissance of the German Humanists* (1967).

ERASMUS

Cornelius Augustijn, *Erasmus: His Life, Works, and Influence* (1991).

Roland Bainton, *Erasmus of Christendom* (1969).

Marjorie O'Rourke Boyle, *Christening Pagan Mysteries: Erasmus in Pursuit of Wisdom* (1977).

Léon-E. Halkin, *Erasmus, A Critical Biography* (1993).

Lisa Jardine, *Erasmus, Man of Letters* (1993). Very challenging.

John Payne, *Erasmus: His Theology of the Sacraments* (1970).

Erika Rummel, *Erasmus as a Translator of the Classics* (1985).

Richard Schoeck, *Erasmus of Europe: The Making of a Humanist 1467- 1500* (1990).

J. Kelley Sowards, *Desiderius Erasmus* (1975).

James Tracy, *Erasmus of the Low Countries* (1996).

PRINTING

Roger Chartier, *The Order of Books: Readers, Authors, and Libraries in Europe between the 14th and 18th Centuries* (1994).

Miriam Chrisman, *Lay Culture, Learned Culture: Books and Social Change in Strasbourg* (1982).

Mark Edwards, Jr., *Printing, Propaganda and Martin Luther* (1994).

Elizabeth Eisenstein, *The Printing Press as an Agent of Change*, 2 vols. (1979).

Notes

1. Cited in Christine de Pisan, *The Treasure of the City of Ladies,* trans. and ed. by Sarah Lawson (New York: Penguin, 1985), p. 17.
2. Cited in Gerda Lerner, *The Creation of Feminist Consciousness: From the Middle Ages to Eighteenseventy* (New York: Oxford University Press, 1993), pp. 144–145.
3. Cited in Julia O'Faolain and Lauro Martines, eds., *Not in God's Image: Women in History from the Greeks to the Victorians* (New York: Harper and Row, 1973), p. 185.
4. Ibid.
5. Cited in James Bruce Ross and Mary Martin McLaughlin, eds., *The Portable Renaissance Reader* (New York: Viking Press, 1970), p. 449.
6. Marguerite de Navarre, *The Heptameron,* trans. by P. A. Chillon (New York: Penguin, 1984), pp. 100–101.
7. François Rabelais, *The Histories of Gargantua and Pantagruel,* trans. by J. M. Cohen (New York: Penguin, 1972), p. 37.
8. Cited in Jonathan Zophy, *Patriarchal Politics and Christoph Kress (1484–1535) of Nuremberg* (Lewiston, N.Y.: Edwin Mellen Press, 1992), p. 78.
9. Albrecht Dürer, *The Writings of Albrecht Dürer,* ed. and trans. by William Conway (New York: Philosophical Library, 1958), p. 158.
10. Cited in Lewis Spitz, Jr., ed., *The Northern Renaissance* (Englewood Cliffs, N. J.: Prentice Hall, 1972), p. 19.
11. Cited in Gerda Lerner, *The Creation of Feminist Consciousness: From the Middle Ages to Eighteenseventy* (New York: Oxford University Press, 1993), pp. 144–145.
12. Cited in Jackson Spielvogel, "Willibald Pirckheimer," in Jonathan W. Zophy, ed., *The Holy Roman Empire: A Dictionary Handbook* (Westport, Conn.: Greenwood Press, 1980), p. 380.
13. Cited in Lewis Spitz, Jr., *The Renaissance and Reformation Movements* (Chicago: Rand McNally, 1971), p. 280.
14. Cited in Ross and McLaughlin, *Renaissance Reader,* p. 411.
15. Ulrich von Hutten and others, *Letters of Obscure Men,* trans. by Francis Griffin Stokes, intro. by Hajo Holborn (Philadelphia: University of Pennsylvania Press, 1964), p. 157.
16. Cited in Rummel, *Handbook,* vol. 2, p. 74.
17. Thomas More, *Utopia,* trans. Paul Turner (Baltimore, Maryland: Penguin, 1965), p. 65.
18. Cited in Spitz, *Renaissance and Reformation,* p. 295.
19. Cited in De Lamar Jensen, *Renaissance Europe: Age of Recovery and Reconciliation,* 2nd ed. (Lexington, Mass.: D. C. Heath, 1992), p. 383.
20. Cited in Lewis Spitz, ed., *The Protestant Reformation* (Englewood Cliffs, N.J.: Prentice Hall, 1966), p. 21.
21. Cited in M. D. Hottinger, *The Stories of Basel, Berne and Zurich* (London: J. M. Dent and Sons, Ltd., 1933), pp. 65–66.
22. Erasmus, *Praise of Folly and Letter to Martin Dorp 1515,* trans. Betty Radice (New York: Penguin, 1971), pp. 152–156.
23. *The Colloquies of Erasmus,* trans. Craig Thompson (Chicago: University of Chicago Press, 1965), p. 223.
24. *The Essential Erasmus,* trans. John Dolan (New York: New American Library, 1964), p. 203.

10

Martin Luther's Revolt

The Man with Seven Heads

Some people thought Martin Luther had seven heads. After all he was a well-published and beloved university professor, a friar, a priest, a heretic (to some), an outlaw, a family man, and a dedicated church reformer (to some). His ideas helped unleash complex economic, intellectual, political, and social forces which are still being felt today. A prolific author, he is one of the first persons in European history whom we can come to know in some detail. The story of his life is intertwined with that of the first phases of the movement known as the Reformation. How did this come to be? Who was this man with seven heads?

Martin Luther's Background

Martin Luther came from an ambitious, hard-working family. His grandfather had been a peasant. His father, Hans, left farm work to become a copper miner and eventually rose to become a part owner of six mines and two copper smelters. Mining was a growth industry in the period, although its expansion ultimately contributed to problems of deforestation and pollution. Hans Luther had married slightly above his station; his wife, Margaret, was a member of a well-educated, middle-class family—the Lindermans. When Martin was born on No-

vember 10, 1483 as the second son, Hans had not yet launched his successful mining career and was desperately searching for work in the mines.

Hans Luther eventually prospered in the rough life of the mines near Mansfeld in Saxony, but life in the Luther household could be difficult. Martin Luther later remembered being beaten by his mother until he bled for "stealing a nut from the kitchen table."[1] He was also punished severely by his father for a boyhood prank, but such discipline was common in a patriarchal age. To be sure, young Martin found a measure of tough love in that hard-working family, as did his four sisters and four brothers.

Luther's parents were determined that at least several of their sons should receive good formal educations as preparatory to prosperous careers. Should young Martin become, say, a lawyer, he would then be able to assure his parents' future and take good care of them in their dotage. This was the plan when Martin was enrolled in the Latin School in his home town of Mansfeld in 1492. Five years later he was sent to school in Magdeburg and a year later to an even better one in Eisenach, where he encountered the dedicated cleric Johann Braun, who became his most important early role model.

In 1501 Martin Luther entered Erfurt University and applied himself to the traditional liberal arts curriculum, receiving his

Hans Brosamer, "Martinus Luther Siebenkopfe." Title page to Johann Cochlaeus's *Sieben Kopfe Martin Luther*, 1529. Foto Marburg/Art Resource.

B.A. degree in 1502 and his M.A. in January 1505. Although he still dreamed of becoming a clergyman, Martin dutifully began his legal studies in the spring of 1505. On July 2, 1505 while returning to law school from a home visit, he was nearly hit by a bolt of lightning. He took a vow, "Help me, St. Anne. I will become a monk."[2] Luther apparently felt he needed all the help the patron saint of miners could give him because he was about to disappoint his miner father and enter an Augustinian Hermit monastery back at Erfurt. A practical man of business, Hans Luther had invested a great deal in the education of his son. Hans now worried that his investment would be wasted if Martin became another poorly paid member of the clery and, therefore, less able to provide for him in his old age.

Less than a year later, an extremely terrified Martin Luther celebrated his first Mass as an ordained priest in the chapel of the Augustinian cloister at Erfurt. He felt unworthy of handling the body and blood of Christ. The celebration was witnessed by his still simmering father and several of his father's cronies. Luther expressed his feelings of unworthiness but explained to his father that he felt compelled to enter the monastery because of his experience with the thunderstorm. Hans Luther countered, "Let us hope it was not an illusion and a deception. Have you not also heard that parents are to be obeyed?"[3] Still the prosperous Hans could not resist showing off by presenting the monastery with an exceptionally generous present of twenty gulden (nearly 20 percent of a typical worker's annual wages).

Despite his pain at the anger his vocational choice had caused his earthly father, Martin Luther persevered in his efforts to achieve religious satisfaction by following a grueling routine in the monastery. His ecclesiastical superior and confessor, Johann von Staupitz (c. 1460–1524), became worried about his brilliant but obviously troubled young colleague. He urged the congenial Luther to continue his academic studies and try his hand at teaching and administrative work. Staupitz also sent Luther as a representative of his order to Rome in the fall of 1510. While Luther found his trip to Rome and his studies to be stimulating, he was still yearning for grace.

On October 19, 1512, Master Luther became Doctor Luther, having received his doctorate in theology. By then he was already well on his way toward becoming one of the most popular professors at Elector Frederick the Wise's University of Wittenberg, a university founded in 1502, the year of Luther's baccalaureate degree from Erfurt. Duke Frederick of Electoral Saxony (1463–1525) was almost as proud of his new university as he was of his fabulous collection of relics, one of the finest in Europe, and the charismatic Luther soon became one of his star faculty members even before his early publications on grace after the Indulgence Controversy of 1517 made him famous throughout the Holy Roman Empire.

THE INDULGENCE CONTROVERSY

At age thirty-four Martin Luther was convinced that he had finally figured out how people's souls were saved. This had been a question that had long troubled him, since he lived in a world where early death was common and most people felt burdened by guilt for their sins. Like many others in the early sixteenth century, Luther was obsessed with religion, worried about his own salvation, and afraid of an angry God.

His duties as a professor of theology at the University of Wittenberg, however, had forced him into a serious examination of the writings of the apostle Paul as well as the Psalms. Luther had become especially intrigued with Paul's letters to the Romans and the concept of "the righteousness of God." Perhaps Luther had been viewing the salvation question from the wrong direction as his mentor Johann von Staupitz had suggested.

Luther assumed that because God is righteous, He, therefore, must punish sinful humanity. As he explained later, "Far from loving that righteous God who punished sinners, I actually hated Him."[4] Then he began to realize that because his "righteous God" is righteous, He mercifully chooses to give some of us the saving gift of faith even though none of us is worthy. In the words of Paul, Luther's great biblical hero, "the just shall live by faith" (Romans 1:17).

Although this discovery of a loving rather than a hateful God changed Luther's entire outlook on life and brought him immense joy, it also brought him into serious trouble with many of his superiors in the hierarchy of the Roman Catholic Church. Martin Luther was certainly not the first theologian to argue for the importance of faith rather than good works as a means of achieving grace. By some estimates at least forty-three other theologians had come to a position somewhat similar to Luther's on the importance of faith for salvation, including the patron saint of his order, Augustine of Hippo in Africa (354–430), and his mentor, Staupitz.

However, the views that Luther now held on the subject in October 1517 were those of a minority of Catholic theologians. Most still argued for the importance of doing good works in order to earn salvation. Furthermore, the doctrine of good works was tied to the often lucrative, papal-controlled practice of selling indulgences.

Indulgences seem to have begun innocently enough as gifts of money to charity as an expression of gratitude for forgiveness. They soon became a way to relax or commute the "satisfaction" or penance imposed as an outward sign of sorrow for sins. The medieval church made a distinction between guilt and punishment for sin. Guilt was atoned for by Christ, but penance could be ordered by a priest. Indulgences were a convenient method for having some of the penalties for sin reduced. They also served as a valued reward for those going on crusade to the Holy Land.

During the thirteenth century, theologians in the service of the papacy formulated the conception of a "treasury of merits." This was a storehouse of the good works of Christ, the saints, and all worthy Christians that the pope could redistribute by means of indulgences. That is to say, Christ and the saints had been better than they needed to be to achieve salvation and, therefore, some of their "excess merit" could be transferred to the spiritual bank accounts of penitent sinners. These indulgences would be used to lessen punishment in purgatory still left after the priest had pronounced absolution. Purgatory, which had been so imaginatively described by Dante in his *Divine Comedy,* was the place where sinners went to expiate sins before going on to heaven.

Many people did not comprehend all the subtleties involved in the church's shifting teachings about indulgences and how the sacrament of penance operated. Some confused eternal punishment with the temporary punishment of purgatory and actually thought they could buy salvation for themselves and, after the fifteenth century, for the dead as well. Some viewed the purchase of an indulgence as a good work sufficient to expiate all sins. As one bold sinner claimed: because I have purchased this indulgence, I can "sleep with" the Virgin Mary and still go to heaven![5]

Since Martin Luther now thought that God saved men and women through his gift of faith, what use were indulgences? As he wrote in his "Ninety-five Theses on the Power and Efficacy of Indulgences" of October 31, 1517, "any truly repentant Christian has a right to full remission of penalty and guilt, even without indulgence letters."

Luther was horrified that so many seemed to be gulled by the sales techniques of crass indulgence sellers such as the cherubic Dominican Johann Tetzel (d. 1519). Tetzel would have been completely at home in our own more materialistic age, outrageously peddling automobiles on television in a voice as loud as his sports coat. Modern advertisers can only marvel at his favorite jingle for selling indulgences:

As soon as a coin in the coffer rings,
Another soul from purgatory springs![6]

What Professor Luther failed to understand completely when he wrote his "Ninety-five Theses" was that Tetzel was at work because of a complicated transaction involving some of the most politically and economically powerful families in Europe. Tetzel was working for Albrecht of Hohenzollern (1490–1545), archbishop of Mainz, Magdeburg, and bishop of Halberstadt. Albrecht was the youngest son of Elector Joachim I of Brandenburg, and his family had borrowed a great deal of money from the Fugger family banking house of Augsburg. The Hohenzollerns wanted to advance Albrecht's ecclesiastical career because that would greatly increase their family's power, prestige, and ultimately their wealth. The purchase of the archbishopric of Mainz meant that the Hohenzollerns controlled half of the four electoral votes needed to become Holy Roman emperor. The Hohenzollerns would eventually become kings of Prussia and emperors of a unified Germany in 1871.

Pope Leo X (r. 1513–1521), scion of another great banking clan, the Medici, had revived a plenary Jubilee Indulgence sale inaugurated by his predecessor, the warrior-pope Julius II, Michelangelo's great patron, in order to continue the extraordinarily expensive rebuilding of St. Peter's Basilica in Rome. Because the Hohenzollerns had shelled out something in the neighborhood of 34,000 ducats for several bishoprics and other favors for the underage Albrecht, that good man of business Pope Leo had graciously allowed half of the proceeds from the sales of this jubilee indulgence to go to the Hohenzollerns and the official papal bankers, the Fuggers of Augsburg. Here, of course, we have an unusually spectacular example of the sale of church offices (*simony*) and the holding of more than one office by a single individual (*pluralism*). Simony and pluralism were corrupt church practices, which had been condemned for over a century before Luther's theses at the Council of Constance and elsewhere.

As a somewhat naive professor at a backwater German university, Martin Luther was not aware of all the complex negotiations involved in Tetzel's sales campaign and all of the powerful vested interests involved. In fact, he rather innocently sent a copy of his "Ninety-five Theses" to Archbishop Albrecht, who later proved to be a sympathetic and reform-minded churchman. However, Luther was suspicious enough about the financial aspects of indulgences to raise the question in his "Theses": Why doesn't the wealthy pope "build this one basilica of St. Peter with his own money rather than with the money of poor believers?"[7]

Martin Luther had intended the "Ninety-five Theses" to touch off an academic debate but never dreamed they would lead to a full-scale movement that became known as the Reformation. However, within weeks of their initial distribution in Wittenberg, the theses had been translated from German into Latin and distributed all over the Holy Roman Empire and eventually beyond. Luther's "Theses" had hit an incredibly sensitive nerve that set off a great storm of controversy.

THE REBEL

In April 1518, Martin Luther journeyed to the center of Germany to attend a convention of Augustinian Hermits at the lovely old town of Heidelberg on the Neckar River. Having a more sharply focused "Twenty-eight Theses on Indulgences," he was eager to defend himself and to share the fruits of his discovery of the importance of the concepts of "salvation by faith alone" and the "sole authority of Scripture" for doctrine.

Rather than being disciplined by his order and cowed into silence, Luther was cheered by his fellow Augustinians, a number of whom later became part of the first generation of evangelical clergy, as Luther's followers were known. A Dominican present at Heidelberg, Martin Bucer, became the leading light of the Reformation in the mighty imperial city of Strasbourg. Johann Brenz, a student at Heidelberg, was also impressed by Luther's performance at the disputation. He later became the leading reformer in the duchy of Württemberg.

Although Luther had already become somewhat of a German folk hero in the empire, the great church bureaucracy in Rome was slower to react. After all, Leo X, who said at his accession to the throne of St. Peter, "God has given us the papacy, let us enjoy it," had numerous pleasures to divert him from his spiritual duties.[8] He was an especially avid hunter and spent a great deal of time traveling from one papal hunting lodge to another. However, as the son of the banker Lorenzo de' Medici, Leo was financially astute enough to know that Luther's attack on indulgences, if left unchecked, represented a serious threat to the church's revenue streams. As sales of indulgences threatened to drop off, the pope understood it was no longer just a matter of "the envy of the monks . . . (Luther) will feel differently when he is sober."[9] Accordingly, on August 7, 1518, Pope Leo X ordered the dissident professor to come to Rome for a hearing.

At this critical juncture Martin Luther asked his prince, Frederick the Wise, for guidance. Reassured by his court chaplain and confessor, George Spalatin (1484–1545), that Luther was no heretic, Frederick allowed the controversial professor to stay in Wittenberg. He also used his influence as one of the seven electors of the Holy Roman emperor and one of the leading lay Christians in the empire to arrange for Luther's

Raphael, *Pope Leo X and the Cardinals Guilio de' Medici and Luigi del Rossi,* Galleria Palatina, Palazzo Pitti, Florence, Italy. Alinari/Art Resource.

hearing to take place on German soil. Not wishing to offend such a pious and powerful prince, Leo X graciously consented to allow the Wittenberg theologian to meet with his envoy, Thomas de Vio, Cardinal Cajetan (1469–1534) at Augsburg in October 1518.

Although apprehensive, Luther was looking forward to this opportunity to meet with the distinguished church administrator and authority on the writings of the great scholastic theologian, Thomas Aquinas. Luther was well acquainted with medieval scholastic thought from his days at Erfurt and was eager to debate his new evangelical theology with the learned cardinal. Meeting at the palace of the Fuggers in the heart of Augsburg where the Dominican vicar-general Cajetan was staying in comfort, the two theologians did not hit it off. The academic

Luther wanted to debate, whereas Cardinal Cajetan demanded submission. To this the courageous and stubborn German theologian would not agree. When friends informed the Wittenberger that he was going to be arrested, Luther wisely left Augsburg for the relative safety of nearby Nuremberg, where he had already impressed a number of members of the town's elite business and humanist circles with his sincerity, good humor, and bravery.

When Luther returned to Wittenberg, he found that although Frederick the Wise was disappointed with the results of the interview with Cajetan, Luther could continue to teach at the university and live in Wittenberg at the Augustinian cloister. Frederick hoped that the controversy would die down in time and Luther agreed to refrain from public disputation and publications on indulgences. However, what neither one of them could foresee was that larger forces had been unleashed by the controversy over indulgences, forces which no human could control. First, however, Frederick had to deal with a new crisis caused by the death of the Holy Roman Emperor Maximilian I in Austria on January 12, 1519.

Choosing a New Caesar

As one of the seven electors of the emperor, Frederick had to help decide who was to replace the affable Maximilian as the heir to the Roman caesars of antiquity, the "descendants of Aeneas," as imperial propagandists argued. Among the candidates were three young kings: Charles I of Spain (b. 1500), François I of France, and Henry VIII of England. All three of these energetic, able Renaissance princes had much to recommend them, but they all had liabilities as well. Charles was Maximilian's grandson, but he already ruled in Spain, which he had inherited from his other grandparents, Isabella of Castile and Ferdinand of Aragon. Charles also had inherited rule over the Low Countries, where he had been raised and educated. Some politicians, including Pope Leo, feared that Charles's election would give the house of Habsburg too much power.

Much the same could be said of electing the ambitious François of France. If the Valois candidate won the imperial title, it would create an empire to rival Charlemagne's (c. 742–814). Few outside the French kingdom wanted that reality. Henry Tudor's candidacy was not really taken seriously as he had no real support among important German princes. Pope Leo was increasingly apprehensive about either a Habsburg or Valois election because both threatened him even in Italy, where Charles was also king of Naples and François ruled Milan.

In desperation the pope now urged Frederick the Wise himself to make a run for the office. The pious Saxon duke was not likely ever to pose a threat to papal power in Italy. Furthermore, Leo told the Saxon that if Frederick would agree to serve as emperor, he could choose "any personal friend" and the pope would make that person a cardinal and endow him with an archbishopric. Should that "personal friend" be Martin Luther, two vexing problems might be solved at once. After all, would Archbishop Martin continue to challenge the authority of the holy mother church?

What Pope Leo failed to reckon with was that Frederick was indeed wise enough not to want to rise above his level of competence. He was perfectly happy as the bachelor duke of Saxony with his relic collection and a congenial mistress. Elector Frederick certainly did not want to inherit the dynastic responsibilities of the emperor, nor did he have the personal resources to fulfill those

obligations. As a Saxon duke, Frederick had a degree of privacy; as an emperor he would be continuously in the spotlight. Frederick wisely declined the pope's generous offer.

The imperial electors were thus forced to choose between Charles and François, accepting huge bribes from both. The Habsburg bribes were funded by the Fuggers of Augsburg, those aggressive papal bankers. On June 28, 1519, they announced that Charles of Habsburg, who had at least some "German blood in him," was their unanimous choice as Holy Roman emperor. Charles promised to respect the "imperial privileges of his German subjects," appoint only Germans to imperial offices, hold imperial diets only on German soil, and revive both the Imperial Council of Regency and the Imperial Supreme Court.[10]

Luther's Rebellion Intensifies

The election of Charles of Habsburg, a staunch supporter of the church, may have solved Frederick the Wise's personal dilemma, but it did little to take care of the problem of Martin Luther. In fact, matters got worse when Luther and several of his colleagues agreed to a debate over their new theology with an ambitious professor from the University of Ingolstadt, Dr. Johann Eck (1484–1543). The debate was held at the University of Leipzig in early July. Eck was a skillful debater, who had earlier been one of the first prominent academic theologians to justify capitalistic practices and was handsomely rewarded for his efforts by a number of grateful patrons including the Fuggers.

Now Eck had a golden chance to defend the truth, earn additional celebrity, and win favor with Rome by crushing the rebellious Wittenberg professor in academic debate. The Wittenberg debate team was at first led by Luther's senior colleague

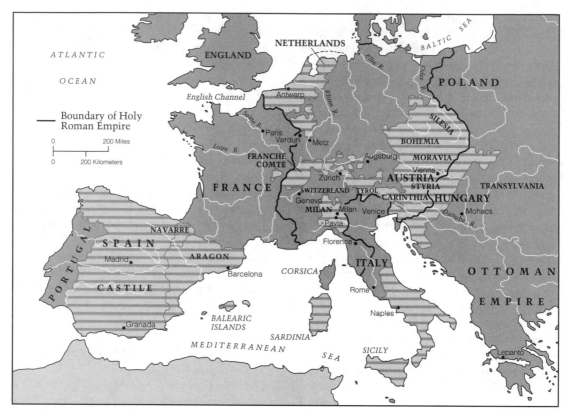

Empire of Charles V (excluding the American colonies).

Andreas von Karlstadt (c. 1480–1541). Luther had already convinced many of his colleagues and students at Wittenberg of the soundness of his position on "justification by faith." However, when Karlstadt seemed to be losing the debate to the wily Eck at every turn, Luther took over for his outmatched friend. Even the brilliant Luther proved to be no contest for Eck, who forced Luther to admit that his doctrines shared a striking number of similarities with those of the convicted heretic Jan Hus. Luther ended up conceding that "We are all Hussites."[11]

Eck's Hussite strategy was a master stroke, for the University of Leipzig had been founded by faculty and students who had fled the University of Prague during the early days of the Hussite revolt a century earlier. Memories of that painful emigration still lingered in the minds of those descendants of refugees who were judging the debate. Getting Luther to admit to "Hussite tendencies" in Leipzig was like getting someone to admit to sympathy with the devil. No wonder Luther lost the debate.

Johann Eck was able to follow up on his debate triumph over Luther by being charged with the responsibility to draft the papal bull *Exsurge Domine* ("Arise Lord"), which gave the Wittenberger sixty days to recant or face excommunication. *Exsurge Domine* was published on June 15, 1520, and included several others against whom Eck had grudges, such as the humanists Ulrich von Hutten and two of Nuremberg's more prominent citizens—the city secretary, Lazarus Spengler (1479–1534) and the patrician humanist Willibald Pirckheimer (1470–1530). Hutten was on Eck's "hit list" because of his defense of Johann Reuchlin, the controversial humanist who advocated Hebrew studies. The Nurembergers were there because of a sprightly little satire, "Cutting Eck Down to Size," which had appeared anonymously earlier in the year. Professor Eck thought Pirckheimer had written it and that Spengler, who had written the first lay defense of his friend Luther, had gotten the satire published. Attacking two of Nuremberg's favorite sons was excessive and contributed to that town's growing dissatisfaction with the Catholic Church. The response of Luther's students in Wittenberg to the papal bull against their hero was to use the bull and other papal decrees as kindling for an openly defiant bonfire.

The Leipzig Debate had already convinced Professor Luther that he was hopelessly at odds with the hierarchy of the church, but that he owed a duty to his protectors and followers to make his evangelical position perfectly clear. He therefore responded with a number of major writings in 1520 addressed to the German laity in which he spelled out his concerns about a number of church doctrines. In his *Appeal to the German Ruling Class,* Luther clarified his conception of the "universal priesthood of all believers" by reemphasizing that we all have a direct relationship with God. According to Luther, baptized believers are in a sense "priests of equal standing" and because of that they should "bring about a genuinely free council" to address the evils that have befallen Christendom which the pope refused to deal with.[12] He also declared in this essay that the parish clergy

Lucas Cranach the Elder, *Luther as an Augustinian Friar,* 1520, engraving. Foto Marburg/Art Resource.

should be allowed to marry; an argument that would also have revolutionary implications.

In his *Babylonian Captivity of the Church of God,* Luther made public his rejection of confirmation, marriage, holy orders, and supreme unction as sacraments on the grounds that they had no basis in the Scriptures. Here Luther was attacking the heart of traditional Roman Catholic piety and practice, the very rituals that had bound the Christian community together. For him, doctrine must clearly be supported by the Bible. If that was not sufficiently outrageous for his enemies, Luther went on in his *Treatise on Christian Liberty,* which was addressed to Pope Leo, to describe the liberating effect upon the Christian of faith in Christ. He argued that "faith alone, without works, justifies, frees, and saves."[13] As for good works, they "do not make a man good, but a good man does good works." These writings were widely published and made Luther and his ideas even more widely known in Germany. Even in a predominantly oral culture, the printing press was making its impact known.

LUTHER VERSUS CHARLES V: THE 1521 DIET OF WORMS

His Holiness Pope Leo in Rome was not persuaded by Luther's writings to change his beliefs and launch a reformation of the church; in fact he was further convinced that Luther was indeed a dangerous and notorious heretic who deserved excommunication and eternal damnation. Accordingly, he initiated a bull of excommunication, *Decet Romanum Pontificem* ("It is Fitting that the Pope") and expected that Charles V, the newly elected emperor, would carry it out.

This provided a bit of a dilemma for the newly crowned Charles, who although a loyal and convinced Catholic knew that the pope had not favored his election as Holy Roman emperor. Charles also knew that he could not afford to offend Luther's protector, Frederick the Wise, or indeed too many of the other German princes, for he needed their continued support for his wars with the French and for a new threat—the Ottoman Turks. The feared Ottomans were already pressing relentlessly up the Danube River and into Charles's Austrian crown lands. His spies had informed him that he would require a great deal of German help to defeat the mighty Ottomans, who had also found vigorous new leadership in the form of Süleyman the Magnificent (r. 1520–1566). Süleyman was a man of immense talents and varied interests. Trained as a goldsmith and a poet, he became an important patron of the arts and a highly successful lawgiver. Süleyman was also deter-

Bernhard Strigel, *Portrait of Emperor Charles V as a Young Man*, Galleria Borghese, Rome. Alinari/Art Resource.

mined to make a great name for himself as a conqueror and the Habsburg lands seemed like inviting targets.

Therefore, Charles V's primary objective at his first German Diet was to win friends and influence people even though he spoke not a word of German. He needed the help of the rich Germans against the threat posed by Sultan Süleyman and the "Turkish plague," as the Nuremberg diplomat Christoph Kress (1484–1535) characterized the Ottomans. So Charles did not feel in a position to turn down Frederick the Wise's polite request that Dr. Martin Luther be given a hearing at the Imperial Diet meeting in Worms in January 1521. The Diet was supposed to have met in Kress's Nuremberg, but an outbreak of the plague there resulted in the meeting site being shifted to the episcopal town of Worms on the Rhine.

Martin Luther dutifully journeyed to Worms, where he took advantage of the presence of some fine Jewish scholars to receive help with his Hebrew. He planned to produce a new translation of the Bible; however, despite his adequate knowledge of New Testament Greek, he still struggled with his Hebrew and the mysteries of the Old Testament. Although Luther was never a full-fledged humanist, he did agree with them that it was essential to get as close to the original sources (*ad fontes*) as possible. Luther was, therefore, an advocate of language studies—one of the central themes of Renaissance humanism.

On April 17, 1521, Luther made his first appearance at 4 P.M. before the assembled magnates of the empire at the palace of the bishop of Worms. When asked if he would retract the contents of his published works, the usually bold Wittenberger asked for a recess to consider his response, to the surprise of many. Screwing up his courage, Luther returned to the Diet late the next afternoon and informed the jewelled and handsomely robed representatives of the imperial ruling classes that:

Unless I am convinced by the testimony of the Holy Scriptures or by some other clear, distinct reason—for I do not believe in the Pope or in councils alone, since they have been often shown to err and contradict themselves—then I am bound by those passages from Scripture that I have quoted. As long as my conscience is bound by the Word of God, I cannot and will not recant because acting against conscience is neither safe nor sound. Here I stand. I can do no other. God help me. Amen.[14]

Martin Luther had affirmed before an audience of the most powerful men in the empire the essence of what he had been sharing with his students and colleagues for several years now. He had put his trust completely in his own interpretation of Scripture over the teaching authority of the pope and the entire hierarchy of the Catholic Church. He would follow the dictates of his own conscience rather than obey a pope whom he viewed as a fallible human.

The recently excommunicated professor found himself at odds with the authorities of the state as well, for in his response to Luther given the very next day, Emperor Charles V declared:

After the impertinent reply which Luther gave yesterday in our presence, I declare that I now regret having delayed so long the proceedings against him and his false doctrines. I am resolved that I will never again hear him talk. He is to be taken back immediately according to arrangement of the mandate with due regard for the stipulation of his safe-conduct. He is not to preach or seduce the people with his evil doctrines and is not to incite rebellion.[15]

Young Charles of Habsburg was not going to "deny the religion of all his ancestors for the false teachings of a solitary monk."[16]

Charles was a shrewd enough politician to delay signing an edict against Luther and his followers until after he had secured financial support for his wars against the French and the Ottomans. His advisors had informed him that the Wittenberger was enormously popular with people all over Germany and with intellectuals throughout Europe, thanks to the thousands of printed copies of his writings that were already in circulation. With help against his enemies assured, Charles issued an edict from Worms on May 26, 1521, that made the professor an outlaw and commanded Charles's subjects not to aid him or his followers. Furthermore, "no one shall dare to buy, sell, read, preserve, or print any of Martin Luther's books."[17]

ANTICLERICALISM

Unfortunately, from the emperor's point of view, the enforcement of the Edict of Worms against Luther proved impossible. Because he had touched such a culturally significant nerve with his attack against indulgences, which in turn played into a long-standing tradition of anticlericalism, Luther and his writings had attained enormous popularity by the close of the Diet of Worms in the spring of 1521. As the papal representative Girolamo Aleander (1480–1542) informed his master in Rome, " . . . all of Germany is in an uproar. Nine-tenths put up the battle cry, 'Luther!' and the other tenth 'Death to the papal court!'"[18]

Although Aleander's claims were greatly exaggerated, there was no question that in the spring of 1521, the now outlawed Wittenberg professor had become a German national hero even if not always a clearly understood one. For example, some humanists initially thought the Wittenberger was one of them, but he was not a humanist in all respects. Luther's fundamental concern was for changing the way that humans understood their relationship with God. He thought that human will had nothing to do with salvation. For Luther it was God's decision, not ours, who is to be given the gift of saving faith. Pressured to prove he was not a Lutheran, in 1524 the great humanist Erasmus challenged Luther's theology of predestination in a pamphlet entitled *On the Freedom of the Will*. Luther responded in Augustinian terms with a 1525 tract, *On the Enslaved Will*.

In 1521 many, including Erasmus, thought of Martin Luther as a German folk hero who wanted to clean up the church and

liberate the empire from the "money-grubbing rapacity" of the Italian-dominated clerical hierarchy. Indeed, if anything can be said to have unified the early Reformation, it was anticlericalism. Anticlericalism is a difficult concept for modern people to grasp partly because in a modern congregation there is little particular reason to be jealous of the privileges of the ministers or priests. In fact the salaries of most modern clerics are far less than the average income of the laity in many Christian churches. In the sixteenth century, a typical priest made more money and lived a better lifestyle than most of his parishioners. For example, the clergy were exempt from taxation and were not citizens of towns, which meant that they avoided unpleasant civic obligations such as sentry duty on the town's walls in bad weather.

Clerical celibacy was another sore point. Some clerics sought intimacy with the wives of parishioners; others kept concubines. Tales of lusty priests seducing women were a staple of European literature, as the highly popular writings of Giovanni Boccaccio and Marguerite of Navarre illustrate, and those who could not read relished gossip about lascivious priests, monks, and nuns. Yet real cases of clerical misconduct caused a great deal of anguish, anger, and resentment, even for those who knew that most clerics kept their vows. To many Europeans even if they liked the clergy they knew personally, the clergy as an abstract body often were considered arrogant, fat, lazy, and lecherous. Although these prejudices did not square with reality in many cases, they were widely held.

LUTHER AT THE WARTBURG CASTLE, MAY 1521 TO MARCH 1522

As for Martin Luther, after the Diet of Worms he had seemingly vanished from the public scene. Frederick the Wise, hoping that his star professor's appearance before the emperor would end the controversy, had an alternate plan in case things went wrong. Duke Frederick's back-up strategy was that Luther would be taken to one of Frederick's more hidden fortresses, the Wartburg, and kept quiet while things cooled down in the empire. The workaholic Luther, disguised as Knight George, kept himself busy at the Wartburg by completing the draft of a translation of the New Testament into highly readable German. It took Luther until 1534 to complete his German Bible because his Hebrew was not as strong as his Greek. Luther's German translation was an enormous intellectual and literary success. Although not the first German Bible, it acquired an enduring popularity and thus helped put the Word of God into the hands of more people than ever before thanks to the printing presses that churned out numerous editions.

Luther's stay at the Wartburg was interrupted by disturbances at Wittenberg in December 1521. The Reformation had continued in his absence as colleagues such as the brilliant humanist Greek scholar Philip Melanchthon (1497–1560) had, among other things, celebrated the first evangelical Lord's Supper. That is, Melanchthon had distributed the wine as well as the bread to the laity, as Luther had recommended in his 1520 pamphlet, *On the Babylonian Captivity of the Church*. Although much of the liturgy remained the same, the Lutherans argued that the Mass was not a sacrifice and that Christ's body and blood were present "in, with, and under the elements," but that the bread and wine remained bread and wine.

Some, however, like his colleague Andreas Bodenstein von Karlstadt, thought the pace of reform was too slow and wanted even more changes to be made. The unstable atmosphere was also intensified by the street corner preaching of one of Luther's

former students, Marcus Stübner, joined by two illiterate weavers from the nearby town of Zwickau. Luther did not rule out the possibility that God might speak through the common man, but he wondered why it was that so many self-proclaimed prophets later proved to be "drunks and liars." Why would God work through them when he could use someone like Professor Luther as his spokesperson? Actually, since the Scriptures, as interpreted by well-educated clergy like himself and his good friend Philip Melanchthon, now spoke so clearly, was there really much of a need for such "prophets"?

As for Professor Karlstadt, he had obviously been carried away with enthusiasm and was persuaded to moderate his course. Luther did preach publicly against the Zwickau "prophets" and urged his followers to moderate their zeal. Such was Luther's stature that a few well-chosen words from him were sufficient to restore a measure of tranquility to Wittenberg. He then promptly returned to the Wartburg Castle until March 1522 when a new round of excess zeal led by the recently married Karlstadt compelled him to return and take leadership of the Reformation in Wittenberg from those whom he dubbed "false brethren." Karlstadt now left Wittenberg for a pastorate in Orlamünde, where he could carry out his own more radical reform program free from the authority of Luther and his cautious prince, Frederick the Wise.

The Knights' Revolt of 1522 to 1524

Despite the bombast of some of his utterances, Luther was at heart a conservative law-and-order man. He had been alarmed that some wanted to use a sword to spread

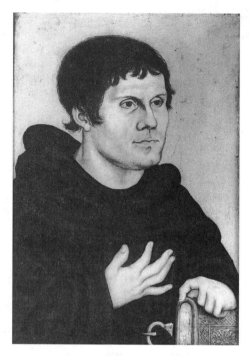

Lucas Cranach the Elder, *Luther as an Augustinian Friar,* c. 1522–1524, courtesy of the Germanisches Nationalmuseum, Nuremberg, Germany.

the Reformation and the Gospel. One of those would-be "swashbuckle Reformers" was the Imperial Knight Franz von Sickingen, who offered his sword to Luther in 1521 at the Diet of Worms. Luther politely but firmly declined the offer but did dedicate one of his writings to Sickingen. The paladin had been converted to the cause of reform by his friend, Ulrich von Hutten (1488–1523), the humanist-knight. One of the authors of the *Letters of the Obscure Men,* Hutten had many grievances with the Catholic Church and favored the subordination of the papacy to the emperor.

Franz von Sickingen (1481–1523)

Like many other members of the lower nobility in the Holy Roman Empire, Hutten and Sickingen had seen their land-based fortunes decline as part of the general economic changes Europe underwent at the beginning of the sixteenth century. With the value of their land holdings falling and expenses—because of inflation—rising, some nobles became robber knights attacking merchants' caravans. Others, like Sickingen, also became soldiers of fortune, selling themselves and their military skills to the highest bidder.

Sickingen had begun his career as a robber baron by attacking the towns of Frankfurt on Main, Metz, and Worms. In April 1515, Emperor Maximilian I declared him to be an outlaw but failed to take the necessary actions to enforce that declaration. The emperor was unwilling to punish the lower nobility, many of whom had friends and relatives at court, in part because he needed some of them as line officers. Military expertise was a valuable commodity. Sickingen soon found his services as a fighter in demand by both King François I of France and his rival Charles of Spain. He accepted the Habsburg's higher bid, but his campaign of 1521 in the first Habsburg-Valois War proved a disaster. The imperial government then defaulted on a loan of 76,000 gulden and Sickingen had to send home many of his unpaid troops with empty promises of future repayment.

During this difficult period in his life, Sickingen was converted to the cause of Martin Luther by a fellow knight, Ulrich von Hutten. Both had been disgusted by attacks against their intellectual hero Johann Reuchlin by the Dominicans of Cologne. They were both envious of the wealth of the Italian-dominated church. When Luther refused Sickingen's offer of military protection, the knight decided on his own means of reform, which included attacking the wealth of the archbishop of Trier in western Germany.

In August 1522, Sickingen launched an attack on the episcopal city of Trier, which found its own champion, ironically, in the form of the pro-Lutheran Margrave Philip of Hesse (1504–1567). Philip, known as the Magnanimous, admired Luther, but like the reformer was appalled at the idea of a violent Reformation and the threat to property posed by Sickingen and his raiders. As a staunch law-and-order man who recognized the threat to privilege posed by the knights, Philip moved to help the archbishop of Trier and others crush Sickingen and his followers. Sickingen's forces were soon driven back from the old episcopal city on the Mosel River.

Sickingen and many of his allies soon found themselves retreating to their home castles, which fell one by one to the artillery of the allied princes and in central Germany to the forces of the Swabian League of princes and cities. Sickingen was killed in 1523 during the siege of his castle at Landstühl. His confederate Hutten fled to the reformer Huldrych Zwingli's Zurich in Switzerland, where he died of syphilis.

Encouraged by the success of the offensive against Sickingen, the army of the Swabian League of towns and princes assembled an army of 1,500 cavalry and 15,000 foot soldiers at Dinkelsbühl in the summer of 1523. The army was commanded by the able and ruthless George Truchsess von Waldburg (1488–1523). They began attacking robber baron castles in Franconia one by one. Thirty in all were destroyed by the forces of the Swabian League. The war against the knights proved a dress rehearsal for the even more destructive Peasants' War soon to follow. These bloody episodes began the awful linkage between Reformation ideas, social upheaval, and political violence, connections which blighted the course of the Reformation.

Chronology

c. 1460–1524	Life of Johann von Staupitz.
c. 1480	Birth of Andreas von Karlstadt.
1483	Birth of Martin Luther at Eisleben.
1484	Birth of Johann Eck.
1497	Birth of Philip Melanchthon.
1505	Thunderstorm and Luther's entrance into an Augustinian monastery at Erfurt.
1507	Luther celebrates his first Mass as a priest.
1512	Luther completes his doctorate in theology.
1513–1521	Reign of Pope Leo X (Giovanni de' Medici).
1517	The "Ninety-five Theses against Indulgences."
1518	Luther meets with Cardinal Cajetan at Augsburg.
1519	Election of Charles of Habsburg as Holy Roman emperor; Leipzig Debate with Johann Eck.
1520	Pope Leo X's bull *Exsurge Domine* gives Luther sixty days to submit; Luther publishes a series of revolutionary pamphlets.
1521	The Diet of Worms; Luther at the Wartburg; Tumult at Wittenberg; Melanchthon's *Loci Communes*.
1522	Franz von Sickingen's campaign against Trier.
1523	Franconian robber knights crushed by Swabian League.

Further Reading

MARTIN LUTHER: BIBLIOGRAPHIES

Kenneth Hagen, et al., *Annotated Bibliography of Luther Studies*, 3 volumes to date (1977–).

Jonathan Zophy, "Martin Luther, 1483–1546," *Research Guide to European Historical Biography*, vol. 7 (1994).

LUTHER BIOGRAPHIES

Roland Bainton, *Here I Stand: A Life of Martin Luther* (1950).

Heinrich Bornkamm, *Luther in Mid-Career, 1521–1530* (1983).

Martin Brecht, *Martin Luther*, 3 vols. (1985–1994). The leading biography.

A. G. Dickens, *The German Nation and Martin Luther* (1974).

Mark Edwards, Jr., *Luther and the False Brethren* (1975).

———, *Luther's Last Battles* (1983).

Richard Friedenthal, *Luther: His Life and Times* (1967).

Leif Grane, *Martinus Noster: Luther in the German Reform Movement, 1518–1521* (1994).

Eric Gritsch, *Martin—God's Court Jester* (1983).

H. G. Haile, *Luther: An Experiment in Biography* (1980).

James Kittelson, *Luther the Reformer* (1986).

Walter von Loewenich, *Martin Luther* (1986).

Bernhard Lohse, *Martin Luther: An Introduction to His Life and Work* (1986).

Peter Manns, *Martin Luther: An Illustrated Biography* (1982).

Heiko Oberman, *Luther: Man between God and the Devil* (1989).

John Todd, *Luther: A Life* (1982).

LUTHER'S THOUGHT

Paul Althaus, *The Theology of Martin Luther* (1966).

Gerhard Brendler, *Martin Luther: Theology and Revolution* (1991).

J. Cargil Thompson, *The Political Thought of Martin Luther* (1984).

Brian Gerrish, *Grace and Reason: A Study in the Theology of Luther* (1962).

Scott Hendrix, *Luther and the Papacy* (1981).

Alister McGrath, *Luther's Theology of the Cross* (1985).

Gordon Rupp, *The Righteousness of God* (1953).

David Steinmetz, *Luther in Context* (1986).

SOME OF LUTHER'S EARLY ASSOCIATES

Calvin Pater, *Karlstadt as the Father of the Baptist Movement: The Emergence of Lay Protestantism* (1993).

Ronald Sider, *Andreas Bodenstein von Karlstadt* (1974).

David Steinmetz, *Misericordia Dei: The Theology of Johannes von Staupitz in Its Late Medieval Setting* (1968).

THE KNIGHTS' REVOLT

William Hitchcock, *The Background of the Knights' Revolt, 1522–1523* (1958).

Hajo Holborn, *Ulrich von Hutten and the German Reformation* (1937).

Notes

1. Cited in Heiko Oberman, *Luther: Man between God and the Devil*, trans. Eileen Walliser-Schwarzbart (New Haven, Conn.: Yale University Press, 1989), p. 87.

2. Cited in James Kittelson, *Luther the Reformer: The Story of the Man and His Career* (Minneapolis, Minn.: Augsburg, 1986), p. 50.

3. Cited in Eric Gritsch, *Martin—God's Court Jester:*

Luther in Retrospect (Philadelphia: Fortress Press, 1983), p. 7.

4. Cited in Hans Hillerbrand, *The Reformation: A Narrative History Related by Contemporary Observers and Participants* (New York: Harper and Row, 1964), p. 27.
5. Ibid., p. 43.
6. Cited in Kittelson, *Luther,* pp. 103–104.
7 Martin Luther, "Ninety-five Theses," in Helmut Lehman and Jaroslav Pelikan, eds., *Luther's Works,* 55 vols. (St. Louis and Philadelphia: Concordia and Fortress Presses, 1955–1975), vol. 31, p. 33.
8. Cited in E. R. Chamberlin, *The Bad Popes* (New York: Dial Press, 1969), p. 248.
9. Cited in Roland Bainton, *Here I Stand: A Life of Martin Luther* (New York: Abingdon, 1950), p. 85.
10. Cited in Jonathan Zophy, *Patriarchal Politics and Christoph Kress (1484–1535) of Nuremberg* (Lewiston, N.Y.: Edwin Mellen Press, 1992), p. 64.
11. Cited in Scott Hendrix, "We Are All Hussites," *Archive for Reformation History,* 65 (1974), p. 134.
12. Cited in Lewis Spitz, ed., *The Protestant Reformation* (Englewood Cliffs, N.J.: Prentice Hall, 1966), p. 55.
13. Ibid., pp. 63–67.
14. Cited in Oberman, *Luther,* p. 39.
15. Cited in Hillerbrand, *Reformation,* p. 94.
16. Ibid., p. 100.
17. Ibid., p. 100.
18. Cited in Kittelson, *Luther,* p. 158.

11

The Spread of Lutheranism

A New Pope and New Hope, 1522–1524

While the Knights' Revolt was brewing, Pope Leo X died and the College of Cardinals elected the reform-minded Adrian of Utrecht as his replacement to the throne of St. Peter. A native of the Low Countries, Adrian was the only non-Italian to be elected in the sixteenth century and the only non-Italian to serve in that office until John Paul II of Poland was elected in 1978. Adrian had been a professor of theology and an administrator at the University of Louvain in the Netherlands before joining the service of the Habsburgs. Emperor Maximilian I hired him in 1510 to tutor his grandson and heir, Charles. Charles loved his tutor and had him promoted to a series of high church offices in Spain. In 1517, at the behest of Charles as king of Spain, Leo X made Adrian a cardinal.

As pope, Adrian VI recognized the need for reform in the church. Although he had supported the condemnation of Martin Luther's teachings by the theological faculty of his former university at Louvain, Adrian opposed the corruption found in the College of Cardinals as well as pluralism, simony, and nepotism. Even though Adrian's call for a general church council to reform abuses and clarify doctrines was rejected by those afraid of change, the pope did appoint a Reform Commission and was prepared to

act on its recommendations when he died of the plague in 1523 after a promising reign of just twenty months. Few realized then that when Adrian VI died, the best hope for a peaceful Reformation died with him. Many in Rome hated Adrian's threat to the status quo and openly celebrated his demise. Although Adrian's successor, Clement VII, was a Medici, he lacked his family's characteristic boldness and thus had no stomach to take on the vested interests that were determined to block change.

THE DIETS OF NUREMBERG, 1522–1524

Back in Germany, three successive Imperial Diets met in the town of Nuremberg between 1522 and 1524. They were all presided over by the emperor's younger brother, Archduke Ferdinand (1503–1564), because Emperor Charles V had pressing business to attend to in Spain and elsewhere. Although educated in Spain, the affable Ferdinand made every effort to learn German and become "one of the boys" with the hard-drinking and partying princes of the empire. This was in direct contrast to his more somber older brother, who always seemed stiff and remote to many and became more and more a Spaniard as he aged rapidly.

The three Imperial Diets at Nuremberg also had pressing business including the "Luther affair" and the enforcement of the Edict of Worms against Luther. However, other matters took priority, for the Ottomans had taken the important fortress city of Belgrade in the Balkans in 1521 and the island of Rhodes in the eastern Mediterranean. If Christendom fell to the Ottoman crescent, it might not really matter whether or not the Edict of Worms against the Lutherans had been enforced or whether capitalist monopolies had been crushed. Archduke Ferdinand found himself in a weak position for pressing the German powers to eliminate the Lutherans. The Habsburgs had to move cautiously. When Ferdinand tried to get the estates to take decisive action against the Lutherans, they answered with lists of grievances against the church and called for a general council to reform the church. The 1524 Diet of Nuremberg decreed that "until a church council should meet, the holy Gospel should be preached according to old and established interpretations."[1] The language was sufficiently vague to allow the followers of Luther and other reformers additional time to continue to win converts despite the horrors associated with the peasant revolts, which raged throughout the German-speaking world from 1524 to 1526.

THE SPREAD OF LUTHERANISM:
THE CASE OF NUREMBERG

After a religious debate, the government of Nuremberg officially adopted Lutheranism in March 1525. This meant that one of the largest of the towns in the empire had become an outpost of Wittenberg in the heart of Germany. As the storage place of the imperial jewelry and regalia and host of three successive Imperial Diets, as well as the seat of the Imperial Council of Regency and the Imperial Supreme Court, Nuremberg was virtually the capital city of the Holy Roman Empire. Therefore, its adoption of

Lutheranism put the Catholic Habsburgs in an extremely awkward position. Understanding how this came to be is important for comprehending the rapid spread of the Reformation, even if other communities adopted the reform for somewhat different reasons and under a bewildering variety of circumstances. Most of the empire's large towns witnessed some sort of reform movement.

The way toward Reformation in Nuremberg had been paved for the introduction of evangelical ideas by an elite humanist group made up of members of the town's intellectual and business elite. It included the patrician Willibald Pirckheimer, the city secretary Lazarus Spengler, the artist Albrecht Dürer, and several leading members of the ruling city council. Therefore, some of the wealthiest and most prominent men in Nuremberg had an early exposure to the ideas of Martin Luther, who twice visited the city in 1518 and made several important friends. In addition to his attacks on clerical abuses, Luther's message offered hope for the release from the burdens of guilt imposed by traditional Catholic beliefs and practices such as regular confessions of sins. As Albrecht Dürer put it:

> In my opinion, it is exactly here that Luther has helped to clarify the situation by making it a point to trust God more than oneself, worldly works, and the laws of human beings. . . . For I believe it is wrong to confuse individuals with a sense of sins, errors, and doubts.[2]

Luther's emphasis on salvation through faith struck a positive chord in the hearts and minds of many Nurembergers. Many also liked his notion of vocation, which stressed that all honest work is useful in serving God. It is little wonder that a number of Nuremberg craftspeople such as the cobbler-poet Hans Sachs saluted Luther as the "Wittenberg nightingale." The lawyer Christoph Scheurl declared in 1520 that "the patriciate, the multitude of other citizens, and all scholars stand on Luther's side."[3] That is why between 1520 and 1522, the city government appointed a series of church officials who had either been Luther's students at Wittenberg or had been converted by his writings. The most prominent of them was Andreas Osiander (1498–1552), who became the pastor of the town's major church and the leading theological advisor to the government.

The appointment of Lutheran preachers not only helped consolidate the hold of Luther's ideas upon the people of Nuremberg, but it also allowed the city government to assert its independence from the pope and its nearby ecclesiastical overlord, the bishop of Bamberg. For centuries, Nuremberg had struggled to become free of the political authority of the neighboring margraves of Brandenburg-Ansbach. A similar pattern developed with respect to the church. In 1474 the city gained the right to nominate candidates for the position of provost at each of its two major parish churches. In 1514 Pope Leo X granted the Nuremberg government full patronage rights over all the city's churches. With the adoption of Lutheranism in 1525, the Nuremberg merchant oligarchy had assumed complete ecclesiastical sovereignty, including the right to supervise the cloistered clergy inside the city and its territory. If the paternalistic patriarchs of the city government could regulate all aspects of the social life of the town, should they not be able to control the religious life of their citizens as well? It was an opportunity for power too tempting to miss and Nuremberg's city council seized the opportunity which Luther's revolt had brought them.

Not everyone in Nuremberg was pleased with the adoption of the reform. Many of the city's monks and nuns resented bitterly the efforts in the spring of 1525 to close their cloisters. The most spirited resistance to the Reformation was offered by the nuns of St. Clare's Convent, led by the learned Abbess Caritas Pirckheimer, the sister of the prominent humanist Willibald Pirckheimer and a skilled Latinist. She used all her political connections and passive resistance to keep her convent open despite Nuremberg's official adoption of Lutheranism. Several daughters of prominent Lutheran politicians had to be dragged from the convent. Finally, the diplomatic Philip Melanchthon interceded on behalf of the nuns after meeting with Caritas. He recommended that the town fathers proceed more carefully with the nuns of St. Clare's, whose piety and learning he admired. Melanchthon recommended that the nuns not be allowed to take new members or receive their Franciscan preachers, but that essentially they be left alone. The Nuremberg government followed Melanchthon's advice and the convent survived until 1590.

The German Peasants' War, 1524–1526

The often fragile nature of social relations in the first decades of the sixteenth century and the potential for class warfare were illustrated by the German Peasants' War. Frequent late medieval agrarian revolts had established a tradition of peasant insurrection. Clerical and noble landlords had ruthlessly exploited their farm workers and violated village rights and customs. Commoners also complained that they were denied access to the markets of their choice, or were forced to sell to their lords at unfairly low prices.

Some areas were overpopulated and some territories such as Alsace, Franconia, and the Upper Rhine suffered failed harvests for nearly two decades. Because a largely agriculturally based economy seldom produced much beyond subsistence, the hunger, disease, ignorance, and collective misery in the 1520s were alarming.

Political grievances were also a major factor in the Peasants' Revolt. The rising territorial states often replaced local communal self-government with the rule of district officials. To create a uniformity of administration and legal practice, customary law was being replaced by Roman law, changes that many peasants found unsettling. Efforts were made in some areas to bind the peasants to the land by reimposing serfdom. New taxes on beer, wine, milling, and slaughtering of farm animals were also deeply resented, as was the insistence of some church officials on the payments of *tithes* (the tenth of one's income) even during times of poor harvests.

The beginnings of the Reformation in Germany only intensified feelings of anticlericalism among the peasantry and some artisans in the towns. Martin Luther's emphasis on the universal priesthood of all believers gave new importance to the role of the laity in the affairs of the church. Some working people interpreted Luther's call for Christian liberty as an invitation to take more control over their own lives. Reform propagandists popularized the ideal of "Karsthans," the evangelical peasant who stood closer to God than a priest. The challenge to the authority of the Roman Catholic Church resulted in some villages insisting on the right to elect their own clergy. Peasants also began to justify their demands not only in terms of traditional law but also in terms of divine law and Scripture. Even some of the so-called "simple folk" of Germany had a sense that change was possible.

Albrecht Dürer, *Market Peasants*, 1512. Woodcut. Foto Marburg/Art Resource.

THE OUTBREAK OF THE REVOLT, MAY 1524

Astrologers had long predicted that 1524 would be a year of disasters and for once they were right. This notion was supported by the popular saying, "He who does not die in 1523, does not drown in 1524, and is not killed in 1525 can truly speak of miracles."[4] On May 30, 1524, subjects of the Black Forest abbey of St. Blasien rebelled against their overlord, declaring that they would pay no more feudal dues and render no more feudal services. This was followed by work stoppages at Stühlingen in the southern

Black Forest on June 24. Here the peasants were incensed by Count Sigismund's restrictions on self-government in the peasant communities. When the count refused to negotiate in good faith, peasant groups, led by the former soldier Hans Müller, began to march through the Black Forest, raising the standard of rebellion. The rebels found sympathy and ready allies among the citizens of the town of Waldschut, led by their reform-minded pastor, Balthasar Hubmaier, the future Anabaptist leader.

The revolt soon spread throughout many parts of southern Germany. Both Archduke Ferdinand of Austria and the Swabian League found it impossible to take immediate steps against the dissidents, for nearly all available military forces were committed to the second Habsburg war with France in northern Italy. The Swabian League was bogged down by its cumbersome organizational and financial structure and Catholic members of the league suspected that towns friendly to Luther, such as Nuremberg, were secretly plotting with the peasant rebels. Although some town artisans were supportive of the peasants, their governments were not. They began sending the Swabian League military aid and money. The league eventually sorted out some of its internal problems and created an effective command structure under George Truchsess von Waldburg, their commander during the war against the Franconian knights of 1523. Then came the news that the Habsburgs had won the Battle of Pavia and captured the French king on February 24, 1525. That allowed some of the Habsburgs' allies to transfer military resources to Germany. With the arrival of fresh troops from the end of the second Habsburg-Valois War, the Swabian League was ready to strike with nearly full force against the rebellious peasants.

THOMAS MÜNTZER (C. 1490–1525)

While the privileged orders were organizing their forces, the radical reformer Thomas Müntzer was hard at work among the dissidents in the Klettgau region for eight weeks. A Saxon native, he had studied at Leipzig, Frankfurt, and Mainz. As early as 1518, he became a partisan of Martin Luther. With the Wittenberger's help, Müntzer secured a pastorate in the town of Zwickau, where he came under the influence of Nicholas Storch, one of the "Zwickau prophets." Increasingly radicalized and frustrated by the slow pace of reform, Müntzer was ousted from Zwickau in April 1521. He fled to Prague, where he also got in trouble with local authorities. In the spring of 1523, Müntzer secured a pastorate at the town of Allstedt in Saxony.

There he fully developed his sense of himself as an Old Testament-style prophet. He began to openly challenge the more conservative Martin Luther for being "slavishly bound to the Gospel" and for not recognizing the continuing revelation of the Holy Spirit.[5] His sermons became increasingly apocalyptic as he foresaw the destruction of the godless by the elect of God and the coming of the reign of Christ on earth. Duke Johann of Saxony, who attended one of his sermons in July 1524, was alarmed by Müntzer's radicalism and ordered him to leave his pastorate. He fled to Mühlhausen, where an ex-priest named Heinrich Pfeiffer was leading a revolution.

Under the spell of Pfeiffer and his associates and his own arrogance, Müntzer now saw the rebellious peasants and their urban artisan allies as God's chosen instruments for the war of the godly against the godless. He moved to Thuringia and then to Saxony urging the peasants in sermons and pamphlets that now was the time to strike.

Urged on by Müntzer, Pfeiffer, and others during February and March 1525, major peasant armies developed in Upper Swabia, Franconia, and Thuringia. Groups of rebels began seizing lands, burning castles, and looting churches and monasteries. Fearing destruction, several town governments cooperated with peasant bands.

The Swabian League under George Truchsess von Waldburg led the counterattack in Franconia. Waldburg's ferocity had been increased by the gruesome death of his cousin Count Ludwig von Helfenstein, who had been forced to walk through a gauntlet of peasant spears along with thirteen other nobles and ten of their servants. Helfenstein and the others were then executed while his former servant Jäcklin Rohrbach piped a tune. When Waldburg captured Rohrbach, he had him bound to a tree by an iron chain long enough to allow the captive to move two feet from the tree. Wood was then piled around the tree and the piper was slowly roasted to death.

Elsewhere, the evangelical Philip of Hesse and the convinced Catholic Duke George of Saxony joined forces on May 15, 1525 to attack rebellious peasants at Frankenhausen, near Luther's birthplace. Thomas Müntzer hurried to Frankenhausen with 300 reinforcements, but even his presence and fiery oratory could not save the day for the outgunned peasants. The bloody Battle of Frankenhausen ended in a complete rout of the peasants and the end of the Peasants' War in Thuringia. The victors arrested Müntzer, viciously tortured him, and later executed him and fifty-two other peasant leaders.

The End of the 1524–1526 Peasants' War

The Swabian League defeated peasant armies at Königshofen (near the Tauber River due west of Nuremberg) on June 2 and at Ingolstadt on June 4. Even with some professional military help, the rebels were no match for the better trained, more powerful, and determined forces arrayed against them. After being crushed in battle, the armies of poor people were often subject to brutal reprisals including exile, fines, blindings, torture, and imprisonment. Margrave Casimir of Brandenburg-Ansbach (1481–1527) was particularly cruel in his treatment of vanquished rebels. He ordered the blinding of sixty rebels at Kitzingen and had to be restrained from doing further damage by his brother, George, who pointed out to him that if Casimir blinded too many of his subjects he would have no one left to wait upon him or work his fields.

George, known for his piety, also persuaded his more temperamental brother that the real cause of the peasants' revolt in Franconia was the lack of uniformity in preaching. George recommended that "unlearned and unsuitable preachers be exiled" and replaced with "pious, honorable Christian preachers who would preach the Word of God purely and cleanly."[6] By this George meant Lutheran preachers. Casimir was eventually persuaded to go along with his brother's plea and on August 30, 1525 he issued an edict exiling all Catholic clergy from Brandenburg-Ansbach and replacing them with Lutherans. Thus, another important territory had been converted to Lutheranism by the actions of its rulers.

Some of the victors, such as Christoph Kress of Nuremberg and one of the Swabian League's military advisors, tried to restrain their more zealous colleagues because many "knew how these people (the peasants) were brought to rebellion and the insufferable burdens with which they have been oppressed."[7] Moderation was also urged because they recognized how much their privileges depended on the hard work of the poor. Kress was able to get punishments lessened, including those levied on the towns of Dinkelsbühl, Heilbronn, Rothenburg on the Tauber, and Windsheim, which Margrave Casimir accused of having collaborated with the rebels. Nuremberg, which had officially adopted Lutheranism after a public debate in March 1525, even loaned some of its smaller neighbors the money to pay their fines to the Swabian League.

Peace came last to Austria, where a rebellion had first broken out in Brixen on May 9, 1525. The rebels plundered religious houses and noble castles and joined in opposition to the payment of church tithes. They elected Michael Gaismair, the bishop of Brixen's former secretary, as their leader. Gaismair proved a surprising combination of practical military strategist and utopian dreamer. Later, outside of Salzburg, he called for the establishment of a Christian, egalitarian, democratic republic that would care for the poor, ensure speedy justice for all, effect coinage and tax reforms, and guarantee the free preaching of the Word of God. By July 1526, forces from the Swabian League and the archbishop of Salzburg defeated Gaismair's motley army. Gaismair escaped to anti-Habsburg Venice, where a Habsburg agent assassinated him in 1532.

The Peasants' War of 1524 to 1526 resulted in the death of approximately 100,000 peasants and artisans. Most of the dead were males, but a few females, such as the runaway serf Margaret Rennerin, joined in the fighting. Sixty women rebels were known to have stormed a convent at Windsheim on May 5, 1525. Other women cooked, did laundry, nursed the wounded, sold goods, and tended camp for the peasant armies. Some worked as prostitutes. Most of the wives and daughters of warring peasants stayed at home and worked the land in their husband's or father's absence.

Many were left with a great sense of loss and betrayal.

MARTIN LUTHER AND THE PEASANTS' WAR

As a child of working people, Martin Luther was sympathetic to the injustices under which many men and women labored. However, he was as opposed to peasant violence as he was to knightly violence. For him, social and economic grievances were to be addressed peacefully and out of Christian love. When the rebels refused to lay down their weapons, he became convinced that the devil was at work among the rebels and in anger he wrote *Against the Robbing and Murdering Horde of Peasants* in May 1525. Luther urged the authorities "to slay, stab, and smite" the rebels lest even more bloodshed follow as the rebellion spread.[8] Of course, the frightened authorities needed no exhortation from Luther to take stern measures against the rebels.

Some peasants felt betrayed by Luther and returned to their traditional Catholic beliefs. Promises to address peasant and artisan grievances at the next Imperial Diet were never kept. The rich and the powerful seldom concern themselves with the problems of the humble folk. In contrast, Martin Luther continued to be concerned about the oppression of the working people and had high hopes that the message of the Gospel about love and charity would lead to an improvement in the way the ruling classes treated those below them on the social scale. His belief was that better Christians would make better masters.

Katherine von Bora (1499–1550)

In the midst of the great crisis of the Peasants' War, the celibate ex-friar Martin Luther married a former nun, Katherine von Bora. At age ten she had been placed in a convent by her recently remarried father, who found, as had so many others, that unwanted children could become "brides of Christ" for smaller dowries than more earthly bridegrooms and their parents usually required. Katherine was not completely fulfilled by convent life, for when she read Luther's writings against clerical vows and monastic celibacy she decided to flee the cloisters. Katherine and twelve of her fellow nuns hid in empty barrels used for transporting smoked herring and bravely made their escape on the eve of Easter 1523.

Three of the nuns were taken in by their families, but Katherine and eight of her "sisters" ended up at Luther's Wittenberg. Runaway nuns who were not great beauties or lacked disposable wealth were becoming an increasingly difficult problem for the early Reformation. Efforts to marry Katherine failed and after two years in Wittenberg, Luther decided to marry her himself. He figured it was a good way to please his father, "spite the devil, and upset the pope."[9] As for Katherine, she liked Luther enough to marry him and eventually grew to love him deeply.

Learning to cherish the forty-two-year-old professor who had spent so much of his adult life in all-male schools and monasteries proved at times to be a difficult task for Katherine. Luther had failed to change the straw in his bedding for a full year prior to their wedding night. The straw was so worn that it decomposed beneath the weight of their lovemaking, which the formerly celibate ex-monk enjoyed enormously. He boasted to friends about his newly discovered, mid-life sexuality: "I now go to bed each night with a beautiful woman and that is my Katie."[10] Six children followed in rapid succession from this union.

Martin Luther proved to be a tender-

Lucas Cranach the Elder, *Portrait of Katherine von Bora*, Uffizi, Florence, Italy. Alinari/Art Resource.

hearted, loving husband and father who shared in parental responsibilities to an unusual degree. The reformer was one of the first husbands to publicly advocate a form of partnership in marriage. He admired his wife's resourcefulness in stretching his modest academic salary so that he could entertain visiting dignitaries and homesick students alike. Katherine took in paying boarders and ran a successful small farm. She brewed excellent beer that Luther enjoyed immensely, though in moderation. Although usually deferring to her more learned husband, she was not afraid to speak her own mind at times even when she disagreed with him.

Partly through his association with Katherine and his daughters as well as through contacts with educated noble-women with whom he corresponded, Luther came to appreciate some of women's gifts. He even became one of the first prominent advocates of elementary schooling for girls and helped women find jobs as elementary schoolteachers. He continued, however, to see women as equal to men "only in Christ." In this world, women were best confined to the domestic sphere, and they were not to assume too many public responsibilities, according to Luther. For example, he admired Argula von Grumbach (b. 1492) for defending him in writing to the faculty of Johann Eck's University of Ingolstadt, but he still did not want even a learned woman like her or Katherine Zell of Strasbourg to be ministers. At his cherished home, Martin Luther remained a benevolent patriarch to the end.

The Emergence of Evangelical Politics

Although religious motivations had been an important factor in the origins of the Reformation, political considerations became a crucial factor in determining the very survival of the various reform movements inside the empire and in the Swiss Confederation. Had Charles V exercised the kind of direct power over his subjects in Germany that he did in Spain, Luther would most likely have been burned as a heretic and his movement suppressed in its infancy. Even the parallel Swiss reform movements of Huldrych Zwingli and his colleagues in Bern and Basel would probably not have been able to hold out had they been completely surrounded by hostile Catholic forces. Further complicating the situation in the empire was the real threat posed by the advancing armies of the Ottomans. There-

fore, the decentralized structure of the Holy Roman Empire and the military and political developments of 1526 and after were of critical importance for the spread of the reform movements.

The Diets of Speyer, 1526 and 1529

As Martin Luther was experiencing the joys and sorrows of wedded life, the estates of the Holy Roman Empire met in the episcopal town of Speyer on the Rhine in late June 1526. Again Archduke Ferdinand presided in place of his absentee brother; again reports reached the dignitaries that the "Grand Turk" was once more on the march. More towns and principalities had turned "Evangelical," so many that Ferdinand had to agree to permit "each one to live, govern, and carry himself as he hopes to answer it to God and His Imperial Majesty."[11] In other words, the principle of "he who rules, his religion" (*cuius regio eius religio*) would be the order of the day until the long-awaited general church council could meet.

Again the main reason for the compromise was the need to gain support for the war against the Ottomans, who now threatened central Hungary, defended by its king and Ferdinand's brother-in-law, Louis II. On August 23, the Diet of Speyer voted to dispatch 24,000 troops (a great force by sixteenth-century standards) to aid Louis against the Ottomans. However, it was too little, too late as Sultan Süleyman's forces crushed the Hungarians and killed King Louis on August 29 at Mohács, along with 500 of his nobles and nearly 20,000 troops. Hungary was devastated and all of Europe now seemed exposed and vulnerable. Fortunately for the Habsburgs, the Ottomans were unable to follow up on this great victory. Noble Ottoman landowners, who served as officers, were obligated to return to their estates at regular intervals to supervise their underlings. This made sustained campaigning over long periods of time an impossibility.

Although the Ottomans did not continue their advance into central Europe, the Evangelicals proceeded to gain converts and to consolidate gains already made. Martin Luther aided the spread of the reform movement by continuing to publish tracts explaining his theology. He also composed hymns mostly based on the Psalms, which enriched Evangelical worship. Perhaps his best-known musical composition is "A Mighty Fortress Is Our God," a hymn based on Psalm 46. The Reformation thus kept spreading in repeated bursts of art (chiefly woodcuts), printed pamphlets, sermons, song, and, above all, word of mouth. If many Germans felt repressed by guilt, they found a form of liberation in Luther's emphasis on the righteousness of God.

As for Luther's opponents, they were embarrassed when segments of Charles V's army in Italy viciously sacked the city of Rome in the summer of 1527. Imperial paymasters had failed to pay Charles's mercenaries in time, and some of them decided to enrich themselves in Rome on the wealth of the church. Pope Clement was a virtual prisoner until order could be restored. That loyal son of the church, Charles V, while deploring the lack of discipline in his army, took advantage of the situation to broker a new understanding with the pope, who had been allied against the emperor's ambitions in Italy.

By the time the German estates met again at Speyer in March 1529, the Habsburgs were determined to deal harshly with the Evangelicals, who seemed in a weaker position than in 1526. By 1529 the Ottoman threat was widely known to be so grave that few would support Philip of Hesse or Duke Johann of Saxony (1468–1532) in threatening to withhold aid for the war against the Ottomans if the religious rights of the Evangelicals were not respected. Johann, known as the Constant, had replaced his brother Frederick (d. 1525) as duke of Saxony and was a committed supporter of Martin Luther. Taking advantage of divisions among the Evangelicals, the Catholic majority voted to revoke the compromise of 1526 on religion and return to "the ancient usages and customs until a general council should meet."[12]

Led by Philip of Hesse, Johann of Saxony, Christoph Kress of Nuremberg, and Jacob Sturm (1489–1553) of Strasbourg, the stunned Evangelicals protested the revocation of "he who rules, his religion" on April 30, 1529. The protest was denied by both Ferdinand and later by Charles V in Spain, but the label *Protestants* remained. The emperor even placed a protesting Evangelical delegation sent to him in Spain under house arrest. Relations between the Evangelicals and the Habsburgs were clearly eroding.

Fearing that the Habsburgs and the German Catholics were going to move against them militarily, Philip of Hesse and others began planning a Protestant military alliance. It seemed to the energetic Philip that theological unity among the Protestants would help facilitate political unity. Therefore, he invited the major Protestant theologians in the empire and Switzerland to come to his town of Marburg for a conference that started on the first of October. Most of the major Evangelical theologians of the day accepted including Martin Luther and his friend Philip Melanchthon. At Marburg, Luther met for the first time the famous leader of the Reformation in Zurich, Huldrych Zwingli. Zwingli had begun his own independent movement for reform at the same time as Luther's revolt. An intensely political theologian, he had extended his influence into other parts of Switzerland as well as into the Holy Roman Empire.

Despite their enormous egos, the Protestant theologians did manage to find many areas of doctrinal agreement, but they could not agree on the subject of the Eucharist. Luther continued to argue for a real presence of Christ in the sacrament; Zwingli favored a symbolic interpretation, and neither would budge on that key issue. They agreed to disagree on the Eucharist and to go their separate ways. Luther never fully trusted Zwingli and believed he was really a radical at heart like Karlstadt. By the time preparations were underway for the next Imperial Diet at Augsburg in the summer of 1530, the Protestants had achieved neither a theological nor a political unified front. They were, however, pleased with the news that at least the Ottomans had failed to take Vienna in the fall of 1529. Most of the politically sophisticated people in the empire recognized that if the Ottomans took well-fortified Vienna, they could easily penetrate into the heart of Germany itself.

The Augsburg Confession of 1530

With the Ottomans now concentrating on taking the rest of Hungary from its new king, the emperor's brother Ferdinand, Charles V announced that he would come to Augsburg, Germany to preside over the next meeting of the Imperial Diet. Charles was determined to deal with the Protestants, but he took a more conciliatory tack this time, addressing Johann of Saxony, for example, as "Dear Uncle." Although many remained skeptical about the emperor's tolerance for varying religious ideas, others were hopeful that if Charles would only give the Protestants a fair hearing, he would

discover what good Christians they were and let them live in peace. The problem, of course, was that Charles had no intention of letting his German subjects reject the pope's authority and, by extension, his own. Emperors saw themselves as representatives of Christ; Charles's grandfather, Maximilian, had dreamed of combining the imperial and papal crowns.

PHILIP MELANCHTHON (1497–1560)

Some took Charles at his word that for this meeting at Augsburg, "animosities would be set aside, all past errors left to the judgment of our Savior, and every man given a charitable hearing."[13] Johann of Saxony decided to take Charles seriously and ordered his theologians to draw up a statement of their Protestant beliefs called a "confession." The chief author of the so-called Augsburg Confession was Philip Melanchthon, Luther's colleague and close friend. Born in Bretten near Karlsruhe, Melanchthon was the son of an armor manufacturer. After the death of his father in 1507, the direction of Philip's education was assumed by his great uncle, the talented humanist Johann Reuchlin. After studies at Heidelberg (B.A., 1511) and Tübingen (M.A., 1514), Melanchthon joined the faculty of the University of Wittenberg in 1518 as an instructor in Greek and the classics. There he became a close friend of Martin Luther, despite the difference in their ages and temperaments.

In 1521 Philip Melanchthon published the first edition of the *Loci Communes*, a much admired basic text for teaching Evangelical theology. Melanchthon was a much more systematic thinker and writer than Luther, who compared his own writings to "grapeshot." Luther very much appreciated his colleague and said of him, Master

Melanchthon "towers above" the doctors of theology. Luther knew his views were well represented by his brilliant colleague. Furthermore, Melanchthon could work inside the walls of Augsburg unlike Luther, who was still an outlaw and had to wait impatiently for news of events from the relative safety of another Saxon castle at Coburg.

The conciliatory Melanchthon worked diligently to provide a confessional statement that surprised Emperor Charles with its mildness. The Zwinglians and others also presented separate theological statements to the emperor. Charles, not willing to play the role of arbitrator of theological disputes, appointed a committee of "qualified theologians" led by Luther's great debate opponent at Leipzig, Johann Eck, to examine the Lutheran statement of belief. Two weeks later Eck returned a 351-page rebuttal to Melanchthon's "Confession." Eck's language was so polemical and abusive that Emperor Charles ordered it toned down and refused to allow the Protestants to see it until it was revised. The emperor still needed Protestant support for his war against the feared Ottomans.

Finally on August 3, 1530, Eck's truncated 31-page report, known as the *Confutation,* was read and it completely maintained the existing papal status quo. Speaking as a stern but kindly father figure, Charles insisted that the Protestants must accept the *Confutation,* renounce their heresies, return to the holy church of Rome, or face his righteous wrath. The Protestant diplomats responded that they must first be allowed to study Eck's report before they could respond. His patience at an end, the emperor refused them even this courtesy and insisted on their immediate obedience to his will.

The Protestants stalled for time and warded off various imperial efforts to divide them with gifts and promises. Many, like the disappointed Elector Johann of Saxony, simply left the diet early and in disgust. Although those who remained did vote to supply the Habsburgs with 40,000 infantry and 8,000 cavalry, the Protestant minority refused to abandon their new religious understandings and prepared to organize themselves militarily in case the emperor decided to back up his deadline of April 15, 1531 for submission with force. The emperor's threats had only served to stiffen the Protestant backbone, although some like the Nurembergers still hoped the situation would not degenerate into a religious civil war.

THE FORMATION OF THE SCHMALKALDIC LEAGUE

The failure of the Diet of Augsburg to heal the religious divisions in the empire led to a renewed effort on the part of Landgrave Philip of Hesse and others to form a military alliance among Protestants in defense of the Gospel. Philip and a number of others believed that if the emperor refused to allow his subjects to worship freely, he could be resisted by them as lesser magistrates, who were also ordained by God if below the emperor in status. Even that committed monarchist Martin Luther was now persuaded that he might have to drop his opposition to taking up arms against the emperor if Charles persisted in his efforts to destroy the religious faith of his Protestant subjects. However, Luther still hoped desperately, even as late as 1542, that peace might prevail. He wrote the Protestant princes:

> Even if somebody were to kill my father or brother, I am not judge or avenger. What need is there for laws and authorities, what need for God, if everybody wanted himself to be judge, avenger, even God over his neighbor, especially in worldly matters.[14]

By then a majority of Protestants had agreed at the town of Schmalkalden in the winter of 1530–1531 to form a military league to protect each other. Eight Protestant princes led by Philip of Hesse and Johann of Saxony and ten cities led by Strasbourg and Ulm had agreed that:

> Whenever any one of us is attacked on account of the Word of God and the doctrine of the Gospel, all the others shall immediately come to his assistance as best they can.[15]

There were some important defections from this show of Protestant military solidarity. Mighty Nuremberg and some of its satellite towns refused to commit themselves to the Schmalkaldic League. Nuremberg was joined in its refusal by its princely neighbor, Brandenburg-Ansbach, now ruled solely by the Lutheran Margrave George. Philip of Hesse and Johann of Saxony still hoped that the Nurembergers and Margrave George would change their collective minds and join the Schmalkaldic League at a later date.

Luther's Declining Years, 1530–1546

People aged much more rapidly in the sixteenth century than they do now. Indeed the average life expectancy then was only about half of what it is now in the United States, where many people expect to live well beyond their seventies. Luther had just turned forty-eight when the Schmalkaldic League was formalized in January 1531. A lifelong workaholic with fluctuating mood swings, he would deteriorate steadily in the last two decades of his life while continuing to be a caring family man, pastor, and professor. Luther had long been a man who seemed to be caught in the tensions between God and the devil. Often in his last years, the devil seemed to be getting the upper hand.

Martin Luther's decline reflected the continual pressures of events in his own life and the life of the world around him. Every year seemed to bring a new load of sorrows. His father died in 1530, followed rapidly, as so often is the case, by the death of his mother in 1531. Even the news that Emperor Charles had agreed to summon a church council within a year and stop his Imperial Supreme Court from proceeding against Protestants or their lands failed to lessen Luther's gloom or improve his health. The emperor had made these concessions to the Protestants because he again needed their help in defending Vienna from the Ottomans. Protestant aid arrived in time to help the Imperials defeat the Ottomans at Grens, sixty miles southeast of Vienna. In June 1533 Sultan Süleyman agreed to a peace treaty with the Habsburgs. Perhaps this time the peace would hold.

As for Martin Luther, his spirits eventually rose again as he fathered several more children, in whom he delighted, and managed to complete his German translation of the Bible in 1534. His completed Bible was a great literary success and helped make him one of the "fathers" of the modern German language. Prior to Luther's day, German was a polyglot language—written and spoken in a bewildering array of dialects. Luther's writings were so popular and written in such a delightful style that later generations of Germans favored his method of using the language. He outpublished his rival reformers by a wide margin. Thus, Luther became one of the German equivalents to Geoffrey Chaucer for English, John Calvin and François Rabelais for French, and Miguel Cervantes for Spanish. If he had done nothing else, the German writings of

Martin Luther would have earned him a prominent place in history.

Yet Luther continued to be troubled by the fact that not everyone agreed with his religious teachings or seemed to have been transformed by them. Even his catechisms designed for young and old had failed to substantially alter the sinful behavior of many, or so the often ailing Luther complained. As the reformer aged he had increasingly identified himself with his biblical hero, the Apostle Paul. Like Paul, Martin Luther felt he had made clear some of God's greatest mysteries. Were people so steeped in pride and sin that they refused to accept the truth now that it had been so wonderfully revealed to them?

THE BIGAMY OF PHILIP OF HESSE

While fighting off painful attacks of uric acid stones, Luther was troubled by reports of the radical and violent Anabaptist takeover of the city of Münster in western Germany. His theological quarrels with opponents and some of his own colleagues in reform continued. In 1540 Luther's secret support for the bigamy of Philip of Hesse was made public and the reformer was mortified. Philip's sixteen-year-old political marriage to Christina, daughter of the Catholic Duke George of nonelectoral Saxony (1471–1539), had never been a happy one. Although Philip had ten children with Christina, he often complained of her coldness, smell, and drinking. Philip was a man of enormous sexual appetites and had further satisfied himself with numerous liaisons with various ladies of the court, despite frequent pangs of conscience. Now in late 1539 he was feeling the first symptoms of syphilis, the same disease that had killed his father. The leader of the Schmalkaldic

League had also fallen in love with one of the ladies of the court, seventeen-year-old Margaret von der Saal, and wanted to marry her.

Landgrave Philip unburdened himself to Luther and several of his ministerial colleagues, including Martin Bucer, the kindly and influential Strasbourg reformer. Earlier in 1526 when Philip wanted to marry another of his favorites, Luther had flatly said no. This time the pastors counseled Philip that a bigamous marriage was better than a divorce. After all, numerous Old Testament patriarchs had several wives and other German princes like Luther's patron Frederick the Wise had enjoyed irregular unions. The problem was that bigamy was against imperial law so Philip was admonished to keep his second marriage a secret and to give Margaret the status of "concubine" in public.

When the landgrave failed to keep his second marriage of 1540 a secret, both he and the pastors were publicly humiliated. Worse yet Philip had to promise Emperor Charles that he would retire from religious politics in exchange for immunity from prosecution on the bigamy matter. Just six years earlier, the landgrave had been instrumental in restoring the Protestant Duke Ulrich of Württemberg to his duchy and further spreading Protestantism. The Schmalkaldic League, which Philip had played a major role in creating, had lost a pillar of strength, and Luther had been part of an attempt to cover up a sordid affair.

LUTHER AND THE JEWS

Things went from bad to worse for Martin Luther when his beloved fourteen-year-old daughter Magdalena died in 1542. "I wish that I and all my children were dead!" he exclaimed publicly a few months after her death as plague raged through Wittenberg.[16] Increasingly the aging Luther was convinced that the Final Judgment was coming and that the sinful world would be destroyed. In his frustration, sorrow, anger, and rage, he now lashed out against the Jews in vitriolic pamphlets such as *Against the Jews and Their Lies* (1542). There he urged the authorities "to burn their synagogues and books, expel them from the cities and commerce if they refuse to convert."[17]

Luther also railed against the Anabaptists, Antinomians (those who denied the need for adherence to the law), Sacramentarians, the Ottomans, and the papacy, publishing *Against the Papacy at Rome Founded by the Devil* in 1545. He also failed to recognize the significance of the opening of the long-sought reform council in 1545 by Paul III (r. 1534–1549), the reform pope. Luther dismissed the gathering of church leaders at Trent as "too little, too late." As we shall see, Luther was completely mistaken.

Of all the harsh polemics in Luther's last years, his tirades against the Jews are particularly unsettling, even without considering to what horrible use they and those of others were put by Adolf Hitler and his partners in the twentieth-century European Holocaust. Here were the toxic fruits of religious fanaticism, bigotry, and cultural, if not racial, anti-Semitism. What is also tragic about Martin Luther's tirades against the Jews is that he had once been a good friend to a number of Jewish communities. In one of his writings, in 1523, he had reminded his growing audience *That Jesus Christ Was Born a Jew.* In an age where many blamed Jews instead of Romans for the death of Christ and believed lies about Jews sacrificing Christian children in ritual murder, Luther had once been a brave defender of Judaism, although he had always believed that Jews were "money grubbers."

With his health in decline, fearful of the Second Coming, and terribly frustrated by the failure of his missionary efforts, Martin Luther indulged in typical expressions of anti-Semitism common to his culture. Although he never urged people to form vigilante mobs to punish "stubborn Jews who fail to embrace the truth of the Christian Gospel while there is still time," Luther failed to intervene when his pious but heavy-drinking patron Duke Johann Frederick of Saxony (r. 1532–1547) exiled the Jews from his lands in 1536.[18] This was the beginning of a hardening of his heart against the Jews, which continued to his final moments. In his last sermon, preached at Eisleben on February 15, 1546, Martin Luther proclaimed that "the Jews are our enemies, who do not cease to defame Christ and would gladly kill us all if they could." However, "we want to practice Christian love toward them and pray that they convert."[19]

Overcome by feelings of weakness, Luther cut short his sermon and retired to his sickbed. There he said "yes" to his colleagues who asked him if he would "stand firm in Christ and the doctrine" he had preached. Three days later at 3 o'clock in the morning, Martin Luther's great heart burst. The man with seven heads was dead at age sixty-three. The Reformation, which he had been so instrumental in launching, would continue to spread even to the northern lands of Scandinavia and beyond.

Lutheranism in Scandinavia

While Philip Melanchthon and other associates of Luther struggled to lead the Lutheran movement in the Holy Roman Empire, Lutheranism also became entrenched in the Nordic lands. Early in Luther's career as a reformer, the last ruler of Scandinavia under the Union of Kalmar, Christian II of Denmark (r. 1513–1523), permitted Lutheran theologians to teach at the University of Copenhagen. Angered by his cruelty and despotic ways, Swedish barons led by Gustavus Vasa successfully revolted against Christian in 1520. They had been outraged by the execution of more than eighty leading members of the Swedish lay and ecclesiastical aristocracy in Stockholm in November 1520. The martryed nobles had called for Sweden's separation from the Danish crown. By 1523 Sweden was reestablished as an independent kingdom.

Christian's similar efforts to weaken the Danish aristocracy led to his replacement as king by his uncle, Duke Frederick of Schleswig-Holstein. Since King Frederick I (r. 1523–1533) was also favorably disposed to Lutheranism, more Lutheran preachers poured into the kingdom. They were led by Hans Tausen, who had studied at Luther's Wittenberg, and later Johann Bugenhagen (1485–1558), a native of the Baltic island of Wollin, who became the pastor of the city church in Wittenberg and a close friend of Martin Luther. A systematic organizer of churches, Bugenhagen helped organize the Evangelical movement in many parts of northern Germany and in Denmark between 1528 and 1543. He also made considerable contributions to the organization of social welfare in Scandinavia. Lutheranism proved exceedingly popular to Scandinavians who had grown tired of political instability and theological wrangling.

Frederick I followed the lead of his subjects and in 1526 openly broke with Rome and allowed the introduction of the Lutheran liturgy into church services. His son and successor, Christian III (r. 1533–1559) was already a staunch Lutheran when he came to the throne. Declaring himself to be the supreme authority in church matters, Christian encouraged the Norwegians to adopt Lutheranism. Not wanting to have their religious beliefs imposed upon them by their neighbors, some Norwegians resisted. Since diversity in religious opinion was not long tolerated in sixteenth-century Europe, Catholic Norwegians found themselves under great pressure to convert to the Lutheran state church. Eventually, all pockets of Roman Catholic resistance were eliminated, and Norway became a bastion of Lutheranism in the north.

The Lutheran Reformation took even longer to become entrenched in Sweden among the common people. Sweden's king, Gustavus Vasa (r. 1523–1560), coveted the wealth of the Roman Catholic Church and wanted the right to appoint its bishops. Breaking with Rome would allow him to do that and he could justify it as good for the souls of his subjects. Shrewdly, Gustavus encouraged reformers such as Olaus Petri (1493–1552), another former Wittenberg student, to evangelize and win converts. Later Petri would fall into disgrace for opposing the king's autocracy. His younger brother, Laurence (1499–1573), was more submissive and became the Lutheran archbishop of Uppsala. After years of careful preparation, King Gustavus Vasa assumed the headship of the church in Sweden in late 1539. Lutheranism offered kings what distant Rome could not—full sovereignty over church and state. Fortunately for monarchs, its doctrines also had broad popular appeal. Gustavus and his theological allies completed the reform in stages. By the Diet of Västeras of 1544, the Lutheran takeover was complete and legalized by royal decree. Sweden became a leading center for Lutheranism. His descendant, Gustavus II Adolphus (r. 1611–1632), would try to defend Protestantism during the Thirty Years' War.

Chronology

1520	Sweden breaks away from Christian II of Denmark.
1522	Adrian VI elected pope.
1523	Clement VII elected pope; Diet of Nuremberg defers action against the Lutherans.
1524	Erasmus publishes *On the Freedom of the Will*; beginnings of Peasants' Revolt.
1525	Battle of Pavia (capture of François I); death of Elector Frederick the Wise, succeeded by his brother Johann; Luther publishes *Against the Robbing and Murdering Hordes of Peasants*; Luther marries Katherine von Bora; Nuremberg turns Lutheran; death of Thomas Müntzer.
1526	Diet of Speyer adopts formula "he who rules, his religion"; Ottomans victorious in Hungary; Denmark breaks with Rome.
1527	Troops of Charles V sack Rome; frequently ill Luther composes hymn "A Mighty Fortress Is Our God."
1529	Evangelical protest at the Diet of Speyer; Marburg Colloquy; Ottomans at Vienna; Luther's German catechism.

1530	Presentation of the Augsburg Confession; formation of the Schmalkaldic League.
1532	Ottomans driven back from Austria; Religious Peace of Nuremberg.
1533–1559	Reign of Christian II; Norway becomes Lutheran.
1534	Publication of Luther's complete German Bible; Philip of Hesse and others restore Protestant Ulrich of Württemberg to his duchy.
1535	Münster Anabaptists.
1539	Sweden, under Gustavus Vasa, breaks with Rome.
1540	Bigamy of Philip of Hesse revealed; Mark of Brandenburg becomes Lutheran.
1542	Death of Magdalena Luther.
1543	Increasingly ill Luther publishes *Against the Jews*.
1544	Diet and Ordinances of Västeras complete Swedish reform.
1545	Paul III opens the Council of Trent; Luther publishes *Against the Papacy at Rome Founded by the Devil*.
1546	Death of Luther at Eisleben.

Further Reading

EARLY REFORMERS

Roland Bainton, *Women of the Reformation in Germany and Italy* (1971). Has useful profiles of Katherine von Bora and others.

James Estes, *Christian Magistrate and State Church: The Reforming Career of Johannes Brenz* (1982).

Clyde Manschreck, *Melanchthon, the Quiet Reformer* (1968).

C. A. Maxcey, *Bona Opera: A Study in the Development of the Doctrine of Grace in Philip Melanchthon* (1980).

R. Emmett McLaughlin, *Caspar Schwenckfeld, Reluctant Radical: His Life to 1540* (1986).

THE SPREAD OF THE REFORMATION

Miriam Chrisman, *Conflicting Visions of Reform: German Lay Propaganda Pamphlets 1519–1530* (1995).

Susan Karant-Nunn, *Zwickau in Transition, 1500–1547: The Reformation as an Agent of Change* (1987).

Bernd Moeller, *Imperial Cities and the Reformation* (1972).

Steven Ozment, *The Reformation in the Cities: The Appeal of Protestantism to Sixteenth-Century Germany and Switzerland* (1975).

Robert Scribner, *For the Sake of the Simple Folk: Popular Propaganda for German Reformation* (1981).

Paul Russell, *Lay Theology in the Reformation: Popular Pamphleteers in Southwest Germany, 1521–1525* (1986).

THE REFORMATION IN NUREMBERG

Harold Grimm, *Lazarus Spengler, A Lay Leader of the Reformation* (1978).

Gerald Strauss, *Nuremberg in the Sixteenth Century*, 2nd ed. (1976).

THE PEASANTS' WAR, 1524–1526

Peter Blickle, *Communal Reformation: The Search for Salvation in Reformation Germany* (1992).

———, *The Revolution of 1525*, trans. Thomas Brady, Jr. and H. C. Erik Midelfort (1981).

Lawrence Buck, "The Peasants' War," in J. Zophy, ed., *The Holy Roman Empire: A Dictionary Handbook* (1980).

Walter Klaassen, *Michael Gaismair* (1978).

Keith Moxey, *Peasants, Warriors, and Wives: Popular Imagery in the Reformation* (1989).

Tom Scott and Bob Scribner, eds., *The German Peasants' War* (1991). An excellent collection of primary source materials with very useful introductions.

Tom Scott, *Freiburg and the Breisgau: Town-Country Relations in the Age of Reformation and Peasants' War* (1986).

Bob Scribner and Gerhard Benecke, eds., *The German Peasant War 1525: New Viewpoints* (1979).

Kyle Sessions, ed., *Reformation and Authority: The Meaning of the Peasants' Revolt* (1968). Primary and secondary materials.

THOMAS MÜNTZER

Michael Baylor, ed. and trans., *Revelation and Revolution: Basic Writings of Thomas Müntzer* (1993).

Eric Gritsch, *Thomas Müntzer* (1989).

Abraham Friesen, *Thomas Muentzer, A Destroyer of the Godless* (1990).

Tom Scott, *Thomas Müntzer* (1989).

POLITICS OF THE EARLY REFORMATION

Thomas Brady, Jr., *Turning Swiss: Cities and Empire, 1450–1550* (1985).

Karl Brandi, *The Emperor Charles V* (1939).

Paula Sutter Fichtner, *Ferdinand I of Austria* (1982).

Hans Hillerbrand, *Landgrave Philip von Hesse* (1967).

Stanford Shaw, *Empire of the Gazis: The Rise and Decline of the Ottoman Empire, 1280–1808* (1976).

Jonathan Zophy, *Patriarchal Politics and Christoph Kress (1484–1535) of Nuremberg* (1992).

SCANDINAVIA

E. H. Dunckley, *The Reformation in Denmark* (1948).

Ole Peter Grell, "Scandinavia," in Andrew Pettegrew, ed., *The Early Reformation in Europe* (1992).

———, ed., *The Scandinavian Reformation: From Evangelical Movement to Institutionalisation* (1995). An important collection of essays by various authors.

Grethe Jacobson, "Nordic Women and the Reformation," in Sherrin Marshall, ed., *Women in Reformation and Counter-Reformation Europe* (1989).

Michael Roberts, *The Early Vasas: A History of Sweden* (1968).

Notes

1. Cited in Jonathan Zophy, *Patriarchal Politics and Christoph Kress (1484–1535) of Nuremberg* (Lewiston, N.Y.: Edwin Mellen Press, 1992), p. 90.
2. Albrecht Dürer, *The Writings of Albrecht Dürer*, William Conaway, ed. and trans. (New York: Philosophical Library, 1958), p. 157.
3. Cited in Gottfried Seebass, "The Reformation in Nürnberg," in Lawrence Buck and Jonathan Zophy, eds., *The Social History of the Reformation* (Columbus, Ohio: Ohio State University Press, 1972), p. 22.
4. Cited in Lawrence Buck, "The Peasants' War," in Jonathan W. Zophy, ed., *The Holy Roman Empire: A Dictionary Handbook* (Westport, Conn.: Greenwood Press, 1980), p. 365.
5. Cited in David Hockenbery, "Müntzer," in Zophy, ed., *Holy Roman Empire*, p. 329.
6. Cited in Tom Scott and Bob Scribner, eds., *The German Peasants' War: A History in Documents* (Atlantic Highlands, N.J.: Humanities Press, 1991), p. 330.
7. Cited in Zophy, *Patriarchal Politics*, p. 120.
8. Cited in Kyle Sessions, ed., *Reformation and Authority: The Meaning of the Peasants' Revolt* (Lexington, Mass.: D. C. Heath, 1968), p. 39.
9. Cited in Roland Bainton, *Women of the Reformation in Germany and Italy* (Minneapolis, Mn.: Augsburg, 1971), p. 26.
10. Cited in Jonathan Zophy, "We Must Have the Dear Ladies: Martin Luther and Women," in Kyle Sessions and Phillip Bebb, eds., *Pietas et Societas: New Trends in Reformation Social History* (Kirksville, Mo.: Sixteenth Century Journal Publishers, 1985), p. 143.
11. Cited in Zophy, *Patriarchal Politics*, p. 137.
12. Ibid., p. 148.
13. Ibid., p. 165.
14. Ibid., p. 183.
15. Ibid., p. 188.
16. Cited in Mark Edwards, Jr., *Luther's Last Battles: Politics and Polemics, 1531–1546* (Ithaca, N.Y.: Cornell University Press, 1983), p. 15.
17. Cited in Heiko Oberman, *Luther: Man between God and the Devil*, trans. Eileen Walliser-Schwartzbart (New Haven: Yale University Press, 1989), p. 290.
18. Edwards, *Last Battles*, pp. 124–136.
19. Cited in Oberman, *Luther*, p. 294.

12

Zwingli, Swiss Reform, and Anabaptism

Almost at the very moment that Martin Luther was embroiled with the church in a debate over indulgences, a similar controversy was raging in Zurich, Switzerland, involving the priest Huldrych Zwingli. A few years later, a classically trained humanist named Conrad Grebel performed the first known adult baptism and initiated the so-called Anabaptist movement, which was violently opposed by Zwingli and his supporters. Despite condemnations from both Protestants and Roman Catholics, the Anabaptist movement spread into central and eastern Europe, although seldom numbering more than 1 percent of the population. After Zwingli's death in 1531, the leadership of the reform movement in Switzerland passed to his successor, Heinrich Bullinger, and to Johann Oecolampadius in Basel before being overshadowed by the powerful movement led by John Calvin in Geneva.

Huldrych Zwingli (1484–1531)

EARLY YEARS

Huldrych Zwingli began life in the rural canton of Glarus in the Swiss Confederation a mere seven weeks after the birth of Martin Luther. His father was a relatively prosper-ous free peasant, eager to provide his sons with the best available education. At age five, young Huldrych was sent to live with his uncle, the vicar of Wesen. His uncle taught him some Latin and then sent him off to grammar school in Basel. When he was twelve, Zwingli transferred to a school in Bern. In 1498 he enrolled at the university of Vienna, whose faculty included the renowned humanist Conrad Celtis. Zwingli had also become interested in the classics and had become a fine musician as well. A virtual one-man band, Zwingli played the lute, harp, viol, reed pipe, and cornet (a precursor of the trumpet).

After four years in the stimulating atmosphere of Vienna, Zwingli transferred to Basel, where he earned his B.A. in 1504 and his M.A. two years later. He was then ordained a priest and became the parish priest of the town of Glarus, where he remained until 1516. To secure his post in Glarus, Zwingli had to buy off a papally appointed competitor for the large sum of 100 florins. While being a conscientious pastor to his congregation in Glarus and several surrounding villages, Zwingli also continued his scholarly pursuits. He studied the Bible diligently, as well as the classical writings and the work of Greek and Latin church fathers. Zwingli also tried to learn Hebrew.

The young priest greeted the writings of Erasmus with great enthusiasm, even making the trip to Basel to meet his intellectual hero in person in 1516. He wrote to the humanist later:

> When I think of writing to you, Erasmus, best of men, I am frightened by the brilliance of your learning, but I am encouraged at the same time by the charming kindness you showed me when I came to see you at Basel not long ago at the beginning of spring. It was no small proof of a generous nature that you did not disdain a man with no gift of speech and an author quite unknown.[1]

Over time Zwingli's self-confidence grew as did his understanding of the biblical materials and ancient languages.

Like his hero Erasmus, Zwingli found a great deal to criticize in the church, although he was much more willing to challenge the authority of the pope than the Dutchman. Zwingli eventually became an outspoken advocate of reform, taking lively interest in Swiss political and military affairs. On several occasions he served as a military chaplain to groups of Swiss mercenaries fighting in various battles against the French for control of Milan. Zwingli showed great courage under fire and came to despise the mercenary system, which corrupted young Swiss when it failed to disable or maim them. Military camp life in the early sixteenth century was very ill-disciplined. Army camps were filled with excessive drinking, gambling, and prostitution. When Zwingli returned from the battle of Marignano of 1515, he began preaching against the evils of the lucrative mercenary system.

In 1516 Zwingli added to his duties by being named rector of the monastic church at nearby Einsiedeln, a position he held for two years. Since Einsiedeln was a center of pilgrimages, he was able to witness how many pilgrims actually came to worship relics and saints. Although Zwingli made his own pilgrimage in 1517, the year of Luther's "Ninety-five Theses," he was increasingly concerned about what he considered abuses in the practices of the church. At Einsiedeln, Zwingli also became involved in a controversy over indulgences with a Franciscan, Bernardin Samson. This controversy did not reach the proportions that Luther's did, but it shows that different people in different areas had come to agree with Erasmus that indulgences were a "cheat."

Not a Frivolous Musician: Zwingli in Zurich

In October 1518 the chance for an even more influential post opened up—that of cathedral priest at the Great Minster in the prosperous trading city of Zurich. With a population of about 7,000, Zurich was considerably larger than the small towns and villages Zwingli had previously served. The ambitious young cleric was keenly interested in the job, but reports circulated against him. Although people in Zurich praised Zwingli for his learning, there were reports that he was "pleasure-seeking and worldly." Even his musical inclinations were viewed with suspicion as "frivolous." Worse, there was a report that Zwingli had "seduced the daughter of an influential citizen" of Einsiedeln.[2]

Zwingli met the charges head on. He wrote to the appointment committee that "some three years ago I firmly resolved not to touch any woman, since Paul stated that it is not good to do so." He admitted that he had slept with the daughter of a barber and that the child she awaited might well be his. He claimed that she had seduced him "with more than flattering words" and that she had sexual relations "with several clerical assistants." As for his music, "I play for myself and delight in the beautiful harmony of melodies and do not desire any recognition."[3] The canons were apparently impressed with Zwingli's defense for on December 11, 1518, they offered him the position over a Swabian competitor, who kept a concubine, had six children, and held several benefices. What happened to the barber's daughter and her child back in Einsiedeln is not known.

THE ADOPTION OF THE REFORM BY ZURICH

Zwingli went on to become an enormously popular preacher and to launch the Swiss Reformation. The citizens of Zurich found that he had an attractive personality, a quick wit, a fine intellect, and a beautiful voice. He soon earned a reputation as a charismatic preacher, whose call for reforms met with a sympathetic response in part because people genuinely admired and respected the messenger despite his previous moral lapses. His stature as a religious and political leader also grew as he became more serious and purposeful. During his first year in Zurich, a ferocious plague hit the city and killed almost a fifth of its population. Among the victims was one of Zwingli's brothers. Zwingli bravely ministered to the sick until catching the illness himself. Surviving the plague, he became a much more earnest and dedicated man with an even greater sense of purpose.

In his early years in Zurich, Huldrych Zwingli read Martin Luther's writings intently and preached directly from the New Testament. In the spring of 1522 some of his parishioners, moved by the emphasis of his sermons on "the Word of God which clearly allows the eating of all foods at all times," broke the church's prohibition against eating meat during Lent. Although Zwingli kept the Lenten fast himself, he defended those who had not from his pulpit and in several of his pamphlets. He wrote in one of them: "If you want to fast, do so; if you do not want to eat meat, don't eat it; but allow Christians a free choice."[4] The ruling Small Council of Zurich issued a decree that the fast be maintained, but it suggested that the matter needed further discussion. Zwingli, a shrewd political animal, had carefully cultivated friendships with many key members of both the council of fifty and the larger council of 200. He understood clearly that reform would not be possible without the support of Zurich's political and economic leadership. In Zwingli's view, both the clergy and the government derive their authority from God; therefore, both the preachers and the magistrates must make sure that God's authority is established over the community.

A public debate was held on January 29, 1523, between Zwingli and Johann Faber, representing the bishop of Constance, who had jurisdiction over Zurich. Zwingli presented sixty-seven articles for reform, which among other things objected to the powers assumed by the pope, argued that the Mass was a symbolic meal of remembrance, and opposed such traditional practices as clerical celibacy, fasting, monasticism, pilgrimages, indulgences, purgatory, and the worship of saints. For him the reformers were engaged in restoring the church to its original "purity" in accordance with what is described in the Acts of the Apostles. Upset by charges that he was a mere imitator of Luther, Zwingli stressed his own contributions to reform, "I began to preach the Gospel of Christ in 1516, long before anyone in our region had heard of Luther."[5] Indeed, Zwingli was much more concerned about the reform of society than Luther, who was more focused on the salvation of individuals.

Later public debates were held and the government of Zurich followed up by ordering other parish priests to follow Zwingli's lead. The collection of tithes was ended; clerical celibacy was denounced; and choral singing and images were removed from Zurich's churches. As Zwingli wrote, "the images are not to be endured, for all that God has forbidden, there can be no compromise."[6] The pattern of removing images as "idolatrous" was repeated in other Swiss cities and later in Calvinist churches. Given Zwingli's love of music, the limitation of congregational singing solely to the Psalms was a cross to bear, but he wanted to be consistent with his interpretation of the practices of the early church. He found some consolation in the arms of a widow with children, Anna Rhinehardt, whom he had secretly married in 1522. Their marriage was made public in 1524, a year before the Mass itself was abolished by order of the Small Council.

The reform Pope Adrian VI attempted to deal with Zwingli more diplomatically than his predecessor Leo X had dealt with Luther. He shared many of the same concerns and withheld papal condemnation. Tragically, Adrian died on September 14, 1523. His successor, Clement VII, was far too dependent on Swiss mercenaries to risk intervention in Swiss affairs. By then Zwingli's friends had spread the reform movement to Basel, Bern, Saint Gall, Schaffhausen, and as far north as Strasbourg. Recognizing the need for an international movement, Zwingli urged his colleagues to join Zurich in an alliance in "defense of the Gospel."

THE MARBURG COLLOQUY

In the autumn of 1529, Zwingli and several of his associates accepted the invitation of Landgrave Philip to attend a major meeting of reformers at Marburg in Hesse. It was the most important meeting of reform leaders held in the sixteenth century. Philip was hoping the conference would result in a common statement of doctrine and a military alliance of reform communities. He feared that Charles V would soon lead the Catholics in a crusade to exterminate the Evangelicals. Zwingli was joined by Luther, Melanchthon, Martin Bucer and Wolfgang Capito of Strasbourg, Johann Oecolampadius of Basel, Johann Brenz of Schwäbisch Hall, Andreas Osiander of Nuremberg, and several others. Never again would such a celebrated group of early sixteenth-century Evangelical theologians be gathered in one place at the same time.

The reformers did find they had a lot of common ground and some of them cemented lasting friendships. Unity dissolved, however, on the thorny issue of the Lord's Supper. All the reformers denied the sacrificial nature of the Catholic Mass and agreed that both the bread and the wine should be given to the laity. Yet Zwingli was unwilling to accept Luther's assertion that Christ was bodily present in the sacrament. He argued that the words "This is my body" were meant only symbolically. The Eucharist is a meal of remembrance; Christ is not present in any form. Neither side would budge from those positions. They finally agreed to disagree. Without complete doctrinal agreement, Luther would not support a military alliance with the Swiss, whom he suspected of secretly being too prone to radicalism and too closely related to the Anabaptists.

ZWINGLI'S LAST YEARS

Returning to Zurich, Zwingli was determined to pressure the five Catholic cantons in the central part of the Swiss Confederation to accept the reform. He believed

Sixteenth-century portrait engraving of Huldrych Zwingli, Bibliotheque de l'histoire du Protestantisme, Paris, France. Giraudon/Art Resource.

Protestantism should be spread by any means necessary. At a January 1530 stormy session of the Swiss Parliament (Diet), Zwingli managed to get the Protestant majority to pass economic sanctions against the Catholics. The Diet prohibited the sale of such basic commodities as wheat, salt, wine, and iron to the Forest Cantons in the mountainous heart of Switzerland. Reformation doctrines had not found such fertile soil in the less urbanized, more mountainous portions of Switzerland, where parishioners were happier with their local clergy and less exposed to the new currents of thought which coursed through Swiss trade and university centers.

In October 1531 the Catholics struck back with a military force of 8,000 marching on Zurich. Taken by surprise, Zwingli rushed to meet them with a much smaller army of about 1,500 troops. Seeing his badly outnumbered soldiers give way, Zwingli put

himself in the center of the Protestant army and took a fatal sword thrust in his throat. With the death of their hero, the Protestant army broke ranks and fled from the field. They lost over 400 including twenty-six Zurich council members and twenty-five Protestant ministers. Catholic soldiers found Zwingli's body, quartered and burned it, and scattered his ashes after mixing them with dung. Luther, who had never trusted Zwingli's political activism, was not overly surprised that Zwingli had died in battle.

Having taught the Protestants a bloody lesson, the Catholics wisely made no attempt to continue the offensive or to disturb the Protestants in their new worship practices. They knew the more populous Protestant areas could raise additional troops if pressured further. What they wanted was the freedom to continue their traditional religious practices. The Peace of Kappel of November 20, 1531 maintained the religious status quo in the Swiss Confederation. Catholic but not Protestant minorities were to be tolerated, and all entangling foreign alliances were forbidden.

Heinrich Bullinger (1504–1575)

Zwingli was ably succeeded by Heinrich Bullinger, who had been exiled from his pastorate at Bremgarten. A native of Bremgarten in the Aargau, Bullinger had earned his bachelor of arts and his master's degrees at the University of Cologne. He then became the head teacher at the abbey school of the Cistercian monastery at Kappel, where he reformed the curriculum of the Latin school along humanist lines. Converted to Protestantism, Bullinger reformed the monastery itself before leaving to take a pastorate in his home town.

Bullinger was an important and influential covenant theologian, who wrote a very valuable *History of the Reformation* and the Second Helvetic Confession (1556), which became one the most accepted of all the Reformed confessionals. A keen intellect, Bullinger stressed the nature of the relationship between an all-powerful God and sinful humans. He also insisted that ordinary people needed to have the Bible interpreted for them by experts. His concerns were much more theological than political so in time Zurich was eclipsed by Bern and then Calvin's Geneva as the center of Swiss Reformed Protestantism. Primarily through correspondence, Bullinger developed a close friendship with John Calvin, who respected his insights and abilities. Contemporaries viewed the sensible Bullinger as one of the leading lights of the reform.

Big Names in the Reform of Basel

The reform movement followed many different patterns in various places. At Basel, a major center of printing with a population of 9,000, the reform was led by Johann Oecolampadius (1482–1531), an able classical and Hebrew scholar. He had studied law at Bologna and theology at Heidelberg and Tübingen. Like Huldrych Zwingli, Oecolampadius was a great admirer of Erasmus and assisted him in the production of his Greek New Testament and an edition of St. Jerome's writings. In 1521 he entered a Briggitine monastery but soon became disenchanted and left the following year. By 1522 he was in close contact with Zwingli and they developed a warm friendship. In June 1523 Oecolampadius secured a position as a professor of theology at the University of Basel.

Oecolampadius also became the preacher at St. Martin's Church, where he enthusiastically promoted reform. In Basel, the magistrates were much slower than they were in Zurich to adopt reform measures. Guild representatives proved particularly reluctant to go along with the religious changes proposed by Oecolampadius, fearing that the town's economic life might suffer. With the help of Zwingli and reformers from Bern, the city council in February 1529 finally made the break with Rome after a major outbreak of iconoclasm. Although Oecolampadius agreed with Zwingli on most points of doctrine, he felt church discipline should solely be a matter of pastoral concern. He was reluctant to use civic officials to enforce faith and morals. Oecolampadius also participated in the Marburg Colloquy and made a good friend of Luther's irenic colleague Philip Melanchthon.

A devoted son, he delayed marriage until after the death of his mother. In his forty-fifth year at the urging of the reformer Wolfgang Capito, he married Wibrandis Rosenblatt (1504–1564), the attractive widow of a Basel humanist, Ludwig Keller. She made him a most comfortable home and they had three children. Wibrandis was a gracious hostess, who also kept up a lively correspondence with the wives of other reformers. They had a lot in common as the first generation of pastors' wives since the early Middle Ages. The network established by the thoughtful Wibrandis was absolutely essential in helping Protestant women married to clergy adapt to their new role and responsibilities, which often included hosting religious refugees. Wibrandis was sensitive to many of the practical realities of the new situation for married clergy fostered by the Reformation. She also enjoyed the company of women and men of faith and intellect.

A year after Oecolampadius's death in 1531, Wibrandis married the humanist-reformer Wolfgang Capito, who had lost his first wife at nearly the same time she had lost her second husband. They moved to Strasbourg and had five children. Following

Capito's demise in 1541, Wibrandis married her third reformer, Martin Bucer, whose wife had died of the plague. After his death in England in 1551, she moved back to the Continent and eventfully died in reformed Basel of yet another outbreak of the dreaded plague. She was widely admired for her good sense, graciousness, problem-solving skills, and supportive nature.

The Rise of Anabaptism

The stress of the early reformers on the importance of reading Scripture gave rise to the problem that the Bible is a complex book that can be interpreted in different ways by different people. In Zwingli's Zurich, for example, a reading group led by Conrad Grebel came to the conclusion that there was no warrant in the Bible for infant baptism. In the Gospel according to Luke, John the Baptist had baptized Jesus as an adult, not as a child. If infant baptism is so essential, why was there no evidence of it in the first two centuries? Why is Scripture itself so silent about it?

CONRAD GREBEL (1498–1526)

Conrad Grebel, a member of a patrician family and a well-educated humanist, concluded that baptism was a sign or symbol of regeneration or the coming of faith by adults who had reached an age of accountability. Grebel and his associates were also concerned about the political activities of Huldrych Zwingli and his willingness to use the power of the state to spread the Gospel. He thought the church should be a voluntary community of believers; no one should be compelled by force to accept the truth of the Gospels. Furthermore, the church should not be an arm of the state or

vice versa. Even at the Zurich Disputation of 1523, Grebel called upon Zwingli to repudiate not only the medieval church but the authority of the city government over religious affairs as well. Since Zwingli had worked long and hard to achieve political influence, he was not about to abandon his efforts at a state-sponsored reform movement.

Grebel and his followers went their own way in trying to establish a form of the church that closely resembled that described in the Acts of the Apostles. They used a simple form of service in private homes and celebrated the Lord's Supper as a meal of solemn remembrance. Grebel's followers tried to follow the Sermon on the Mount as closely as possible. Then, in January 1525, Grebel performed an adult baptism on George Blaurock as a public symbol of his coming into a new understanding (covenant) of God. Blaurock, a former priest, then baptized others.

Since the first group of people who were baptized as adults in 1525 had already been baptized as Catholic children, their enemies called them Anabaptists or Rebaptists. This brought them under the penalty of Roman law, which prescribed death for those who rebaptize. The Romans tended to view religion as a community rather than an individual matter. The Anabaptists, who believed that like the early Christians they were destined to suffer, called themselves "Christians," "Saints," or "Brethren." They saw themselves as outside the mainstream of society or at least as an alternative to it. Inherent in Anabaptism was the idea that man's law had no force for those whom God had saved (*antinomianism*). Some Anabaptists taught that faith takes precedence over marital vows. They allowed even single women to convert and had some female prophets such as Ursula Jost and Barbara Rostock, who were active in Strasbourg.

Tragically, the Anabaptist movement

began in the midst of the Peasants' War in the Holy Roman Empire (1524–1526), which greatly added to the fears of the authorities about social upheaval. Although most Anabaptists were pacifists, enemies such as Martin Luther believed they were "wolves in sheep's clothing." He linked them with fanatics like Thomas Müntzer and Hans Hut. In Zurich, Zwingli was distressed that his former disciple Grebel had moved so far from his teachings about the role of civil government and the importance of infant baptism. He believed false reports about their dissolute behavior and condemned them in a tract called *Against the Tricks of the Katabaptists.*

After a public disputation on adult baptism in Zurich, the city council ordered Grebel and his followers to leave the city. When Anabaptists continued to win converts in the countryside, the Zurich government on March 7, 1526 made rebaptism punishable by death according to Roman law. Grebel was imprisoned for five months before escaping. He died of the plague later in that same year. Other Anabaptists were arrested, burned at the stake, and sometimes symbolically punished by drowning, as was the case with most captured female Anabaptists. Yet the movement continued to attract new members, many of whom were impressed by the clarity of the Anabaptist message and the courage of the "suffering saints."

Michael Sattler (c. 1490–1527) and the Schleitheim Statement

Michael Sattler was one of the bravest of the Anabaptist suffering saints. He had been a prior in a monastery at Freiburg in Breisgau before converting to Lutheranism. In 1525 Sattler arrived in Zurich and became an important convert to Anabaptism. After being expelled from the city, he became an evangelist outside Zurich and later in the Strasbourg area and then at Horb in Württemberg. In 1527 Sattler presided over a conference of Anabaptists meeting at Schleitheim near Schaffhausen in southern Germany. For that conference, he drew up a brief statement of basic Brethren beliefs for those at Schleitheim. It was never intended as a public confessional statement.

According to the Schleitheim Statement:

1. Baptism was to be given to all those who had learned repentance and amendment of life and who truly believe their sins were taken away by Christ.

2. After having professed to be brothers or sisters, all those who fall into error and sin, shall be warned twice in secret and excommunicated upon the third offense.

3. Those who wish to participate in the Lord's Supper must first be baptized.

4. The baptized were to separate themselves from the "evil and wickedness, which the devil planted in the world."

5. A pastor in the church must have a good reputation with those outside the church. (Members of the Brethren were still being accused of having joined with rebellious peasants as did the radical theologian Thomas Müntzer).

6. No member of the church was to bear arms in any cause.

7. No member of the church was to take an oath.[7]

Although the Schleitheim Statement was not accepted as definitive by all Anabaptists, it does give us a sense of some of their early beliefs. Anabaptists came to see themselves primarily as local "gathered communities" and, therefore, they did not need a binding, public confessional declaration. They left that for the state-churches of the larger Catholic and Protestant denominations.

Shortly after his return to Horb from Schleitheim, Sattler, his wife, and several others were arrested. The imperial authorities, fearing the continued spread of the Brethren, were determined to make an example of the unrepentant Sattler. After a two-day trial in which he defended himself and his beliefs with great courage and intelligence, the gentle Sattler was cruelly tortured by having pieces of his body torn with red hot tongs before he was burned at the stake. His devoted wife was drowned eight days later, after having turned down an offer of amnesty and a comfortable retirement home if she would recant.

Balthasar Hubmaier (c. 1480–1528)

Balthasar Hubmaier helped provide intellectual leadership for the early Anabaptists. A gifted former student of Luther's opponent at Leipzig, Johann Eck, Hubmaier earned a doctorate in theology and became a chaplain and vice-rector of the University of Ingolstadt by 1515. He left the university for an important Cathedral pulpit at Regensburg and then, after a controversy over pilgrimage revenues, a more modest one at Waldshut on the Rhine. Impressed by the writings of Zwingli, he made his own intensive studies of the New Testament and came to the conclusion that there was no basis for the practice of infant baptism. In April 1525 he had himself baptized by an associate of Grebel's. After resigning his clerical position, Hubmaier was chosen by his congregation to continue as their minister. He also married Elizabeth Hüglein.

Later that year he responded to Huldrych Zwingli's published attacks on the Brethren with a highly influential book, *Concerning the Christian Baptism of Believers.* This became known as one of the most intelligently argued statements of the Brethren position on adult baptism. Forced to flee from Waldshut by Archduke Ferdinand, the Hubmaiers fled to Zurich, where he was arrested, tortured, and forced to recant his Anabaptist beliefs. He was then banished to Nikolsburg in southern Moravia, where he succeeded in converting two of the local barons, who encouraged him to continue his ministry. Thousands of others were converted by Hubmaier's congenial personality, incisive mind, and clear message.

Hubmaier continued his writing and was one of the first to call for religious toleration, thereby atoning to an extent for his own role in the expulsion of Jews from Regensburg earlier in his career. He disagreed with most other Anabaptists on support of the state and the necessity at times of defensive warfare. His views on baptism were circulated widely in Brethren circles. When his old enemy, Archduke Ferdinand, became king of Bohemia in February 1527, Moravia came under his authority. Hubmaier and his wife were soon arrested. Brought to Vienna, he was tortured and then burned at the stake after refusing to recant. His wife, Elizabeth, was drowned and another 105 of Hubmaier's followers were executed.

Charisma and Fanaticism at Münster

Despite the persecutions of the early Anabaptists, the movement continued to spread throughout the Holy Roman Empire and into the Low Countries, although it never numbered more than 1 percent of the European population during the sixteenth century. In an age that valued conformity and suspected all deviance from the norm, Catholics and other Protestants continued to believe the worst about the Anabaptists. A strange outbreak of fanaticism in the Westphalian city of Münster in 1534 seemed to support even the greatest fears that people like Martin Luther and others had about them.

After a period of unrest over plague, crop failures, and an unpopular bishop, Münster's city council appointed Lutheran ministers to the town's parish churches in 1532. Protestants of all sorts flocked to the city as a safe haven. Among them were disciples of Jan Matthys, a fanatical Dutch baker. Claiming to be the prophet Enoch, Matthys preached that the Day of Judgment was coming and that the elect must prepare for Christ's return and the rule of the saints in the millennium. While most other Millenarians were pacifists, the tall and bearded Matthys preached that the elect must take up the sword against the ungodly. Several of his more enthusiastic followers had run naked through the streets of Amsterdam proclaiming the imminent coming of Christ; they were quickly seized and butchered.

Then in February 1534 Jan of Leiden (c. 1509–1536), a tailor, arrived in Münster, which was to become the city of God proclaimed by his spiritual leader, Jan Matthys. The handsome, illegitimate son of a Dutch mayor, Jan of Leiden was sent to help prepare for the coming of the great prophet Matthys and his followers. In new elections, the municipal council was replaced by one dominated by "immigrants, shoemakers, tailors, furriers, and other artisans."[8] Conservatives who could fled the city but were replaced by the coming of Matthys himself and more of his disciples. Münster was proclaimed to be the New Jerusalem, which would be spared when the rest of the world was destroyed at Easter. All those who ac-

cepted Matthys as their prophet were rebaptized, private property was abolished, and laws were promulgated for "perfection of the saints."

Franz von Waldeck, the former bishop of Münster, returned with a besieging army made up of Catholic and Protestant recruits. The rule of working-class fanatics in Münster frightened many throughout Europe, who listened to the wild tales about the city with great fascination. Yet the New Jerusalem held out, protected by its thick walls and the desperate courage and faith of its defenders. Then Matthys had a vision that he claimed instructed him to leave the city's walls and attack the bishop, which would lead to a glorious victory. On Easter Sunday of 1534, Matthys was pierced by a spear while leading a small raiding party outside the protective walls of the city. Apparently, he had misinterpreted his vision.

The Fall of "King" Jan

With Matthys dead, Jan of Leiden moved quickly to take full control over Münster and reassure the faithful. First, he ran naked through the streets, fell into a trance, and proclaimed himself to be the new prophet and king of Zion. He began to force the council to issue even more revolutionary decrees, including one which established Old Testament style polygamy. Jan of Leiden himself led the way by eventually taking fifteen wives, including the lovely widow of Matthys. His loyal followers continued to defend the city, despite the hardships imposed upon them by the siege, such was their desperate faith in Jan of Leiden and their fear of the attackers' wrath. While others suffered, King Jan, his leading lieutenants and their harems lived remarkably well.

After sixteen months of siege, Münster

Heinrich Aldegrever, Portrait engraving of Jan van Leiden (1536). Foto Marburg/Art Resource.

was finally taken. Its besiegers had been reinforced by the army of Philip of Hesse, a Protestant prince. Its defenders were starving and disease ridden except for their leaders, including King Jan. Most of the men, women, and children, who remained alive in the town were ruthlessly slaughtered. Jan of Leiden was exhibited throughout northern Germany before being mutilated with red hot tongs and hung with several of his associates in cages above the walls of Münster as a warning to others of the dangers of fanaticism and trust in false prophets.

Menno Simons (1496–1561)

Anabaptism survived the great trauma of the Münster episode because most of its leaders were not self-serving powermongers like Matthys or Leiden. The movement soon found renewed leadership under Menno Simons, an often self-effacing man of genuine faith and deep piety. Born in the Low Countries, Simons worked as a parish priest for twelve years before coming to the conclusion that many Catholic doctrines were insufficiently supported by Scripture. In 1527 he was shocked by the reports of the execution of the first Anabaptist martyr in the Low Countries. While Simons could find no warrant for infant baptism in Scripture, he was not willing to take the risk of converting. Then came the terrible news of the debacle at Münster. Simons felt partly responsible for having "disclosed to some of them the abominations of the papal system."[9] Although terribly misled, the Münsterites had been willing to die for their version of the faith. Did he lack similar courage?

In October 1536, Menno Simons was baptized and began a career as a highly influential Anabaptist preacher. When exiled from Groningen in 1539, he continued his ministry in the Dutch province of Friesland. Two years later, Simons was forced to flee to Amsterdam. Late in 1543 he left Holland for the north of Germany, where he would spend the rest of his life. Intent on calling the Brethren back to their original vision, the pacifist Simons expounded his views in a series of important books, including *Christian Baptism* (1539) and *Foundations of Christian Doctrine* (1540). He stressed the new birth in Christ of Brethren believers and the importance of living as Christ taught. For Simons, the church was an "assembly of the righteous" at odds with the world.[10] His voluminous writings were printed in many languages and he soon became the best known Anabaptist theologian of the century. However, since many of the early Anabaptists had become suspicious of learned doctors after the extermination of the first generation of educated Anabaptist clergy such as Grebel, Hubmaier, Sattler, and Pilgram Marpeck, Simons downplayed his own academic background and intellectual tendencies. At one point he told his supporters that "Scripture does not need interpreting; it needs only to be obeyed."[11] His followers became known as Mennonites.

The Hutterites and the Community of Goods

Many Anabaptists held that the Christian was only a steward and not the owner of the property she or he possessed. Christians should be compelled by brotherly and sisterly love to share with anyone in need, especially those of the same faith. Hutterites made the belief in the "community of goods" an indispensable mark of discipleship and the church.

The Hutterites trace their beginnings to Nikolsburg, Moravia, where under the leadership of Jacob Wiedemann they began to practice the sharing of goods in 1528. They were named after Jacob Hutter (d. 1536) from the Austrian Tyrol. He had been converted to Anabaptism by the preaching of Conrad Grebel's associate George Blaurock. A staunch pacifist, Hutter argued that the Anabaptists were a threat to no one: "We have no physical weapons, such as spears or muskets. We wish to show, by our words and deeds, we are true followers of Christ."[12] Despite such protestations, Hutter had to flee from persecution in the Tyrol. He and and a loyal band of followers arrived in Moravia in 1533. Hutter then began reorganizing the Moravian Brethren into

tight-knit congregations with common ownership of all goods as based on the Acts of the Apostles, the fifth book of the New Testament.

After Jacob Hutter's arrest and execution in 1536, the Hutterites found new leadership in Peter Riedemann, who wrote the influential *Confession of Faith*. Written while Riedemann was in prison in Hesse in 1545, the *Confession* became the definitive statement of Hutterite beliefs. Riedemann argued that only fallen persons have a desire to own things. God did not intend for humans to appropriate property for their own selfish purposes. A true Christian disciple will have no problem in forsaking private property. Despite continued persecutions, the Hutterites spread into Slovakia, Hungary, Transylvania, and the Ukraine. In the nineteenth century, many Hutterites moved to the United States in an effort to maintain their communal existence.

Believing in a voluntary association of the faithful as opposed to a state-supported church, the Hutterites, Mennonites, and other Anabaptist groups remained for the most part scattered, small, and struggling. No great prince offered them his or her protection. Most of their members remained working people. Although the Anabaptists never became a majority in any one area, they did make up 10 percent of the population of the Low Countries at one point. The movement spread into Eastern Europe, throughout the Holy Roman Empire, and eventually to the Western Hemisphere. While trying to renounce the world, the Anabaptists usually became a force in promoting religious freedom. Their courage when persecuted and their usually gentle lives of faith eventually won a measure of acceptance from a world all too ready to fear that which was different.

Chronology

c. 1480–1528	Life of Balthasar Hubmaier.	**1525**	First adult baptisms in Zurich.
1482–1531	Life of Johann Oecolampadius.	**1527**	Schleitheim Conference and Statement.
1484	Birth of Huldrych Zwingli.	**1528**	Bern adopts the reform.
c. 1490–1527	Life of Michael Sattler.	**1529**	Basel adopts the reform; Marburg Colloquy.
1496–1565	Life of Menno Simons.		
1504–1564	Life of Wibrandis Rosenblatt.	**1531**	Death of Zwingli; Peace of Kappel.
1504–1575	Life of Heinrich Bullinger.	**1534**	Anabaptists take control of Münster.
1519	Zwingli begins his ministry in Zurich.	**1535**	Fall of Münster; death of Jan of Leiden.
1522	Breaking of the Lenten fast in Zurich.	**1536**	Death of Jacob Hutter.
1523	First Public Disputation in Zurich.	**1540**	Publication of Simons's *Foundation of Christian Doctrine*.
1524	The Mass abolished in Zurich.	**1545**	Peter Riedemann's *Confession of Faith*.
		1556	Publication of Bullinger's *Second Helvetic Confession*.

Further Reading

ZWINGLI

Ulrich Gabler, *Huldrych Zwingli* (1986).

Charles Garside, Jr., *Zwingli and the Arts* (1966).

Gottfried Lochner, *Zwingli's Thought: New Perspectives* (1981).

G. R. Potter, *Zwingli* (1976).

W. P. Stephens, *The Theology of Huldrych Zwingli* (1986).

Robert Walton, *Zwingli's Theocracy* (1971).

Lee Palmer Wandel, *Always Among Us: Images of the Poor in Zwingli's Zurich* (1990).

BULLINGER

Aurelio Garcia Archilla, *The Theology of History and Apologetic Historiography in Heinrich Bullinger: Truth in History* (1992).

J. Wayne Baker, *Heinrich Bullinger and the Covenant* (1980).

Paul Rorem, *Calvin and Bullinger on the Lord's Supper* (1989).

EARLY SWISS REFORM

Irena Backus, *The Disputations of Baden, 1526 and Berne, 1528: Neutralizing the Early Church* (1993).

Hans Guggisberg, *Basel in the Sixteenth Century* (1982).

Lee Palmer Wandel, *Voracious Idols and Violent Hands: Iconoclasm in Reformation Zurich, Strasbourg, and Basel* (1995).

ANABAPTISM: GENERAL STUDIES

Michael Baylor, ed. and trans., *The Radical Reformation* (1991). A valuable collection of sources.

Claus-Peter Clasen, *Anabaptism: A Social History* (1972).

Kenneth Davis, *Anabaptism and Asceticism* (1974).

William Estep, *The Anabaptist Story* (1996).

Hans Hillerbrand, *A Bibliography of Anabaptism, A Sequel* (1975).

Joyce Irwin, ed., *Womanhood in Radical Protestantism* (1979). Important essays.

Cornelius Krahn, *Dutch Anabaptism: Origin, Spread, Life, and Thought, 1450–1600* (1968).

Franklin Littel, *The Anabaptist View of the Church*, 2nd ed. (1958).

Michael Mullett, *Radical Religious Movements in Early Modern Europe* (1981).

Werner Packull, *Hutterite Beginnings: Communitarian Experiments during the Reformation* (1995).

————, *Mysticism and the Early South-German-Austrian Anabaptism Movement* (1977).

John Rempel, *The Lord's Supper in Anabaptism: A Study in the Christology of Balthasar Hubmaier, Pilgram Marpeck, and Dirk Philips* (1993).

James Stayer, *Anabaptists and the Sword* (1972).

J. Denny Weaver, *Becoming Anabaptist: The Origins and Significance of Sixteenth Century Anabaptism* (1987).

George Williams, *The Radical Reformation*, expanded 2nd ed. (1991).

INDIVIDUAL ANABAPTIST LEADERS AND VARIETIES

Stephen Boyd, *Pilgram Marpeck: His Life and Theology* (1992).

Cornelius Dyck, *An Introduction to Mennonite History*, rev. ed. (1981).

Hans-Jürgen Goetz, *Profiles of Radical Reformers* (1982).

Leonard Gross, *The Golden Years of the Hutterites* (1980).

H. Wayne Pipkin and John Yoder, *Balthasar Hubmaier, Theologian of Anabaptism* (1989).

Calvin Redekop and Samuel Steinter, *Mennonite Identity* (1988).

C. Arnold Snyder, *The Life and Thought of Michael Sattler* (1984).

Gary Waite, *David Joris and Dutch Anabaptism, 1524–1543* (1990).

Jerold Knox Zeman, *The Anabaptists and the Czech Reform in Moravia, 1526–1628: A Study of Origins and Contacts* (1969).

Notes

1. Cited in Andrew Johnson, *The Protestant Reformation in Europe* (New York: Longman, 1991), p. 91.
2. Cited in Hans Hillerbrand, ed., *The Protestant Reformation: A Narrative History Related by Contemporary Observers and Participants* (New York: Harper and Row, 1964), pp. 114–115.
3. Ibid., p. 116.
4. Cited in Johnson, *Reformation*, p. 92.
5. Cited in Hillerbrand, *The Reformation*, p. 125.
6. Cited in Lee Palmer Wandel, *Voracious Idols and Violent Hands: Iconoclasm in Reformation Zurich, Strasbourg, and Basel* (New York: Cambridge University Press, 1995), p. 81.
7. Adapted from Lewis Spitz, ed., *The Protestant Reformation* (Englewood Cliffs, N.J.: Prentice Hall, 1966), pp. 89–96.
8. Cited in Hillerbrand, *The Reformation*, p. 254.
9. Ibid.
10. Cited in Alister McGrath, *Reformation Thought: An Introduction*, 2nd ed. (Oxford: Blackwell, 1993), p. 202.
11. Quoted by John Roth, "Panel on Sixteenth-Century Confessionalism," Sixteenth Century Studies Conference, Toronto, Canada, October 28, 1994.
12. Cited in McGrath, *Reformation Thought*, p. 203.

13

John Calvin and Calvinism

The reform movement in Switzerland found new and dynamic leadership in the considerable personage of John (Jean Cauvin) Calvin (1509–1564). A Protestant reformer of the second generation, Calvin was a brilliant theologian, a powerful preacher, a caring pastor, a skilled legalist, and something of an organizational genius. Not only did he accomplish a thorough reform of the city of Geneva, but Calvin used that Swiss city as a base from which missionaries were sent out to much of the rest of Europe. Calvinism eventually outstripped Lutheranism as the largest denomination within the ranks of Protestantism.

Calvin's Early Years

John Calvin began life in the town of Noyon in northern France. His mother, Jeanne, known for her beauty and her piety, was the daughter of a successful innkeeper. She died when John was only three. His notary father, Gerard, soon remarried, but little is known about his second wife. Young John was educated by private tutors and attended an endowed school in Noyon attended by the sons of the aristocratic Montmor family. He soon exhibited a keen intelligence and a facility with Latin.

Calvin's father, who had become secretary to the bishop of Noyon, used his connections to obtain a cathedral chaplaincy and other benefices for John, all of which supported his continued education. At the age of fourteen, Calvin was sent to a college of the University of Paris, with the Montmor boys as companions and schoolfellows. His radiant personality and fine manners helped make him a number of close friends and he excelled in his studies. He soon transferred to the College of Montaigu, where Erasmus had studied and complained about the food and the scholastic theology. Calvin found the environment there much more stimulating, partly because he came into contact with some of the finest minds in Paris including the great humanist and Greek scholar Guillaume Budé and possibly the literary titan François Rabelais. A true intellectual, Calvin blossomed in the stimulating atmosphere of Renaissance Paris.

Calvin had been preparing for the priesthood, but in 1528 shortly after receiving his M.A. at age eighteen, he suddenly left Paris to study law at Orléans. By this time, his father was having difficulties in his relations with the cathedral chapter in Noyon over disputed accounting records. These problems apparently influenced Gerard Calvin to reconsider his son's future. Although he was more enamored of humanistic studies than the law, the dutiful son continued his study of law until his father's death in 1531. He had completed all work for his license as a lawyer, but instead of practicing law, Calvin returned to Paris to continue his classical scholarship.

Immersing himself in Greek and Hebrew studies, John Calvin published his first book, a *Commentary on Seneca's Treatise on Clemency* in 1532. Calvin's work on the Roman Stoic reveals his impressive knowledge of classical literature and philosophy. Deeply religious, he was particularly attracted to the Stoic belief in divine providence. During this period, Calvin also underwent "a sudden conversion" to Protestantism. Forbidden Protestant books and ideas circulated widely among Calvin's friends. His father's problems with the church may also have played a part in his souring on the Catholic Church and his decision to give up his benefices. He later wrote of his conversion: "And first, since I was too obstinately devoted to the superstitions of Popery to be easily extricated from so profound an abyss of mire, God by a sudden conversion subdued and brought my mind to a teachable frame."[1]

THE FLIGHT FROM PARIS

In 1533 John Calvin was forced to flee Paris. His friend Nicholas Cop, son of the royal physician and recently elected rector of the university, gave a convocation address at the opening of the fall semester that had a decidedly Protestant tone to it. Cop not only defended Marguerite of Navarre's mystical poem *The Mirror of a Sinful Soul,* which had been condemned by the faculty of theology, but he emphasized the role of grace in salvation. The brilliant Calvin was known to have helped Cop write the address and was advised to leave the city to avoid arrest. He spent the first half of 1534 at Saintonge in the home of a student friend whose parents had a good library.

When pranksters broke into the royal palace of King François I in October 1534 and posted Protestant slogans on his bedroom door as well as throughout Paris, the king responded with even more persecutions of Protestants in France. Some of the posters called the Mass an "execrable blasphemy, pretending to be a sacrifice to God."[2] Calvin fled France for Strasbourg, where he met the talented reformers Martin Bucer, Matthew Zell, and Katherine Zell. He then moved on to Basel, which had become Protestant in 1529, and there met another important humanist turned reformer, Wolfgang Capito, who would later join Bucer and the Zells in Strasbourg. In Basel during March 1536, Calvin published the first edition of his masterwork, *The Institutes of the Christian Religion,* which he spent the rest of his life expanding.

Calvin's Theology

A brilliant summary of Protestant theology, *The Institutes* helped establish Calvin at age twenty-six as one of the leading Protestant minds in Europe. He later translated it into French and kept expanding it in numerous editions until his death. Even the aging Martin Luther found the book most impressive. Its lucid and facile style had much the same influence on the formation of modern literary French as Luther's translation of the Bible had on German. Its success was rivaled only by the ribald writings of the ex-monk and humanist François Rabelais. Like Luther, Calvin used the printing press to great advantage.

Probably Calvin's most significant contribution to the emergence of Protestant theology was his sublime conception of the majesty of God. For him the divine creator is so overwhelming and awe-inspiring that humans by contrast seem insignificant, sinful, and unworthy. Nevertheless, this majestic God is a God of love, who planned the whole universe to the end of time, selecting some humans for salvation and some for damnation. Like Luther, Calvin was strongly influenced by the writings of St. Augustine and gave priority to the role of God in the salvation of humanity. He believed that faith unites the believer to Christ and begins a process of regeneration, which makes the believer more Christlike.

Calvin described his doctrine of double predestination in the *Institutes* with great clarity, as the following illustrates.

> Predestination we call the eternal decree of God by which He determined in Himself what would have to become of every individual of mankind. For they are not all created with a similar destiny, but eternal life is foreordained for some and eternal damnation for others. Every person, therefore, being created for one or the other of these two ends, we say is predestined to life or to death.[3]

Although Calvin shared many of these ideas with other reformers, few have expressed Protestant beliefs with such lucidity and power. A prolific author, he supplemented the various editions of the *Institutes* with numerous biblical commentaries, polemics, treatises, and letters.

Calvin differed from both Luther and Zwingli in his understanding of the sacrament of the Eucharist. He took a position midway between Luther's conception of the real presence of God in the sacrament and Zwingli's symbolic presence. Instead, Calvin argued for a "spiritual" presence. He stressed that there is such a close connection between the symbol (the bread) and the gift which it symbolizes that we can "easily pass from one to the other. For why should the Lord put in your hand the symbol of his body, unless it was to assure you that you really participate in it?"[4]

With the first edition of the *Institutes* published, Calvin set out for Italy to visit the court of Renée, duchess of Ferrara and daughter of King Louis XII of France. Renée (1510–1575) was known for her learning and her sympathies with reformers. He stayed barely a month in Ferrara because Renée's more conservative husband, Duke Ercole I (d. 1559), refused to let her turn their court into a refuge for religious dissenters. Renée kept up a lifelong correspondence with Calvin, and when her husband died she joined the Calvinists in France and provided safe havens for many of them. John Calvin then returned to France to bring a brother and sister to safety in Strasbourg but was forced to take a detour by marauding troops involved in the third of the Habsburg-Valois wars (1536–1538) and ended up in Geneva in July 1536.

THE CALL TO GENEVA

The Swiss city of Geneva, an active commercial town of 10,300 inhabitants, had become a center for religious refugees from France and Italy. It had previously been ruled by a rapacious bishop as a fief of the Holy Roman Empire. The duke of Savoy, whose territory surrounded the town, also claimed influence in the city. Nearby Bern had sent the preacher Guillaume Farel (1489–1565) to urge the Genevans to free themselves from the authority of both the bishop and the house of Savoy and save their souls by adopting the Protestant version of reform. This combination of religious and political motivations was too appealing to reject. After a public debate between Protestant leaders and Catholic clergy in June 1535, a majority of the male citizens voted to "abandon all papal ceremonies and abuses, images, and idols."[5] Yet the Genevans also resisted Farel's efforts to dampen their enthusiasm for amusements and make the city more "godly."

The fiery Farel wanted Calvin's help in further changing the community and begged him to stay. Contemplating a quiet life of scholarship, Calvin was reluctant to become involved in the turbulent waters of reform on a daily basis. Farel admonished him, "You are following only your own wishes, and I declare in the name of God Almighty, that if you do not assist us in this work of the Lord, God will punish you."[6] Overcome by guilt and a stoical sense of duty, Calvin agreed to stay and help Farel reform Geneva. He was made "Reader in Holy Scripture to the church of Geneva." With his encouragement, the Mass was replaced with simple services of prayer, sermons, and the singing of the Psalms. In January 1537 the hard-working and legalistic Calvin submitted his *Articles Concerning the Government of the Church,* a *Confession,* and a *Catechism,* for purposes of instruction.

Calvin and Farel proposed that his confession be made mandatory for all citizens by public profession and oath. They insisted that the reformed church had the right to scrutinize the lives of its members and to punish impenitent sinners. After considerable debate, these stern and intrusive measures were adopted by a majority of the city's ruling councils. Calvin also insisted that Geneva's existing ordinances against licentious dancing, card-playing, theater-going, drunkenness, gambling, and swearing be enforced and applied equally to all, regardless of social standing. As one cynical wit commented, "You can do anything you want in Geneva as long as you do not enjoy it."[7]

Political leaders began hearing rumblings of discontent from some prominent Genevans who resented the power over their lives assumed by two French immigrants. Calvin and the councils began to dis-

agree publicly on whether the church or the state should administer church discipline. The crisis escalated in February 1538 when Calvin refused the government's order to administer the Lord's Supper in the Bernese manner with unleavened bread. Calvin and Farel were expelled from the city.

The Reform in Strasbourg

Calvin and Farel first went to Bern, then to Zurich, and finally ended up in Basel. Farel then accepted a call from his former parish at Neuchatel and Calvin accepted one from his friend Martin Bucer to return to Strasbourg. Strasbourg was a busy and prosperous commercial town of about 20,000 people, located at the crossroads between Germany, France, Switzerland, and the Low Countries. As an imperial city, it technically owed allegiance to the Holy Roman emperor but was independent for all practical purposes. Strasbourg was one of the more than fifty imperial cities which had recognized the Reformation in the sixteenth century. As early as 1521 it had exhibited Lutheran sympathies. Later Strasbourg came under the influence of the moderate reformer, Martin Bucer, who was sympathetic to a variety of Protestant views including those of Huldrych Zwingli.

MARTIN BUCER (1491–1551)

A former Dominican friar with humanist leanings, Bucer had attended Martin Luther's 1518 meeting with the Augustinians at Heidelberg and been profoundly impressed. He left the monastery and became a priest at Landstühl, the parish of Franz von Sickingen, a knight. After the failure of Sickingen's Knights' Revolt, Bucer and his young wife, a former nun, moved to Weissenberg and later to Strasbourg in 1523. Supported by theologically sophisticated politicians such as the ex-cleric Jacob Sturm, the reformers eventually persuaded a reluctant city council to abolish the Mass in 1529. Like Zwingli, Bucer believed that the magistrates had the obligation to help reform the church.

Blessed with a fine mind and a unique vision, Martin Bucer tried to make Strasbourg a center of reform that was relatively open to a variety of religious opinions. Anabaptists, Spiritualists, and refugees from Catholicism such as the former abbot Peter Martyr Vermigli (1500–1562) found hospitality and sanctuary there. Vermigli claimed that Bucer's home was "like a hostel, receiving refugees for the cause of Christ."[8] Bucer did not think the breach with Rome had to be permanent and hoped that one day unity would be restored. Over time, he lost that hope but continued to mediate between his fellow Protestants on various disputed points of doctrine. Bucer was ably assisted in his reform efforts by the humanist Wolfgang Capito, Casper Hedio, and Matthew and Katherine Zell among others.

KATHERINE ZELL (C. 1497–1562)

Katherine Zell was one of the most important female leaders of the early Reformation. Inspired by the writings of Martin Luther, Katherine had married the ex-monk Matthew Zell in 1523 in a service presided over by Martin Bucer. They became a ministerial team because of her strong religious interests and the admiration her much older husband had for her abilities. The daughter of a respected carpenter, Katherine had been tutored at home and possibly at a vernacular school. She developed a fondness for liturgical reform and theology. When her two babies died in infancy, she threw herself

into her husband's ministry with great energy. She sheltered large groups of religious refugees, administered relief to the poor, visited the sick and infirm, wrote theological tracts, published hymns, and delivered a public address at the funeral of her husband in 1548, in an age when women were seldom allowed to speak in public.

Martin Bucer, Wolfgang Capito, and the Zells had a lot to teach John Calvin about how to be a successful pastor. Calvin served as the pastor of a congregation of fellow French refugees. He also attended Protestant meetings at Frankfurt on the Main, Hagenau, Worms, and Regensburg. There he met many of the leaders of German Protestantism including Philip Melanchthon, whom he admired greatly, and Gasparo Contarini, the reform-minded cardinal. At age thirty Calvin also accepted Bucer's suggestion that he marry Idelette de Bure, the widow of a Dutch Anabaptist. The marriage proved a happy one though both were troubled with ill health. She was further weakened by childbirth and the death of their only child and died six years later in 1549.

Calvin's Return to Geneva

Calvin reluctantly returned to Geneva in September 1541 to complete his reform work. Genevan leaders had promised that this time they would fully support his disciplinary efforts and treat him with the respect he deserved. He was appointed pastor of St. Peter's parish and given a substantial salary and a large house. The ruling elite in Geneva had decided they needed the astute Calvin's firm hand in creating a truly reformed city and were willing to pay a high price to bring him back. Calvin's leadership was challenged in 1546 when a prominent member of the elite Small Council accused him of being "a wicked man, who preaches false doctrine." Calvin demanded a public apology and that his accuser march through the streets of Geneva in disgrace. This was done but other members of the Genevan old-guard rose up to challenge Calvin's authority from time to time. Calvin also found that he could not trust many of his ministerial colleagues, especially those who had remained in Geneva during his and Farel's exile.

THE MICHAEL SERVETUS CASE

Public opposition to Calvin within Geneva virtually came to a head in 1553 with the trial and burning of Michael Servetus (c. 1509–1553). Servetus was a Spanish scientist, lawyer, physician, and amateur theologian. He was the first person to postulate the pulmonary circulation of the blood. Turning to theology, Servetus was interested in building the Jewish case for Christianity. In his *On the Errors of the Trinity* (1531), Servetus seemed to cast doubt on the divinity of Christ, traditionally a sensitive issue for Christians. After failing to convince the reformers of Basel and Strasbourg of the correctness of his views, he was arrested by the Catholic Inquisition and condemned "as a case of total heresy." He later escaped from prison and arrived in Geneva on his way to refuge in Italy.

Servetus was recognized in Geneva and immediately turned over to the authorities for trial as a heretic. He had earlier sent Calvin a copy of the *Institutes* with the Spaniard's "corrections" written in the margins. After a lengthy trial at which Calvin testified extensively and was counterattacked by Servetus, the Spaniard was found guilty and burned at the stake. Calvin graciously attempted to minister to him in his cell and recommended the less painful pun-

ishment of beheading but was overruled by the authorities. Calvin gained prestige with some for having moved against a talented but arrogant man believed to be a dangerous heretic. However, the death of Servetus appalled his former colleague Sebastian Castellio (1515–1563), who was banished from Geneva in 1545 for his insistence on drawing a distinction between essential and nonessential doctrines. Castellio had also asserted that the biblical Song of Songs was a true love song and not an allegory.

Castellio argued in his 1554 treatise, *Whether Heretics Should Be Persecuted*, that to kill a man "is not defending a doctrine, it is merely killing a man." He understood that the root cause of intolerance was arrogance and pride:

> Men are puffed up with knowledge or a false opinion of knowledge and look down upon all others. Pride is followed by cruelty and persecution so that now scarcely anyone is able to endure another who differs from him. Although opinions are almost as numerous as men, nevertheless there is hardly any sect which does not condemn all others and desire to reign alone.[9]

Tragically, Castellio's words of wisdom were not heeded by Calvin or very many other leaders of the time. Religious toleration was not an acceptable concept for most in the sixteenth century, who saw only a lack of religious fervor in those willing to allow a range of religious thought. Such laxity, it was believed, jeopardized souls by exposing people to the risk of "false teachings." Heresy was thought to be a "cancer" that had to be eliminated at all costs. As for Castellio, he died a professor of Greek at Basel under suspicion in 1563, having dared to question such basic theological issues as predestination.

The Threat of the Libertines

Two years after the execution of Servetus, Calvin faced his gravest political threat when a native Genevan, Ami Perrin, tried to take over the government of Geneva by force. Perrin was an influential member of the Small Council and an early supporter of Calvin. However, he fell out with Calvin over the latter's insistence that church discipline should be enforced uniformly against all members of Genevan society. In 1546, Perrin's father-in-law, François Favre, also a member of the Small Council, had been excommunicated for immoral conduct. Perrin's wife, Francesca, also attempted to defy Calvin's insistence on equal justice for all and was exiled for disobeying some of Geneva's laws against dissolute public behavior.

Ami Perrin himself was arrested later in 1546 when it was discovered that he had entered into negotiations with the French king on his own authority. His political allies rallied behind him and he was acquitted and returned to office. In 1548 Perrin's faction was victorious in the elections for the town council. Calvin called them the "Libertines" and argued against their attempts to relax ecclesiastical discipline. An uneasy truce existed for seven years between Calvin's friends and foes on the city councils. The Libertines also broadened their support base in Geneva by stirring up resentment among the older inhabitants against the increasing number of religious refugees who were fleeing France in ever greater numbers.

When the Calvinists won the majority of seats on the Small Council in the spring of 1555, Perrin, who was then a captain of the town militia, attempted a coup against the government and called for the massacre of the French. His followers were promptly put down, but Perrin managed to escape from the city with three companions. This was the last great political challenge Calvin had to face in Geneva. He now felt secure enough to become a citizen of the city eighteen years after he had first settled in Geneva.

Discipline in Calvin's Geneva

Always concerned with the practical aspects of reform, John Calvin helped establish what his Scottish disciple John Knox called, "the most perfect school of life that was ever on earth since the days of the apostles."[10] Among the many things about Calvin's Geneva that Knox admired were its clean streets devoid of beggars and its well-organized churches. Calvin's legal training and orderly mind were invaluable in organizing the Genevan church and in dealing with societal problems. Calvin's *Ecclesiastical Ordinances* of 1541 established four orders of offices: pastors, teachers, elders, and deacons. Ministers were to preach the word, administer the sacraments (baptism and the Eucharist), and admonish their parishioners both publicly and privately. Teachers were to "instruct the faithful in sound doctrine." Elders were laymen whose primary function was to "oversee everybody" and maintain proper order and discipline. The deacons were to help the poor, comfort the sick, and care for widows and orphans. All these things were done with greater efficiency in Calvin's Geneva than almost anywhere else in Europe.

Discipline especially was rigorously maintained over all segments of society. The chief instrument of enforcement in Calvin's Geneva was the Consistory, made up of twelve elders and five pastors and presided over by a member of the Small Council. This made the Consistory at once an agency of both the church and the state. Calvin believed that both the magistrates and the ministers were agents of God with similar purposes, although different tools: "For the church has not the right of the sword to punish or restrain, has no power to coerce, no prison nor other punishments which the magistrate is wont to inflict."[11]

The chief difference between Calvin's Geneva and most other places in Europe was the thoroughness of the Genevan Consistory in attempting to enforce morality. Geneva's city fathers also tried to deal with some of the root causes of crime such as poverty. Relief was carefully administered for the poor, for Calvin argued that "we should be moved to pity when we see any poor folks in adversity and provide for them according to our ability."[12] Even Geneva's prostitutes were organized under the leadership of a "queen" and carefully regulated with regular medical inspections after efforts to eliminate the practice failed.

CALVIN AND WOMEN

All these public functions, however, were carried out solely by men; even the "queen" of the prostitutes reported to a male official. A thorough patriarch, Calvin argued that in the early church "a woman was not allowed to speak in church, and also not to teach, to baptize, or to offer."[13] He was apparently unimpressed with the many women deaconesses in the early church or the significance of the prophet Joel's (2:28) statement that "your sons and your daughters shall prophesy." Biblical heroines such as Deborah and Judith were "exceptional women." Calvin did think that salvation was open to both sexes and approved of religious education for girls. Women were to read the Bible

only in private, but he did allow female singing in church, despite the criticism of some members of the government.

Calvin held views on women rulers which were quite similar to his colleague John Knox, who got in considerable trouble with Queen Elizabeth I of England for his misogynist diatribe *Against the Monstrous Regiment of Women.* Calvin apologized to the powerful English queen for the tenor of Knox's comments, but his own thoughts in a letter to Heinrich Bullinger of April 28, 1554, reflect ideas similar to the Scotsman's. Calvin wrote:

> About the government of women I expressed myself thus: since it is utterly at variance with the legitimate order of nature, it ought to be counted among the judgements with which God visits us. . . . For a gynaecocracy or female rule badly organized is like a tyranny, and is to be tolerated until God sees fit to overthrow it.[14]

Obviously, Calvin was a shrewd enough political animal to not share his real thoughts on this subject with Queen Elizabeth, whose support he needed to help Calvinist communities elsewhere in Europe.

CALVIN THE MAN

During his lifetime Calvin acquired a reputation for severity and somberness. A closer examination reveals that his image as a "blue-nosed Puritan" is based more on polemics than reality. Although he was deeply concerned about sexual improprieties, particularly adultery, those who knew him well—such as his ministerial colleague and biographer Theodore Beza—found him to be a kind and gentle man with "a singular good wit greatly given to the service of God."[15] Beza pointed out that Anabaptists

Anonymous, *Portrait of John Calvin*. SEF/Art Resource.

ried a much younger woman when he was sixty-four. He worried about "what will the sneerers say, and what will the simple think, but that the preachers wish to have the law for themselves."[18]

For many years after his return to Geneva in 1541, Calvin had felt a strong sense of anxiety and isolation. He found that he could not trust many of his ministerial colleagues with the major exception of Pierre Viret (1511–1571). Viret had converted Lausanne to Protestantism and then joined Farel in the early reform in Geneva. Calvin's loneliness increased in 1549 with the death of his wife, Idelette. He wrote of her, "I have lost the best companion of my life. . . . While she lived, she was the faithful helper of my ministry. . . . Her greatness of spirit means more to me than a thousand commendations."[19]

were exiled from Calvin's Geneva and not executed as they were in most other places. Despite his frail health and many struggles, Calvin was a good pastor, companion, and friend. As Calvin himself wrote in the *Institutes:* "We are nowhere forbidden to laugh or to be satisfied with food or to be delighted with music or to drink wine."[16]

Calvin's opportunities to delight in wine or music were limited by the many struggles of his life. His latter years were especially troubled by bouts of ill health and a number of scandals which plagued his family and friends. His brother's wife was found guilty of adultery with one of the reformer's servants and his stepdaughter Judith was also found guilty of adultery. Calvin viewed extramarital sex as a threat to society and all good order. He argued that "fornicators and adulterers should not be tolerated" because they "rob the honor of everything."[17] Calvin was also upset when Guillaume Farel, his former colleague, mar-

Theodore Beza (1516–1605) and the Genevan Academy

Although he never returned to France, Calvin kept a close eye on developments there and sent out teams of missionaries to his homeland. Many of those missionaries were trained in the Genevan Academy that Calvin founded in June 1559. Calvin also had a strong concern that the church be led by well-educated men. The academy emphasized instruction in languages, the liberal arts, philosophy, and theology. Calvin recruited Theodore Beza, who came from the provincial French nobility, to serve as the academy's rector. Calvin had first met Beza in 1529 when Calvin was studying law briefly in Bourges. Beza had received much of his legal training at Orléans, where Calvin had also studied law. Beza later earned a licentiate in law from Bourges. After a number of years pursuing humanist learning and worldly pleasure in Paris, Beza took a religious turn and visited Calvin in Geneva in 1548. He then joined Pierre Viret on the faculty of the academy in Lausanne as a professor of Greek before agreeing to serve in Geneva. Beza may have had an even better command of Greek than Calvin. Like Calvin, he was a fine, largely self-taught theologian with a strong concern for helping others.

The academy was divided into two sections: a high school and a college. To some extent, it was modeled after a very successful school at Strasbourg developed by Johann Sturm (1507–1589). Sturm was the leading educator in the Reformation period and was much admired by Martin Luther and many others. In the Genevan high school, young males were taught French, Latin, and Greek grammar and literature, as well as elements of logic. Students in the college learned Greek, Hebrew, philosophy, and theology. The academy was supported by the public treasury and did not charge tuition. Many of its early students came from various parts of France to which a number returned as Calvinist missionaries. By Calvin's death in 1564, the Genevan Academy enrolled 1,200 students in the high school and 300 in the college, which eventually became the University of Geneva. Its faculty included François Hotman, one of the foremost legal theorists of the century.

Theodore Beza, who continued to teach theology at the academy between 1564 and 1595, was named by the dying Calvin to succeed him in Geneva as head of the Company of Pastors. Beza was highly respected as a biblical scholar and had completely absorbed and supported Calvin's theological system. His aristocratic background served him well with the social elite of Geneva and as a diplomat. Beza reluctantly became the leading force in the church of Geneva and helped spread international Calvinism.

The Spread of Calvinism

John Calvin's clearly articulated theology and well-organized churches had enormous appeal. Calvin and Beza continued to supply a steady stream of well-trained missionaries to start congregations in nearby France and elsewhere throughout Europe. Geneva offered itself as a successful model of a reform community, and its printing presses supplied an abundance of materials for the new centers of Calvinism. Calvin and Beza both kept up an active correspondence with those who were spreading the movement including their close friend Pierre Viret, who became a leading missionary in France. Beza also served ably as a missionary and diplomat in France and attended a number of Calvinist religious conventions (synods) before he returned to succeed Calvin in Geneva.

Although France held a special place in the hearts of Calvin and Beza, they also encouraged missionary efforts in other parts of Europe. The clarity of the Calvinist organizational structure had great appeal in the Low Countries, especially in the French-speaking areas. A Belgic Confession of Faith was drafted as early as 1561. Later, as we shall see in Chapter 17, Calvinism became deeply rooted in the Dutch-speaking portions of the Netherlands. In 1560 Elector Frederick III, count Palatine of the Rhine, converted to Calvinism and established his electorate as a major center of Calvinism inside the Holy Roman Empire. Three years later his theologians drew up the Heidelberg Catechism, which joined Heinrich Bullinger's second Helvetic Confession of 1556 as the most influential doctrinal guides for Calvinist congregations east of the Rhine. A Protestant academy founded at Heidelberg threatened to overshadow the Genevan Academy as a trainer of Calvinist missionaries.

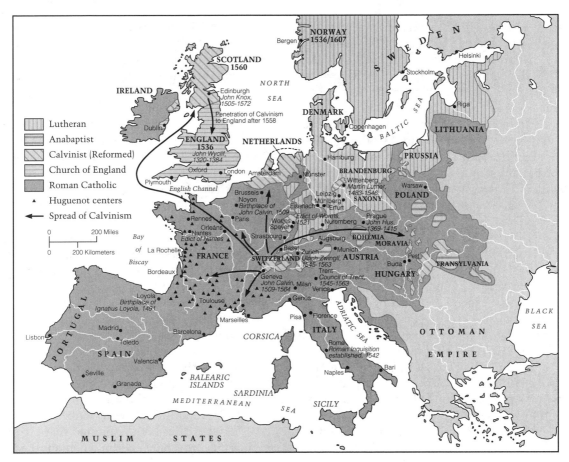

Protestant and Catholic Centers

A Failed Calvinist Reformation in Brandenburg

In 1613 the Hohenzollern Elector Johann Sigismund of the Mark of Brandenburg attempted to convert his north German electorate from Lutheranism to Calvinism in a "second Reformation." Educated at Heidelberg and Strasbourg, Johann Sigismund had become convinced of the superiority of Calvinism to Lutheranism. He thought that although Martin Luther "has done much to set the gospel free, yet he has remained deeply stuck in the darkness of the papacy."[20] Sigismund favored the Calvinist spiritual interpretation of the Lord's Supper and the less elaborate liturgy of the Swiss reformers. The Lutheran Mass was too close to that of the Catholics for Johann Sigismund's taste. Calvinist churches used hymns based on the Psalms and removed traditional art. For political as well as religious reasons, the elector wanted to draw closer to the Calvinist Palatinate.

However, Elector Johann Sigismund's efforts to promote Calvinism failed as Lutheranism was too popular and too deeply entrenched into the fabric of society to be dislodged. Lutheranism had officially been adopted by the Mark of Brandenburg in 1540 under Johann Sigismund's grandfather, Joachim II (r. 1535–1571). He in turn had been strongly influenced by his mother, Electress Elizabeth (1485–1545), the sister of Christian II, the Lutheran king of Denmark. Defying her philandering Catholic husband, Elizabeth had taken communion in both kinds during Easter of 1527 from a Lutheran minister. When he learned of his wife's defiance, Elector Joachim I considered divorcing her or incarcerating her for life. Elizabeth's uncle, Duke Johann the Constant of Saxony, offered her sanctuary, which she accepted, fleeing Berlin disguised as a peasant.

An enraged Joachim demanded that she be returned at once, but Johann the Constant refused. Joachim then appealed to the 1529 Diet of Speyer for the restoration of his "property." The Diet took no action against powerful electoral Saxony and Elector Johann wondered aloud whether it was "possible for a good Catholic to keep concubines while his legitimate wife had to be fed in Saxony."[21] The crisis continued as Joachim became the leader of the Catholic League of Halle, formed in opposition to the Protestant Schmalkaldic League. He also sought to bind his sons to Catholicism by threatening them with disinheritance in his will should they not be faithful to "the old Christian faith."

Meanwhile, the exiled electress lived on in poverty and battled mental illness. She stayed for a time with Martin and Katherine Luther. Her son, Joachim II, succeeded his father in 1535 and invited his mother to return. Elizabeth refused as long as he remained Catholic. Although long attracted to Luther's doctrines, Joachim II resented the reformer's continuing verbal attacks on his uncle, Archbishop Albrecht of Mainz. He also hoped that a general church council could achieve harmony between Lutherans and Catholics in the empire. However, the pressure of events soon got the better of his intention to achieve a degree of religious toleration.

Joachim's younger brother, Hans of Küstrin, embraced the reform and joined the Schmalkaldic League in 1538. Influenced by Prince George III of Anhalt, a fellow moderate and a recent convert to Lutheranism, and Philip Melanchthon, Joachim II issued a new church ordinance in 1540 that brought him reluctantly into the Protestant camp. His ordinance barely passed muster with the Wittenbergers and Joachim himself continued to collect relics. He continued his efforts at mediation and was a strong supporter of the 1541 Regensburg Colloquy between, among others, Philip Melanchthon and Cardinal Gasparo Contarini, a Catholic moderate reformer. In 1545 his brother Hans arrived in Lichtenberg with 500 horses to bring his mother back from exile. He paid her debts and settled her at Spandau. She was allowed the minister of her choice and freedom of worship. Her health failing, Elizabeth requested that Elector Joachim bring her to Berlin. There she died in that same year and was buried beside her Catholic husband from whom she had fled twenty-seven years earlier.

Despite Joachim II's best efforts to steer a course between Rome and Wittenberg and to work out a compromise with Emperor Charles V during the crisis of the Schmalkaldic War and its aftermath, Brandenburg became thoroughly Lutheran. When Johann Sigismund and his court tried to turn the electorate to Calvinism, he found fierce opposition not only from Lutheran pastors but also from their congregations. Neighboring Prussia, which the Hohenzollerns sought to incorporate into their holdings, also was firmly committed to Lutheranism. Therefore, Elector Johann Sigismund found that he could not force

Calvinism down the throats of his subjects. He and his court worshiped as Calvinists, but the rest of the electorate stayed Lutheran.

CALVINISM TRIUMPHANT

While Calvinism failed to dislodge Lutheranism from the Mark of Brandenburg, it continued to advance elsewhere on all fronts. Further to the east, for example, Calvinism had grown rapidly in Poland and in Hungary in the 1550s (for a while, it was the leading denomination in Hungary).

Calvinism also had strong minority followings in Bohemia and England (the Puritans). Scotland became Calvinist (the Presbyterians) during the reign of Mary, Queen of Scots, as discussed in Chapter 15. Emden in the Low Countries became almost a second Geneva, serving as a base for the spread of the reform. Various Calvinist groups and missionaries spread from Europe to the rest of the world, and Calvinism became one of the strongest set or group of traditions within Protestantism. Its appeal has proved universal and enduring. For such a slender man, John Calvin has indeed cast a wide shadow.

Chronology

1485–1545	Life of Elizabeth of Brandenburg.
1489–1565	Life of Guillaume Farel.
1491–1555	Life of Martin Bucer.
c. 1497–1562	Life of Katherine Zell.
1509	Birth of John Calvin.
1511–1571	Life of Pierre Viret.
1516	Birth of Theodore Beza.
1523	Marriage of Matthew and Katherine Zell.
1528	Calvin earns his M.A. in the arts at Paris and begins law school.
1529	Strasbourg adopts the reform.
1532	Calvin publishes his *Commentary on Seneca's Treatise on Clemency*.
1533	Calvin forced to flee Paris.
1534	Affair of the Placards.
1535	Geneva adopts the reform under Farel and Viret.
1536	First edition of Calvin's *Institutes of the Christian Religion*; Calvin begins his ministry in Geneva.
1538	Calvin and Farel exiled from Geneva; Calvin begins his pastorate in Strasbourg.
1539	Calvin marries Idelette de Bure.
1540	Adoption of Lutheranism in Brandenburg.
1541	Calvin returns to Geneva; publication of the *Ecclesiastical Ordinances*.
1549	Death of Idelette Calvin.
1553	Trial and execution of Michael Servetus in Geneva.
1554	Castellio's *Whether Heretics Should Be Burned*.
1555	Ami Perrin's attempted takeover of Geneva fails.
1556	Bullinger's Second Helvetic Confession.
1558	Theodore Beza and Pierre Viret flee Lausanne for Geneva.
1559	Founding of the Geneva Academy.
1560	Elector Frederick III of the Palatinate converts to Calvinism.
1563	Publication of the Heidelberg Catechism.
1564	Death of Calvin.
1605	Death of Theodore Beza.

Further Reading

CALVIN: BIOGRAPHIES

William Bousma, *John Calvin* (1988). The leading biographical study.

Alister McGrath, *A Life of John Calvin* (1990).

T. H. L. Parker, *John Calvin, A Biography* (1975).

Ronald Wallace, *Calvin, Geneva, and the Reformation* (1988).

Francois Wendel, *Calvin: The Origin and Development of His Religious Thought* (1963).

CALVIN'S THOUGHT

Jane Dempsey Douglas, *Women, Freedom, and Calvin* (1982).

Richard Gamble, ed., *Calvin and Calvinism,* 14 vols. (1992). A vast collection of scholarly articles.

Timoth George, ed., *John Calvin and the Church: A Prism of Reform* (1990).

B. A. Gerrish, *Grace and Gratitude: The Eucharistic Theology of John Calvin* (1993).

W. Fred Graham, *The Constructive Revolutionary: Calvin's Socio-Economic Impact* (1989).

Harro Höpfl, *The Christian Polity of John Calvin* (1982).

Elsie McKee, *Elders and the Plural Ministry: The Role of Exegetical History in Illuminating John Calvin's Theology* (1988).

William Naphy, *Calvin and the Consolidation of the Genevan Reformation* (1994).

Jeannine Olson, *Calvin and Social Welfare* (1989).

Robert Schnucker, ed., *Calviana: Ideas and Influence of Jean Calvin* (1988). Valuable essays by a variety of leading scholars.

David Steinmetz, *Calvin in Context* (1995).

John Lee Thompson, *John Calvin and the Daughters of Sarah* (1992).

Thomas Torrance, *The Hermeneutics of John Calvin* (1988).

OTHERS INVOLVED IN THE GENEVAN REFORM

Jerome Friedman, *Michael Servetus* (1989).

Robert Lindner, *The Political Thought of Pierre Viret* (1964).

Jill Raitt, *The Eucharistic Theology of Theodore Beza* (1972).

CALVINISM

Brian Armstrong, *Calvinism and the Amyraut Heresy* (1969).

Phyllis Mack Crew, *Calvinist Preaching and Iconoclasm in the Netherlands, 1544–1569* (1978).

Alastair Duke, Gillian Lewis, and Andrew Pettegree, eds. and trans., *Calvinism in Europe, 1540–1610: A Collection of Documents* (1992).

W. Fred Graham, ed., *Later Calvinism: International Perspectives* (1994). A valuable collection of essays.

Henry Heller, *The Conquest of Poverty: The Calvinist Revolt in Sixteenth-Century France* (1986).

Robert Kingdon, *Adultery and Divorce in Calvin's Geneva* (1994).

———, *Geneva and the Consolidation of the French Protestant Movement* (1967). By the leading authority.

John T. McNeill, *The History and Character of Calvinism* (1967).

Eric Monter, *Calvin's Geneva* (1967).

Richard Muller, *Christ and the Decree: Christology and Predestination in Reformed Theology from Calvin to Perkins* (1986).

Bodo Nischan, *Prince, People, and Confession: The Second Reformation in Brandenburg* (1994).

Andrew Pettegree, *Emden and the Dutch Revolt: Exile and the Development of Reformed Protestantism* (1992).

Minna Prestwich, ed., *International Calvinism, 1541–1715* (1985). Important essays by a variety of scholars.

Stephen Strehle, *Calvinism, Federalism, and Scholasticism: A Study of the Reformed Doctrine of the Covenant* (1988).

STRASBOURG

Jane Lorna Abray, *The People's Reformation* (1985).

Thomas Brady, Jr., *Ruling Class, Regime and Reformation at Strasbourg* (1978).

Amy Nelson Burnett, *The Yoke of Discipline: Martin Bucer and Church Discipline* (1994).

Miriam Usher Chrisman, *Strasbourg and the Reform* (1967).

James Kittelson, *Wolfgang Capito From Humanist to Reformer* (1975).

Elsie McKee, *Reforming Popular Piety in Sixteenth-century Strasbourg: Katharina Schütz Zell and Her Hymnbook* (1995).

Lewis Spitz and Barbara Sher Tinsley, *Johann Sturm on Education: The Reformation and Humanist Learning* (1995).

W. P. Stephens, *The Holy Spirit in the Theology of Martin Bucer* (1970).

William Stafford, *Domesticating the Clergy: The Inception of the Reformation in Strasbourg 1522–1524* (1976).

Notes

1. Cited in Andrew Johnson, *The Protestant Reformation in Europe* (New York: Longman, 1991), p. 99.
2. Cited in Lewis Spitz, *The Renaissance and Reformation Movements* (Chicago: Rand McNally, 1971), p. 415.
3. John Calvin, *Institutes of the Christian Religion*, trans. by Ford Lewis Battles, ed. by John T. McNeill, 2 vols. (Philadelphia: Westminster Press, 1960), vol. 2, p. 926.
4. Cited in Alister McGrath, *Reformation Thought: An Introduction*, 2nd ed. (Oxford: Blackwell, 1993), p. 182.
5. Cited in De Lamar Jensen, *Reformation Europe: Age of Reform and Revolution*, 2nd ed. (New York: D. C. Heath, 1992), p. 136.
6. Cited in Hans Hillerbrand, ed., *The Protestant Reformation: A Narrative History Related by Contemporary Observers and Participants* (New York: Harper and Row, 1964), p. 179.
7. James Tillema, April 1964.
8. Cited in Roland Bainton, *Women of the Reformation in Germany and Italy* (Minneapolis, Mn.: Augsburg, 1971), p. 88.
9. Cited in Lewis Spitz, ed., *The Protestant Reformation* (Englewood Cliffs, N.J.: Prentice Hall, 1966), p. 108.
10. Cited in John T. McNeill, *The History and Character of Calvinism* (New York: Oxford University Press, 1967), p. 178.
11. Cited in Alister McGrath, *Reformation Thought: An Introduction*, 2nd ed. (Oxford: Blackwell, 1993), p. 216.
12. John Calvin, *Sermons from Job*, trans. Leroy Nixon (Grand Rapids, Michigan: William Eerdmans, 1952), p. 199.
13. Cited in Julia O'Faolain and Lauro Martines, eds., *Not in God's Image: Women in History from the Greeks to the Victorians* (New York: Harper and Row, 1973), p. 202.
14. John Calvin, *Letters of John Calvin*, ed. and trans. by Jules Bonnet, 4 vols. (Edinburgh, Scotland: Thomas Constable, 1855–1857), vol. 3, pp. 35–38.
15. Cited in Hillerbrand, *Reformation*, pp. 206–207.
16. Calvin, *Institutes*, vol. 1, pp. 720–721.
17. Calvin, *Sermons from Job*, p. 186.
18. Calvin, *Letters*, vol. 3, pp. 473–474.
19. Ibid., vol. 2, pp. 202–203.
20. Cited in Bodo Nischan, *Prince, People, and Confession: The Second Reformation in Brandenburg* (Philadelphia: University of Pennsylvania Press, 1994), pp. 94–95.
21. Ibid., pp. 120–121.

14

The Reformation in England to 1558

King Harry's Trouble with Women

The word on the streets of Catholic Dublin in the summer of 1530 was that "King Harry of England was having trouble with his women."[1] People were referring, of course, to King Henry VIII of England, a remarkable Renaissance prince who had been seeking a divorce from his wife, Queen Catherine of Aragon (b. 1485) since 1527. Henry wanted to end his marriage because after eighteen years of marriage he had been blessed with only one surviving child, a daughter, Mary (b. 1516). All the rest of his offspring died before birth or within a few days of their birth. Their deaths had confirmed Henry's fear that he had been living in sin, albeit with a woman who was a model of piety.

By the spring of 1527, the king had become convinced that God was denying him a son to punish him for having married his brother's widow. Even if Henry had been less of a misogynist, when he looked back into English history, he saw only one ruling female, and that was the "imperious" Matilda (1102–1167), daughter of King Henry I (r. 1100–1135), whose right to rule had been challenged by her more popular cousin Stephen of Blois (1135–1154). This contest for the throne eventually led to nine

years of civil war that ended when Stephen was allowed the throne on the condition that upon his death it go to Matilda's son, the future Henry II. By this time neither faction had been able to decisively defeat the other, and Stephen's only son had died.

Henry VIII, a talented lay theologian with a tender conscience and a monstrous ego, came to the conclusion that his marriage to Catherine was contrary to the injunction in Leviticus 20:21: "If a man takes his brother's wife, it is impurity; he has uncovered his brother's nakedness, they shall be childless." Queen Catherine was the widow of Henry's older brother Arthur (d. 1502), who had died of consumption four months after their marriage. Not wanting to lose Catherine's considerable dowry or the prestige of marrying into the house of Ferdinand and Isabella of Spain, Henry's father, the frugal King Henry VII, succeeded in convincing the Spanish to agree to the second marriage despite the fact that the twelve-year-old Henry was six years younger than his bride.

Henry VII also had to get a special papal dispensation from Pope Julius II to permit a marriage that so clearly violated the injunction in Leviticus. His theologians argued that Deuteronomy 25:5 permitted the nuptials:

When brothers shall dwell together, and one of them dies without children, the wife of the deceased shall not marry to another; but his brother shall take her, and raise up seed for his brother.

At length the papacy was convinced to permit the marriage and Henry and Catherine were finally wed on June 11, 1509, a few weeks after the death of Henry's father.

The marriage was generally considered a happy one despite the age difference. Catherine was a good, well-educated, intelligent, and pious woman, and Henry was a remarkably talented young prince. Not only was he a warrior and a statesman, but he was a gifted athlete, an active hunter, a mu-

Hans Holbein, *Henry VIII* (c. 1536). Photo courtesy of the National Portrait Gallery, London, United Kingdom.

sician, and a poet. A loyal son of the church, he had been named "Defender of the Faith" by Pope Leo X in 1521 for his writings against Martin Luther. Now in 1527 his conscience and his vanity were disturbed by his failure to have a son and heir. Perhaps the church had been wrong; perhaps he should never have violated Leviticus by marrying his brother's widow. Henry was desperate to have a legitimate male heir.

Cardinal Thomas Wolsey (1471–1530)

King Henry now turned for help to his great friend and the head of his government, Cardinal Thomas Wolsey. A veritable mountain of flesh with a lively mind, Wolsey was one of the most talented men in England. The son of a successful butcher, Wolsey had gone on to a university career at Oxford and rose eventually to become a chaplain to King Henry VII. Following the death of the first Tudor king, Wolsey entered the service of Henry VIII and proved invaluable as a judge and councillor, despite his lack of a legal background. A gifted administrator whose talents allowed Henry to neglect governing for the pleasures of the hunt, the dance, and playing soldier, Wolsey eventually became head of the government as lord chancellor.

As the king's favorite, Wolsey also advanced in the church. By 1527 he was the greatest pluralist in the church, serving as papal legate, archbishop of York, and abbot of St. Albans. Wolsey also held three other bishoprics and three deputy bishoprics. He supplemented his already enormous income with bribes and extortions. Arrogant and sensual, Wolsey loved power, eating well, fornicating, and living sumptuously. The stately palace at Hampton Court west of London is one of his great monuments. Possessed of great wit and a gift for management, Wolsey knew that he still owed his fabulous rise to power and wealth to his king. Even his dazzling accomplishments in administration and foreign policy, where he had helped make England a power to be reckoned with on the Continent, would begin to pale if he failed Henry in the matter of the divorce.

"Breaking Up Is Hard To Do": The Problem of the Divorce

Getting the papacy to grant Henry an annulment of his marriage was going to be very difficult. As fate would have it, Emperor Charles V's army in Italy had just sacked Rome in the summer of 1527, and Charles was the nephew of Henry's queen. Pope Clement VII was still a virtual prisoner of Charles's army and Queen Catherine did not want her marriage to Henry Tudor to end. The thought that she had been "living in sin" with Henry for eighteen years appalled the queen, who was widely respected in England and elsewhere for her religiosity. Emperor Charles was not about to let the pope agree to the disgrace of his aunt even if it meant breaking up the English-Habsburg alliance.

Pope Clement VII was also not willing to admit that the original dispensation that had allowed Henry's marriage to Catherine was illegal. Such an admission would challenge the "fullness of power" (*plenitudo potestatis*) doctrine upon which great medieval lawyer-popes such as Innocent III (1161–1216) had built the authority of the papal monarchy. Even Wolsey did not seem to push the case as hard as he might have for fear of offending the Sacred College of Cardinals. After all, his sole remaining ambition was to become the next pope and he would need the goodwill of many of the

cardinals. He did try to get the case transferred to England and his own jurisdiction. Although agreeing to this for awhile to gain time, Pope Clement had no intention of giving up the power of the papal court over marriages, and he took the case back after failing to persuade Henry to drop the matter.

The case dragged on and on as Henry's and Catherine's relationship continued to deteriorate under the pressure of his eagerness to remove her as his queen. His desire to end the Spanish marriage was further fueled by an attractive, dark-haired, younger woman with whom he had fallen in love and lust, Anne Boleyn (b. 1506). Having previously sampled the favors of Anne's married, older sister, Mary, Henry was keen to wed the bright-eyed, intelligent, sophisticated beauty, who had picked up some of the graces of the French court. She held out the promise of sons and renewed youth for the middle-aged lion. Anne insisted on a clear understanding of marriage before sex, not wishing to be as easily discarded as other mistresses such as her sister had been. With great skill, she held the king at bay for over five years until a promise of marriage had been secured.

In his fury over Cardinal Wolsey's failure to achieve the divorce, Henry ruthlessly turned on his former favorite and stripped him of his office as lord chancellor in 1529. Even the cardinal's sudden gift of Hampton Court to the king failed to appease the wrath of the ruthless and morbid Henry. Only Wolsey's death of a heart attack a year later saved him from dying at the chopping block for "treason." In his play *Henry VIII*, William Shakespeare has Wolsey saying: "Had I served my God with half the zeal I served my king, he would not in mine old age have left me naked to mine enemies." Although the quote may not be historically accurate, the sentiment rings true.

Replacements for Wolsey

New helpers now emerged to assist the king in the running of England. To replace the worldly cardinal as lord chancellor, Henry selected Sir Thomas More (1478–1535), the gifted humanist and lawyer, celebrated author of the visionary *Utopia*, and veteran politician. What an ornament he would be to Henry's inner circle. More recognized the dangers of serving Henry as chancellor, but did not think he could turn down his sovereign. As a man of great conscience, Thomas More was unwilling to become a tool in the process of disgracing Queen Catherine. He would serve his master in other ways for the time being such as by persecuting Protestants and suppressing English translations of the Bible.

Help with the annulment problem now came from an ambitious young cleric named Thomas Cranmer (c. 1489–1553). A graduate of Cambridge University and sympathetic to Continental reform ideas, Cranmer proposed that the universities should rule on Henry's divorce case. This idea was tried, and although the king got a mixed verdict from the academicians, he was pleased with Cranmer's intelligence and willingness to be of service. Cranmer had also impressed Anne Boleyn, another advocate of church reform. She used her influence to have her lover appoint Cranmer archbishop of Canterbury following the death of William Warham in 1532. As archbishop, Cranmer dutifully pronounced the dissolution of Henry's marriage to Catherine of Aragon, and in June 1533, he married the king to Anne Boleyn.

THOMAS CROMWELL (1485–1540)

Thanks in part to the work of another shrewd servant of the crown, Thomas Cromwell, the king's marriage was widely accepted in England despite the continued popularity of Catherine of Aragon. A cloth worker's son who got into trouble as a teenager, Cromwell had been forced to flee England. He became a mercenary soldier in Italy, then turned to a prosperous career in international trade. The hard-working, ambitious, and talented Cromwell eventually returned to England and married a woman for her money but proved a dutiful husband and son-in-law. Even after his wife's death, Cromwell continued to support his mother-in-law. In 1516 he entered the employ of Cardinal Wolsey, who recognized his considerable gifts and used him as an attorney and his chief man of business. In 1523 he was elected to the House of Commons. A largely self-made lawyer, Cromwell was one of the few who stayed loyal to the great cardinal

After Hans Holbein, *Thomas Cromwell*. Courtesy of the National Portrait Gallery, London, United Kingdom.

even after his fall. He soon entered into the king's service and eventually became the king's leading advisor and principal secretary.

It was the precedent-minded Cromwell who persuaded Henry VIII to make his reformation a legal one. Cromwell, a stout, sober student of the Bible, was convinced that England should break with the papacy. In so doing, Henry could not only obtain his divorce, but he could also enhance his power as well. Henry could become "supreme head of the church" in England and attain full sovereignty. In Cromwell's vision, England could become a godlier and more powerful state. This would also enhance his own stature as the king's most "devoted servant."

Exploiting Anticlericalism

Because of the general strength of the old church, Henry and Cromwell began their move toward reform by allowing their publicists to stir up anticlericalism, already a staple in many parts of England as in other European lands. The corrupt pluralist Wolsey was an obvious target for ridicule. Yet it would take a considerable effort to turn public opinion in England away from the Catholic Church, which was healthy and vigorous for the most part. The church's rich traditions in art and music had a particularly firm hold on the popular mind.

The king's propagandists felt compelled to bring up a nasty case from 1514 involving a merchant named Richard Hunne, which still rankled many in England as a telling example of clerical abuse. Hunne had refused to pay the mortuary fee to a priest for burying one of his infant sons. The merchant was sued for this a year later in the bishop of London's court. Hunne countersued in the Court of King's Bench. Bishop

Richard Fitzjames of London then instituted heresy proceedings against Hunne, accusing him of possessing a Lollard Bible and other forbidden writings.

On December 2, 1514, Hunne was sent to the bishop's prison and found two days later hanging from a beam. Hunne's jailer and a representative of the bishop of London were implicated in the merchant's death. To cover up their involvement, church officials argued that Hunne had committed suicide and continued their suit against his estate. They also had Hunne's body burned as a heretic. This raised an outcry with the public, and the jailer and the bishop's vicar were arrested. The jailer escaped from his holding cell and the vicar blamed him for murdering Hunne. The bishop of London pleaded immunity from punishment and begged Cardinal Wolsey to protect him. The case had now gone to Parliament, which ordered the vicar to pay a huge fine. Wolsey pleaded for forgiveness and understanding for the church, but he also maintained that clerics must continue to be immune from civil punishment.

Other anticlerical tales were allowed to circulate during this period when Cromwell was working hard to cultivate public opinion in advance of the planned break with Rome. In 1529 Simon Fish's scurrilous anticlerical pamphlet, "The Supplication of Beggars," appeared. Fish wrote that monks were after "every man's wife, every man's daughter, and every man's maid."[2] Fish urged the king to prohibit clerical begging and allow the true Gospel to be preached. Anne Boleyn personally brought the former Oxford student's writings to the attention of the king, as she did other reformers' works.

Members of Parliament had also expressed anticlerical sentiments in 1529, when they attacked the privileges of church courts, pluralism, and nonresident bishops like Wolsey. The Richard Hunne case was brought up as a great symbol of church corruption. William Warham, archbishop of Canterbury, responded by holding several assemblies of the English clergy, who apologized for wrong doings, declared Henry to be the English church's "supreme head and protector," and voted gifts of 118,000 pounds to help defray Henry's divorce expenses. Since the church already controlled about a fourth of the land in England, it could well afford to be generous in order to save its privileges.

The Legal Reformation

Thomas Cromwell was determined to make Parliament—and through it the public—full partners in reform. As a lawyer, he knew that to become permanent, the Reformation needed the force of law. It could not rely on just the whim of mercurial sovereigns such as King Henry VIII. Therefore, Cromwell continued his efforts to make Parliament a major participant in the process of reform and to institutionalize the Reformation. In 1532 he succeeded in getting it to approve the Act of Annates, which stopped certain church revenues from going to Rome. In March 1533 Parliament passed the Act in Restraint of Appeals, which declared England to be "an empire" that did not need to appeal church legal matters to Rome. The new Act of Succession was also issued by Parliament to give precedence in inheritance to the children of Henry and his new bride, Queen Anne.

On September 7, 1533, Anne Boleyn gave birth to her first child—a girl named Elizabeth. She was to become, arguably, the greatest monarch in English history, but at the time of her birth her father was deeply disappointed and did not even bother to attend her christening. He still did not have

the legitimate son he desperately wanted. Anne tried to reassure him that she was still young enough to have many sons. She also encouraged him on his path of Reformation. Among her carefully chosen chaplains was Matthew Parker (1504–1573), the future Protestant archbishop of Canterbury under Elizabeth.

The Act of Supremacy of 1534 made Henry "supreme head of the church in England." This was far more than Sir Thomas More could stand. He had already resigned his position as lord chancellor in May 1532, deeply concerned about the direction Henry, Cromwell, Cranmer, and the queen were moving the kingdom. When he would not agree to recognize the succession of Elizabeth over Mary, Henry had him arrested for treason. He was executed on July 7, 1535, and his severed head was prominently displayed on London Bridge as a warning to any other subject who might put his loyalty to the pope above his obedience to the king.

More died blessing King Henry, his old intellectual friend whom he genuinely admired, and was joined in martyrdom by John Fisher, the brave bishop of Rochester, another prominent foe of the Reformation. More and Fisher were among the few who openly resisted Henry's break with Rome despite the high level of satisfaction with the old church. The king was so popular and powerful and anticlericalism was so strong that Cromwell was able to lead the kingdom away from the authority of Rome without much public protest. Catherine of Aragon, although treated with increasing cruelty by the frustrated Henry, refused to encourage her supporters who wished to foment rebellion. At her death on January 7, 1536, Henry crowed, "God be praised, the harridan is dead!"[3]

In 1536 Cromwell took another major step toward reform on the continental model by securing the Act of Dissolution, which completed the process of closing 560 of England's monasteries begun under Wolsey as a fund-raising measure and ceded their lands to the crown. To add to the confusion, monks were still required to keep their vows. The spendthrift king was pleased at these additional revenues and promised to make up for the loss to various charities and schools. The further closing of the monasteries and continued agricultural problems in the north contributed to an uprising known as The Pilgrimage of Grace. Although not as great a threat to law and order as the German Peasant Revolts of 1524 to 1526, Henry moved quickly to crush the rebellion of "priests and gentlemen" in the summer of 1536.

UNLUCKY IN LOVE:
HENRY'S MATRIMONIAL DIFFICULTIES

By 1536 the death of Catherine of Aragon removed the basis for Henry's quarrel with the papacy. It was also clear that the king was uncomfortable with some aspects of Protestant theology and practice. Some in the old church still hoped Henry might revert back to the authority of Rome. For that reason there was a two-year delay in publishing in England the 1536 bull that excommunicated the English king. Even before, Henry had turned against Anne Boleyn, who had miscarried a male fetus in January 1536. The king now thought God had damned his second marriage, and charges of treasonous adultery were brought against Anne. She was executed at the chopping block inside the Tower of London on May 19, 1536.

Her replacement, the mild-mannered and submissive Jane Seymour (b. 1509), finally presented Henry with a legitimate son in 1537, the future King Edward VI. Sadly for Henry, Jane died shortly after giving

birth. Thomas Cromwell, now earl of Essex, was increasingly concerned about the king's misgivings about the Reformation. He decided that a political marriage to a Protestant dynasty might be just the thing to help save the Reformation in England. Since no daughter of a staunch Protestant house was then made available to the aging British lion, Cromwell settled on Anne (b. 1515), eldest daughter of Duke Wilhlem of Cleves. The Erasmian Wilhelm joined Henry in having reservations about some aspects of both Protestantism and traditional Roman Catholicism. Cleves, like England, was at odds with Charles V; therefore, the marriage would help cement an anti-imperial alliance and at least not bring Henry any closer to Rome.

Since the sensual Henry was not about to marry a woman he had never seen, the king's favorite court artist, Hans Holbein of Augsburg, was dispatched to Cleves to paint Anne. The German was noted for the high quality of his portraits. Holbein's likeness sufficiently pleased the king that he allowed his ambassadors to finalize their negotiations, and Anne was sent to England by her brother to marry Henry in 1539. When the two finally met, neither apparently liked what they saw. Holbein's miniature portrait had hidden the effects of smallpox on Anne's complexion, and the king referred to her cuttingly as the "Rhenish mare." Anne of Cleves probably did not consider Henry much of a prize either for he was already well into the process of moving from a svelte 32-inch waist to a gargantuan 52-inch waist. The marriage was quickly annulled, and Anne was given a handsome country estate and a sufficient income to live upon, lest her brother be incensed. She was also invited to court for holidays, treated as a beloved relative, and officially referred to as the "king's sister."

Someone had to bear the brunt of the king's wrath over the Cleves fiasco, and this

Hans Holbein, *Anne of Cleves*. Photo courtesy of the National Portrait Gallery, London, United Kingdom.

time the talented Thomas Cromwell was the victim. Henry was eventually persuaded by Cromwell's enemies that he was a dangerous heretic who must be removed from office. Despite his invaluable services to the crown and his fervent pleas for mercy, Cromwell was duly executed in the exact spot where Anne Boleyn had previously lost her head.

Disappointed in love for at least the fourth time, the aging king vowed never to marry and promptly fell in love with a lively young beauty, Catherine Howard. He married the high-spirited Catherine in 1540, shortly after Cromwell's execution. By then he had issued his "Six Articles" of 1539, which reaffirmed his essential Catholicism on such issues as clerical celibacy, the real presence of Christ in the sacrament, the withholding of the cup from the laity, and the importance of oral confession. The "Six

Articles" were opposed by the secretly married Thomas Cranmer but to no avail. For Henry, the Reformation had gone far enough and he wanted to revel in the robust sensuality of his pretty young wife.

Unfortunately for Henry, Catherine Howard found him insufficient to satisfy her sexual and romantic longings and she invited at least one man of the court to share her royal bed while Henry was away. Catherine had also had sex with another lover prior to her marriage to the king. Enemies of the Howard clan eventually dared to report Catherine's treasonable liaisons and premarital experience, and she was duly executed in 1542 along with both of the men who had shared her favors. A year later Henry married his sixth and last wife, the matronly and charming Catherine Parr (1512–1548).

A cultivated woman of good sense, Catherine had been twice widowed before winning the affections of the declining and disappointed king. She proved to be a good companion to Henry and a good nurse, which he needed very much in his last four years of life as his world grew smaller. A Protestant sympathizer and a compassionate woman, Catherine also proved to be a wonderfully nurturing stepmother to Henry's children, who badly needed some stability and maternal love after the deaths of so many of their mothers and stepmothers. Queen Catherine seems to have done a great deal to repair some of the psychic damage done to the royal offspring.

The Reformation under Edward VI (1537–1553)

When that master manipulator Henry VIII died in 1547, he was succeeded by his ten-year-old son, Edward. Although Edward was a bright youth with a great fondness for

Protestant theology, England was in fact ruled by a Council of Regents led by the king's ambitious uncle, Edward Seymour (c. 1506–1552). The handsome Seymour, who soon became the duke of Somerset and lord protector, had the Catholic "Six Articles" repealed and with the support of the frail young king moved England solidly into the Protestant camp. Seymour was particularly zealous in attacking Catholic shrines. His brother, Thomas, quickly married Edward's Protestant stepmother, Catherine, and envied his brother's power. Being named an admiral in the English navy was insufficient to satisfy his grandiose dreams of power. The admiral's later "romping" with the fourteen-year-old Princess Elizabeth put her in a compromising position and was obviously an expression of his interest in promoting his own ambitions. Elizabeth's stepmother intervened after catching her husband kissing the princess in a more than stepfatherly manner and sent her to a safer haven elsewhere.

Despite these behind-the-scenes maneuvers, Edward VI's reign witnessed the full flowering of Protestantism in the realm. Archbishop Thomas Cranmer was now allowed to introduce his wife, a niece of the Lutheran reformer of Nuremberg Andreas Osiander, at court for the first time. Even more important, Thomas Cranmer was ordered to isssue his Protestant manual of worship, *The Book of Common Prayer*. The Act of Uniformity of 1549 made the prayer book's use mandatory for religious services throughout the kingdom. Cranmer also published "Forty-two Articles of Religious Belief," which further clarified the triumph of Protestantism in England.

THE TYNDALE BIBLE

The use of the English Bible of William Tyndale (1494–1536) and Miles Coverdale

(1488–1568) was now fully encouraged and Lollard descendants of John Wycliffe and others could openly read the Scriptures in English. Tyndale was the first person to translate the New Testament and the Pentateuch from their original languages into English. He was also the first to print an English version of the Bible. Ordained a priest, Tyndale was educated at Oxford, where he took his M.A. in 1515. He then moved to Cambridge before leaving seven years later for London. There Tyndale became immersed in the writings of Martin Luther and determined to make his own contribution to the cause of reform by making the Bible available to the laity.

Finding it impossible to work on an English Bible in England because of the prejudices against "Lollardy," Tyndale moved to Germany in 1524 and then to the Low Countries, where he published his new translations in 1525. His translations were widely circulated back in England despite official condemnation. Tyndale never lived to see the eventual royal acceptance of his work, for he was arrested by officials of the Holy Roman Empire in Antwerp and burned at the stake for heresy in 1536. His loyal follower, Miles Coverdale, completed the English translation of the Old Testament. Their Bible became known as the Great Bible when printed by Thomas Cromwell and sanctioned by Henry VIII in 1539. An act of Parliament in 1543 restricted its use until the reign of Edward VI.

THE FALL OF EDWARD SEYMOUR

While the Protestant reform proceeded apace, Edward Seymour found himself in political difficulties. Unfortunately, he was not the most efficient of administrators and there were still many, especially in the north, who resisted the new religion. In 1549 a rebellion led by Robert Kett, a Protestant tradesman, broke out at Norwich and elsewhere. Seymour had continued Henry VIII's 1542 policy of debasing the coinage, which helped fuel inflation. The continuing problem of converting farm lands to more profitable sheep runs, which required less labor, also contributed to rural unrest. Usually a good soldier, Seymour gave the command to John Dudley, another ambitious member of the council, who put down the revolt, and Kett and 1,000 of his followers were executed. Seymour was blamed for a loss of nerve and the continuing economic problems and was replaced as head of the council of regency by Dudley, who had long coveted more power.

The Rise and Fall of John Dudley (c. 1502–1553) and Lady Jane Grey (1537–1554)

Dudley, who became duke of Northumberland, had ousted Seymour in 1547 promising to improve administration, end public commotion, and halt Seymour's foreign adventures in Scotland and France. Seymour had wished to bring about the union of the English and Scottish crowns, one of Henry VIII's fondest wishes. France was allied with Scotland and determined to keep the Scots out of English hands. They sent a powerful army to defend Scotland's northern border in 1549 and inflicted a humiliating defeat upon England. Dudley also continued the Reformation knowing that the priggish and bigoted King Edward would never abandon his Protestantism and that too many powerful people in England agreed with the young king.

By the winter of 1553 it was becoming increasingly clear that the king was dying of what proved to be tuberculosis. Mary,

daughter of Catherine of Aragon and a loyal Catholic, was to inherit the crown under the terms of the Succession Act of 1543 and Henry VIII's will. Her accession meant a Catholic restoration was certain. This placed John Dudley's future in question, and he took steps to ward off this potential disaster before the dying Edward expired. He married his oldest son, Guilford, to the convinced Protestant Lady Jane Grey, a theologically sophisticated sixteen-year-old Tudor cousin. She was forced into the marriage by her parents. King Edward, also wanting to avoid a Catholic restoration, agreed in writing to disinherit his sisters and left the crown to Lady Jane and her heirs before his death on July 6, 1553.

Dudley had thought of almost everything, except that he neglected to secure Princess Mary, around whom opposition could rally. She was removed from London by several Protestant politicians, who could not bear the thought that the legitimate succession should be violated and that the Dudleys would remain in power. John Dudley was believed to have been converting some of the wealth of the crown to his own personal use for some time and was disliked by some who were jealous of his power and talent. Mary's rescuers took her to Suffolk, where she was surrounded by loyal Catholic gentry. Her followers marched on London and the Dudleys and their unwilling accomplice, Lady Jane, were arrested and later executed for treason. Mary exhibited a merciful heart in not executing a larger number of traitors.

At age thirty-seven, Mary became queen of England. Her heart was set on finding happiness for herself and her people. To do that, the religious history of her brother's six-year reign must be reversed. Roman Catholicism must be restored to England so that the souls of the English people could be rescued from eternal damnation.

The Reign of Mary I, Tudor, 1553–1558

Like all the children of Henry VIII, Queen Mary had been well educated in languages and was intelligent. She also had a good heart, strong religious convictions, and was very well intentioned. Unfortunately, Queen Mary was also very rigid and did not always receive or follow the best of advice. Her chief advisor was her cousin, Cardinal Reginald Pole (1500–1558), whom she made archbishop of Canterbury in place of the Protestant Thomas Cranmer. Pole was a well-respected churchman, but he, in his fervent zeal to restore what he considered to be the true faith, did not always exhibit the best judgment in the face of the new realities in England. Cranmer was arrested for treason and burned at the stake as a heretic. Under judicial torture, he had recanted his Protestant beliefs and then denied his denial. When brought to the stake at Smithfield, he put his right hand in the flames so he could write no more recantations.

Reginald Pole and others urged Queen Mary to deal harshly with heretics. Pole, like Mary, was kindhearted and merciful, but as a matter of public policy he felt it was essential to exterminate heresy by publicly burning prominent Protestants as an example to others. Unfortunately for the archbishop's intended purposes, most of the Protestant leaders had already fled to the Continent upon the accession of Mary. The result was that most of the 287 or so Protestants executed for religious treason in the queen's six-year reign were comparatively small fish, with a few notable exceptions such as Thomas Cranmer and Hugh Latimer (1485–1555), the Protestant bishop of Worcester and a major figure in the reform. The queen's policy thus did not destroy English Protestantism as she had hoped but earned her the unhappy title "Bloody Mary."

Even worse from the point of view of the public was Mary's decision to wed Emperor Charles V's son Philip rather than one of several English candidates. Mary wanted a staunch Catholic and the blond-haired, blue-eyed, devout, and intelligent Philip more than filled the bill. However, the proposed match touched off strong antiforeign feelings in the realm. Many could not stomach the notion of England having "a Spanish king," and 3,000 joined Sir Thomas Wyatt (son of a famous poet of the same name) of Kent in attempting to overthrow the government. Wyatt's forces did succeed in pen-

After Antonio Moro, *Portrait of Mary I. Tudor,* Bibliotheque Nationale, Paris, France. Giraudon/Art Resource.

etrating into London in February 1554 before their defeat. The ringleaders of the revolt were executed as well as Lady Jane Grey and her husband, even though they had not been involved in the uprising. Wyatt had rebelled in the name of the queen's sister Elizabeth, who disavowed the rebels and worshipped publicly as a Catholic.

At long last Philip of Spain arrived in England in July 1554 and the marriage was celebrated. While the middle-aged Mary was very pleased with her younger and equally pious husband, their union was not blessed with children. Finally, in September 1554 Philip departed England to attend to business in Flanders. Two years later he succeeded his father as king of Spain. The disconsolate Mary was left eagerly looking for the signs of a child. She was also having difficulties with Parliament over her program for the restoration of Roman Catholicism. Those who had purchased church lands had no intention of returning them to the church, but Mary was finally able to get Parliament to repeal many of the Reformation statutes passed under her late brother. She also ap-

pointed new Catholic bishops and made one of them, the vindictive Stephen Gardiner (c. 1493–1555), her lord chancellor. On the positive side, the queen completed some of the fiscal reforms begun by John Dudley.

For the most part, however, Queen Mary's six-year reign must be judged a failure. Her persecutions of Protestants and her unpopular marriage helped to undermine the cause of Roman Catholicism in England. She had no great successes in foreign policy, even having to abandon Calais to the French. The port of Calais was the last English toehold on the Continent after the close of the Hundred Years' War. Its loss in 1558 hurt English pride. Philip made only a brief return to England in 1557 and failed to impregnate Mary. She died of uterine cancer on November 17, 1558. Her good friend Cardinal Pole died twelve hours later. Neither had lived long enough to permanently reestablish Catholicism as the official state religion of England. Their creation of Protestant martyrs and generally unsuccessful policies had in fact made the situation worse for practicing Catholics.

Chronology

1502	Catherine of Aragon marries Arthur Tudor of England, who dies four months later.		Parliament; Simon Fish's "Supplication of Beggars."
1509	Catherine marries King Henry VIII.	1531	Convocation of the English clergy declares King Henry VIII "Supreme Head of the Church" in England.
1514	Richard Hunne case.		
1521	Henry VIII named "Defender of the Faith" by Pope Leo X for his written attack on Martin Luther.	1532	Act of Annates; Thomas More resigns as chancellor.
1527	Henry requests a papal annulment of his marriage to Catherine of Aragon.	1533	Act in Restraint of Appeals; Henry marries Anne Boleyn; birth of future Queen Elizabeth I; Act of Succession.
1529	Cardinal Thomas Wolsey ousted as lord chancellor; First Reformation	1534	Act of Supremacy.

(continued)

1535	Executions of Sir Thomas More and Bishop John Fisher.
1536	Death of Catherine of Aragon; Act of Dissolution of the monasteries; suppression of the Pilgrimage of Grace; death of William Tyndale.
1537	King Henry VIII marries Jane Seymour, who dies shortly after giving birth to future King Edward VI.
1539	Henry weds Anne of Cleves; English Bible sanctioned; Henry reaffirms Catholic doctrines by issuing "Six Articles."
1540	Execution of Thomas Cromwell; aging Henry weds youthful Catherine Howard.
1543	Henry VIII weds his sixth and last wife, Catherine Parr.
1547	Death of Henry VIII; accession of Edward VI; Council of Regency dominated by Edward Seymour.
1549	Act of Uniformity makes Archbishop Thomas Cranmer's *The Book of Common Prayer* and "42 Articles" mandatory in English churches.
1551	Kett's Rebellion suppressed; John Dudley replaces Seymour as head of king's Council of Regency.
1553	Failing health of Edward VI; Guilford Dudley marries Lady Jane Grey; death of Edward VI; overthrow of Dudleys; accession of Queen Mary I.
1554	Thomas Wyatt's revolt; Queen Mary weds Philip of Habsburg; Parliament repeals the Act of Supremacy; England received back in the good graces of the Catholic Church; Reginald Pole serves as archbishop of Canterbury; Philip leaves England.
1555	Persecutions of Protestants intensify; death of Hugh Latimer.
1556	Death of Thomas Cranmer.
1557	Brief return of Philip II, now king of Spain.
1558	Calais lost to the French; deaths of Queen Mary and Cardinal Reginald Pole.

Further Reading

THE ENGLISH REFORMATION AND THE EARLY TUDORS

Susan Brigden, *London and the Reformation* (1989).

A. G. Dickens, *The English Reformation*, 2nd ed. (1989). Still one of the best overviews.

Eamon Duffy, *The Stripping of the Altars: Traditional Religion in England, 1400–1580* (1992). Argues that the late medieval English church was strong and vigorous.

G. R. Elton, *England under the Tudors*, 3rd ed. (1991).

———, *Reform and Reformation: England 1509–1558* (1977). Valuable surveys by a master historian.

Ronald Fritz, ed., *Historical Dictionary of Tudor England, 1485–1603* (1991). An outstanding reference work with contributions from a host of able scholars.

Charles Gray, *Renaissance and Reformation England, 1509–1714* (1973).

John Guy, *Tudor England* (1988). One of the best recent surveys.

Christopher Haigh, *English Reformations: Religion, Politics, and Society under the Tudors* (1993).

Felicity Heal and Rosemary O'Day, eds., *Church and Society in England Henry VIII to James I* (1977).

Richard Helmholtz, *Roman Canon Law in Reformation England* (1990).

J. D. Mackie, *The Early Tudors, 1485–1558* (1994).

Richard Rex, *The Theology of John Fisher* (1991).

John Scarisbrick, *The Reformation and the English People* (1984).

Arthur Slavin, *The Precarious Balance: English Government and Society, 1450–1640* (1973). Still very sound.

Leo Solt, *Church and State in Early Modern England, 1509–1640* (1990).

Carl Trueman, *Luther's Legacy: Salvation and the English Reformers, 1525–1556* (1994).

Penry Williams, *The Tudor Regime* (1979).

Joyce Youings, *Sixteenth-Century England* (1984).

———, *The Dissolution of the Monasteries* (1971).

KING HENRY VIII

Carolly Erickson, *Great Harry* (1980).

Henry Kelly, *The Matrimonial Trials of Henry VIII* (1976).

Stanford Lehmberg, *The Later Parliaments of Henry VIII* (1977).

Helen Miller, *Henry VIII and the English Nobility* (1986).

Richard Rex, *Henry VIII and the English Reformation* (1993).

John Scarisbrick, *Henry VIII* (1968). Still the most important biography.

Lacey Baldwin Smith, *Henry VIII: The Mask of Royalty* (1971). A fascinating psychological study.

HIS QUEENS AND MINISTERS

R. W. Chambers, *Thomas More* (1958).

G. R. Elton, *Reform and Renewal: Thomas Cromwell and the Commonweal* (1973).

Antonia Fraser, *The Six Wives of Henry VIII* (1992).

Peter Gywn, *The King's Cardinal: The Rise and Fall of Thomas Wolsey* (1993).

E. W. Ives, *Anne Boleyn* (1986).

Karen Lindsey, *Divorced, Beheaded, Survived: A Feminist Reinterpretation of the Wives of Henry VIII* (1995).

Richard Marius, *Thomas More, A Biography* (1985).

Garrett Mattingly, *Catherine of Aragon* (1944).

Lacey Baldwin Smith, *A Tudor Tragedy: The Life and Times of Catherine Howard* (1961).

Retha Warnicke, *The Rise and Fall of Anne Boleyn* (1989). Revises many of our understandings.

OTHER FIGURES IN THE REFORM

David Daniell, *William Tyndale: A Biography* (1994).

Thomas Mayer, *Thomas Starkey and the Commonweal* (1990).

Diarmaid MacCulloch, *Thomas Cranmer* (1996).

Donald Smeeton, *Lollard Themes in the Reformation Theology of William Tyndale* (1986).

THE REIGNS OF EDWARD VI AND MARY I

Barrett Beer, *Northumberland, the Political Career of John Dudley* (1973).

Carolly Erickson, *Bloody Mary* (1978).

Dale Hoak, *The King's Council in the Reign of Edward VI* (1976).

W. K. Jordan, *Edward VI*, 2 vols. (1968, 1970).

David Loades, *John Dudley: Duke of Northumberland* (1997).

———, *The Reign of Mary Tudor* (1979). The leading study.

Alison Plowden, *Jane Grey and the House of Suffolk* (1986).

Notes

1. Quoted by Thomas Clarke, "Irish Awareness during the Reformation," paper presented at The Sixteenth Century Studies Conference, St. Louis, Missouri, October 27, 1978.
2. Cited in Lewis Spitz, ed., *The Protestant Reformation* (Englewod Cliffs, N.J.: Prentice Hall, 1966), p. 150.
3. Cited in Karen Lindsey, *Divorced, Beheaded, Survived: A Feminist Reinterpretation of the Wives of Henry VIII* (Reading, Mass.: Addison Wesley, 1995), p. 114.

15

A Tale of Two Queens: Elizabeth I of England and Mary of Scotland

Queen Mary was succeeded by her twenty-four-year-old sister, Elizabeth, the daughter of Anne Boleyn. It was under Elizabeth I that the Reformation came to full flower in England. The Reformation in Scotland came to fruition during the reign of Elizabeth's staunchly Catholic cousin, Mary, Queen of Scots. Nine years younger than Elizabeth, Mary of Scotland eventually became the leading candidate to succeed her unmarried cousin as queen of England. She dreamed of restoring Catholicism to both monarchies. The two queens found themselves locked in a dangerous competition.

The Young Queen Elizabeth

Like her sister, Mary Tudor, Elizabeth was well-schooled in languages, knowing some Greek, Latin, French, and Spanish. Elizabeth had been tutored by, among others, Roger Ascham (1516–1568), a Cambridge scholar and one of the foremost pedagogues of the Renaissance. Ascham believed that Latin grammar and literature were the foundations of a sound humanist education. Elizabeth, his greatest pupil, demonstrated a

keen mind and an aptitude for learning. Later she even learned to talk to her sailors in a language they could understand.

Unlike her older sister, Elizabeth had a talent for survival and could demonstrate great flexibility when needed. With the help of her stepmother, Catherine Parr, she had warded off the dangerous advances of Thomas Seymour as a teenager. Elizabeth had also survived the threat of confinement and possible death in the Tower of London during the reign of her sister when she had been accused of attempting to undermine the queen's restoration of Catholicism. Elizabeth had learned the lessons of caution and discretion at an early age. Such lessons served her well as queen.

The young queen also learned to judge character and not let emotions interfere with matters of state. Elizabeth usually made shrewd appointments to office. One of her best choices was William Cecil (1520–1598), an experienced officeholder, as her principal secretary and later lord treasurer. Cecil, although a very able official, found he could never dominate the queen but that he could work most effectively with her. Although sometimes disagreeing with her on such matters as the need for Elizabeth to marry, he was always completely loyal to his prodigious sovereign and held her in deep affection and respect. His talented son, Robert, the earl of Salisbury (1563–1612), served both Elizabeth and her successor with distinction.

Both Elizabeth and Cecil were naturally cautious and careful in spending money, qualities essential in a modest monarchy with limited resources. England could hardly have stood another prodigal like Henry VIII. While Elizabeth and the able Cecil usually agreed on the main outlines of policy, serving her was not without its moments of trauma. She was capable of serious outbursts of ill temper—some real, some staged. More problematic was Elizabeth's difficulty in making up her mind on a variety of issues. Possessed of a very complicated intelligence, she anticipated a myriad of ramifications to most policy decisions. Elizabeth also understood that many problems would solve themselves if one delayed taking action long enough. Still her labored style often frustrated her ministers, including her astute principal secretary from 1573 on, Francis Walsingham (1530–1590), who nevertheless remained in awe of her intelligence and vast knowledge.

THE ELIZABETHAN RELIGIOUS SETTLEMENT

Although frequently appearing indecisive, the astute young queen recognized early in her reign that the religious question had to be dealt with immediately. Religion was a crucial matter to most people in England and the country had already been through too many shifts between Catholicism and Protestantism, as had Elizabeth herself. There were many issues to be sorted out. If England returned to the Protestant fold, it would be threatened by potentially hostile Catholic powers such as France and Spain. Yet most of the English, including the queen, had no wish to continue their religious allegiance to Rome. What emerged was a compromise between the Marian exiles who returned after a period of association with Calvinist Protestants on the Continent and Elizabeth's own desire for a settlement that would be more centrist Protestant.

Elizabeth had Parliament recognize her as sole "supreme governor of this realm in all things ecclesiastical and temporal" in the Act of Supremacy of 1559. Unlike her more arrogant father, she refused the title of "supreme head" of the church because that dignity belonged to God alone. Parliament also issued the Act of Uniformity in 1559, which further reestablished a Protestant church, but a state church in which many Catholics could worship in relative comfort of conscience. Thomas Cranmer's "Forty-two Articles" of religious belief were trimmed to "Thirty-nine Articles" and issued in 1563. Only the two Protestant sacraments of the Eucharist and baptism were retained. The Act of Uniformity also mandated the use of a modified version of Cranmer's *The Book of Common Prayer*. She named her mother's former chaplain, the moderate Matthew Parker, as archbishop of Canterbury.

The Elizabethan settlement had features designed to appeal to both Catholics and Protestants. It permitted the clergy to marry as they did in Protestant lands, but it also continued the traditional episcopal system. Church ritual retained its ceremonial splendor, which Elizabeth enjoyed, but its theology embraced a number of evangelical innovations such as the emphasis on salvation by faith over good works. Elizabeth's religious agreement, while leaning toward Protestantism, was moderate enough and sensible enough to please the overwhelming majority of her subjects.

The queen especially desired an end to religious wrangling and civil unrest. Not wanting to establish "windows into men's souls," Elizabeth settled for outward conformity and obedience to law. This she generally achieved, although her Reformation had too many elements of "popery" to please those mostly Calvinist Protestants who would "purify" the English church and society. They became known collectively as the *Puritans* and would increase in influence and numbers throughout her reign. A few Protestant extremists wanted to separate themselves completely from the church of England, but they too would have to bide their time.

Some uncompromising Roman Catholics also were not happy with aspects of Elizabeth's religious program, which they considered too Protestant. In 1570, Pope Pius V (r. 1566–1572) excommunicated the queen and absolved her subjects of their obligations to her. Nevertheless, most Catholics stayed loyal to the increasingly popular "virgin queen." Repeated attempts by some Catholic gentlemen to replace the "English Jezebel" with her Catholic cousin, Mary of Scotland, only served to further discredit the church of Rome and its more loyal adherents. Mary's execution in 1587 and the defeat of the Spanish Armada of 1588 sealed the fate of Catholicism in England. Elizabeth's government executed 183 religious dissidents, but those executions were not as unpopular as Mary Tudor's in part because they were spread over a forty-five-year reign. The well-intentioned but unfortunate Mary Tudor has had to bear the epithet "bloody," while her more popular sister's persecutions have been largely downplayed.

GLORIANA: THE SUCCESSFUL QUEEN

Elizabeth's enemies were faced with the great problem of her developing status as a beloved cultural icon and her considerable success as an administrator. Fiscally conservative, the queen usually managed to avoid bothering the all-male Parliament for additional revenues, which pleased them a great deal. "Gloriana" put herself on public display to great advantage with her brilliant speeches to Parliament, pageants, and processions around the country. Her subjects loved those glimpses of their glamorous queen and her brilliantly clad court. She was capable of personally charming almost anyone.

Beneath the style, there was also a great deal of substance. Elizabeth was able to sponsor new efforts at colonization, aid rebels in the Netherlands, defeat the Spanish invaders, subdue Irish rebels, enhance economic development, revise the laws dealing with poor relief, and offer encouragement to brilliant artists such as the matchless playwrights William Shakespeare (1564–1616) and Christopher Marlowe (1564–1593), and the poets Edmund Spenser (c. 1552–1599), and Mary (1561–1621) and Philip Sidney (1554–1586). Seldom had one European monarchy seen such a concentration of talent. Queen Elizabeth's usual course was to avoid costly foreign entanglements and military display, using her status as Europe's most eligible single female to neutralize potential aggressors. After all, why would anyone attack England if he had hopes of gaining it by marrying Elizabeth?

Elizabeth decided early in her reign that she would never share power and her bed with a man. She liked being a ruling queen and had no wish to run the risks of her mother, her stepmothers, and her sister—all of whom had suffered for the sake of their relationships. Physical problems may have compounded the issue. Elizabeth did enjoy both flirting and dancing but had no desire to make herself vulnerable to another human being. She did have her court

Federigo Zuccaro, *Portrait of Elizabeth I* (known as the "Sieve" Portrait). Pinacoteca Nazionale, Siena, Italy, Scala/Art Resource.

favorites—men such as Robert Dudley, son of the traitor John Dudley, the dashing Christopher Hatton, and Walter Raleigh (c. 1552–1618), the founder of a colony off the coast of North Carolina. Raleigh later wrote a *History of the World*, while in prison during the reign of James I. The married Dudley was a particular friend whom she made master of her horses. When Dudley's wife died under mysterious circumstances in 1560, many believed the queen would marry her beloved "Robin." Wanting to avoid all hints of scandal, Elizabeth continued her friendship with Dudley but remained perpetually single.

The decision to remain a single woman married to her career was unique for the period and provided its own set of pressures. Scurrilous gossip about the queen's personal life became a staple of Elizabethan life.

Her advisors continually pressured her to marry and assure the succession. Elizabeth held them and her various suitors at bay, and demonstrated that England could prosper under its "Virgin Queen," even if one favorite, Robert Devereux, earl of Essex (1567–1601), had to be executed for treason.

Essex's treachery was particularly galling for he was the stepson of her beloved Robert Dudley and she had lavished favors upon him. A serious Irish revolt broke out in 1598, and Hugh O'Neill, earl of Tyrone (c. 1547–1616), defeated an English army at the Battle of Blackwater River. Elizabeth sent an army led by Essex to Ireland to quell the revolt. His command was a disaster; instead of fighting Tyrone, Essex lavished knighthoods on 59 gentlemen contrary to the queen's instructions. Blaming his failures on the queen and her Privy Council, Essex returned to England without permission and later plotted to force the government to replace the trusted Robert Cecil with himself. One of Essex's supporters was the earl of Southampton, Shakespeare's great patron; both were found guilty of treason and executed.

For the most part, the queen's judgment of people was sound and her policies worked. England kept its independence and prospered under her rule. Embarrassing and soul-wrenching reversals on religious policy were avoided throughout her long reign. The aging Elizabeth was able to continue impressing many of her subjects and many of the crowned heads of Europe well into her sixties. Near the end of her rule in 1601, after some particularly stormy sessions of Parliament over the Essex crisis and various monopolies granted by the queen, the elaborately bejewelled Elizabeth informed her subjects:

> Though God has raised me high, yet this I count the glory of my crown, that I have

reigned with your love. . . . Your prosperity has been my chief concern. . . . My heart was never set on worldly goods, but only for my subjects' good.[1]

The sly Elizabeth was such a great actress and politician that it is likely she actually believed these words as did many of those parliamentarians who heard them. Here was a performer worthy of the age of Marlowe and Shakespeare.

Mary Stuart and the Reformation in Scotland

As for Elizabeth's neighboring monarchy to the north, Scotland also experienced the rise of a Protestant movement. The way to Reformation in Scotland, as in England, was paved by anticlericalism, remnants of Lollardy, and to some extent Renaissance humanism. Lutheran ideas had infiltrated into Scotland during the reign of King James V (r. 1513–1542) despite the outlawing of Luther's writings in 1525 by the Scottish Parliament. The English Bible of William Tyndale was also popular in mountainous and rugged Scotland.

The Spread of Protestant Ideas

Part of the reason for the appeal of Protestant notions in Scotland was a high level of dissatisfaction with the Roman Catholic Church. There was widespread resentment of its financial power since the church held about a third of the landed wealth in Scotland at this time and its leadership insisted on strictly enforcing the payment of tithes. This wealth was enjoyed primarily by the upper clergy; an estimated 10,000 Scottish priests labored without regular church incomes (benefices). The higher clergy added to their unpopularity by tending to side with the crown in quarrels with the Scottish barons.

Disputes between the crown and the nobility grew more and more frequent as King James was followed in power by his French wife, Mary of Guise (1515–1560). A devout Catholic, Mary served as regent for her infant daughter, Mary, Queen of Scots (b. 1542). The widowed queen was determined to bring Scotland more firmly into the orbit of her native France and her militantly Catholic family, the Guises. Most of the barons were equally determined to keep Scotland an independent kingdom.

Reformation ideas had been spread by attractive figures such as Patrick Hamilton (d. 1528). Hamilton was a humanist of noble blood and related to the king. He had studied at Paris, Louvain, and several places in Germany before becoming a teacher at the University of St. Andrews in 1523. There he openly taught Lutheran ideas until cited for heresy by the archbishop of St. Andrews. Hamilton found refuge in Luther's Wittenberg before returning to Scotland in 1528. He was then tried and burned for heresy, a grim lesson for other would-be Lutherans.

Despite the dangers of spreading Lutheranism, another charismatic preacher emerged in the person of the handsome George Wishart. Wishart had visited a number of Protestant communities on the Continent and had returned in 1543 to advocate many of the positions of Huldrych Zwingli. It was Wishart who converted John Knox (1502–1572) to Protestantism. Knox was a peasant's son who had become a disillusioned Catholic priest and would later become the charismatic leader of the Reformation in Scotland. In 1546 David Beaton, cardinal and archbishop of St. Andrews, had Wishart tried and burned for heresy. The cardinal was reported to have laughed out loud as the popular Wishart writhed in agony.

Determined on revenge, a number of Wishart's friends entered Beaton's castle at St. Andrew's in May 1546 and murdered the cardinal in his bedroom. The assassins then draped the cardinal's body, which they had urinated on, over his castle wall as a public expression of defiance. Holding the archbishop's fortress in the name of King Henry VIII of England, the rebels called John Knox to join them as their preacher. They held out until July 1547, when a squadron of French warships summoned by the queen-regent took over the castle and dispatched the rebels to French prison ships. Their preacher, John Knox, was sentenced to life as a galley slave on French ships plying the Mediterranean.

THE RISE OF KNOX, THE "THUNDERING SCOT"

After serving as a bound oarsman for nineteen months, Knox managed to escape and made his way to England. There the "thundering Scot" became a very popular preacher during the reign of the Protestant Edward VI. With the Catholic Mary Tudor's accession in 1553, Knox fled England for the Continent and spent time at Frankfurt on the Main in Germany and the Geneva of John Calvin.

Knox was especially dazzled by Calvin's reformed Geneva. He was keen for a chance to reform his native Scotland along the lines laid out so successfully by John Calvin in Geneva. The problem was that Catholic women still ruled in England and Scotland. In chauvinist and Protestant anger, Knox published his "First Blast Against the Monstrous Regiment of Women." He declared that to "promote a woman to have rule in any realm is repugnant to nature, contumely to God, a thing most contrary to His revealed will and ap-

proved ordinance, and a subversion of all good order, equity, and justice." As for Mary of Guise, she was an "unruly cow saddled by mistake."[2]

Knox's flagrant display of misogyny did not sit well with Mary Tudor's successor, Elizabeth I, and she wrote John Calvin, rebuking him for the tirade of his Scottish disciple. An embarrassed Calvin apologized to the queen and assured her that Knox's comments were in no way directed at a Protestant queen such as herself. Elizabeth was somewhat mollified and agreed in 1559 to send an English army to drive the French out of Scotland. During the ensuing war, Mary of Guise died. Her forces were defeated by the English and their pro-Protestant Scottish allies. The Treaty of Edinburgh of July 6, 1560, which concluded the hostilities, assured the triumph of Protestantism. Catholicism was outlawed by an act of the Scottish Parliament on August 24, 1560.

As for John Knox, he had been called back to Scotland in 1558 by a delegation of Scottish Protestants. He soon became the enormously popular preacher at St. Giles's Cathedral in the heart of downtown Edinburgh. There his energetic preaching, punctuated by his habit of pounding his fists, reduced many pulpits to rubble. His congregations loved the show but also found a great deal of substance in his sermons. A tireless worker of deep faith and courage, Knox also wrote a *Confession of Faith*, a *Book of Common Order*, a *First Book of Discipline*, and eventually *A History of the Reformation in Scotland*, which contributed to his reputation as one of the heroes of the movement.

MARY, QUEEN OF SCOTS

If John Knox was the greatest hero of the Reformation in Scotland, the lovely and talented daughter of Mary of Guise was his an-

French School, *Portrait of Mary Stuart, Queen of Scots,* Prado, Madrid, Spain. Alinari/Art Resource.

tagonist. Mary Stuart had been out of Scotland during most of the turbulent years of the Scottish Reformation. She had been married to the heir to the French throne, the future François II (r. 1559–1560) since 1548. Now in 1561 the eighteen-year-old widow with glorious auburn hair returned to Protestant Scotland to reclaim her throne. Intelligent and well educated, Mary was astute enough to recognize that she was going to have to accept Protestantism for the moment while worshipping privately as a Roman Catholic, much to the dismay of John Knox. However, beneath her surface charm, the steely Mary Stuart was determined to achieve a Catholic restoration.

Unlike Elizabeth I, who feared the pos-

sibility of being dominated by a husband, Mary wanted to remarry and have children. Her uncles proposed Don Carlos, son of Philip II of Spain. She declined the suggestion upon learning that Don Carlos was mentally unstable. Then a strange suitor from England appeared in the handsome personage of Robert Dudley, the earl of Leicester. Dudley had been Elizabeth of England's great favorite. Elizabeth probably was interested in having her beloved "Robin" as a spy in Mary of Scotland's bed. This possibility no doubt also occurred to Mary, who was not interested in marrying one of Elizabeth's ex-suitors, so instead she turned to another gentleman in Dudley's entourage, Charles Stuart, Lord Darnley (1545–1567).

Darnley had many qualities to recommend him. He was handsome and tall, which made him an ideal dance partner for a willowy queen such as Mary. Darnley was of royal blood, a grandson of King Henry VII, but most importantly to the devout Mary, he was a fellow Roman Catholic. He could be her partner in turning Scotland away from the Protestant plague. They were married in July 1565.

The prospect of a Catholic restoration horrified Mary's half brother, James Stuart, the earl of Moray, who raised the flag of revolt and was joined by a number of other Protestant lords. Moray's revolt failed and he and many of his coconspirators fled to safety in England. Queen Mary promptly confiscated their lands and proceeded with her plans to restore Catholicism with the help of the pope and Philip II of Spain. However, her real partner in plotting was her secretary, an Italian musician named David Rizzio (c. 1533–1566). Shortly after her honeymoon, Mary had discovered that her passionate Darnley was "a man of mystery with no secret."[3] In short, she had been blinded by passion and had married a boring blockhead, something her royal cousin would never do. As early as 1558, Elizabeth had informed Parliament: "I have long since made a choice of husband, the kingdom of England."[4]

More and more Mary turned to the agreeable company of the amusing Rizzio. Darnley grew insanely jealous and in March 1566 he and a number of henchman broke in upon the pregnant queen and stabbed her suspected lover to death. Mary fled the crime scene at her palace of Holyrood House in Edinburgh on horseback not knowing if Rizzio's death would be enough to satiate the blood lust of Darnley. She eventually found a replacement for Rizzio in the arms of the dashing James, earl of Bothwell (c. 1536–1578), a Protestant. His charms and his willingness to convert to Catholicism were enough for Mary to fall passionately in love with him.

However, Mary still had a murderously jealous husband to deal with as well as an infant son, the future King James VI of Scotland, who also became James I, king of England (b. June 1566). A skilled political actress herself, Mary fooled Darnley into thinking that she had forgiven him for the murder of Rizzio. The queen also tenderly nursed him as he tried to recover from a bout of venereal disease that had so disfigured his once handsome face that he wore a veil. However in February 1567, the house that Darnley was recuperating in blew up, and he was found strangled in the garden. Apparently Darnley had heard mysterious sounds of barrels of gunpowder being put into position and had attempted to escape by crawling out of his bedroom window.

Although legally acquitted of the crime, the queen's lover, Bothwell, was obviously guilty. When he quickly divorced his wife and married the queen in May of that year in a Protestant ceremony, it was more than John Knox and the Scottish people could bear. They flew to arms against the "wicked Jezebel" and her "evil lover." The queen's forces were soon defeated and Bothwell fled to the Continent. Mary was imprisoned for her role in the murder of Darnley, partly on the basis of possibly forged incriminating letters. She was also forced to abdicate in favor of her young son with Moray being named as regent.

MARY'S LIFE AND DEATH IN ENGLAND, 1568–1587

In May 1568 Mary managed a daring escape from prison and, deciding to try her luck with English gentleman Catholics, she fled to England, where she was soon arrested upon the orders of her cousin and rival, Elizabeth I. Mary's arrival on English soil put Elizabeth in an awkward situation. She did not want to outrage Scottish Protestant sensibilities by attempting to restore the convicted Catholic murderess to her throne. Elizabeth also did not want to turn Mary over to her subjects for execution; the death of a fellow sovereign would establish a dangerous precedent.

The solution that Elizabeth came up with was to play for time, an approach she took to many problems. After all, Mary might catch a cold in a drafty English country house and die of natural causes. Maybe Mary was innocent of the death of Darnley and might one day be sent back to Scotland. Elizabeth ended up keeping Mary in forced detention in a succession of country estates for nineteen years. Mary was not permitted to leave England or to come to court. Elizabeth was not going to permit Mary to gain adherents at the center of power nor was she going to risk face-to-face comparisons with her dangerous and glamorous cousin. On one occasion Elizabeth asked a courtier who had returned from a recent visit to Mary how the two queens compared in height. The embarrassed courtier grudgingly conceded that Mary was, indeed, somewhat taller than Elizabeth. Gloriana responded, "she is too tall; I myself am of a perfect height."[5]

Mary was kept in relative isolation and her host jailers were rotated lest they succumb to her fatal charm. She was never again to see her beloved Bothwell. The passionate earl died ten years later having gone insane in a Danish prison.

The exiled queen grew increasingly impatient in her gilded cages. In 1571 she entered into a plot with a group of Catholics led by Thomas Howard, the duke of Norfolk. Norfolk wanted to marry the Queen of Scots and return her to the throne of Scotland. In time, Mary would inherit the English throne as well. Others secretly hoped they could hasten the restoration of Catholicism by facilitating the death of Elizabeth. The marriage of Mary and Norfolk, supplemented by an invasion from Spain, was to signal an uprising of English Catholics. The Ridolfi Plot, named for one of its members, Roberto Ridolfi, a Catholic banker from Florence, soon fell apart and the duke of Norfolk was imprisoned and later executed in 1572 for treason.

In 1586 another Catholic conspiracy, this one led by Anthony Babington, was uncovered by Francis Walsingham's spies. This time Mary Stuart had agreed in writing to support the assassination of her cousin and replace her as queen of England. Obviously, Elizabeth could not ignore Mary's treasonous role. She reluctantly allowed her trial and execution at the chopping block in February 1587. Mary had paid the ultimate price for her impatience. Consequently, King Philip II of Spain, a Catholic crusader, felt compelled to send his forces against England to attempt a forceable conversion as we shall see in greater detail in Chapter 17.

Meanwhile, Mary's son, James, was raised as a Calvinist Protestant. James was as vain of his abilities as an amateur theologian as Henry VIII had been. It was James who later, as Elizabeth's successor, sponsored a beautifully lyric translation of the Bible—the so-called King James Bible. Some called him the "wisest fool in Christendom" for his arrogance. Be that as it may, the English and Scottish kingdoms, united after 1603, would move into the seventeenth century firmly in the Protestant camp.

Chronology

1528	Execution of Patrick Hamilton.		1554	Knox forced to leave Catholic England of Mary Tudor.
1533	Birth of Elizabeth Tudor.			
1542	Birth of Mary Stuart; death of King James V of Scotland.		1558	Death of Queen Mary Tudor; accession of Elizabeth I; Knox publishes his "First Blast Against the Monstrous Regiment of Women" and returns to Scotland.
1546	Execution of George Wishart; murder of Cardinal David Beaton and seizure of his castle by Protestants.			
1547	Recapture of the archbishop's castle; John Knox sentenced to French prison galleys.		1559	Acts of Supremacy and Uniformity in England; civil war in Scotland; Protestants aided by Elizabeth I; Mary Stuart is queen of France.
1548	John Knox escapes from the galleys; Mary Stuart engaged to marry future King François II of France.		1560	Deaths of Mary of Guise, Amy Rosbart Dudley, and François II of France; Catholicism outlawed by

	Scottish Parliament; Knox becomes preacher at St. Giles.	**1568**	Mary escapes from Scotland to England; Queen Elizabeth of England keeps Mary in forced detention.
1561	Widowed Queen Mary Stuart returns to Scotland.		
1564	Births of William Shakespeare and Christopher Marlowe.	**1571**	The Ridolfi Plot against Elizabeth I.
		1572	Execution of the duke of Norfolk.
		1578	Death of the earl of Bothwell.
1565	Queen Mary marries Henry, Lord Darnley.	**1585**	Raleigh founds a colony on Roanoke Island, North Carolina.
1566	Darnley and others murder David Rizzio; Queen Mary gives birth to future Scottish and English King James.	**1586**	Babington Plot against Elizabeth I.
		1587	Execution of Mary for plotting against Elizabeth.
		1588	Defeat of the Spanish Armada.
1567	Darnley is murdered; Mary marries Bothwell; Scots revolt against Mary and Bothwell; Bothwell escapes to the Continent; Mary forced to abdicate and name her son James VI as her successor; Mary imprisoned for the death of Darnley; birth of Robert Devereux.	**1598**	Death of William Cecil, Lord Burghley; Irish revolt.
		1601	Execution of Robert Devereux, the earl of Essex.
		1603	Death of Elizabeth I; accession of Protestant James I of England and VI of Scotland.

Further Reading

THE REFORMATION IN ENGLAND AFTER 1558

Stephen Brachelow, *The Communion of Saints: Radical Puritan Thought and Separatist Ecclesiology, 1570–1625* (1988).

James Bryant, *Tudor Drama and Religious Controversy* (1984).

Patrick Collinson, *The Religion of the Protestants: The Church in English Society 1559–1625* (1982).

Alan Dures, *English Catholicism 1558–1642: Continuity and Change* (1983).

Richard Greaves, *Religion and Society in Elizabethan England* (1981).

Norman Jones, *The Birth of the Elizabethan Age, England in the 1560s* (1994).

Diarmaid MacCulloch, *The Later Reformation in England 1547–1603* (1990).

Peter Marshall, *The Catholic Priesthood and the English Reformation* (1994).

ELIZABETH I

Susan Bassnett, *Elizabeth I: A Feminist Perspective* (1988).

J. B. Black, *The Reign of Elizabeth I, 1558–1603*, 2nd ed. (1994).

Carolly Erickson, *The First Elizabeth* (1983).

Christopher Haigh, *Elizabeth I: Profile in Power* (1988). Less admiring of her than most studies of the queen.

T. E. Hartley, *Elizabeth's Parliaments: Queens, Lords and Commons, 1559–1601* (1991).

Paul Johnson, *Elizabeth I: A Study in Power and Intellect* (1974).

Carole Levin, *The Heart and Stomach of a King: Elizabeth I and the Politics of Sex and Power* (1994). A fresh approach.

Wallace MacCaffrey, *Elizabeth I* (1994).

——, *Queen Elizabeth and the Making of Policy, 1572–1588*, 2nd ed. (1994). Meticulous scholarship.

John Neale, *Queen Elizabeth I: A Biography* (1934). Still valuable.

D. M. Palliser, *The Age of Elizabeth: England under the Later Tudors, 1547–1603* (1983).

Conyers Read, *Mr. Secretary Cecil and Queen Elizabeth* (1955).

Lacey Baldwin Smith, *Elizabeth I* (1975).

The Scottish Reformation

Frank Bardgett, *Scotland Reformed: The Reformation in Angus and the Mearns* (1992).

Keith Brown, *Bloodfeud in Scotland 1573–1625: Violence, Justice and Politics in an Early Modern Society* (1986).

Ian Cowan, *The Scottish Reformation* (1982).

Gordon Donaldson, *All the Queen's Men: Power and Politics in Mary Stewart's Scotland* (1983).

———, *The Scottish Reformation* (1960).

———, *Mary, Queen of Scots* (1974). Three studies by a leading authority.

Antonia Fraser, *Mary Queen of Scots* (1969). A lively account.

Richard Greaves, *Theology and Revolution in the Scottish Reformation: Studies in the Thought of John Knox* (1980).

Richard Kyle, *The Mind of John Knox* (1984).

Michael Lynch, *Edinburgh and the Reformation* (1981).

James McGoldrick, *Luther's Scottish Connection* (1989).

W. Stanford Reid, *Trumpeter of God: A Biography of John Knox* (1974).

Jenny Wormald, *Court, Kirk, and Community: Scotland 1470–1625* (1981).

Other Topics

Brendan Bradshaw, *The Dissolution of the Religious Orders in Ireland under Henry VIII* (London, 1974).

Patrick Collinson, *The Elizabethan Puritan Movement* (1990).

Felicity Heal, *Hospitality in Early Modern England* (1990).

Colm Lennon, *Sixteenth-Century Ireland* (1995).

Jennifer Loach, *Parliament under the Tudors* (1991).

Roger Manning, *Village Revolts: Social Protest and Popular Disturbances in England, 1509–1640* (1987).

Martha Skeeters, *Community and Clergy: Bristol and the Reformation c. 1530–c. 1570* (1993).

Glanmor Williams, *Renewal and Reformation: Wales c. 1415–1642* (1987).

Notes

1. Cited in Lacey Baldwin Smith, ed., *Elizabeth I* (St. Louis, Mo.: Forum Press, 1980), pp. 38–39.
2. Cited in Lewis Spitz, *The Renaissance and Reformation Movements* (Chicago: Rand McNally, 1971), p. 465.
3. Phrase used by Professor Norman Rich to refer to Louis Napoleon in a class at Michigan State University in the spring of 1966. I think it holds true for Darnley as well.
4. Cited in Helga Harriman, *Women in the Western Heritage* (Guilford, Conn.: Dushkin Publishing, 1995), p. 198.
5. Cited in Lacey Baldwin Smith, *Elizabeth Tudor: Portrait of a Queen* (Boston, Mass.: Little Brown, 1975), p. 73.

16

The Catholic Reformation

It is relatively easy to get the impression from the anticlerical tone of much popular Renaissance literature and the propaganda of the reformers that almost everyone in Europe had serious grievances with the Roman Catholic Church in the sixteenth century. Nothing could be farther from the truth. While perhaps as many as 40 percent of Europeans became Protestant, many areas remained Catholic and some sovereigns that had changed to Protestantism regretted it and returned to the umbrella of the papacy. A majority of Europeans seemed to find that the church of Rome met their spiritual needs. Many loved the rich ceremonial and liturgical life of the Catholic Church; others admired the institution for its care of the poor and the sick; intellectuals continued to admire the rich theological tradition of Catholicism. Above all, most Europeans seemed to believe their souls had the best chance of being saved by staying Catholic and adhering to the church's teachings and sacraments.

It is interesting to note how many humanists stayed loyal to the church, even when they agreed with Luther and others that there was a great deal that needed to be changed about church thought and practice. As the learned jurist Ulrich Zasius put in a letter of 1519:

I agree with much in Luther and admire him . . . But there are in his teachings some blemishes which I dislike. His assertion, for example, that we sin even when we perform a good work is a misplaced proposition. . . . He thinks it proved that the Pope is not universal bishop by divine right. I cannot say emphatically enough how much this displeases me.[1]

Others like Erasmus found the dogmatism and inflexibility of many of the early reformers to be offensive, and many other perceptive observers joined him in fearing that the reform movement would destabilize European society; in other words, the cure of radical reform might prove worse than the disease of church corruption and clerical abuses.

Reform in Spain

Looking back through history, thoughtful persons could observe that the Roman Catholic Church has always had periods of trouble followed by periods of renewal. Even before Martin Luther's call for change, many Roman Catholics were actively working to reform the church. In Spain, for example, the scholarly Cardinal Francisco Jiménez de Cisneros (1436–1517) had imposed stricter discipline upon the clergy and helped wage war against heretics with the founding of the Spanish Inquisition in 1480. A relatively unknown Franciscan, Jiménez saw his career skyrocket when Queen Isabella of Castile found that his religious passion matched her own. He became her confessor and leading spiritual advisor. Through her influence Jiménez rose to become Grand Inquisitor, governor of Castile, and the first churchman of Spain as archbishop of Toledo.

As primate of Spain, Cardinal Jiménez took many paths to reform. To improve the quality of clerical learning, he founded the University of Alcalá near Madrid in 1509 and sponsored the publication of a Polyglot (multilingual) Bible with papal approval. The Polyglot Bible featured Hebrew, Greek, and Latin texts in parallel columns for ready comparisons. Jiménez also sponsored translations into Spanish of such great mystical works as Ludolf the Saxon's *Life of Christ* and Thomas à Kempis's *Imitation of Christ*. Both became major influences on the development of Ignatius of Loyola, the founder of the Society of Jesus. Before his death, Jiménez had helped Spain become the center of a version of reformed Catholicism, a place where Protestants, fearful of the Inquisition, could make few inroads.

The price of attempting to create a religious monolith was terribly high. Forced to flee Spain rather than give up their religious and cultural traditions, thousands of people saw their lives destroyed. Thousands of Jews, Moors, Protestants, and others suspected of heresy were brought before the Inquisition and hundreds were executed by the royal government in horrific and elaborate public ceremonials. Many prominent churchmen and women had brushes with the terror of the Inquisition, including Ignatius of Loyola. Isabella's and Jiménez's attempts to purge Spain of non-Catholics left a terrible legacy and contributed in many ways to the eventual decline of Spain. Even if other sovereigns had been willing to put their swords in the service of the Catholic Church, it is doubtful that the Spanish situation could have been replicated anywhere else in Europe. The Catholic Church in Spain had wealth and firm support from the crown.

Efforts at Reform in Italy

In Italy an informal group of dedicated clerics and some laymen and laywomen were worshipping together, sharing ideas, doing works of charity, and hoping for internal church reform. First founded in Genoa in 1497 by Catherine Fieschi (later Saint Catherine of Genoa), the Oratory of Divine Love spread to Rome early in the reign of Pope Leo X and later to other parts of Italy. Among its more prominent members were the poet Vittoria Colonna, Gasparo Contarini (later a cardinal), Gianpietro Carafa (later Pope Paul IV), Jacob Sadoleto (later a bishop), and Gaetano Thiene (one of the founders of the Theatines). They were disappointed that although the Fifth Lateran Council summoned to Rome by Pope Julius II in 1512 and continued by Pope Leo had identified many abuses in the church, so little was being done to implement the reforms recommended by the council. The first Medici pope, Leo X, seemed preoccupied with his pleasures (chiefly hunting and art) and hurling condemnations at the rebellious monk Luther.

Since the Roman Catholic Church was structurally a monarchy, even though in theory all power came from God and was invested also in the "body of the faithful," the members of the Oratory realized that there were limits to what could be achieved at the grassroots level or even at their level of prominent laity and promising clerics. Hopes for papal leadership were renewed in 1522 with the accession of Adrian of Utrecht, a Dutchman. As we have seen, Adrian was serious about change and appointed a re-form commission but died in 1523 before he could put its recommendations into action. His successor, the second Medici pope, Clement VII (r. 1523–1534), was too timid and vacillating to accomplish anything substantial in the way of reform. Although he was a man of some integrity and ability, he was overwhelmed by such challenges as the Sack of Rome of 1527 and the loss of Henry VIII's England.

New Reform Orders: Capuchins, Theatines, and Ursulines

The founding of new religious orders had traditionally been a source of renewal and reform in the Catholic Church. Yet the Fourth Lateran Council in 1215 had discouraged the establishment of new orders as Pope Innocent III enhanced the papal monarchy and tightened his grip on all agencies of the church. In 1525 two members of the Oratory, Gaetano Thiene and Gianpietro Carafa, persuaded Pope Clement VII to allow the creation of a new order called the Theatines. Thiene was a monk from Vicenza and the tempestuous Carafa was bishop of Chieti. The Theatines were a religious society made up of regular priests who took vows similar to those of monks and mendicant friars. In this way Theatines were able to continue their parish ministries while enjoying a more regulated devotional life. They concentrated on study, meditation, preaching, and good works and earned a great reputation as advocates of improvement.

Other new orders sprang up including the Company of Saint Ursula, founded by Angela Merici of Brescia (1474–1540). Orphaned at age ten, she became a Franciscan tertiary when she was thirteen. *Tertiaries* were laypersons attached to a religious house who followed lives of austerity. At age twenty-three Angela had a vision that she would found a religious congregation devoted to service, teaching, and curing. After the death of her guardian uncle, she began her exemplary career of service and teaching among the poor of Brescia. In 1535 Merici founded the Company of Saint Ursula, named for the legendary British princess who was martyred while on the way to her wedding, allegedly along with 11,000 virgin companions. The Ursulines were to dedicate themselves as "consecrated virgins" to prayer and charitable work. They usually lived at home with their parents, wore no special habit, and concentrated on teaching young girls.

Not until four years after the death of their founder in 1540 were they officially recognized by the reform-minded pope, Paul III, with some alterations. The patriarchs who dominated the church wanted to keep religious women firmly under their control and protection. Some were concerned about safeguarding dowries and possible inheritances. Pope Paul made the Ursulines wear habits and in 1566 they were cloistered. In 1612 Pope Paul V ordered the Ursulines to follow the Augustinian rules. Even though the rules developed by Angela Merici were discarded and the Ursulines were put under masculine control, they continued to be a strong force for the education of women. Ursuline schools could be found all over Italy and elsewhere.

The Capuchins came out of the Franciscan tradition and were recognized as an independent order by Pope Clement VIII in 1528. Matteo da Bascio (d. 1552) had gathered the first group of Capuchins and introduced wearing beards and the distinctive painted hoods (*capucchio*) from which the order derived its name. Bascio served only briefly as their vicar-general before returning to the Observant Franciscans. Bernardino d' Asti (1484–1554) eventually became the leader of the Capuchins and played a major role in drafting their constitution. His work was almost undone when his successor Bernardino Ochino (1487–1564) fled to Geneva in 1542 and became a Protestant. Pope Paul III considered abolishing them, but a church investigation vindicated their orthodoxy. Their supporters included Vittoria Colonna.

Despite these difficult beginnings, the Capuchins managed to grow rapidly after 1574 when they were allowed to serve outside of Italy. They worked as military chaplains, preachers, and missionaries. More than any other group, they worked courageously with plague victims. They generally lived in small hermitages near the towns where they begged for their daily bread. Despite their austere lives and work among the poor, the Capuchins attracted a large membership. They numbered 8,803 by 1600; a century later there were 27,336 Capuchins.

Ignatius of Loyola (1491–1556) and the Society of Jesus

The most prominent of the new church orders that came into existence was the Society of Jesus founded by the remarkable Ignatius of Loyola (Inigo López de Recalde). The last of thirteen children, Ignatius was born at the castle of Loyola in the Basque territory of northern Spain in the Pyrenees Mountains. He received the customary limited education of the lesser nobility before being sent to the household of the chief treasurer of King Ferdinand of Aragon at age thirteen. When his master died in 1517, the red-haired Ignatius entered into military service under the viceroy of Navarre.

Ignatius of Loyola served only a few months as a military volunteer until the battle of Pamplona between France and Spain on May 20, 1521, when a cannonball shat-

tered his right leg and badly wounded his left. Because they grew crooked, Loyola's legs were set twice and rebroken twice, each time without the benefit of modern anesthetics. He was left with a limp for life and his brief stint as a soldier was over. While recuperating, Loyola found little pleasure in the usual chivalric tales that he once loved to read. Instead, he was forced to find consolation in reading the lives of saints. Ignatius's inner voice gradually brought him to the conviction that God wanted him to follow the way of St. Francis and St. Dominic.

Once his health was sufficiently restored, Loyola set out for the Benedictine monastery of Montserrat in Catalonia. He planned a pilgrimage to Jerusalem. After spending an entire night in vigil before a statue of the Virgin Mary, Ignatius put down his sword and dagger and took up instead a beggar's staff and clothing. He spent three days confessing his sins before heading to the small town of Manresa near Barcelona. An outbreak of the plague forced him to remain there for almost a year. At Manresa, Loyola was greatly influenced by Thomas à Kempis's *Imitation of Christ* and his own inner experiences in finding God. He used those experiences in writing his famous *Spiritual Exercises.*

The pilgrim finally arrived in the Holy Land in the autumn of 1523, where he hoped to spend the rest of his life "helping souls." Because of pressure from Ottoman authorities, the Franciscans who were in charge of looking after Christian pilgrims told Loyola he would have to leave. Bitterly disappointed, he returned to Barcelona, where he studied Latin grammar with children less than half his age. Begging for his food, Ignatius shared what he had obtained with other street people. In 1526 he enrolled for theology classes at the University of Alcalá. Wearing his pilgrim's garb, Loyola contin-

Juan Martinez, *St. Ignatius.* Sculpture, University Chapel, Seville, Spain. Foto Marburg/Art Resource.

ued his begging and began to teach people a version of his *Spiritual Exercises.* Rumors began to circulate that he and his associates were "enlightened ones" (*alumbrados*), members of a suspect mystical movement. He was hauled before the Inquisition of Toledo, where he spent forty-two days in prison waiting for a verdict.

Declared innocent by the Inquisition, Ignatius continued his studies at the University of Salamanca, where he was examined for heresy by local Dominicans. Again found innocent, the Spaniard then tried his luck in Paris in 1528. He earned his licentiate in theology in 1534 and his M.A. in 1535. Loyola was in Paris during the period of Nicholas Cop's controversial rectorial address and subsequent flight with Calvin, so

very likely he was exposed to "Lutheran ideas." Protestantism in any form never had any appeal for Ignatius of Loyola.

THE FOUNDING OF THE SOCIETY OF JESUS

On August 15, 1534, Ignatius and six friends vowed to spend their lives helping souls. One of them was Francis Xavier, who later became an incredibly successful missionary to the Orient; another was Diego Lainez, who succeeded Loyola as the second head of the Society of Jesus. These seven men formed the nucleus of what became one of the most influential religious organizations in history and profoundly changed the life of the Roman Catholic Church.

Ignatius of Loyola guided all his fellow-founding Jesuits, and several others who joined them, through his *Spiritual Exercises.* In January 1537 Ignatius and his associates met in Venice, hoping to take a ship to Jerusalem. They spent their time in such charitable activities as nursing the sick, cleaning, removing garbage, digging graves, and burying the dead. Pope Paul III agreed to bless their trip to the Holy Land and provided funds. On June 24, 1537, Ignatius and six of his friends were ordained priests. The political situation in Palestine prevented them from making their journey, so instead Loyola and several others went to Rome to offer their services to Pope Paul III. The pope appointed several of them to teaching positions at the University of Rome. Ignatius helped many prominent persons through the *Exercises,* including Cardinal Gasparo Contarini, who helped persuade the pope to sanction the Society of Jesus in September 1540.

THE ORGANIZATION OF THE JESUITS

Ignatius of Loyola was elected as the first superior general of the Society of Jesus. By

PAVLO III PONTIFICI MAXIMO

DE SOCIET IESV AB IPSO RECEPTA ET CONFIRMA TVOP TIME MERITO

Anonymous, *St. Ignatius before Pope Paul III*, Gesu, Il, Rome, Italy. Scala/Art Resource.

1550, as membership expanded, the society was grouped into four provinces—Italy, Portugal, Spain, and India. Each province was governed by a provincial, who was responsible directly to Ignatius, who governed all other Jesuits. At the death of the superior general, the Jesuits would meet in General Congregation to elect his successor. The Jesuits set high standards for admission wanting only men of sound intelligence, good character, and good health. They came from a variety of backgrounds as Loyola wished to combine diversity with quality. Under pressure from Pope Paul III in 1545, he reluctantly permitted a few "devout women" to join, but this experiment was abandoned two years later. In 1554, Juana of Austria (d. 1573), the deeply pious and talented daughter of Emperor Charles V, sometime regent of Spain, forced Ignatius to admit her as a secret member.

The society placed great emphasis on the vow of obedience. Loyola admonished his fellow Jesuits that if the hierarchichal church "defines anything to be black which to our eyes appears to be white, we must declare it to be black."[2] Members were to cut earthly ties and devote themselves entirely to the society, whose primary purpose was to help souls. Jesuits also took vows of chastity and poverty. After an exacting two-year period of testing, they were given rigorous academic training to help prepare them for careers as priests, preachers, teachers, chaplains, missionaries, diplomats, or in whatever way they might serve the greater glory of God. If there were sufficient numbers of them, they might live in a house, but Jesuits were not cloistered like monks or nuns. The world was their home.

Although Ignatius of Loyola had no intention of being a church reformer, his leadership of the society proved inspirational to many as did his incredible manual of meditation, *The Spiritual Exercises*. Loyola helped the Jesuits ward off the attacks from church leaders, jealous of the society's privileges or, like Pope Paul IV (Carafa), eager to control them. Because of his own prejudices, Paul IV was unhappy with Ignatius's willingness to accept former Jews, such as his successor, Diego Lainez, the son of a Jewish merchant from Castile. Paul confined the Jews of Rome to a ghetto in 1555.

The success of the Jesuits in all their various callings attracted criticism. The society was particularly successful as educators. Their schools were much more innovative than most rival schools, dividing pupils into classes by age and ability, and using better catechisms, textbooks, and methods of examination. They were very involved in higher education as well. Loyola saw education as a key tool in the fight against heresy. As he wrote in a letter of August 13, 1554:

> The heretics have made their false theology popular and presented it in a way that is within the capacity of the common people. . . . Their success is largely due to the negligence of those who should have shown some interest; and the bad example and the ignorance of Catholics, especially the clergy, have made such ravages in the vineyard of the Lord. . . . To put a stop to these evils, we must multiply the colleges and schools of the Society in many lands. . . . We must write answers (to the Protestants) in pamphlet form, short, lively, and well-written. This must be done by learned men well grounded in theology, who can write for the multitudes.[3]

THE JESUIT LEGACY

By the time of Ignatius of Loyola's death in 1556, there were already thirty-five Jesuit colleges. The membership of the Society of Jesus itself had grown from the original seven to about 1,000 members. A number of these early Jesuits became leading theologians and debaters, such as Robert Bellarmine (c. 1542–1621) and Francesco Suárez (1548–1617). Jesuits also excelled as mis-

sionaries. For example, the dynamic Dutchman Peter Canisius (1521–1597) had enormous success in winning back many Protestants to Catholicism in the Holy Roman Empire and Poland. Canisius also wrote a catechism that became an extremely important learning tool as well as a crucial statement of Catholic belief.

Ignatius of Loyola's close friend Francis Xavier (1506–1552) converted thousands of Asians to Christianity despite numerous hardships. Xavier was particularly impressed by the Japanese: "they are a people of excellent morals—good in general and not malicious."[4] Ignatius had wisely advised Jesuit missionaries to learn the language of the country where they were living. The courage, faith, and hard work of Jesuit missionaries resulted in widespread conversions to Catholicism in Europe and throughout the world. In all, the Society of Jesus has been one of the greatest legacies of the period of the Catholic Reformation.

Teresa of Avila (1515–1582)

The Catholic Church not only gained added strength from the creation of new orders, but it also witnessed a revival of existing orders. The Carmelites in Spain, for example, found vigorous new leadership during the sixteenth century in Teresa of Avila and Juan de la Cruz, her famous disciple. Teresa grew up in the fortified town of Avila as part of a prosperous merchant family. Her grandfather, Juan Sanchez, had converted from Judaism to Christianity but still had been publicly shamed by being hauled before the Inquisition in Toledo. When she was thirteen, she suffered the death of her devout mother and the loss of her oldest sister to marriage. Teresa responded to these losses by running with a fast crowd and getting into minor forms of trouble.

Her worried and doting father reacted by placing her in a nearby Augustinian convent, known for its strict discipline. Teresa remained in the convent for a year and a half and thrived on its disciplined love. After a bout of illness and despite objections of her father, she joined a Carmelite house in Avila in 1535 and remained there for the next twenty-six years. At first her longing for her family made her confinement difficult, even though her convent allowed her numerous creature comforts. Teresa suffered persistent ill health until she was in her early forties. She also came under the influence of a Dominican priest, Domingo Banes, who taught her that God can be loved in and through all things. Reading St. Augustine's *Confessions* also had a serious impact upon her development.

After a series of visions that reprimanded her for her worldly concerns, Teresa decided to return to a life of austerity. In 1562, she left her monastery to embark on a life of service to others. With four companions, Teresa founded a new convent dedicated to St. Joseph in Avila, one which renounced worldly goods and followed a strict form of discipline. Although greeted with deep suspicion, Teresa eventually won the support of the reform-minded bishop of Avila, and her order of Discalced ("barefoot" to suggest a life of poverty) Carmelites was officially recognized in 1562.

During the remaining twenty years of her life, Teresa wandered throughout Spain establishing convents and reforming others. On her travels, she met Juan de la Cruz, a Carmelite monk, who became her most ardent disciple. "Although he is small, he is great in the sight of God," she said of him.[5] He became spiritual director of the Discalced house of St. Joseph's in 1572 but was seized and thrown into prison for nine months by his unreformed Carmelite brothers. Juan (1542–1592) was a major poet who

also wrote some of the most inspiring works of mystical literature, including his *The Dark Night of the Soul*, *The Ascent of Mount Carmel*, and *The Living Flame of Love*.

Teresa's publications, such as her *Way of Perfection* and *Interior Castle*, also became religious classics. Her writings, including a partial *Autobiography*, tell of her own life of struggle, persecutions endured, her many doubts, and the triumph of her faith. In her 1562 *Autobiography*, she described one of her visions as follows:

> Almost always Our Lord appeared to me as He rose from the dead, and it was the same when I saw Him in the Host. Only occasionally, to hearten me if I was in tribulation, He would show me His wounds, and then would appear sometimes on the Cross and sometimes as He was in the garden. . . . I found myself dying of the desire to see God. . . . This love came to me in mighty impulses which robbed me of all power of action.[6]

For all her religiosity, she was also a sound woman of business and a born political intriguer. By the time of her death, Teresa had founded thirty reformed Carmelite houses for both women and men. However, controversy swirled about her throughout her life because some church leaders, having been deceived by a number of frauds, doubted the nature of her visions. At several points, Teresa was even accused of "Lutheran tendencies." As she wrote, "I was startled by what the devil stirred up against a few poor little women."[7] Despite the attacks from her critics, she found great support from King Philip II, other Spanish grandees, and influential church leaders in Rome, who recognized her administrative and spiritual talents.

Always self-deprecating, Teresa of Avila would have been astonished that in 1622 the church made her a saint. As she had

Bernini, *Ecstasy of St. Teresa*, S. Maria della Vittoria, Rome, Italy. Alinari/Art Resource.

written about her life in the community at Seville, "one of the things that makes me happy here is that there is no suggestion of that nonsense about my supposed sanctity."[8]

Pope Paul III and Reform

As important as the work of lay and clerical reformers was, the Catholic Church would never have succeeded in undertaking such a thorough reform without the support of the papacy and many in the college of cardinals. In 1534 Cardinal Alessandro Farnese, a smart and aging aristocrat, became Pope Paul III (r. 1534–1549). As a churchman who had first been made a cardinal during the scandalous pontificate of Alexander VI (Borgia), Paul was well aware of church corruption and the need for change in the face

of the Protestant and Ottoman threats. Realizing that "fish stink from the head down," a reform commission of 1537 chaired by Contarini recommended a number of reforms in the College of Cardinals itself and the elimination of the selling of church offices, which had grown from 625 at the time of Sixtus IV (r. 1471–1484) to 2,232 by the time of Leo X (r. 1513–1521).

A conservative majority of the College of Cardinals, however, was unwilling to make the necessary changes and the papacy had become financially dependent on the revenues from venal offices. What was needed was an increase in the number of reform-minded cardinals and new sources of revenues. Paul III's first round of appointments to the College of Cardinals included no major reformers and two of his own grandsons, both teenagers. It seemed to many in Rome that Paul III was going to be just another nepotistic Renaissance pope determined to take care of his own family first. Yet in his next series of appointments, the pope promoted a number of earnest reformers to the cardinalate, including Gianpietro Carafa, Reginald Pole (archbishop of Canterbury under Queen Mary Tudor), Jacopo Sadoleto, Gasparo Contarini, and others. They pressured the pope to follow through on reform measures, despite the opposition of those in high places who had a large financial stake in existing practices.

AN IRENIC REFORMER: GASPARO CONTARINI (1483–1542)

Gasparo Contarini was an especially fine choice for a cardinal's hat. The seventh son of an illustrious Venetian family, he studied philosophy at Padua before becoming a member of the Venetian government and diplomatic corps. He followed Emperor Charles V to Germany and attended the Diet of Worms of 1521. In 1528 Contarini represented Venice's interests at the court of Pope Clement VII. Thus, he was able to witness firsthand the rise of Protestantism and the papal response. Although sympathetic to some of the ideas of the Protestants, Contarini remained a convinced Catholic who was committed to reason and peaceful reform. Although a layman, he left his position in the Venetian government to accept a cardinalate in 1535 because he hoped he could do something worthwhile for the church in a time of great need.

Two years later Contarini presented the pope with a report on church reform, which was rejected by the majority of the papal court as impractical. Although disappointed, he continued to urge his friend, Paul III, to carry on with efforts at reform and even compromise with the Protestants. In 1541 Cardinal Contarini was named as legate to an important meeting at Regensburg with leaders of the Protestant movement. Sponsored by Emperor Charles V, the Regensburg Colloquy sought to find common theological ground between Catholics and Protestants. Working in harmony with Martin Bucer, Johann Eck, and Philip Melanchthon, Contarini was able to help draft a statement on justification and other matters, which contained both Catholic and Evangelical ideas. However, the temper of the times was such that the Regensburg formula was rejected by all groups. Contarini then served as a reform legate in charge of Bologna.

The Council of Trent 1545–1563

Despite the failure of both Catholics and Protestants to accept the spirit of compromise manifest at Regensburg, Pope Paul III pressed on with his version of reform. In 1542 he established the Inquisition in Rome

as recommended by the militant reformer, Cardinal Carafa of Naples. Carafa served as its first inquisitor-general. The influence of the hardliner Carafa caused the vicar-general of the Capuchins, Bernardino Ochino, to flee Italy, along with the prolific and skilled theologian Peter Martyr Vermigli. They both ended up as wandering preachers in various northern Protestant communities before Vermigli found a chair for a while in theology at Oxford during the reign of Edward VI.

Balanced against these important defections from Catholicism, Pope Paul III also chartered the Jesuits and the Ursulines. His most famous accomplishment was his calling of a general reform council of the church, which began meeting in the Italian Alpine

Titian, *Portrait of Pope Paul III*, Museo Nazionale di Capodimonte, Naples, Italy. Alinari/Art Resource.

town of Trent in March 1545. Although Emperor Charles V had long called for a reform council, his rival, François I, and the French bishops were opposed, fearing the loss of the French church's privileges. Still hoping for peace between the great powers, Paul III had the vision and courage to go ahead with "a general, holy council" despite their political pressure and his fears of the Ottomans. "We must do this," he informed church leaders because "all the world is in fear and sorrow."[9]

The opening sessions of the Council of Trent were attended by four legates and cardinals, four archbishops, thirty-one bishops, five generals of church orders, and fifty theologians and canonists. The ailing Luther, who had often called for such a reform council, called this one "too little, too late." The Wittenberger was wrong, for although the Council of Trent was forced to meet off and on for eighteen years before concluding, it proved to be the most important church council in a thousand years. Paul III had devised measures to control its voting and membership. Unlike the Council of Constance (1414–1418), the delegates at Trent voted as individuals, not as nations. This way the big Italian delegation made up the largest voting block and their loyalty to the papacy could generally be relied upon.

Before Trent would finally conclude its important work in 1563, four popes would come and go, and the council would suffer many misadventures. Plague forced the council to adjourn to Bologna in March 1547. When Carafa became Pope Paul IV in 1555, he refused to continue the council, believing that he as papal monarch could best revive the church. Paul IV issued his own reform decrees such as the one setting up the Index of Prohibited Books in 1559. Paul's papal list of "unholy and dangerous books" included the complete writings of Calvin, Luther, Zwingli, Knox, and other reformers. It also condemned certain writings of Erasmus, Machiavelli's *The Prince*, Rabelais's *Pantagruel*, and the Koran.

Prohibited works listed between 1559 and 1596 also included Dante's *On Monarchy*, Boccaccio's *Decameron* (unless expurgated), four of the humanist Petrarca's sonnets, four of Lorenzo Valla's major works, the ribald Aretino's works, the poetry of the courtesan Veronica Franco, the Latin edition of Guicciardini's *History of Italy*, Castiglione's *The Courtier*, and many other Renaissance classics. Authors were condemned sometimes for their words and sometimes for their lives and in some cases for both. While debate continues on how successful the Index was in helping to halt the spread of Protestant doctrines, there is no question that it had a chilling effect on the freewheeling exchange of ideas that had been such a stimulating part of the Renaissance.

THE CONCLUSION OF THE COUNCIL
OF TRENT AND ITS IMPACT

With Carafa's death in 1559 and peace between Henri II of France and Philip II of Spain, the Council of Trent reconvened in 1562 with the blessing of Pius IV (r. 1559–1565), the new Medici pope. Under the aegis of the tactful Cardinal Morone, Trent finally came to closure in 1563. Among its great work was the reaffirmation and clarification of major church doctrines. There had been enormous confusion among Catholics about what exactly was the official church teaching about, for example, purgatory prior to the start of the Reformation. Different popes, councils, and theologians had said different things at different times. After Trent issued its concluding statements, the official church positions on such matters as the seven sacraments, transubstantiation, communion in one kind for the laity, auricular confession, celibacy, monasticism, purgatory, indulgences (reaffirmed but sellers outlawed), the invocation of saints, and the veneration of saints were perfectly clear.

Trent declared that good works were necessary for salvation, but that faith was also crucial. The apostolic succession was reaffirmed. Scripture was to be valued equally with tradition as sources of doctrine. The authority of the church to interpret Scripture against the rampant individualism of Protestant interpreters was affirmed: "No one shall presume to interpret Scripture contrary to that sense which Holy Mother Church . . . has held and now holds."[10] The doctrinal statements of Trent concluded by making it clear to Protestants that they must accept the teaching authority of the church without deviation or be "accursed."

In the area of church practice, the Council of Trent admitted the existence of a great deal of corruption and issued stern measures to help clean it up. Pluralism, simony, nepotism, absenteeism, immorality, and ignorance among the clergy were all condemned and combatted. Pluralists had to give up their multiple benefices. Priests were ordered to reside in their parishes. Bishops were made more responsible for the discipline of their clergy. More masculine control was put over female religious orders and houses. To improve the education of the clergy, seminaries were to be established in each diocese. The supremacy of

Aerial view of St. Peter's Basilica, columns by Bernini, dome by Michelangelo, Vatican State. Alinari/Art Resource.

the pope over prelates increased. As King Philip II of Spain wryly commented, "I sent bishops to Trent and they came back parish priests."[11]

Although the church has had a long history of reform councils, what was particularly striking about the Council of Trent is how many of its decrees were in fact carried out and how much it changed the church despite pockets of resistance often in rural parishes. While the sale of offices and pluralism were never completely eliminated, as illustrated by the case of the underage pluralist, Joseph Clemens (1671–1723), archbishop of Cologne and a member of the great house of Wittelsbach, such abuses were substantially reduced.

Pius IV continued the spirit of reform by implementing the Tridentine reforms and by continuing the tradition of appointing reformers to high office, such as his talented nephew, Carlo Borromeo (1538–1584), who was made a cardinal and archbishop of Milan at age twenty-one. Borromeo's appointment initially looked like nepotism as usual, but he soon proved the cynics wrong with his administrative skills and devoted

work among the poor. His reform activities included writing a very influential catechism and a very sensible redesign of the confessional, which allowed for greater privacy.

Stimulated by the work of the reformers and the new and revived religious orders, the Catholic Church seemed ready for a new era of glory. Artists such as Michelangelo (1475–1564), Artemisia Gentileschi (1593–c. 1632), Gian Lorenzo Bernini (1598–1630), and Giovanni Palestrina (c. 1525–1594) were already transforming that feeling of renewed piety into a stunning series of artistic masterpieces as the Renaissance gave way to the age of the Baroque. The church had been reformed in head and numbers, while withstanding the first onslaughts of Protestantism and the Ottomans. Tragically, there were still convinced Catholics and Protestants who were willing to use any means necessary to promote their vision of the truth. The spirit of reason and compromise so wonderfully exemplified by Cardinal Gasparo Contarini was soon swept away and the age of religious wars launched in earnest.

Chronology

1436–1517	Life of Cardinal Francisco Jiménez des Cisneros.	1521–1597	Life of Peter Canisius.
1474–1540	Life of Angela Merici.	1522–1523	Reign of Pope Adrian VI; Commission on Reform.
1480	Spanish Inquisition established in Seville.	1528	Clement VIII recognizes the Capuchins.
1483–1542	Life of Cardinal Gasparo Contarini.	1534–1549	Reign of Paul III.
1491	Birth of Ignatius of Loyola.	1537	Commission on Reform of the Church.
1506–1552	Life of Francis Xavier.	1538–1584	Life of Carlo Borromeo.
1512–1517	Fifth Lateran Council.	1540	Paul III charters the Jesuits.
1515	Birth of Teresa of Avila.	1541	Regensburg Colloquy.
1517	Oratory of Divine Love begins in Rome.	1542	Inquisition established in Rome; Bernardino Ochino flees to Geneva.

1544	Chartering of the Ursulines.	**1559**	Establishment of the Index of Prohibited Books.
1545	Opening of the Council of Trent.	**1559–1565**	Reign of Pius IV.
1555–1559	Reign of Pope Paul IV (Carafa).	**1563**	The Council of Trent concludes.
1556	Death of Loyola; Diego Lainez elected as Jesuit general.	**1582**	Death of Teresa of Avila.

Further Readings

GENERAL

Louis Chatellier, *The Europe of the Devout: The Catholic Reformation and the Formation of a New Society* (1989).

N. S. Davidson, *The Counter-Reformation* (1987).

Jean Delumeau, *Catholicism Between Luther and Voltaire: A New View of the Counter-Reformation* (1977).

H. O. Evennett, *The Spirit of the Counter-Reformation* (1968).

Marc Forster, *The Counter-Reformation in the Villages: Religion and Reform in the Bishopric of Speyer, 1560–1720* (1992).

Barbara McClung Hallman, *Italian Cardinals, Reform, and the Church as Property* (1985).

Hubert Jedin and John Dolan, eds., *History of the Church*, Vol. 5, *Reformation and Counter Reformation* (1980).

Martin Jones, *The Counter Reformation: Religion and Society in Early Modern Europe* (1995).

Michael Mullett, *The Counter Reformation and the Catholic Reformation in Early Modern Europe* (1984).

Marvin O'Connell, *The Counter-Reformation* (1974). One of the more readable surveys.

John Olin, ed., *Catholic Reform from Cardinal Ximenes to the Council of Trent, 1495–1563: Illustrative Documents and a Brief Study of St. Ignatius Loyola* (1990).

——, ed., *The Catholic Reformation: From Savonarola to Ignatius Loyola* (1990). Useful collections of documents.

John O'Malley, ed., *Catholicism in Early Modern Europe: A Guide to Research* (1988). An in-valuable collection of bibliographical essays by leading scholars.

Frederic McGinness, *Right Thinking and Sacred Oratory in Counter-Reformation Rome* (1995).

Nelson Minnich, *The Fifth Lateran Council (1512–17): Studies on Its Membership, Diplomacy and Proposals for Reform* (1993).

G. W. Searle, *The Counter Reformation* (1974).

Philip Soergel, *Wondrous in His Saints: Counter-Reformation Propaganda in Bavaria* (1993).

A. D. Wright, *The Counter-Reformation* (1982).

NEW RELIGIOUS ORDERS AND IGNATIUS OF LOYOLA

Wiliam Bangert, *History of the Society of Jesus* (1972).

Richard De Molen, ed., *Religious Orders of the Catholic Reformation* (1994). Scholarly essays by a variety of contributors.

John W. O'Malley, *The First Jesuits* (1993). An important survey.

A. Lynn Martin, *The Jesuit Mind: The Mentality of an Elite in Early Modern France* (1988).

W. W. Meisner, *Ignatius of Loyola: The Psychology of a Saint* (1992). A Freudian interpretation.

INDIVIDUAL REFORMERS

Jodi Bilinkoff, *The Avila of Saint Teresa* (1989).

Robert Birely, *Religion and Politics in the Age of Counter-Reformation* (1982).

Philip Caraman, *St. Angela. The Life of Angela Merici* (1964).

Stephen Clissold, *St. Teresa of Avila* (1982).

John P. Donnelly, *Calvinism and Scholasticism in Vermigli's Doctrine of Man and Grace* (1976).

Elisabeth Gleason, *Gasparo Contarini: Venice, Rome and Reform* (1993).

Pamela Jones, *Federico Borromeo and the Ambrosiana: Art Patronage and Reform in Seventeenth Century Milan* (1993).

Philip McNair, *Peter Martyr in Italy: An Anatomy of Apostasy* (1967).

José Nieto, *Mystic, Rebel, Saint: A Study of St. John of the Cross* (1979).

Anne Jacobson Schutte, *Pier Paolo Vergerio; the Making of an Italian Reformer* (1977).

Carol Slade, *St. Teresa of Avila: Author of a Heroic Life* (1995).

George Tavard, *Poetry and Contemplation in St. John of the Cross* (1988).

THE INQUISITION AND INDEX

Paul Grendler, *Culture and Censorship in Late Renaissance Italy* (1981).

Henry Kamen, *Inquisition and Society in Spain in the Sixteenth and Seventeenth Centuries* (1985).

———, *The Phoenix and the Flame: Catalonia and the Counter- Reformation* (1993).

———, *The Spanish Inquisition* (1965).

William Monter, *Frontiers of Heresy* (1990).

Edward Peters, *Inquisition* (1988).

THE COUNCIL OF TRENT

H. O. Evennett, *The Cardinal of Lorraine and the Council of Trent* (1940).

Herbert Jedin, *History of the Council of Trent*, trans. Ernest Graf, 2 vols. (1957–1961).

Notes

1. Cited in Hans Hillerbrand, ed., *The Reformation: A Narrative History Related by Contemporary Observers and Participants* (New York: Harper and Row, 1964), p. 428.
2. *The Spiritual Exercises of St. Ignatius*, trans. by Anthony Mottola (New York: Image Books, 1964), p. 428.
3. Cited in Hillerbrand, *Reformation*, pp. 446–447.
4. Cited in John O'Malley, *The First Jesuits* (Cambridge, Mass.: Harvard University Press, 1993), p. 76.
5. Cited in Theodore Rabb, *Renaissance Lives: Portraits of an Age* (New York: Pantheon Books, 1993), p. 107.
6. *The Life of St. Teresa by Herself*, trans. J. M. Cohen (New York: Penguin, 1957), pp. 206–208.
7. Ibid., pp. 268–270.
8. Ibid., p. 19.
9. Cited in Hillerbrand, *Reformation*, pp. 460–461.
10. Cited in Alister McGrath, *Reformation Thought: An Introduction*, 2nd ed. (Oxford: Blackwell, 1993), p. 156.
11. Cited in DeLamar Jensen, *Reformation Europe: Age of Reform and Reconciliation*, 2nd ed. (Lexington, Mass.: D. C. Heath, 1992), p. 216.

17

An Age of Religious Warfare, 1546–1660

The willingness to tolerate a diversity of opinion on some matters of religious doctrine and practice displayed by people like Cardinal Gasparo Contarini, Sebastian Castellio, or Marguerite of Navarre was not in tune with the prevailing sentiments of many in the sixteenth century. For many, to tolerate other opinions on matters of faith was a sign of weak religious convictions, or worse, a tendency toward heresy. Not only did the age suffer from an excess of religious and social intolerance, but there was a tendency on the part of many prominent individuals of the period to declare themselves correct on all major points of doctrine and to demonize their opponents. Martin Luther, for example, regularly referred to the pope as "the devil incarnate" and "a brothel keeper."[1] When some of his theological colleagues disagreed with him on points of doctrine which he considered clearly established, they were castigated as "false brethren" and sometimes worse. Luther's Catholic and Protestant opponents replied in kind. Even Philip Melanchthon, Luther's close friend and partner in reform, admitted that he was at times "a violent physician," while excusing his rhetorical excesses as caused by "the magnitude of the age's disorders."[2]

What made the bombast of the theologians particularly dangerous was that many of those in political power shared their intolerance of the ideas of others. Emperor Charles V, for example, referred to the Lutheran Reformation as an "evil movement, which seduces the people with false doctrines and incites rebellion."[3] While some political authorities saw in the Reformation an opportunity for them to take over church authority and property, others saw the reform movement as a threat to law, order, and their own power. Charles's son, Philip II of Spain, was typical of those who thought forced conversions were the only way to prevent souls from being damned for all eternity. Most Protestant princes agreed with Philip's position. Many on all sides of the Reformation were willing to use coercion as a way to solve religious and political problems. They believed that religious differences in a state caused factionalism and made the state ungovernable. Religious fanaticism coupled with political power proved to be an explosive mixture in the already fragile economic and social environment of the sixteenth and seventeenth centuries. The end result was wave after wave of widespread death and destruction.

The Empire Strikes Back: The Schmalkaldic War, 1546–1548

Having survived the tremors of the Peasants' War and the assault of the Ottomans on Hungary in 1526, Emperor Charles V was determined to deal firmly with the growing Evangelical movement. Landgrave Philip of Hesse, Duke Johann the Constant of Saxony, and Jacob Sturm of Strasbourg were equally determined to protect their new religious understandings by armed alliance against the emperor if necessary. The failure of peaceful efforts to come to terms with the emperor at the Diet of Augsburg of 1530 resulted in a meeting of Protestant leaders at the town of Schmalkald in the Thuringian forest in December 1530. There eight princes and ten cities agreed to defend each other if attacked because of their religion.

The signatory powers had come to agree with Landgrave Philip of Hesse and others who argued that lesser magistrates had the right to resist the emperor if he refused to protect or abused the religious rights of his subjects. Some legal theorists asserted that, according to both canon and civil law, anyone who is attacked unjustly has the right to self-defense. Philip of Hesse concurred with that opinion: "Since I must protect my subjects . . . must I wait to protect them after they are dead; what good is that?"[4]

THE DEFECTION OF NUREMBERG AND BRANDENBURG-ANSBACH

Brandenburg-Ansbach and Nuremberg disagreed with the landgrave about their right to resist the emperor by force of arms. They refused to support their fellow Protestants by allying themselves against Charles V and the Catholics. Although unwilling to commit themselves to use the sword against their sovereign, they promised to study the matter and assist by legal means other Protestants who were being proceeded against by the Imperial Supreme Court. The magistrates of Nuremberg and some of their advisors still had grave doubts about whether or not it was lawful to resist their emperor by violent means. Even Martin Luther, as a man of peace, still hoped the Evangelicals would not have to arm themselves against the emperor, whom many still viewed as a "father." As late as 1542 he warned the Protestant princes not to be so quick to take up the sword, even in a just cause. He informed the members of the Schmalkaldic League:

> Even if somebody were to kill my father or brother, I am not judge or avenger. What need is there for laws and authorities, what for God, if everybody wanted himself to be judge, avenger, even God over his neighbor, especially in worldly matters.[5]

The wealthy merchants in control of Nuremberg also worried that the formation of an anti-Catholic league would escalate tensions. Rising tensions might eventually result in a war that would destroy international trade, the basis of Nuremberg's prosperity. Brandenburg-Ansbach, Nuremberg's neighbor and ally, followed the imperial city's lead on this matter. Despite these important defections, the Schmalkaldic League was able to add additional members and become a force to be reckoned with.

A TRUCE WITH THE OTTOMANS

The Schmalkaldic League was saved from an immediate test of strength by the advance of the Ottomans toward Vienna in the summer of 1532. Horrified by the Ottoman advance, Emperor Charles arranged for a truce with the Protestants at Nuremberg. He agreed to summon a church council within a year, quash all cases against Protestants pending in the Imperial Chamber Court, and postpone the question of confiscated church property. In return the Protestants sent troops, weapons, and money to aid the Habsburgs in their campaign against the forces of Süleyman the Magnificent. The imperial forces defeated the Ottomans sixty miles southeast of Vienna at Grens. The sultan sent raiding parties throughout Austria but withdrew the bulk of his army. In June 1533 the Ottomans made peace with the Habsburgs, allowing Charles's brother, Ferdinand, to continue to hold the western part of Hungary in exchange for the payment of tribute to the sultan.

The Ottomans joined with sea raiders from Algeria and Tunisia in naval attacks on the Mediterranean coast of Italy and Spain. Charles V defended his empire and succeeded in capturing Tunis in North Africa in 1535. His great enemy, François I of France, shocked Europe by concluding a treaty with Sultan Süleyman that gave France the right to trade inside the Ottoman Empire. King François then marched into Savoy, which he claimed through his mother. His real objective was the rich duchy of Milan. Emperor Charles then counterattacked in French Provence and Languedoc. None of these attacks succeeded, and finally in 1538 the warring kings agreed to peace at Nice.

IMPERIAL INITIATIVES

The emperor then resumed his efforts to find a peaceful resolution to the religious differences in the Holy Roman Empire. He pressured the papacy to sponsor a general reform council, which finally bore fruit with the convening of the Council of Trent in

1545. Even before that, Charles had sponsored discussions between Catholic and Protestant theologians at Speyer, Hagenau, Worms, Leipzig, and Regensburg in 1540 and 1541. Although many areas of agreement were found, fundamental divisions remained.

In that same period, the truce with France collapsed as François I sent naval units to support the Muslims in their war in the Mediterranean and then sent French troops into the Low Countries. A Habsburg fleet was destroyed by a storm off the coast of Algiers in October 1541. Süleyman the Magnificent then resumed his conquests in western Hungary and the Danube valley. Inside the Holy Roman Empire, additional territories became Protestant and even the archbishop of Cologne, Herman von Wied, allowed Martin Bucer and Philip Melanchthon to introduce Protestantism into his lands in 1542.

Faced with enormous pressures on all sides, Emperor Charles managed to conclude a new alliance with King Henry VIII of England and attacked the duchy of Cleves, a recently acquired ally of the French. He then continued his offensive in the west, marching to within sight of Paris. A startled François I quickly agreed to peace at Crépy in September 1544. An armistice with the Ottomans soon followed.

When it became apparent that the Council of Trent was not going to solve the religious fissures in Germany, Charles concluded that it was time to use military force to hold his empire together while his truces with France and the Ottoman Empire held. The death of Martin Luther in February 1546 removed a strong voice for peace in the empire and made the emperor doubly eager to strike rapidly should the Lutherans be in disarray. First, Charles shored up support among various Catholic princes in the empire such as the powerful duke of Bavaria.

Then Charles won the support of the ambitious Protestant Duke Moritz of ducal Saxony (r. 1541–1553) by promising him the electoral title, which then was lodged in the hands of his cousin, Johann Frederick (d. 1554), the heavy-drinking duke of electoral Saxony. Moritz was soon called a "Judas" by his fellow Protestants.

THE BATTLE OF MÜHLBERG, 1547

Duke Moritz invaded electoral Saxony in November 1546, which caused Elector Johann Frederick to abandon his Schmalkaldic League allies in the south and rush to his homeland's defense. The gout-afflicted emperor was thus able to increase his forces and assume control of much of the Rhineland and southern Germany. Meanwhile, Johann Frederick was enjoying military success against both Moritz and King Ferdinand (Charles's brother). The emperor moved north to relieve Moritz and managed to surprise Johann Frederick at the Battle of Mühlberg on the Elbe River on April 24, 1547. The elector had only a third of his army with him and was captured during the battle. He was forced to cede his electoral title and much of his land to Moritz. Philip of Hesse surrendered a short time later. The Schmalkaldic League had been utterly humiliated, and the emperor seemed poised to realize his dream of forcing the Protestants to return to the church of Rome.

THE AUGSBURG AND LEIPZIG INTERIMS

The victorious emperor followed up his military success by presenting the 1547–1548 Imperial Diet of Augsburg with a document known as the *Augsburg Interim*, which was to give the empire a temporary religious policy until the Council of Trent could com-

Titian, *Emperor Charles V at Mühlberg*, Prado, Madrid, Spain. Alinari/Art Resource. This is an idealized image because, in reality, Charles had to be carried on a litter throughout much of the campaign because of painful attacks of gout.

plete its work. For the most part, it restated traditional Catholic doctrines but offered a few concessions to the Protestants, such as permitting clerical marriages with papal dispensation and allowing for communion with both bread and wine. Although formally accepted by a majority of the estates at Augsburg, hardly anyone was satisfied with it. Pope Paul III felt too much had been conceded to the Protestants; militant Protestants considered it far too Catholic. Philip Melanchthon and Julius Pflug, the irenic Catholic bishop of Naumburg, at the urging of Duke Moritz of Saxony, drafted a more Protestant *Leipzig Interim*, but that too was rejected by the many hardliners on both sides.

Splits in Lutheranism

The arguments over the Augsburg and Leipzig *Interims* marked the first major fissures in the Lutheran movement after the death of Luther. Philip Melanchthon was criticized severely for his willingness to compromise on what he considered nonessentials of doctrine and practice. For example, Melanchthon was willing to accept the episcopal system in the interest of religious peace. His opponents were led by a fiery Slav, Flacius Illyricus (1520–1575) and Nicholas von Amsdorf (1483–1565). Flacius was a former humanist educated at Venice, Basel, and Tübingen. He argued that there were no nonessentials in Lutheranism. Flacius soon left his position as a professor of Hebrew at Wittenberg for Magdeburg, where he became one of the most outspoken leaders of the Gnesiolutherans or conservative Lutherans.

Nicholas von Amsdorf was born at Torgau in Saxony to a noble family. A nephew of Johann von Staupitz, Amsdorf earned his licentiate in theology from Wittenberg, where he studied under Martin Luther and Philip Melanchthon. One of the first converts to Lutheranism, Amsdorf accompanied Luther to the Leipzig debate in 1519 and to Worms in 1521 and served on the faculty of his alma mater. He later helped reform Magdeburg, Goslar, and Einbeck before becoming the Lutheran bishop of Naumburg/Zeitz in 1541. A close friend and advisor to Elector Johann Frederick, Amsdorf was driven into exile during the Schmalkaldic War. He considered Melanchthon too open to compromise. Therefore, he helped found a new university at Jena because he thought Wittenberg was too much under the influence of the "Philippists," as the supporters of Melanchthon were called.

The Schmalkaldic War and its after-math had revealed the fragile nature of Lutheran unity. Another victim of the war and its aftermath was Katherine Luther. She had been forced to flee Wittenberg several times when it was threatened by imperial troops. Then in the fall of 1550, an attack of the plague hit Wittenberg and with two of her children, Katherine had set out for Torgau. Her horses bolted and she was thrown from her wagon into a ditch filled with cold water. Nursed for three months by her daughter, Margaret, age eighteen, Katherine Luther died on December 20, 1550. Her last known words were, "I will stick to Christ as a burr to a top coat."[6]

The Religious Peace of Augsburg of 1555

Meanwhile Emperor Charles found himself abandoned by his ally, Duke Moritz of Saxony. Moritz had become impatient with the emperor's refusal to release his father-in-law, Philip of Hesse, from prison in the Low Countries. More importantly, he found it difficult being accepted as the ruler of Lutheran Saxony while being known as the "betrayer of the Gospel." To demonstrate his Lutheranism, he called upon Philip Melanchthon to restore the University of Wittenberg along strictly Lutheran lines. Moritz helped revive the Schmalkaldic League by taking in new members and joining in an alliance with the new king of France, Henri II, who invaded the empire from the west and seized the fortress cities of Metz, Toul, and Verdun. In 1552 Duke Moritz, at the head of a Protestant army, marched on Charles V at Innsbruck. The imperial forces were taken by surprise and the emperor was forced to flee and agree to peace negotiations.

Worn out and bitterly disappointed by the failure of his imperial policies, Charles turned over German affairs to Ferdinand, his brother and successor. Earlier, he had attempted to bypass Ferdinand and have his son, Philip, succeed him in both Spain and the empire. Ferdinand, who had for so many years served his brother as regent in the empire, refused to accept this and threatened a Habsburg civil war. Charles backed down and agreed to support Ferdinand as the Habsburg candidate for the imperial dignity. It was King Ferdinand who presided over the Diet of Augsburg, which met from February to September 1555.

The recess of the Diet of Augsburg provided a measure of religious peace for the empire, which lasted almost until 1618. By its terms, the Lutheran estates in the empire were given legal recognition and permitted to retain all their acquired territories. Imperial cities that had adopted Lutheranism had to allow and protect the rights of minority Catholics to worship in the Catholic churches that had been reopened after the 1548 *Interim*. In princely territories, the ruler decided the religion of all his subjects. Only Catholicism and Lutheranism were recognized by the Religious Peace of Augsburg. Every ecclesiastical prince who became Protestant would forfeit his title, lands, and privileges.

Emperor Charles V was not happy with the concessions his brother had been forced to make to the Lutherans in the Holy Roman Empire, but his years of trying to hold his vast, multinational empire together had left him exhausted. A month after the Diet of Augsburg ended, the ailing emperor turned over his authority in the Low Countries to his son, Philip. In 1556 he became the first Holy Roman emperor to abdicate. He then turned over his Spanish possessions to Philip and retired to a palace near the Jeronimite monastery of Yuste in southwestern Spain, where he died two years later.

The Religious Wars in France

The Holy Roman Empire was not the only part of Europe to become a battleground because of religious differences. Hatred of religious pluralism was also a staple of French society and a matter of royal policy. Despite the vigorous persecutions of King François I and his son, Henri II, Calvinism made slow but steady progress in France. John Calvin had been sending out missionaries trained in Geneva for many years trying to convert his fellow French to his brand of Protestantism. Young Henri II was even less tolerant of the Huguenots (French Protestants from the Swiss-German term *Eidgenossen* or confederates) than his father had been. Upon coming to the throne in 1547, he had created a special committee (called the "Burning Chamber") of the Parlement of Paris to suppress heresy.

THE REIGN OF HENRI II (R. 1547–1559)

Although he had been married at age fourteen to Catherine de' Medici, Henri's constant companion and most influential advisor was his beloved mistress, Diane de Poitiers, a well-read and politically astute woman. She viewed the Huguenots as representing a threat to her lover's authority and joined Charles de Guise, archbishop of Rheims, in urging Henri to be severe with them. In spite of these persecutions, the well-organized Huguenot movement continued to grow and came to include even members of the nobility such as the king's cousins from the house of Bourbon. Because the king was distracted by yet another round of war with Habsburg Spain, suppression of the Calvinists proved impossible.

In 1559 King Henri II finally agreed to

François Clouet, *Henri II of France*. Louvre, Paris, France. Giraudon/Art Resource.

peace with Spain by signing the very important Peace of Cateau-Cambrésis. In order to create "perpetual peace," Henri's daughter, Elizabeth of Valois, was married to King Philip II of Spain, who had recently lost his second wife, Queen Mary Tudor of England. As part of the festivities surrounding the royal nuptials, a great tournament was held in late June in which King Henri, a veteran jouster, eagerly participated. On the last joust of the day, the king was struck in the eye by a piece of his opponent's shattered lance. Twelve days later Henri II died of complications from his wound.

The Power of Catherine de' Medici (1519–1589)

Henri's beloved and influential mistress, Diane de Poitiers, was dismissed from the court by order of Queen Catherine de' Medici, whose sickly fifteen-year-old son, François II (r. 1559–1560), took the throne. Educated by nuns, Catherine was the daughter of Lorenzo de' Medici (1492–1519), nephew of Pope Leo X. She became a dominant figure in the reigns of her three sons. Catherine shared many of the common prejudices against the Huguenots, who in 1559 had held a major synod or convention. She also hoped that religious civil war could be avoided.

Queen Catherine was disappointed by the growing militancy displayed by both sides as well as by the growing influence exerted over her young son by the house of Guise, fanatical champions of Catholic orthodoxy. Rumors circulated that the Protestants planned to burn down the city of Paris and, if that failed, to kidnap the king at Amboise and force him to recognize their religion or to abdicate in favor of the Bourbons. The conspiracy of Amboise was discovered, and its ringleaders were harshly punished in the spring of 1560. The incident left an important legacy of fear in the minds of many Catholics, including the queen mother.

The Saint Bartholomew's Day Massacre

When the young king died unexpectedly in December 1560, the savvy Catherine was named regent for her nine-year-old son, Charles IX (r. 1560–1574). She supported a policy of moderation and easing of the persecutions against the Calvinists. The queen also sponsored discussions between Catholic and Protestant theologians at Poissy in 1561 and St. Germain-en-Laye early in 1562. Despite the clear presentations of Calvinist theology by Theodore Beza and the willingness of some moderate Catholics to compromise, neither group could find common ground on the nature of the "true church" and the importance of images. Extremism dominated as France drifted toward religious civil war. Because of apocalyptic fears, the failure of compromise, religious bigotry, and desires for power by various factions, a series of isolated clashes between Catholics and Protestants led to a general outbreak of religious warfare in 1562, which lasted, on and off, for the next ten years.

Finally by 1572, it appeared that both Protestants and Catholics were ready to end the bloodletting. The Peace of Saint Germain was to be followed by a great celebration on Saint Bartholomew's Day, August 24. There was much to celebrate for the king's sister, Marguerite of Valois, had just married Henri of Navarre, the dashing young Huguenot leader. Surely this happy union would put an end to the religious civil wars in France.

The religious peace and the wedding of Marguerite and Henri attracted thousands of Huguenots to Paris, including their most influential leader, Gaspard de Coligny, admiral of France. Weddings between prominent families were great occasions. Coligny had been urging the king to intervene in the Low Countries against Philip of Spain. Assassins, possibly encouraged by Henri, duke of Guise, plotted Coligny's murder in revenge for his alleged agreement to the murder of Henri's father in 1563. The admiral's attackers initially succeeded only in wounding him, and the Protestant leaders demanded that the culprits be punished. On the night of August 23, fearing a Huguenot plot against the crown, King Charles gave the order to exterminate the Protestant leadership in Paris.

On the morning of Saint Bartholomew's Day, a detachment of the king's Swiss Guard led by the duke of Guise broke down the door to Coligny's house and murdered him in the ensuing scuffle. The duke of Guise then urged his followers to begin killing other nearby Huguenots: "kill them, kill them all, it is the king's command!"[7] The murder of Coligny sparked a general slaughter of Huguenots in Paris, which spread to the countryside over the next several weeks. Thousands were murdered. Henri of Navarre escaped the assassin's blade by promising to convert to Roman

Anonymous, *Portrait of Catherine de' Medici.* Palazzo Medici Riccardi, Florence, Italy. Alinari/Art Resource.

Catholicism. He was detained for three months in Paris but eventually managed to escape to the countryside to rally the surviving Huguenot forces.

When news of the massacre reached Madrid, the usually dour Philip II could not repress a smile. In Rome, special church services were held to commemorate the massacre. However, many Catholics were appalled by the level of hatred and violence in France. Protestant leaders such as Elizabeth of England protested the new outbursts of religious and political violence in the French kingdom. Many Protestant propagandists blamed Catherine de' Medici ("the wicked Italian queen") for the massacre, but it is unlikely that she condoned such extensive atrocities after years of trying to maintain peace between Huguenots and Catholics and her general high level of political astuteness. Guilt probably added to the instability and poor health of King Charles IX, who died two years after the massacre.

The Reign of Henri III (r. 1574–1589)

Charles was succeeded by his twenty-three-year-old brother, Henri III. An intelligent prince, Henri was in much better physical health than either of his elder brothers and had commanded royal armies in victories over the Huguenots when he was only eighteen. In 1573 he had been elected king of Poland, but he was unhappy there and eagerly fled the country after learning of the death of his brother. As king of France, Henri resumed the war against the Calvinists, but in April 1576 he agreed to a truce that recognized the legality of Protestantism.

This unprecedented display of toleration gravely upset the duke of Guise and other hardline Catholics determined to exterminate the Huguenots. Eventually Henri

of Guise formed the Catholic League with support from Spain and the papacy. It became a powerful force and helped to contribute to the next agonizing round of religious and civil wars. Some of the misery of the period is shown in the revival of flagellants, not seen in France in large numbers since the time of the Black Death in the middle of the fourteenth century.

In June 1584, the duke of Anjou, younger brother of the king, died. Openly homosexual, Henri III showered his affections and favors—such as choice lands, titles, and honors—on a series of handsome young men. To pay for his extravagant court and the expenses of the civil wars, the intelligent but erratic king raised taxes on the already strained peasantry and confiscated the estates of some nobles. With the death of the last Valois heir, the Huguenot Henri of Navarre was next in line for the throne of France. Henri was the son of Antoine of Bourbon, king of Navarre, who vacillated between Catholicism and Protestantism. His mother, Jeanne d'Albret (1528–1572), daughter of Marguerite of Navarre, was a staunch Protestant. When chided by a papal legate for her support of the Huguenots, she responded, "Your feeble arguments do not dent my tough skull. I am serving God and He knows how to sustain his cause."[8]

Political Theorists

With Jeanne d'Albret's energetic son destined to inherit the throne of France, Protestant political theorists turned from justifying rebellion against royal authority to writing in praise of the monarch as the embodiment of sovereignty. For example, in *Six Books of the Commonwealth* (1576), the lawyer Jean Bodin argued that the chief end of the state was the preservation of peace, justice, and private property, which can best be done

Engraving of Flagellants, 1583, Bibliotheque Nationale, Paris, France. Giraudon/Art Resource.

where sovereignty is not divided as in a monarchy. Although "all princes of the earth are subject to the laws of God and of nature, and even to certain human laws common to all nations," they are not subject to the authority of others.[9] Moderate intellectuals called *politiques* ("politicals") hoped that a way could be found to assure religious coexistence between Catholics and Protestants.

One of the foremost of the *politiques* was Michel de Montaigne (1533–1592). Montaigne was the son of a prosperous merchant family in the area of Bordeaux. His father taught him to read, write, and speak Latin. Educated in the law, he became a magistrate in the Parlement of Bordeaux (superior court) until ill health forced him into a life of study and writing. He is best

known for his series of *Essays*, which explored the human condition and acknowledged the limitations of human reason. In the face of the upheavals caused by the religious civil wars in France, Montaigne urged moderation: take the "middle way, wide and open."[10] Be yourself and let others be themselves was his plea. After an extended period of travel in Europe searching out the healing qualities of mineral baths, he returned to Bordeaux and served two terms as mayor.

THE WAR OF THE THREE HENRIES, 1587–1589

Tragically, Montaigne's pleas for toleration were ignored and France soon found itself

Portrait of Montaigne, copy of a seventeenth-century original. Private Collection. Giraudon/Art Resource.

shrewd Catherine de' Medici, Henri III learned of the defeat of the Spanish Armada and determined to rid France of Guise and his Spanish backers. He invited Guise and his brother, the cardinal of Lorraine, to a secret meeting and had them murdered on December 22, 1588 as traitors to the crown. King Henri was in turn denounced as a tyrant and a traitor by the Catholic League and soon fled to the camp of his Protestant rival, Henri of Navarre, whom he agreed to accept as his heir. The king then met with his estates at Blois and presented them with a reorganized government. With the help of Navarre, Henri III planned to retake Paris, but he was assassinated on August 1, 1589, by a friar who thought the king was a traitor for being willing to accept a Protestant as his successor. The surviving Henri (Navarre) now declared himself to be king of France as Henri IV, but Paris refused to recognize his authority. Half of the kingdom was in the hands of the Catholic League and its Spanish allies.

in another nasty round of civil war. The ensuing conflict was known as the War of the Three Henries, named after its three major participants: King Henri III, Henri, duke of Guise, and Henri of Navarre. In the autumn of 1587, Huguenot forces led by Henri of Navarre routed a royal army at Coutras near Bordeaux. The scar-faced Henri of Guise had more success against Protestant mercenaries in the northeast, but was angered by the king's failure to send him royal troops. He then marched on Paris in May 1588, forcing the king to flee to Chartres for safety. Wildly popular in the capital as the champion of militant Catholicism, Guise was proclaimed "king of Paris."

While Guise was planning his next move in consultation with the aging but still

HENRI OF NAVARRE AS KING OF FRANCE, 1589–1610

A five-year struggle followed as the Catholics and Spain were determined that a Huguenot would never be allowed to hold the throne of St. Denis. King Philip II of Spain dispatched his best general, Alexander Farnese, duke of Parma (1545–1592), from the Low Countries to France. He lifted Henri IV's siege of Paris in the summer of 1590. However, when Parma died from wounds in battle in 1592, Spanish power in France ebbed. The king's pragmatic fifth reconversion to Catholicism in 1593 further undermined the Catholic League's willingness to resist Henri's authority. Thinking that "Paris is well worth a Mass," Henri realized that he could never truly be king of France if his religion was different from 90 percent of his subjects. The Catholic majority needed to have its fears of the Huguenot minority alleviated, or so the king was advised by his leading counselor, the duke of Sully, who remained a Protestant.

A short bundle of charm and vitality, the gallant king eventually became one of the most popular sovereigns in French history. He faced a mountain of debt, a country ravaged by two decades of civil war, and enemies on all sides. Even his Bourbon dynasty was not secure, as he and Marguerite of Valois had failed to conceive a son after twenty-one years of marriage. Henri petitioned Pope Clement VIII (r. 1592–1605) for both absolution and a divorce. Fearing a repeat of the English experience under Henry VIII, Jesuits in Rome persuaded the pope to grant both. In return, Henri promised to be a loyal servant of the church. In 1600 the king, notorious for his many love affairs, married Marie de' Medici of Florence in a politically motivated match. They eventually produced a legitimate male heir, the future Louis XIII.

Not until his long war with Spain had ended in 1598 and several of his rebellious nobles had been subdued by bribery and/or force was King Henri IV able to give a large measure of civil and religious liberty to his Protestant subjects. In his Edict of Nantes of 1598, Henri granted religious liberty to French Huguenots. They would be allowed seventy-five fortified towns plus other fortified places in which to exercise freedom of religion in addition to the right to worship in the lands of Huguenot nobles. Huguenots were declared eligible for public office and guaranteed the right to use schools and other facilities on an equal basis with Catholics. The edict also declared Catholicism to be the official state church and re-

stored to it its former income, possessions, and rights. Although it did not satisfy extremists, the Edict of Nantes was usually enforced by the king until his death in 1610. It did provide a strong measure of peace to a land long devastated by religious and civil war.

With the aid of his able superintendent of finances, the duke of Sully, Henri launched a major economic reform program. Government debt was reduced, tax collecting improved, roads and bridges were rebuilt, farm land was reclaimed, grain export restrictions were eased, and silkworm cultivation was introduced into southern France. The king genuinely hoped to improve the quality of life for the peasantry to the extent that every peasant family would have a chicken in the pot for Sunday dinner. This promise was never fulfilled for all areas, but it is significant that Henri and Sully made the effort. Few other sixteenth-century rulers were overly concerned about the welfare of the working masses. Little wonder that so many French people came to revere him as "Henri the Grand" and mourn his death to a monk-assassin, who apparently doubted the sincerity of his Catholicism.

Henri's reputation might have suffered had he realized some of his later military ambitions for expansion to the east. It is intriguing to note that at the time of his murder, Henri IV was planning to establish a sort of "united states of Europe." Given the state-building mentality of the time and the jealousy of French power, it is not likely that Henri could have achieved his grand design through diplomacy. To create such a confederation of territorial states by military means would have meant a series of bloody conflicts with the Habsburgs and others. The king's early death kept his subjects from paying the full price of their sovereign's ambitions.

Philip II's Crusades

Although many had doubts about the extent of Henri IV's commitment to Catholicism, no one had any about that of Philip of Habsburg. Philip of Spain was the most powerful ruler of the late sixteenth century. His father, Charles V, had bestowed the lion's share of his vast empire upon Philip. In addition to mighty Spain, Philip had inherited the Burgundian Low Countries, Luxembourg, Franche-Comté, Naples, Sicily, Sardinia, Corsica, the Balearic Islands, Milan, and all of the Spanish holdings along the western coast of Africa and in the Western Hemisphere. In 1580 Philip conquered Portugal in the name of his Portuguese mother and added Portugal's huge eastern empire to his dominions. He also sponsored the colonization of the Philippines, which are still named after him. The introverted Spanish sovereign could claim legal authority over more of the earth's surface than any other monarch in history.

THE CHARACTER OF THE KING

Philip II of Spain was a very complex individual. Cautious, hard working, and patient, he was notorious for his attention to details. Because he was afraid to trust his subordinates, almost every state document of importance passed through his hands, which made the inner workings of his government cumbersome indeed. He treated servants and nobles alike with equal courtesy. As a young prince, he was quite the ladies' man. Later, he became devoted to his children. Philip of Spain was also a major friend of the arts and learning. Sofonisba Anguisola and Titian were just two of the many artists to benefit from his good taste and eye for talent. He also established academies to promote mathematics and the sciences.

Titian, *Portrait of Philip II*, Prado, Madrid, Spain. Alinari/Art Resource.

At the core of Philip's being was a deep sense of religious duty. Religion was his solace from the deep tragedies of his personal life and the difficulties of his governmental responsibilities. In rapid succession he lost his mother, father, sister, four wives, one daughter, and four sons. His sense of obligation to Catholicism added additional burdens to his already troubled soul. Philip took it upon himself to use the wealth and power of his vast empire to restore the dominion of the Roman church over as much of Europe as possible. Furthermore, he thought it was his divine mandate to protect Christendom from the forces of Islam.

WAR AGAINST ISLAM

Philip II distrusted the thousands of Moriscos (nominally Christian Moors) who lived in his southern Spanish provinces and had gradually been reverting to Islamic practices. On occasion, some Moriscos had aided some of the Muslim sea raiders. Philip and others feared that they would one day open the gates of Spain to the Muslims of North Africa. In January 1567, the king issued a royal decree ordering the Moriscos to cease practicing Islam and using the Arabic tongue. The Moriscos of Granada responded by revolting against the authority of Philip's government. Aided by Arab allies from Algiers and other Muslim lands, the rebellion dragged on for two years. Both sides committed unspeakable atrocities.

Finally, Philip's illegitimate half brother, Don Juan of Austria (1547–1578), succeeded in crushing the rebels. By a royal edict of 1570, the Moriscos of Granada were ordered to leave their homes and settle among the Christians of Castile and Aragon. In 1609 Philip issued an edict that expelled them from all of Spain. Before that, the monarch had experienced an even greater triumph against the Ottomans at the naval battle of Lepanto, despite humiliating defeats in the Low Countries, England, and France.

In 1566 Sultan Süleyman the Magnificent died and was succeeded by his son, Selim II (r. 1566–1574), who was eager to get out from under his illustrious father's considerable shadow. To do that Selim thought he needed to make his own reputation as a conqueror. Selim's ambitions were opposed by an aggressive new pope, Pius V (r. 1566–1572), who called for a new crusade against the Ottomans. The pope's calls for holy war took on extra significance when Selim's forces conquered the island of Cyprus in 1570. Philip II joined with Venice and the pope in a new Holy League. A huge fleet was assembled under the command of Philip's half brother, Don Juan of Austria, in the fall of 1571.

On October 7 the Christian fleet engaged the Ottomans in the Bay of Lepanto off the eastern coast of Greece. The battle involved over 400 galleys and 160,000 participants. The Christians had 1,815 naval guns, which destroyed at least 70 Ottoman galleys. The battle raged for three hours and resulted in a major victory for the Holy League. Not until the seventeenth century would the Ottomans be able to resume their naval war against Christian Europe in the Mediterranean on a full scale. The youthful Don Juan became the romanticized military hero of the moment among Christians. His brother, Philip II, thought that God was indeed on his side and was encouraged by the great victory at Lepanto to attempt new crusades, this time against various Protestants, whom he also viewed as spawn of the devil.

THE REVOLT OF THE LOW COUNTRIES

The Spanish Lowlands (Netherlands) were the richest part of Philip II's vast empire. The Netherlanders had taken a large portion of the herring trade and international commerce from their rivals. Their farmers were some of the most efficient in Europe. However, Philip, unlike his father, Charles V, was considered to be an unsympathetic foreigner who taxed their prosperous trade and commerce for the benefit of Spain. Emperor Charles V, after all, had been born in Ghent and grown up in the Flemish-speaking provinces of Flanders and Brabant. Although Philip's policies were not that much different from his father's, the Netherlanders never trusted Philip as much as they had his predecessor. The area was already suffering through a series of economic and social crises in the 1560s when Philip II decided to move against the Protestants. In 1566 he outlined his policy to the Spanish ambassador at Rome: "I neither intend nor desire to be the ruler of heretics. If things cannot be remedied as I wish without recourse to arms, I am determined to go to war."[11]

Philip's policy of repression touched off a war which resulted in the independence of more than half of the Low Countries. Tensions that had been slowly increasing between the king and his subjects escalated when the Habsburg king sponsored a much-needed reorganization of the church in the Netherlands in 1565. The existing structure was cumbersome and awkward and left a lot of freedom of action to local magnates, who enjoyed their privileges. Philip pressured the church to create fifteen new bishoprics, which was protested by a group of nobles led by William of Nassau, prince of Orange (1533–1584). In August petitions were sent to the king asking for an easing of the religious persecutions. When he refused, William of Orange and several others resigned from the Council of State.

In April 1566 a large body of the lesser nobles presented a request to Philip's regent and half sister, Margaret of Parma, that the king allow the States General to deal with the religious problem. During their interview with the regent, one of Margaret's counselor's referred to the rowdy nobles as "those beggars." The label was quickly adopted by the leaders of the opposition as an appropriate reflection of the contempt in which the Netherlanders were held by the ruling Spanish. In the summer of 1566, bands of rebels began desecrating Catholic churches, smashing stained glass windows, altar paintings, and statues.

Philip II dispatched the "Iron duke" of Alba (1507–1582) from Genoa to the Netherlands. Alba arrived in Brussels with an imposing army of 10,000 mostly Spanish and Italian troops in August 1567 and promptly set up a "Council of Blood," which took swift and brutal actions against suspected heretics. Margaret of Parma resigned protesting Alba's severity. Alba was named to replace her and continued his reign of terror for six years. Thousands were put to death. The duke further antagonized the Dutch by levying a permanent sales tax.

William of Orange found refuge in Holland and Zeeland, where he led resistance to the authority of Alba. He proved a worthy opponent for the Spanish and came to be widely respected for his courage, intelligence, and tactical abilities. William married Charlotte de Bourbon, the daughter of a French duke, who made a fine home for his children from two previous marriages and ran his estates with great efficiency. He was also aided by daring Dutch privateers, called "Sea Beggars," who attacked the coastal towns and crippled Spanish shipping and communications. Alba was recalled in 1573, but the revolt continued under other governors when the rebels refused to lay down their arms, even though Philip offered to cease the hated sales tax.

In 1578 the king turned to his talented young nephew, Alexander Farnese (1545–1592), the son of Margaret of Parma. An astute diplomat, Parma managed in 1579 to persuade ten of the southern provinces to reaffirm their loyalty to Philip II and "maintain good government and the Catholic church" in the Union of Arras.[12] William of Orange countered by organizing the seven northern states into their own Protestant Union of Utrecht, which continued the revolt with great vigor. William was assassinated by a hireling of Philip II in the summer of 1584. The rebels found capable new leaders such as William's son, Maurice of Nassau (1567–1625) and the shrewd lawyer Jan van Oldenbarneveldt (1547–1619).

The Dutch rebels also persuaded Elizabeth I of England in 1585 to send them an army of 6,000 men under the command of her favorite, Robert Dudley, earl of Leicester. Elizabeth had been sending the rebels money, and at times she allowed the "Sea Beggars" to use English ports. The fall of Antwerp and Brussels to the Spanish made the situation appear even more threatening. Leicester had to be withdrawn a year and a half later for incompetence, one of the queen's rare lapses in her judgment of men and situations. Despite the mixed blessings of English help, the Dutch under Maurice of Nassau succeeded in driving out the last remnants of the Spanish forces. Finally in 1609, eleven years after Philip II's death, Spain agreed to a twelve-year truce. The full independence of the Calvinist United Provinces was formally recognized in 1648 as part of the general treaties at the conclusion of the central European phase of the Thirty Years' War (1618–1648). Philip II's agents were able to preserve Catholicism only in the southern provinces of the Low Countries.

As for the United Provinces, they soon became the world's leader in commercial activity. In the course of the long war with Spain, they had seized the richest part of the Portuguese empire in the East Indies. The products of the East poured into Dutch ports and were exchanged for goods from all over Europe. Dutch ships were some of the best designed in the world and could carry more than any of their competitors. The French finance minister, J. B. Colbert, estimated that the Dutch came to control 75 percent of Europe's merchant marine by the second half of the seventeenth century. Quality products manufactured in the Low Countries were also in high demand, including new optical instruments. Amsterdam became a major center of finance.

The wealth of the Netherlands was reflected in the high levels of patronage and support for major artists such as Judith Leyster (1609–1661), Frans Hals (c. 1581–1666), Jan Vermeer (1632–1675), Rembrandt van Rijn (1606–1669), and many others. Rembrandt is often considered the greatest painter of the seventeenth century and one of the very best of all time. Dutch artists painted not only religious subjects but also portrayed the lives of people of all stations. Obviously the expanding merchant class had plenty of money to invest in art. With the innovative ideas of the jurist Hugo Grotius (1583–1645) in international law and Baruch Spinoza (1632–1677), a Jewish lens grinder, in philosophy, along with numerous scientific and technological breakthroughs, the seventeenth century proved to be a golden age for the enterprising Dutch.

THE SPANISH ARMADA OF 1588

The most grandiose of King Philip II's crusading efforts was his attempt to restore wayward England to the Roman Catholic fold. His first move had been to marry England's Catholic queen, Mary Tudor. This was done in 1554, two years before the start of his own rule over the Spanish empire. Mary's marriage to the future king of a feared and hated rival power and her bloody persecutions of English Protestants diminished her popularity and that of her beloved church in England. Moreover, the marriage failed to produce a Catholic heir. When the unhappy Mary died in 1558, Philip sought to continue his influence in England by trying to court Mary's sister and successor, Elizabeth.

For her part, Elizabeth was determined to marry no one, as we have seen. She loved being queen and having power. Marriage to an ambitious consort meant giving up or sharing power. She loved being a sovereign and saw no reason to give up her free-

Rembrandt van Rijn, *Self-Portrait* (c. 1657).
Kunsthistorisches Museum, Vienna, Austria.
Foto Marburg/Art Resource.

dom and authority. Therefore, the "Virgin Queen" refused to marry despite the pressures of her advisors such as William Cecil, who were desperate that she marry in order to produce an heir. Philip of Spain was too important a suitor to spurn outright, so Elizabeth strung him along for a number of years as she would do other suitors throughout her long reign. By the 1570s, Philip was fully aware that she would never marry and instead sought other means for bringing England back to Catholicism. He was encouraged by Catholic exiles and others to liberate England from the Protestant "Jezebel."

Philip's anger at Elizabeth was only increased by her aid to his rebellious Dutch subjects and by the attacks on his shipping by English privateers such as Francis Drake (c. 1540–1596) and John Hawkins (1532–1595).

When a Spanish fleet defeated a French fleet in the Azores in 1583, its commander, the marquis of Santa Cruz, urged Philip to follow up his success by launching a naval offensive against England. The cautious Spanish monarch was tempted but thought he still lacked sufficient resources to be successful in such an elaborate enterprise. When Elizabeth sent an army to the Low Countries in 1585 and aided the Huguenots in France, Philip felt compelled to order Santa Cruz and the duke of Parma to draw up their plans for an invasion of England.

With the execution of Mary Stuart, queen of Scots, on February 7, 1587, Philip had an additional excuse for launching his invasion. The staunchly Catholic Mary had been Elizabeth's heir, but with her death a Protestant succession through Mary's son, James, who was being reared a Calvinist in Edinburgh, seemed likely. Mary had encouraged a number of conspiracies against her cousin's life during her long captivity in England, and Elizabeth's patience with her taller and more glamorous rival had at last run out. Philip hailed Mary as a great Catholic martyr and swore to avenge her death. However, numerous delays kept his grand fleet from sailing. Those delays allowed Sir Francis Drake the opportunity to singe the beard of the king of Spain by attacking part of the Spanish fleet at Cadiz harbor in April 1587 and damaging or capturing some thirty vessels, plus valuable war materials, such as wood for the casks which would hold some of the armada's supplies of fresh water and food.

In February 1588, the armada's experienced commander, Santa Cruz, died before the fleet was ready to sail. Philip then appointed a very reluctant duke of Medina Sidonia (1549–1592) to take Santa Cruz's place. Although lacking in naval experience, the duke was a fine administrator and by May 1588 he set sail from Lisbon with a fleet of 130 vessels, 20,000 soldiers, 10,000 sailors, and 2,000 guns. They sailed "in the confident hope of a miracle."[13] The English in the meantime had put together a fleet of 190 ships, which rode lower in the water and had more long-range firepower than the Spanish fleet.

The Spanish fleet, somewhat damaged by storms, reached the English Channel at the beginning of August and hoped to be able to gain temporary control of the seas and transport the army of the duke of Parma from the Netherlands to England. Elizabeth of England met with her assembled home-guard troops at Tilbury. Decked out in full armor, Gloriana promised them that she would herself lead them into battle should the Spanish army land in England. The queen proudly informed her soliders: "I know I have but the body of a weak and feeble woman; but I have the heart and stomach of a King and of a King of England too."[14] Elizabeth knew how to manipulate the prejudices of her audience to full advantage. Such a brave queen seemed well worth dying for.

Meanwhile the Spanish and English fleets had encountered each other in the channel, but neither side had suffered great damage. When the armada reached Calais, Medina Sidonia learned that Parma could not reach the coast with his army. Since the Spanish had a shortage of boats that could navigate the shallow coastal waters off Calais, the chances of a successful rendezvous were somewhat limited. Without the transport needed to carry their troops and weapons across the channel, the Spanish would not be able to invade England. In a real sense, the mission had been defeated with most of the mighty Spanish fleet still intact.

On the night of August 7, the English ignited eight of their ships and sent them into the anchored Spanish fleet. The Spaniards feared the burning ships were filled with gunpowder and would explode like bombs in their midst. Dutch rebels had used exploding "hell burners" against the Spanish with great effect years before. Terrible memories of such fire ships lingered among the Spanish and Medina Sidonia gave the order to cut anchors and scatter for safety. The following day the English attacked the armada before it could fully regroup and inflicted heavy damage. Rather than sail back into the channel, the Spanish gambled on sailing northward around Scotland, Ireland, and then back home to Spain. Medina Sidonia heroically kept much of his fleet together, despite foul weather, a lack of charts of the treacherous North Sea, and terrible illnesses from insufficient food and water. Less than half of the Spanish fleet ever sailed again.

The defeat of the 1588 armada did not end the war between England and Spain. The next year Francis Drake led a counterattack against Spain with a huge fleet of 120 ships. Half of them and their crews were lost. Six years later, the Puritan Drake led another expedition against the Spanish, this time to the West Indies, where he hoped to capture a Spanish treasure fleet and destroy Spanish bases in the Americas. Drake's final raid proved a great disaster and he died before returning to England. In 1596 the English did manage to sack Cadiz, which was bravely defended by Medina Sidonia, who burned the fifty ships that the English had hoped to capture. King Philip sent armadas against England later in 1596 and the following year, but they were driven from the channel by terrible storms. The long and expensive naval duel between England and Spain proved indecisive, except that England kept its Protestantism and its independence. Philip II died in 1598 wondering why God had not blessed more of his crusades with success.

The Thirty Years' War, 1618–1648

The Religious Peace of Augsburg of 1555, which had brought to a close the first round of armed conflict in the empire between Catholics and Lutherans, proved to be an uneasy truce. Since the signing of the treaty, the Calvinists had made strong headway in several areas of Germany including the Palatinate, and they demanded legal recognition. Furthermore, lands of the Catholic Church were constantly being secularized in Protestant areas, particularly in the north, in violation of the treaty. At the same time Catholics, led by the dukes of Bavaria and the Jesuits, became increasingly aggressive in their desire to regain what they had earlier lost to the Protestants.

Growing political and religious tensions led a group of Evangelical princes and cities to found a Protestant Union in 1608. In response, the Catholics organized a military league under the energetic Duke Maximilian I of Bavaria (1573–1651). Maximilian had been educated at the Jesuit University of Ingolstadt and was determined to use his power to promote Catholicism. Outside the Holy Roman Empire, antagonisms between France and the Habsburgs threatened to erupt into war at any moment. Only the death of the anti-Habsburg leader, King Henri IV, in France, prevented the outbreak of a general European war over a succession dispute in Cleves-Jülich in 1610. A greater crisis soon developed in Bohemia in 1617 when Archduke Ferdinand of Styria, nephew of Holy Roman Emperor Matthias (r. 1612–1619), was designated as king by the Bohemian estates.

As a militant Catholic crusader, Ferdinand was determined to eliminate Protestantism from his domains. He clashed immediately with Bohemia's largely Protestant nobles, who also resented Ferdinand's efforts to increase his authority at the expense of their local privileges. A gathering of Protestant Czech nobles met in Prague in the spring of 1618 to condemn Habsburg policy. Some of them, as a form of protest, tossed two of the Habsburg officials and a secretary out of an upper window of the royal castle in Prague on May 23, 1618, into a dry moat fifty feet below. Their falls were broken somewhat by castle wastes and manure, and all three survived the humiliating, terrifying, and smelly experience, but their master, Ferdinand, was furious with the Czechs for defying his authority.

Hours after learning that Ferdinand had been elected Holy Roman emperor, the Bohemians deposed him as their king and offered the throne to the young Count Frederick V, the Calvinist elector of the Palatinate. The Bohemian rebels were soon joined by Protestants from neighboring Austria, Moravia, Silesia, and Lusatia. However, Frederick's Protestant father-in-law, King James I of England, refused to back him. The Dutch and the German Protestants also offered no real help to Frederick in whom they had little confidence. In fact, the Lutheran duke, Johann Georg of Saxony, sided with the emperor, in part motivated by a desire for territorial gain and a hatred of Calvinism. Commanded by Duke Maximilian of Bavaria and Count Johann von Tilly (1559–1632), the Catholic League's army crushed the Bohemian uprising at the Battle of White Mountain near Prague on November 8, 1620. Hundreds of Bohemian nobles were executed and their estates confiscated. Frederick fled and eventually found refuge in the Hague in the United Provinces. His homeland, the Palatinate, was overrun by Bavarian and Spanish soldiers. In September 1622, Tilly's troops stormed Heidelberg and the first phase of the war was over. Frederick's electoral title was given to Maximilian of Bavaria, who had long coveted the electoral dignity. Duke Johann Georg of

Saxony was rewarded with the province of Lusatia.

DANISH INTERVENTION, 1623–1630

Leadership of the Protestant resistance passed to King Christian IV of Denmark. The ambitious Danish king intervened partly in order to save his coreligionists but primarily to acquire some Catholic bishoprics in northern Germany. England, France, and the United Provinces all encouraged his intervention but did not provide any substantial financial or military aid. The imperial forces gained yet another brilliant general in the person of Albrecht von Wallenstein (1583–1634), a soldier of fortune who had successfully married for money. An avid believer in astrology, yet shrewdly calculating, Wallenstein is one of the more complex individuals to emerge from the period. Eager to increase his landholdings, Wallenstein offered Emperor Ferdinand II (r. 1619–1637) an army of 20,000 troops. Under Wallenstein and Tilly, imperial forces won a series of victories over Christian and eventually subjugated all of northern Germany as far as Jutland.

On May 22, 1629, the Danish king renounced his ambitions in Germany but was allowed to retain his hereditary lands. Emperor Ferdinand decided to follow up on his generals' victories and turn the Holy Roman Empire into a centralized Habsburg monarchy. He declared the rights of the dukes of Mecklenburg to be forfeited because they had supported King Christian IV of Denmark. The emperor then gave their duchy to the grasping insomniac Wallenstein, who was not even a prince of the empire. Ferdinand had issued the Edict of Restitution on March 6, 1629. It threatened the very existence of Protestantism by prohibiting Calvinist worship and ordering the restoration to the Catholic Church of all church properties that had been secularized since 1552.

Even committed Catholic princes in the empire such as Maximilian of Bavaria became alarmed about the emperor's intentions. They had benefited from the loose, decentralized nature of the Holy Roman Empire, and many were also concerned that Wallenstein's immense army of mercenaries could no longer be controlled. At the Diet of Regensburg in the summer of 1630, Catholic and Protestant princes joined hands to demand that the emperor dismiss Wallenstein and force him to disband his army. Powers outside the empire, including France and Sweden, were also concerned about Ferdinand's ambitions.

SWEDISH INTERVENTION, 1630–1635

A staunch and determined Lutheran, Gustavus II Adolphus (1594–1632) regarded Ferdinand's growing might in northern Germany as a threat to Lutheranism generally and to his own empire more specifically. Although not populous, Sweden had an efficient government and valuable deposits of iron and copper, resources in great demand by the militarists of the age. Handsome, well educated, fluent in seven languages, and fond of music and poetry, the king of Sweden was the model of a Renaissance prince. One of the ablest military leaders and tacticians of his day, the so-called "Lion of the North" landed in Pomerania in July 1630 with a well-equipped, experienced army. With gold from France and allies among the German Protestants, Gustavus Adolphus won an overwhelming victory over Tilly at Breitenfeld near Leipzig on September 17, 1631. In the spring of 1632, the victorious Protestants marched into the Rhineland, then south into the heart of Bavaria, deliber-

The Thirty Years' War and English Civil War

ately devastating the countryside in the spring of 1632.

With the Catholic position deteriorating rapidly, Ferdinand II recalled the intense Wallenstein and made him supreme commander. Early in September 1532 the imperial forces held their own in a clash with

Gustavus Adolphus outside of Nuremberg. Wallenstein then moved to Saxony, where he planned to spend the winter. The Swedish king followed him and the two armies met in a furious battle at Lützen (near Leipzig) on November 16, 1632. Gustavus Adolphus was mortally wounded in

Anonymous, *Engraved Portrait of Gustavus Adolphus, King of Sweden.* Foto Marburg/Art Resource.

the battle, but his enraged soldiers forced the Imperials to withdraw into Bohemia. The king's able chancellor, Axel Oxenstierna, continued the war. Wallenstein opened negotiations with the Swedes and Saxons, hoping to create an independent state for himself. One of his Irish captains, outraged by Wallenstein's treachery, murdered him on the night of February 25, 1634.

Wallenstein's death helped restore unity among the Imperials, who were now led by the future Ferdinand III, the young heir to the throne. The Habsburgs' position was also strengthened by the refusal of some of the Protestants, such as Duke Johann Georg of Saxony, to cooperate fully with the Swedes. A war between Russia and Poland also drew off some of the Swedish forces. On September 6, 1634 an Imperial

army, reinforced by Spanish troops, crushed the Swedish army outside of the town of Nördlingen. Almost all of southern Germany now fell back into the hands of the Imperialists. Johann Georg of Saxony signed a peace treaty at Prague with Emperor Ferdinand II, which suspended the Edict of Restitution but prohibited military alliances among the princes and with foreigners.

THE FRANCO-SWEDISH PHASE (1635–1648) AND AFTERMATH

Following the Swedish defeat at Nördlingen, France, under its brilliant Machiavellian first minister, Cardinal de Richelieu (d. 1642), felt compelled to intervene with troops. France had been sending money to the Protestant anti-Imperialists since the early phases of the war because it feared encirclement by the Habsburgs of Spain in conjunction with their cousins in Vienna. Even Pope Urban VIII (r. 1623–1644) gave his blessing to French intervention because he too feared the rise of Habsburg power, which might be used against the papal interests in Italy. Reasons of state had come to supplant religious considerations at least to some extent in the international arena.

Although the coming of French forces did not immediately turn the tide of the war, it did eventually make the Imperial defeat inevitable. Spain, with its communications in Germany disrupted, was soon further weakened by an uprising in Catalonia in Spain and the rebellion of proud Portugal in 1640. On May 19, 1643, the French won a stunning victory over the Spanish at Rocroi on the border of the Spanish Netherlands. The recently crowned Emperor Ferdinand III (r. 1637–1657) now found himself increasingly isolated in the empire as Frederick Wilhelm, the young elector of Prussia, made a separate peace with Sweden in 1640.

Other Protestant leaders also defected from their alliances with the emperor.

On Christmas of 1641, Ferdinand III agreed to begin peace negotiations with the French at Münster and with the Swedes at Osnabrück. Separate discussions were held between Protestants and Catholics. These cumbersome arrangements made the peace process drag on for years. A final settlement of the German phase of the conflict was not reached until 1648 at the Peace of Westphalia, as all sides jockeyed for more favorable conditions. The western phase of the conflict between France and Spain was not ended until the Peace of the Pyrenees of 1659. Other ongoing regional conflicts were also winding down. Peace agreements between Sweden and Denmark were finally reached in 1660, the same year that Sweden settled a conflict with Poland. Russia and Poland made peace in 1667.

France emerged from the wars as the dominant European power. It had gained the fortress towns of Metz, Toul, Verdun, Philippsburg, and most of Alsace in 1648. In 1659 France received Artois, Cambrai, Roussillon, and a claim to the Spanish throne through the marriage of Louis XIV of France to Philip IV's daughter, Maria Teresa. The 1648 agreements at Westphalia also recognized the independence of the Dutch Netherlands from Spain, as we have seen. The Swedes gained the southern end of the Swedish peninsula, western Pomerania, the bishoprics of Bremen and Verden, and Wismar, plus cash. Sweden was now officially recognized as the leading power in the Baltic.

Inside the devastated Holy Roman Empire, the Religious Peace of Augsburg of 1555 was reaffirmed and extended to Calvinists. The territorial independence and sovereignty of each of the empire's roughly 300 states were recognized. German princes could now once again legally conclude alliances with foreign powers. From the peak of power in 1629, the Habsburg emperor had been reduced to a figurehead in the Holy Roman Empire. His cousin in Spain had also lost a great deal. The Spanish kingdom had fallen a long way from the proud days of Philip II. What had begun as a religious conflict wound up as a chapter in Europe's continuing dynastic power struggles. Political violence was only one of the many legacies of the Reformation Era.

Chronology

1531	Formation of the Schmalkaldic League.	1547	Charles V victorious at Mühlberg.
1532	Religious truce at Nuremberg; Ottomans defeated east of Vienna.	1548	Augsburg and Leipzig *Interims*.
1535	Fall of Tunis to Charles V; renewed Habsburg-Valois conflict.	1552	Moritz of Saxony and Henri II of France attack Charles V.
		1555	Religious Peace of Augsburg.
1542–1544	Fourth Habsburg-Valois War.	1556	Abdication of Charles V.
1546	Death of Luther; beginning of Schmalkaldic War.	1558	Death of Charles V.
		1559	Peace of Cateau-Cambrésis;

	death of Henri II in France; Huguenots in Convention in Paris.	1609	Truce between Dutch rebels and Spain; birth of Judith Leyster.
1560–1572	Dominance of Catherine de' Medici.	1610	Death of Henri IV of France.
1561–1562	Colloquies at Poissy and St. Germain-en-Laye.	1618	Beginning of the Thirty Years' War.
1566	Beginning of the Revolt in the Low Countries.	1629	Defeat of Christian IV of Denmark; Edict of Restitution.
1571	Battle of Lepanto, naval defeat of the Ottomans.	1630	Gustavus II Adolphus of Sweden enters the Thirty Years' War.
1572	Saint Bartholomew's Day Massacres in France.	1632	Death of Gustavus Adolphus.
1574–1589	Reign of Henri III in France.		
1579	Union of Arras; division of the Low Countries.	1634	Death of Wallenstein.
		1635	France commits troops to the Thirty Years' War.
c. 1581–1666	Life of Frans Hals.		
1582	Murder of William of Orange.	1648	Treaties of Westphalia; recognition of the independence of the United Provinces.
1585	Fall of Brussels and Antwerp to Spanish.		
1587–1589	War of the Three Henries.	1659	Peace of the Pyrenees between France and Spain.
1588	Spanish Armada attacks England and is defeated.	1660	Peace between Denmark and Sweden; peace between Sweden and Poland.
1598	Peace between France and Spain; Edict of Nantes.	1667	Peace between Poland and Russia.
1606–1669	Life of Rembrandt.		

Further Reading

GENERAL STUDIES OF WARFARE

Frederic Baumgartner, *From Spear to Flintlock: A History of War in Europe and the Middle East to the French Revolution* (1991).

Jeremy Black, *A Military Revolution?* (1991). Important discussion of a major historiographical issue.

Christopher Duffy, *Siege Warfare: The Fortress in the Early Modern World* (1997).

David Eltis, *The Military Revolution of the Sixteenth Century* (1995).

Jack Goldstone, *Revolution and Rebellion in the Early Modern World* (1993).

John Guilmartin, *Gunpowder and Galleys: Changing Technology and Mediterranean Warfare at Sea in the Sixteenth Century* (1974).

John Hale, *War and Society in Renaissance Europe* (1985).

Michael Mallet, *Mercenaries and Their Masters: Warfare in Renaissance Italy* (1984).

Geoffrey Parker, *The Military Revolution* (1988).

Kenneth Setton, *Western Hostility to Islam and Prophecies of Turkish Doom* (1992).

Frank Tallett, *War and Society in Early Modern Europe, 1495–1715* (1992). Argues against the notion of a military revolution.

Janice Thomson, *Mercenaries, Pirates, and Sovereigns: State-Building and Extraterritorial Violence in Early Modern Europe* (1994).

GERMANY AND THE SCHMALKALDIC LEAGUE AND WAR

Thomas Brady, Jr., *Protestant Politics, Jacob Sturm (1498–1553) and the German Reformation* (1995). A full-length study of a pivotal figure in the rise of the Schmalkaldic League.

Carl Christensen, *Princes and Propaganda: Electoral Saxon Art of the Reformation* (1992).

Christopher Friedrichs, *Urban Society in an Age of War: Nördlingen* (1979).

Hajo Holborn, *A History of Modern Germany: The Reformation* (1961).

Robert Kolb, *Nikolaus von Amsdorf (1483–1565): Popular Piety in Preserving Luther's Legacy* (1977).

H. C. Erik Midelfort, *Mad Princes of Renaissance Germany* (1994).

Luther Peterson, "Melanchthon on Resisting the Emperor," in Jerome Friedman, ed., *Regnum, Religio et Ratio* (1987).

M. J. Rodriguez-Salgado, *The Changing Face of Empire: Charles V, Philip II, and Habsburg Authority, 1551–59* (1988).

Steven Rowan, *Ulrich Zasius: A Jurist in the German Renaissance, 1461–1531* (1987).

Kristin Zapalac, *"In His Image and Likeness": Political Iconography and Religious Change in Regensburg, 1500–1600* (1991).

FRANCE AND THE RELIGIOUS WARS

Frederic Baumgartner, *France in the Sixteenth Century* (1995).

———, *Henri II, King of France, 1547–1559* (1988).

Philip Benedict, *Rouen during the Wars of Religion* (1981).

David Buisseret, *Henry IV* (1984).

Natalie Davis, *Society and Culture in Early Modern France* (1965).

———, *The Return of Martin Guerre* (1983). Fascinating account of an imposter.

Jonathan Dewald, *The Formation of a Provincial Nobility* (1980).

Barbara Diefendorf, *Beneath the Cross: Catholics and Huguenots in Sixteenth-Century Paris* (1991).

Julian Franklin, *Jean Bodin and the Rise of Absolutistic Theory* (1973).

Janine Garrison, *A History of Sixteenth-Century France, 1483–1598: Renaissance, Reformation, and Rebellion* (1995).

Mark Greengrass, *France in the Age of Henri IV* (1984).

Malcom Greenshields, *An Economy of Violence in Early Modern France* (1994).

Mack Holt, *The Duke of Anjou and the Politique Struggle during the Wars of Religion* (1986).

De Lamar Jensen, *Diplomacy and Dogmatism: Bernardino de Mendoza and the French Catholic League* (1964).

Donald Kelley, *The Beginnings of Ideology* (1981).

Robert Kingdon, *Myths about the St. Bartholomew's Day Massacres* (1988).

Emmanuel Le Roy Ladurie, *Carnival in Romans* (1980). Intriguing study of popular violence.

J. Russell Major, *Representative Government in Early Modern France* (1980).

Raymond Mentzer, Jr., *Blood and Belief: Family Survival and Confessional Identity among Provincial Huguenot Nobility* (1994).

Robert Muchembled, *Popular Culture and Elite Culture in France*, trans. by Lydia Cochcrane (1985).

Donald Nugent, *Ecumenism in the Age of Reformation: The Colloquy of Poissy* (1974).

Nancy Roelker, *Queen of Navarre: Jeanne d'Albret* (1968).

J. H. Salmon, *Society in Crisis: France in the Sixteenth Century* (1975). A valuable synthesis.

N. M. Sutherland, *The Huguenot Struggle for Recognition* (1980).

Michael Wolfe, *The Conversion of Henri IV: Politics, Power, and Religious Belief in Early Modern France* (1993).

Philip II's Spain

Fernand Braudel, *The Mediterranean and the Mediterranean World in the Age of Philip II*, 2 vols. (1972).

William Christian, *Local Religion in Sixteenth-Century Spain* (1981).

Carlos Eire, *From Madrid to Purgatory: The Art and Craft of Dying in Sixteenth-Century Spain* (1994).

J. H. Elliot, *Imperial Spain* (1963).

Maureen Flynn, *Sacred Charities: Confraternities and Social Welfare in Spain* (1989).

Alastair Hamilton, *Heresy and Mysticism in Sixteenth-Century Spain: The Alumbrados* (1993).

Henry Kamen, *Philip of Spain* (1997). The leading biography.

———, *Spain 1469–1714*, 2nd ed. (1991).

Marvin Lunenfeld, *The Council of the Santa Hermandad* (1970).

John Lynch, *Spain 1516–1598* (1991).

———, *The Hispanic World in Crisis and Change, 1598–1700* (1992).

William Maltby, *Alba* (1983). A fascinating portrait of the soldier-statesman.

Helen Nader, *Liberty in Absolutist Spain: The Habsburg Sale of Towns* (1991).

Sara Nalle, *God in La Mancha* (1993).

Peter Pierson, *Philip II* (1989).

Ruth Pike, *Aristocrats and Traders: Sevillian Society in the Sixteenth Century* (1972).

I. A. A. Thompson, *War and Government in Habsburg Spain, 1560–1720* (1976).

Michael Weisser, *The Peasants of the Montes* (1976).

The Dutch Revolt and Its Aftermath

Alastair Duke, *Reformation and Revolt in the Low Countries* (1990).

Jonathan Israel, *Dutch Primacy in World Trade, 1585–1715* (1989).

———, *The Dutch Republic: Its Rise, Greatness, and Fall 1477–1806* (1995).

Guido Marnef, *Antwerp in the Age of Reformation: Undergrown Protestantism in a Commercial Metropolis, 1550–1577* (1995).

Sherrin Marshall, *The Dutch Gentry, 1500–1650* (1987).

Geoffrey Parker, *Spain and the Netherlands* (1979).

Simon Schama, *The Embarrassment of Riches: An Interpretation of Dutch Culture in the Golden Age* (1987). Magisterial synthesis.

Marjolein 't Hart, *The Making of a Bourgeois State: War, Politics, and Finance during the Dutch Revolution* (1993).

James Tracy, *Holland under Habsburg Rule* (1990).

Martin van Gelderen, ed., *The Dutch Revolt* (1993). A useful collection of documents.

The Spanish Armada

Felipe Fernandez-Armestro, *The Spanish Armada* (1988).

Colin Martin and Geoffrey Parker, *The Spanish Armada* (1988).

Garrett Mattingly, *The Armada*, 2nd ed. (1988). Beautifully written classic.

Wallace MacCaffrey, *Elizabeth I: War and Politics 1588–1603* (1992).

Peter Pierson, *Commander of the Armada: The Seventh Duke of Medinia Sidonia* (1989).

The Thirty Years' War

Gerhard Benecke, ed., *Germany in the Thirty Years' War* (1979). A valuable collection of excerpts from primary sources.

Bodo Nischan, "The Thirty Years' War," in J. W. Zophy, ed., *The Holy Roman Empire: A Dictionary Handbook* (1980).

Geoffrey Parker, *The Thirty Years' War* (1984).

J. V. Polisenký, *The Thirty Years' War* (1971).

Michael Roberts, *Gustavus Adolphus*, 2nd ed. (1992).

John Theibault, *German Villages in Crisis: Rural Life in Hesse-Kassel and the Thirty Years' War, 1580–1720* (1995).

Notes

1. Cited in Mark Edwards, Jr., *Luther's Last Battles: Politics and Polemics, 1531–46* (Ithaca, N.Y.: Cornell University Press, 1983), pp. 182–183.
2. Cited in Lewis Spitz, *The Protestant Reformation* (Englewood Cliffs, N.J.: Prentice Hall, 1966), p. 72.
3. Cited in Jonathan Zophy, *Patriarchal Politics and Christoph Kress (1484–1535) of Nuremberg* (Lewiston, N.Y.: Edwin Mellen, 1992), p. 14.
4. Cited in William J. Wright, "Philip of Hesse's Vision of Protestant Unity and the Marburg Colloquy," in Kyle Sessions and Philip Bebb, eds., *Pietas et Societas: New Trends in Reformation Social History* (Kirksville, Mo.: Sixteenth Century Journal Publishers, 1985), pp. 165–166.
5. Cited in Zophy, *Patriarchal Politics*, p. 183.
6. Cited in Roland Bainton, *Women of the Reformation in Germany and Italy* (Minneapolis, Mn.: Augsburg, 1971), p. 42.
7. Cited in Barbara Diefendorf, *Beneath the Cross: Catholics and Huguenots in Sixteenth-century Paris* (New York: Oxford University Press, 1991), p. 99.
8. Cited in Bonnie Anderson and Judith Zinsser, *A History of Their Own: Women in History from Prehistory to the Present*, 2 vols. (New York: Harper and Row, 1988), vol. 1, p. 233.
9. Cited in G. R. Elton, ed., *Renaissance and Reformation 1300—1648*, 3rd ed. (New York: Macmillan, 1976), p. 145.
10. Cited in De Lamar Jensen, *Reformation Europe: Age of Reform and Revolution*, 2nd ed. (Lexington, Mass.: D. C. Heath, 1992), p. 255.
11. Cited in H. G. Koenigsberger, "The Politics of Philip II," in Malcolm Thorp and Arthur Slavin, eds., *Politics, Religion, and Diplomacy in Early Modern Europe: Essays in Honor of De Lamar Jensen* (Kirksville, Mo.: Sixteenth Century Journal Publishers, 1994), pp. 180–181.
12. Cited in Jensen, *Reformation*, p. 290.
13. Cited in Garrett Mattingly, *The Armada* (Boston: Houghton Mifflin, 1959), p. 217.
14. Cited in Lacey Baldwin Smith, *Elizabeth Tudor: Portrait of a Queen* (Boston: Little Brown, 1975), p. 69.

18

The Legacy

History is, among many other things, a dialogue between the past and the present. Therefore, it seems appropriate to end this book by discussing some of the ways in which the Renaissance and Reformation movements influenced our world. What changed as a result of these movements? What ideas and institutions grew out of this period of time? Although the Renaissance and Reformation era introduced an abundance of changes in European society, ranging from the introduction of double-entry bookkeeping to the use of forks in dining, this concluding chapter will focus on only some of the major developments which emerged from this era.

Religious Life

Clearly the world of 1648 was quite different in many respects from the one we encountered in 1300. At that time almost all of the peoples living in western Europe were nominally Roman Catholics with just a small number of Jews and Muslims. By 1648 the religious unity of what was called Christendom was gone forever. Large numbers of western Europeans no longer looked to Rome exclusively for spiritual guidance. Clergy in Protestant areas had a different status than Catholic clergy. Many of them were now free to marry and forced to take on the obligations of citizens including the

paying of taxes. They still performed the remaining sacraments, preached, and comforted the sick and dying, but they were not a part of such a privileged estate. The Reformation changed many aspects of life not just for the clergy but for the laity as well.

THEOLOGICAL DIVISIONS
AND SOCIAL DISCIPLINE

The second half of the sixteenth century continued to witness theological disputes and efforts to create a more "godly" and disciplined society. After the death of Martin Luther in 1546, Lutheranism had broken into two major camps as we have seen. The followers of Luther's close friend Philip Melanchthon (Philippists) argued with the followers of Flacius Illyricus and Nicholas von Amsdorf (Gnesiolutherans) over such issues as the nature of the Eucharist or whether Lutheran churches should use a version of the old Catholic episcopal system. Disputes among Lutherans also broke out over whether adherence to divine law was necessary for salvation (Antinomianism) and whether humans could do anything toward earning salvation (Synergistic Controversy). The Gnesiolutherans held firmly to their belief in salvation by grace alone, completely denying that good works contributed anything toward salvation. Philippists believed that piety and learning contribute to regeneration. Some of the heat went out of the disputes with the successive deaths of some of the major protagonists (Melanchthon in 1560, Amsdorf in 1565, and Flacius in 1575).

Lutheran princes who hoped to use Lutheranism to enforce social discipline were increasingly disturbed by the failure of the theologians to come to common ground on doctrine. If they could not discipline themselves, how could they discipline their flocks? That is why many such as Duke Christoph of Württemberg (1515–1568) eagerly supported the efforts of Jacob Andreae (1528–1590) and others to achieve doctrinal unity. The son of an itinerant Bavarian blacksmith, Andreae rose to earn a doctorate in theology and become a Lutheran pastor in Stuttgart. Later Andreae was named a counselor to Duke Christoph and in 1561 chancellor of his alma mater, the University of Tübingen.

A prolific writer, he wrote a "Formula of Concord" in 1577 that helped to unify many of the various Lutheran factions. It was included in *The Book of the Concord* of June 1580 along with Melanchthon's Augsburg Confession, the Apology (Defense) of the Augsburg Confession, the Schmalkaldic Articles, and Luther's Large and Small Catechisms. *The Book of the Concord* was eventually supported by eighty-six princes and town governments and between eight and nine thousand theologians. The princes were led by Elector Augustus of Saxony (1553–1586), who was determined to put a stop to theological divisions among Lutherans. All of the major questions raised in the various doctrinal controversies were discussed and refuted. Lutheranism had finally achieved a great deal of doctrinal cohesion.

The period also saw increased efforts to create state churches that enforced social discipline upon their subject populations. Major confessional statements such as the

Calvinist *Second Helvetic Confession* of 1566, the Calvinist *Heidelberg Catechism* of 1563, and the Lutheran *Book of the Concord* of 1580 were used to attempt to impose discipline and order on society. In his preface to the *Heidelberg Catechism*, Elector Frederick III of the Palatinate explained some of his motives for adopting it. He wrote:

> We have finally recognized and undertaken to fulfill Our divinely ordained office, vocation, and governance, not only to keep peace and order, but also to maintain a disciplined, upright, and virtuous life and behavior among Our subjects, furthermore and especially, to instruct them and bring them step by step to the righteous knowledge and fear of the Almighty and His sanctifying Word as the basis of all virtues and obedience.[1]

Thus, Frederick and other princes sought to use the Reformation as a means of consolidating their power and imposing social control upon their subjects. Church ordinances and regulations could be used to make more "godly" cities and territories while strengthening the hand of patriarchal secular authorities. In many areas, this took the form of closing brothels, regulating poor relief, and indoctrinating the young. As enforcers of morality under the authority of a prince or city council, Protestant clergy in the Holy Roman Empire became servants of the state. Teams of clergy and civic officials attempted to enforce discipline through periodic visitations, which examined the conduct of parish pastors and their congregations.

How successful they were in instilling piety and morality is a matter of spirited debate. The quest to establish "godly" communities did not seem to succeed. Traditional modes of belief and dissolute behavior persisted despite the exhortations of the preachers and their secular colleagues.

Excessive drinking, gambling, illicit sex, and public violence continued to be staples of male bonding and common features of European town and village life. Dancing could not be eliminated in Calvinistic Geneva or elsewhere. Even some of the married Protestant clergy were found in violation of the new discipline ordinances.

Apparently much more successful were the efforts to improve individuals and society through expanded educational opportunities for males and females. Building on the work of Renaissance humanism, many Protestant leaders were interested in increasing biblical literacy to make better Christians and persons. They founded new primary schools for both boys and girls, established Latin schools at the secondary level, and developed academies and colleges for the training of pastors and male church workers. Educational growth also occurred in Roman Catholic areas through the efforts of the Society of Jesus and other groups that stressed the importance of education. Although these efforts made only a slight dent in Europe's massive illiteracy, there is no question that the improvement of education was one of the most important heritages of the Renaissance and Reformation, along with the efforts to improve social welfare systems.

MARRIAGE IN PROTESTANT EUROPE

One of the areas of daily life most profoundly affected by the Reformation was the institution of marriage. No longer a sacrament among Protestants, marriage still occupied a place of great importance. Protestants championed marriage as spiritually preferable to celibacy. While there was variance among various groups in their regulation of marriage, most Protestants stressed the importance of parental consent and al-

lowed the possibility of divorce with remarriage for adultery or impotence. In some areas, divorce was also permitted for refusal to have sexual relations, abandonment, deadly abuse, or affliction with an incurable disease. While Protestants permitted divorce under certain circumstances, their leaders attempted to discourage the breakup of families. Marriage courts tried to settle marital disputes before permitting divorce. Overall, divorce was still a rarity in the pretwentieth-century world.

Many of the reformers argued that marriage was the "natural" vocation for women and urged husbands to treat their wives and children in a kindly manner. The Reformation affirmed patriarchy time and time again as wives were continually admonished to be obedient to their husbands. Protestant marriage courts did punish both male and female adulterers. They also attempted to make sure divorced husbands paid child support. Premarital sex, a common practice, was also discouraged in most Protestant areas as was infanticide. The stability of the patriarchal family was considered an important foundation of the patriarchal state.

MARGARET FELL (1614–1702) AND WOMEN AS PREACHERS

Protestant women lost a great deal with the closing of most convents and the strengthening of patriarchy, yet some were able to gain access to newly founded grammar schools. Reformers such as Martin Luther stressed "biblical literacy" and he helped establish schools for girls. Although Lutheran girls were not in school as long as boys so as not to interfere with their domestic chores, the schools did open some windows of learning for those outside of the cloistered world. Since there were not enough male

Albrecht Dürer, *The Moor Katherine* (1521). Uffizi, Florence, Italy. Foto Marburg / Art Resource.

schoolteachers available, some schools were forced to hire some literate women as teachers, which opened yet another profession to women.

The ministry, however, remained forbidden to women in Protestant as well as Catholic territories. While some Anabaptist women were allowed to administer baptism and preach, the larger Protestant groups were adamantly opposed to the practice except in baptismal emergencies. As the magisterial reformer John Calvin put it, "The custom of the church, before St. Augustine was born, may be elicited first of all from Tertullian (church father, c. 160–230), who held that no woman in church is allowed to speak, teach, baptize, or make offerings; this

in order that she may not usurp the functions of men."[2]

Not until the rise of the Society of Friends (Quakers) in the seventeenth century in England were women such as Margaret Fell given the opportunity to preach in public. An offshoot of the Puritan movement, the early Quakers based their religion on the exposition of the biblical revelation by ministerial authority. They favored plain living and speaking, exacting conscience, and a complete avoidance of sensuous and formal liturgy.

As a young woman Margaret Fell had been converted to "enlightenment" by George Fox (1624–1691), one of the principal leaders of the Quakers in 1652. After the death of her first husband, Margaret married Fox in 1669 even though she was prosperous. With her second husband and other Quaker missionaries constantly traveling and sometimes being imprisoned, Margaret Fell, who usually remained at the society's headquarters at Swarthmoor Hall, became known as the "nursing mother of the church." She also did missionary work as well as preaching, writing tracts, and trying to persuade King Charles II that the Friends, those "rude" disciples, were no threat to law and order and should be released from prison and not persecuted.

Her pleas failed and Margaret Fell found herself imprisoned as a religious dissenter from 1664 to 1668 and again from 1670 to 1671. During her first stint in prison, she wrote and published a tract called *Women's Speaking Justified*. In it, Fell argued that "the Lord God in creation, when he made man in his own image, he made them *male* and *female*."[3] Her words seemed to echo those of the early feminist writer Christine de Pizan (1365–c. 1429) centuries earlier. Fell also asserted that as God's creatures, women had the obligation to speak in church and elsewhere when the Holy Spirit moved them. She cited chapter and verse of the Old and New Testaments, naming every woman who was recorded as having prophesied, spoken, or argued. Other Quaker women followed in the bold steps of Margaret Fell. Not until the twentieth century were women admitted to the ministry in some of the other Protestant denominations. Most fundamentalist groups of Protestants still have an all-male clergy, as do the Roman Catholics and the Eastern Orthodox.

ROMAN CATHOLICISM REVIVED

In Catholic areas, old institutions and worship practices survived and many in the church felt reinvigorated. The Catholic Church had not only survived the Protestant defections but had emerged with new energy after the reform Council of Trent. Able leaders had emerged and new organizations such as the Society of Jesus and the Ursulines had further strengthened the church. Doctrines had been clarified and reaffirmed and there was now little question about what good Catholics were to believe and practice. Corruption in church practices had been greatly reduced. The Catholic Church, while still dominated by aristocrats, was no longer as nepotistic or simoniacal as it had been prior to the Reformation. By and large the education of the clergy had been substantially improved. Even scholasticism had been reinvigorated. The post-Tridentine church not only enforced greater discipline upon the clergy, it also attempted to impose social discipline upon society as well.

In the late sixteenth and continuing into the seventeenth centuries, the Catholic Church was able to make some spectacular conversions. For example, Protestantism had made deep inroads into Poland during the first half of the sixteenth century. By the beginning of the seventeenth century,

Poland was a Roman Catholic bulwark led by active reformers such as the Jesuit theologian and court preacher Peter Skarga (1536–1618) and others. Jesuits may have played a key role in the decision of Sweden's free thinking Queen Christina to abdicate in 1654 and to turn away from Lutheranism. In the Holy Roman Empire, where the ranks of the Catholic clergy had been thoroughly depleted in the first decades of the Reformation and where even the archdiocese of Cologne threatened to turn Protestant in 1547 and again in 1583, reformed Catholicism slowly began to make a comeback.

In the seventeenth century, reformed Catholicism made a spectacular series of princely conversions ranging from Duke Wolfgang Wilhelm of Palatine-Neuberg to Elector Frederick August of Saxony. Even important intellectuals such as Angelus Silesius (1624–1677) made surprising conversions to Catholicism. Following his conversion, Silesius gave up his position as personal physician to the Protestant duke of Württemberg and eventually found new employment as physician to Emperor Ferdinand III. Ordained a priest in 1661, he became a leading propagandist for the Catholic Reformation and one of the era's leading lyrical poets. Catholicism also made a comeback in a number of south German imperial cities such as Augsburg, Dinkelsbühl, and Ulm. Those biconfessional towns showed that a community could have adherents of different denominations living in relative harmony with each other. This too was an important lesson of the era.

Witchcraft and Its Suppression

Although there were pockets of toleration in some parts of Europe, not many Catholic or Protestant communities were willing to allow witchcraft by the end of the sixteenth century. European witchcraft was considered to be a dangerous mixture of heresy (treason against God) and sorcery (the magical power to do evil deeds through formulas and rituals). Witches were believed to have made a pact to deny God and serve the devil. Satan then gave the witch the power to cause illness and sometimes even death in humans and animals, bring on bad weather, and destroy fertility in humans or plants. Territorial states also felt threatened by witchcraft as a form of local power that denied the authority of the divinely sanctioned hierarchy.

Such beliefs were well grounded in the popular culture of the time. Many people believed they lived in a world where supernatural forces abounded; some worked for good, some for evil. If God could act in human history, so could Satan and his minions. Alarmed by reports of diabolic activities, the recently elected Pope Innocent VIII (r. 1484–1492) commissioned two Dominicans—Jacob Sprenger and Heinrich Kramer—to draw up the first comprehensive handbook on witchcraft and demonology. Their handbook on witchcraft and demonology was entitled the *Malleus Maleficarum* (*The Hammer of Witches*) and came out in 1486. It would be used to help witch-hunters and courts that handled witchcraft cases identify the signs of witchcraft.

Laced with misogyny, the *Malleus Maleficarum* sums up much of the worst in Western thought about women. For example, Sprenger and Kramer wrote:

> Woman is more carnal than man. . . . She always deceives. . . . What else is woman but a foe to friendship, an inescapable punishment, a necessary evil, a natural temptation, a desirable calamity, a domestic danger, a delectable detriment, an evil of nature, painted with fair colors. . . . To conclude, all witchcraft comes from carnal lust, which in women is insatiable.[4]

With such a mindset helping guide those males charged with identifying, trying, and sentencing suspect witches, it is hardly surprising that the overwhelming majority of the 50,000 to 75,000 persons executed for witchcraft during the sixteenth and seventeenth centuries were women. Yet witch persecutions were not just manifestations of animosity between men and women; they could also involve tensions between women, such as between a new mother and her midwife or between a conflicted mother and her maid. The witch craze tapped into all sorts of cultural, political, social, and psychological forces present in early modern Europe.

Despite the fact that the revised Imperial Law Code of 1532 made witchcraft a capital offense punishable by death, the witch trials did not involve large numbers of people until the end of the sixteenth century. For decades, Catholics and Protestants were too busy fighting each other to bother with witches. However, as Europe continued to be troubled with periodic famines, inflation, and social tensions, the temptation to use accused witches as scapegoats proved impossible to resist in both Catholic and Protestant territories. The majority of the witch prosecutions took place inside the Holy Roman Empire, with France a close second. Bohemia, Poland, and Switzerland were also active in witch hunting. Fewer prosecutions took place in the British Isles, the Low Countries, and Scandinavia. Catholic Spain and Italy had very few witch trials and very few of their prosecutions resulted in executions. Those areas had long experience in dealing with heretics and many of those accused of witchcraft failed to qualify as such when scrutinized by experienced inquisitors.

Because of the widespread belief in the powers of witches, magic, and the frequent use of torture in judicial proceedings, once started the witch-hunts were hard to stop.

When tortured, accused witches confessed to all sorts of diabolical activities. As one convicted witch in Bamberg wrote his daughter in 1628, "I confessed in order to escape the great anguish and bitter torture, which it was impossible for me to bear longer."[5]

Leading authorities such as the political theorist Jean Bodin were convinced that witch-hunts were an absolute necessity. Those who argued that pacts with the devil were frauds and that witches were really harmless and confused old women, such as the German physician Johann Weyer (1550–1578), were themselves accused of being witches. Why would one defend a witch unless one were a witch? In 1623 Pope Gregory XV commanded that anyone who made a pact with the devil or who practiced black magic that resulted in death should be turned over to the secular courts and put to death.

CRITICS OF THE WITCH CRAZE

Among those who dared to criticize the belief in witches were Michel de Montaigne and the seventeenth-century essayist-swashbuckler Cyrano de Bergerac. In a famous letter of 1654 about witches Bergerac wrote: "No, I do not believe in witches, even though several important people do not agree with me; and I defer to no man's authority, unless it is accompanied by reason and comes from God."[6] He found that most of the so-called witches were "crack-brained" shepherds and "ignorant" peasants. Given his renowned skill with a sword, few were willing to challenge Bergerac or accuse him of being a witch to his face.

In fact, the attitude of skepticism about the alleged powers of witches came to be more and more prevalent. Educated people increasingly began to seek natural explana-

tions for things that had previously been attributed to supernatural forces. Courts began demanding more conclusive evidence about evil deeds and the pact with the devil and putting greater limitations upon the use of torture. The same legal authorities who had once vigorously prosecuted witches now began to doubt that some of the people brought before them actually were witches. Some wondered why secular courts were wasting their time on a matter that belonged to the church.

Executions for witchcraft fell off rapidly, especially as economic conditions improved in many parts of Europe toward the end of the seventeenth century. King Louis XIV issued an edict in 1682, which successfully curtailed witchcraft trials in France, the same year in which the last accused witch was legally executed in England. Accused witches were still occasionally executed legally in the Holy Roman Empire until 1775 and in Glarus, Switzerland until 1782. The belief in the powers of the devil and witches persisted in the minds of Europeans, especially those in the working classes, but at least those in power no longer were so eager to prosecute suspected witches.

The Rise of Western Science

ASTROLOGY, ALCHEMY, AND MAGIC

The rise of science played a role in the declining belief in witchcraft and is one of the most important legacies of the Renaissance and Reformation period. However, an understanding of the workings of nature and the universe free from such time-honored traditions as astrology, magic, and theological considerations took a long time to achieve. Most Renaissance intellectuals continued to believe, as had most ancient Greek thinkers, that matter was made up of four basic elements: air, earth, fire, and water. Each of those elements in turn possessed characteristics drawn from four basic qualities: heat, cold, dryness, and moistness. Those qualities were related to the four medical humors that determined health: choleric, melancholic, phlegmatic, and sanguine. Even the planets, as they slid past each other in concentric spheres pulled by angels, partook of these same qualities. Thus, Saturn was believed to be cold and dry whereas Mars was hot.

Furthermore, the movement of the planets and stars was believed to have an impact on life on earth. As the planets moved in relationship with each other and the still earth, their movements caused changes in the lives of humans, animals, and crops. By calculating the correct movement of the planets, astrologers could forecast when plagues or famines would occur and determine when was the best time to conceive a child, plant a crop, or go to war. Thus, astrologers such as Nostradamus (1503–1566) or John Dee (1527–1608) were in great demand by governments as well as by private citizens. Nostradamus found employment with Queen Catherine de' Medici and fooled her and many others by predicting events *after* they had occurred. John Dee, an outstanding alchemist and mathematician, served both Queen Elizabeth of England and Holy Roman Emperor Rudolf II (r. 1576–1612). The mentally unbalanced Rudolf was particularly fascinated by astrology and kept a large stable of astrologers on hand, including the astronomers Tycho Brahe and Johann Kepler.

A few bold skeptics such as the humanist-philosopher Giovanni Pico della Mirandola noticed in the 1480s that the accuracy of astrological weather predictions was low. He once kept a weather diary and found that the astrologers were correct for only seven out of one hundred days. He dared to write a "Treatise Against Astrology" in which he noted that "Plato and Aristotle, the leaders of the (philosophy) profession, considered astrology unworthy of discussion."[7] He recommended that physicians be trusted more than astrologers on matters of health when they contradicted each other. Yet Pico's reservations about astrology were a minority opinion even among learned humanists. Astrology seemed a useful and time-tested science. Its teachings had been supported by many revered sages and Christian theologians. It was taught in the universities along with astronomy. Almanacs filled with astrological lore and predictions continued to be in great demand throughout the Renaissance and beyond.

Next to astrology and physics, alchemy continued to be a leading science of the day. It had long been observed that many substances in nature change over time. For example, flowers bloom and wilt and change colors. Even basic substances can be altered by heating or cooling. Many alchemists became intrigued with the idea of transforming base metals such as lead into gold. In attempting to do so, however, they learned a great deal about the properties of various substances and developed much of the equipment used by later chemists. The first general discussion of how to produce compounds, solutions, distillates, crystallizations, and fusions was the 1597 *Alchemy* of the German physician-poet-historian Andreas Libavius (1540–1616). Although critical of the "magical superstitions" of the influential physician-theorist Paracelsus, Libavius maintained his belief in such traditional alchemical lore as the philosopher's stone, which was thought to be able to change base metal into gold. Science still had not freed itself from magic. The universe still seemed best explained by the astrologers and the mystics.

NICHOLAS COPERNICUS (1473–1543)

All this slowly began to change during the Renaissance with the work of scientists and scholars such as Nicholas Copernicus, Andreas Vesalius, and those who followed them. At the heart of the world view of the astrologers was the earth-centered view of the universe fostered by a host of scholars in the wake of the Hellenistic astronomer, Claudius Ptolemy (second century A.D.). Ptolemy's system placed the earth at the center of the universe. This seemed to satisfy the senses, appeal to human egoism, and agree with certain sentences in the Bible. After all, Joshua had ordered the sun, not the earth, to stand still (Joshua 10:12). Before Ptolemy, Aristotle had postulated that the planets move in circular and uniform orbits in crystalline spheres.

Copernicus, a Polish mathematician, came to the conclusion that while Aristotle was essentially correct, Ptolemy had erred in placing the earth at the center of the solar system. The son of a merchant, Nicholas Copernicus had been educated in theology and law at the University of Cracow. For ten years after that he studied astronomy, mathematics, canon law, Greek, and medicine at various universities in Italy. Returning to Poland, Copernicus spent the last thirty years of his life as a canon of Frauenberg Cathedral and physician to his uncle, the bishop of Ermeland. In his spare time, he continued to observe the stars and make mathematical calculations despite his poor eyesight. His calculations led him to the startling conclusion that the venerated Ptolemy was wrong about the location of earth and its lack of rotation.

His great book, *On the Revolution of the Celestial Spheres,* was completed in 1530 but circulated in manuscript form only until the year of his death, 1543. Copernicus was quite concerned that even his mild revision

of Ptolemy might not sit well with the Catholic Church. He humbly dedicated his book to Pope Paul III with the hope that it would not be considered too upsetting to church dogma. Some Catholics did find his views upsetting; so did most Protestants who became aware of them. Although it was the Lutheran pastor and astronomer, Andreas Osiander, who first published Copernicus's major work, he did so with a disclaimer. Martin Luther, who was supportive of the new work done in botany, exclaimed, "That fool (Copernicus) will upset the whole science of astronomy."[8] In the short run, Luther was wrong, for even most advanced scholars found Copernicus's mathematical proofs to be inadequate and his theory as problematic as Ptolemy's.

BRAHE AND KEPLER

While a few bold thinkers such as the controversial Italian philosopher Giordano Bruno (c. 1548–1600) embraced Copernicus's theory of a sun-centered solar system, most advanced thinkers remained unconvinced. Even the great Danish nobleman and astronomer Tycho Brahe (1546–1601), found a great deal in Copernicus that was unsatisfactory. Brahe, who had lost his nose in a duel as a young man, made his astronomical career in 1572 by providing the most accurate description of the appearance of a nova, a star that seems to suddenly appear because of a rapid increase in light output and then fades away after several months. His book, *On the New Star,* came to the attention of King Frederick II, who rewarded Brahe with the lordship of the island of Hveen and a generous stipend. There Brahe built the laboratory palace of Uraniborg, with multiple observatories, a giant quadrant, a great brass-plated globe for the mapping of observations, equipment for alchemy experiments, and rooms for visiting students and colleagues.

Although Brahe did not think the earth could rotate as Copernicus had argued, he still believed that the earth was near the center of the universe. He also rejected the old Aristotelian notion of crystalline spheres. Instead the keen-eyed Brahe concluded that while the other planets revolve around the sun, the sun and the other planets revolve around the earth.

Brahe's greatest student was a German, Johann Kepler (1571–1630). Kepler, the son of a soldier and an encouraging mother, studied mathematics and theology at the University of Tübingen. There he was very much influenced by Michael Maestlin, the most celebrated astronomer in the empire and an advocate of the Copernican system. In 1594 after taking his M.A., Kepler became a teacher of mathematics at a school in Graz, Austria. There he amazed the locals with his knowledge of astrology and mathematics. His calendars seemed to predict events with uncanny accuracy. Kepler became fascinated with the mystery of planetary motions and published his pro-Copernican *Mysteries of the Cosmos* in 1597, which was based heavily on Brahe's work.

He sent copies of his book to many of the leading mathematicians, scientists, and princes in Europe. Impressed by his mathematics, Tycho Brahe invited him to become his assistant in Denmark. A few years later, Kepler joined Brahe at the court of Emperor Rudolf II in Prague, a ruler obsessed with astrology. Kepler worked with the Dane for less than a year before Brahe's death and succeeded him as imperial astronomer and mathematician, a post with a generous salary. Kepler continued the compilation of Brahe's planetary tables, to which he added some of his own data, which he published in 1627.

Kepler's most famous work was his *The New Astronomy* of 1609, which contained his famous discovery that planetary orbits are ellipses, not circles as Copernicus and most ancients taught. He also demonstrated that the speed of a planet is greater when it is closer to the sun and slower when it is farther away. Not everything was new in his astronomy, for he continued to believe in astrology and in the ancient Pythagorean notion of the harmony of the spheres. After the forced abdication of the increasingly unstable Emperor Rudolf in 1612, Kepler continued as imperial astronomer and mathematician but moved to Linz as a professor of mathematics. He stayed in Linz for the next fourteen years despite periodic persecutions because of his Lutheranism.

Devoted to his mother, Kepler made several trips to his native Swabia in 1620 and 1621 in order to defend her from accusations of witchcraft. Because he often found his imperial pay in arrears, Kepler went to work in 1628 as an astrologer for Albrecht von Wallenstein, the famous imperial general. After Wallenstein's dismissal from imperial service, Kepler moved to Regensburg, where he died still seeking some of his imperial back pay. By the time of Kepler's death in 1630, he had laid the basis for a clearer understanding of the nature of the solar system and the mathematical relationship of its various parts.

GALILEO GALILEI (1564–1642)

The nearsighted Kepler had not been able to support his theories fully by observation. That honor went to Galileo Galilei, who made great use of the Dutch invention of the telescope. Galileo was the son of a minor Florentine noble turned cloth merchant. Excelling in school, he became a brilliant mathematician, an accomplished musician, and a talented artist and author. After abandoning

Justus Susterman, *Portrait of Galileo*. Tarre del Galla, Villa Galetti, Florence, Italy. Foto Marburg/Art Resource.

the study of medicine at Pisa, Galileo took a post in 1592 as a professor of mathematics at the University of Padua, where he remained for the next eighteen years. In 1593 he invented an open-air thermometer. While at Padua, Galileo also discovered the law of the pendulum and used it to measure time.

In 1609 he devised a telescope from a Dutch lens grinder's model. Galileo used his telescope to identify shadows on the moon's surface as mountains, valleys, and plains. As he wrote in his famous book of 1610, *The Starry Messenger,* "The surface of the moon is not perfectly smooth, free from inequalities, and exactly spherical, as a large group of philosophers considered."[9] Galileo also discovered that four satellites swung around the planet Jupiter, just as the moon circles the earth and that the stars are more numerous and farther from the earth than

had previously been assumed. The curious Florentine was also the first to see sunspots with a telescope.

Although some ridiculed Galileo's new discoveries, others applauded him for his challenges to previous understandings of the workings of the solar system. His growing reputation and talent for flattery won him a new position as philosopher and mathematician to Grand Duke Cosimo II of Florence. He had proposed earlier that the newly discovered satellites of Jupiter be named "the Medicean stars." In 1611 Galileo traveled to Rome to explain his discoveries to church leaders. Many were impressed with Galileo and his pro-Copernican theories including the head mathematician of the Jesuits as well as Cardinal Maffeo Barberini, the future Pope Urban VIII (r. 1623–1644).

There were also men in high places, however, who found Galileo's barbed criticisms of the ideas of revered authorities such as Aristotle and Ptolemy to be dangerous and his personality to be combative. Many theologians were still wedded to the use of Aristotelian forms of logic to support church doctrine. Denounced by the Roman Inquisition in 1616, Galileo was told to abandon and cease to defend and teach as fact the Copernican notion that the sun is the center of the universe and that the earth moves around it. Galileo refused to do this and in 1623 he published a treatise entitled *The Assayer,* which argued that knowledge of nature is acquired by observation and mathematics, not by merely reading ancient authorities.

The work was dedicated to Galileo's friend, Maffeo Barberini, who had just become Pope Urban VIII. Calling Galileo a "great man whose fame shines in the heavens and goes far and wide on earth,"[10] the pope presented the astronomer with costly gifts and a pension for the support of his illegitimate son. Urban refused to lift the censorship of the Inquisition, however, and advised Galileo to avoid theological arguments and treat Copernicanism as a theory. Galileo then returned to Florence and completed his *Dialogue Concerning the Two Chief World Systems, Ptolemaic and Copernican.* Failing to get permission to publish in Rome, Galileo arranged to have the book published in Florence in 1632. This act of defiance enraged the pope and others in Rome, who summoned the aging scientist to appear before the Inquisition in Rome. There he was interrogated and forced to deny his support for Copernicus. Galileo was ordered to retire to his home in Florence and to avoid saying or writing anything that might cause "suspicion."

Although forced to give up on astronomy, the aging scientist resumed his important work in mechanics, which he had first begun in his youth. His last book, *Dialogues Concerning Two New Sciences,* published in 1638, dealt strictly with mechanics and physics. One of his most important discoveries was the law of inertia, which demonstrated that a moving body will continue in motion in a straight line at a uniform speed unless it is acted upon by another force to alter its direction or speed. This discovery contradicted Aristotle's notion that the "natural" state of a body is rest and anticipated the work of Isaac Newton (1642–1727).

The wonderful story that Galileo dropped unequal weights from the leaning tower of Pisa to demonstrate that bodies fall at a uniform rate is apparently the stuff of legend. It is true, however, that Galileo kept

Tito Lessi, *Galileo Telling His Son of the New Science,* Osservatorio, Italy. Alinari/Art Resource.

experimenting to the end of his life, even though he had become totally blind.

MEDICINE AND ANDREAS VESALIUS (1514–1564)

If Copernicus started a process that eventually led to more people such as Galileo looking to the stars with greater objectivity and precision, so Andreas Vesalius helped to advance medicine. The Renaissance had inherited a wealth of medical knowledge from the ancient Greeks and medieval Muslims. The development of the printing press meant that the works of thinkers such as Hippocrates and Galen were now available to a larger audience than ever before. Some of it was useful such as the notion that diseases had natural causes and could be treated by rational means and improvements in diet. Some of it was harmful, such as the notion that the human body contained four basic fluids: blood, phlegm, red or yellow bile, and black bile. The proper balance of these four humors was believed necessary for maintaining proper health as shown in the complexion. Thus, bloodletting was commonly used to correct the problem of imbalance among the humors.

The balance of the humors and life cycles was also believed to be linked to the movements of the heavenly bodies. Therefore, Renaissance doctors commonly used astrology to determine the best time for treatment and the type of treatment. Further problems arose from the very training most Renaissance physicians received. Medical schools still used the writings of the prolific second century A.D. Greek physician Galen as their guide to anatomy. Galen had made a number of astute judgments about human anatomy, but his work was fundamentally flawed by his belief that the human organs were similar to those of animals. Galen also

incorrectly concluded that women were men turned outside in. The ovaries were "smaller, less perfect testes" and females were less "perfect than men."[11]

Out of deference to the classical and Christian belief in the sanctity of the human body, most dissections prior to the fourteenth century had been limited to dogs, pigs, and when available apes from North Africa. Only the anatomical treatise of 1316 by the Italian Mondine di Luzzi was based on the dissection of humans.

Given the limitations of the ancient and medieval knowledge of anatomy, it is easy to see why the work of Leonardo da Vinci (1452–1519) and Andreas Vesalius was so revolutionary. Leonardo, the artist-scientist, had to study human anatomy and other natural things in order to portray them accurately. As he wrote in his *Treatise on Painting*, "We rightly call painting the grandchild of nature and related to God."[12] For him, painting was a branch of science which sought to communicate with precision the miracles of nature.

Andreas Vesalius was born in Flanders and studied at universities in Louvain, Paris, and then Padua in Italy. Only Italian universities were using human cadavers and conducting autopsies. Vesalius, a superior medical student, was invited to join the faculty at Padua at age twenty-three. Instead of reading Galen's description of the organs to his students while a barber-surgeon located each one, Vesalius used the scalpel himself and reverently pointed out errors in Galen. News of his dissections spread, and they became public events.

Then in 1543 he published his *On the Fabric of the Human Body*, which carefully described in words and detailed drawings the parts, organs, and functions of the human body. Regrettably, Vesalius repeated some of Galen's errors, most notably his description of the circulation of the blood. He accepted

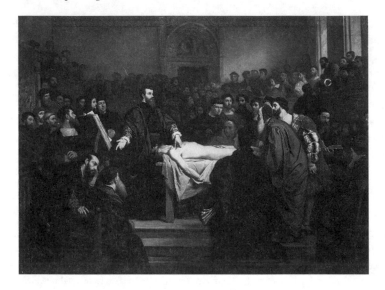

Edouard Jeana Conrad, *Andre Vesalius Teaching at Padua*. Musee des Beaux-Arts, Marseille, France. Giraudon/Art Resource.

wholesale Galen's notion of the "septum" as a wall dividing the heart, which he considered porous and thus facilitating the passage of the blood from the veins to the arteries. The Spanish heretic Michael Servetus actually had a better understanding of the circulatory system, whose workings were not fully explained until the work of the English physician William Harvey (1578–1657), who also studied at Padua.

Despite its flaws, Vesalius's book had the most accurate anatomical drawings of the time and his understanding of human anatomy represented a considerable advancement. Although the book was criticized by some clerics, it soon became an invaluable guide to physicians and surgeons all over Europe. Shortly after the publication of his masterwork, he left Padua to spend the last twenty years of his life as a court physician to Emperor Charles V and his son, Philip II of Spain. Andreas Vesalius continued his medical research and made several more valuable contributions to the art of surgery. He also published several new editions of the still admired work of Galen.

THE SCIENTIFIC METHOD AND FRANCIS BACON (1561–1626)

Galileo's and Vesalius's interests in experimentation were eventually echoed throughout Europe, particularly after Francis Bacon helped to popularize the scientific method. Bacon was the son of Lady Anne and Sir Nicholas Bacon, lord keeper of the Great Seal under Queen Elizabeth I. A child prodigy, he became a favorite of the queen and the court with his prematurely wise and witty conversation. At age twelve, Francis entered Trinity College, Cambridge, where he studied classical philosophy and developed his distaste for Aristotelianism. According to Bacon, Aristotelianism did not do enough to improve the human condition.

Francis Bacon continued his studies of philosophy but also had a successful career as a lawyer and member of Parliament. Although never able to win favor with Queen Elizabeth as an adult, he advanced rapidly under the reign of her successor, James I, becoming lord chancellor in 1616. Then came an equally dramatic fall as Bacon was

Andreas Vesalius, *Musculature Structure of a Man.* Sixteenth-century print. Collection of Fratelli Fabbri, Milan, Italy. Bridgeman/Art Resource.

most of the traditional scientific lore, Bacon stressed the importance of careful observation of nature and arriving at conclusions based on evidence. He had high hopes for an "alliance, so far unconcluded, between the experimental and the rational methods."[13] Although Bacon seldom experimented himself, placed little emphasis on the mathematical dimension of physics, and discovered no new scientific laws, his work as a philosopher of science in popularizing the scientific method was of fundamental importance.

Bacon's call for greater use of experimentation and reason echoed a similar call made centuries earlier by the Oxford Franciscan Roger Bacon (d. 1292 and not related to Francis Bacon). The major difference was that by the seventeenth century the Western world was more ready to listen. Religious objections began to lessen when church officials came to recognize that scientists were not interested in undermining belief in God but only in discovering more precisely how God's creation worked. Almost all of the major scientists of the first phases of the so-called scientific revolution were devout Christians and skilled secular theologians. As the eighteenth-century poet Alexander Pope later expressed it, "The state of Nature was the reign of God."[14]

Part of the reason for that change in attitude was that the new science was quickly shown to have practical applications. The telescope, for example, could be used by generals and admirals to see the movements of their enemies. Merchants could get advance word on which commercial ships were going to arrive safely in harbor from their long-distance journeys. Such foreknowledge could then be used to make profits or avoid losses in the commodities market.

Given the technological advances made possible by the new science, especially for business and warfare, it is hardly

charged with bribery, imprisoned, and later banished from the court. Although he was subsequently pardoned, his political career was over. Despite the failure of his political ambitions, Bacon made many significant contributions to philosophy and the rise of science. He sought to organize all existing scientific knowledge and use it to better the human condition.

As part of this ambitious scheme, Bacon published his *Novum Organum* (*The New Method*) in 1620. He argued for a new method of reasoning based on induction from data. Urging his readers to disregard surprising that governments became interested in fostering scientific development. A Royal Society for the advancement of science was chartered in England by King Charles II in 1662. An Academy of Sciences was founded by Louis XIV's astute finance minister, Jean-Baptiste Colbert, four years later. Similar organizations followed throughout Europe and the rest of the world. These organizations and others patterned after them furnished laboratories, granted subsidies, brought scientists together to exchange ideas, published their findings, and encouraged scientific achievement generally.

WOMEN SCIENTISTS

Unfortunately, scientific development was not fostered among women. Even those enlightened parents who encouraged their daughters to read and write often considered science to be an "inappropriate, inelegant, and unfeminine subject" for girls and women.[15] Women were still not admitted to the universities or the newly created scientific academies with rare exceptions. Those who made contributions to the rise of science seldom had their work acknowledged. For example, Anne Finch, the Viscountess Conway (1631–1679), has only recently had her contributions to the ideas of the philosopher Gottfried Wilhelm Leibniz (1646–1716) acknowledged. Leibniz is best known as the coinventor with Isaac Newton of differential calculus. Newton in turn became known to French audiences largely through the translation of the talented mathematician Emilia du Chatelet (1706–1749), perhaps the leading woman scientist of her century. Yet she is still best known as the mistress of the literary giant Voltaire.

Margaret Cavendish, duchess of Newcastle (1617–1673), was the most prolific female scientific author of the seventeenth century. She produced fourteen books on everything from natural history to atomic physics. Because of their special privileges, noblewomen like Cavendish and Chatelet could sometimes get around some of the restrictions placed on their sex. A few of the early female scientists rose from more humble stations. Maria Sibylla Merian (1647–1717) came from an artistic family and worked as a housewife before leaving her husband to join a religious sect. A lifelong collector of insects and plants, Merian published six collections of engravings of European flowers and insects, which were far more scientifically accurate than their rivals. Toward the end of her life she journeyed from Amsterdam to Suriname in the interior of South America to study plant and insect life for two years. The resulting book of sixty copperplates with commentaries cemented her reputation as a leading naturalist. Her *Metamorphosis of the Insects of Suriname* came out in Dutch and Latin to critical acclaim.

RENÉ DESCARTES (1595–1650)

The advancement of science by men and women was clearly one of the greatest legacies of the Renaissance and Reformation. The rise of science also contributed directly to the intellectual revolution known as the Enlightenment. The Frenchman René Descartes was a key figure in both the rise of science and the pre-Enlightenment. Born into the French nobility, Descartes was educated in a Jesuit college. Young René showed great talents in mathematics, philosophy, and theology. At age fifteen, he invented an adding machine. Later Descartes would devise analytical geometry, a method of combining and interchanging algebra and geometry. Determined to educate himself "from the great book of the world," Descartes traveled to Paris and then to the Low Countries, where he enlisted for a time in the army of Maurice of Nassau. After a lengthy period of wandering about northern Europe, the accomplished Frenchman retired to Holland where he could think and write in peace.

One of the finest fruits of his reflections was his famous *Discourse on Method* of 1637. There he made an eloquent defense of the value of abstract reasoning. Descartes argued that it was necessary to question all authority, no matter how venerable and revered. The only thing he could not ultimately doubt was that he doubted (*cogito ergo sum*—"I think, therefore, I am"). Where could this ability to doubt come from? For Descartes, it must come from God, the supreme substance. "I myself am a substance. I should not, however, have the idea of an infinite substance, seeing as I am a finite being unless it were given me by some substance in reality infinite."[16]

Using reason "to the best of my power," Descartes became certain of the existence of God, himself, and the external world. Since reason is identical to all people, whereas the senses vary, it is the best guide to universal truth. From a few simple self-evident truths, Descartes believed he could come to understand much of the whole of God's creation: "Give me extension and motion and I will create the universe."[17] Although other scientists such as Galileo and Isaac Newton demonstrated many of the weaknesses of Cartesian physics including the belief that the planets were held up by celestial fluids, there is no question that Descartes's emphasis on the use of deductive reasoning made a major contribution to the world of the Enlightenment and the continued advance of science.

Political Changes

If reason could be used to guide humans in understanding the world of nature, could it also have its uses in the world of politics? Here the answers seemed less clear. The Renaissance and Reformation era had produced a rich diversity of political thought and practice. Some political theorists such as François Hotman in France (1524–1590) had argued against absolutism; others such as Jean Bodin and King James I of England (r. 1603–1625) had argued strongly for the divine right of kings to rule. During the period the feudalized monarchies of Europe had seen their sovereigns extend their authority and build their bureaucracies, legal systems, and militaries. The rise of territorial states and divine-right absolutist monarchies was a major trend of the period. Yet republican oligarchies continued in parts of Italy and in the Dutch United Provinces.

THE CONSTITUTIONAL STRUGGLE IN ENGLAND, 1642–1688

In England, the divine-right pretensions of James I's son, Charles I (r. 1625–1649), would be challenged by the rise of Parliament and those who believed in placing limitations upon the authority of the crown. As early as 1565, Sir Thomas Smith, a professor of Roman law at Cambridge, had argued that "the most high and absolute power of the realm of England consists in the Parliament."[18] Common law theorists such as Sir Edward Coke (1552–1634) repeatedly stressed the limits to royal power and the need for the king to be subject to the laws made by Parliament. Adding to the atmosphere of crisis, a fierce Irish revolt broke out in 1641. In 1642 a civil war broke out in England between those loyal to the crown and those

Sir Peter Lely, *Portrait of Oliver Cromwell.*
Galleria Palatina, Palazzo Pitti, Florence.
Alinari/Art Resource.

who sided with Parliament. Parliament found strong leadership in the person of Oliver Cromwell (1598–1658), a Puritan gentleman farmer and a former member of Parliament.

As a Puritan, Oliver Cromwell was a descendant of those who wished to "purify" the English church of what they saw as vestiges of "popery." King Charles Stuart and his Catholic queen, Henrietta Maria, were far too "high church" for the likes of Cromwell, who favored independent congregations and simple services. The king's archbishop, William Laud (1573–1645), emphasized the "visibility and catholicity" of the Church of England.[19] He sought to ele-

vate worship over preaching and drive the Puritans from the established church. All this was resisted with great determination by men such as Oliver Cromwell. Cromwell believed himself to be doing the Lord's work in fighting against the king and his supporters. He raised a well-disciplined army of men who "had the fear of God before them."[20] Cromwell led them to victory after victory until Charles's forces were totally defeated. Guided by Cromwell, a High Court of Justice found King Charles guilty of treason and the king was beheaded on January 30, 1649.

The House of Lords and the monarchy were abolished and England was ruled by a small minority in the House of Commons backed by the victorious parliamentary army. They faced opposition from radicals such as the Levellers, who believed in freedom of speech, toleration, democracy, and a reduction in social and economic distinctions. Cromwell moved to crush the Leveller movement as it spread into the army. He also invaded Ireland in August 1649 when Irish rebels proclaimed Charles II, son of Charles I, as their king. His forces attacked the rebel strongholds of Drogheda and Wexford, massacring their garrisons. In the following year, Cromwell's forces devastated Catholic Ireland, where about a third of the population was killed outright or died of starvation. For Cromwell, the Catholic Irish who opposed "his godly authority" were servants of Satan. Resistance to Cromwell's authority in Ireland ended but at a high price in a legacy of hatred, much of it along religious lines.

The Irish campaign was followed by one against the Presbyterian Scots, who had also proclaimed Charles II as their king. Scottish defiance was completely ended by September 1651. Cromwell then turned to London, where a growing rift had developed between Parliament and the army. As commander-in-chief of the army, he dismissed Parliament in 1653 and instituted the so-called Protectorate with himself as lord protector. Although several new parliaments came and went, the incorruptible Cromwell ruled England with an iron hand until his death in 1658.

A year and a half after the lord protector's death, the monarchy was restored in the personage of Charles II (r. 1660–1685). Relations between the high church king and Parliament soon deteriorated and finally in 1688 Charles's openly Catholic brother, James II, was bloodlessly overthrown, and a Protestant king and queen, William III of the Dutch Netherlands and Mary II (James's daughter) assumed the throne. A new coronation oath was devised for William and Mary that required that they swear to abide by the decisions of Parliament as well as by the ancient laws of England. This was followed by a Declaration of Rights of 1689, which spelled out, among other things, Parliament's authority to depose a monarch and choose a new one. The so-called Glorious Revolution of 1688 thus marked the complete ascendancy of representative government in England and the complete establishment of a Protestant state church.

THE RISE OF ABSOLUTISM

In vivid contrast with England, the Continental states of Austria, Brandenburg-Prussia, France, Russia, and Spain developed autocratic monarchies with expanding bureaucracies in the seventeenth and eighteenth centuries as did Sweden in Scandinavia. Monarchs such as Charles XII of Sweden (r. 1689–1718) and Frederick II, the Great, of Prussia (r. 1740–1786) used their abilities as successful generals not only to

increase the size of their realms, but also to gain control over governmental institutions by keeping their states in an almost constant state of military readiness. In Russia, Czar Ivan IV, the Terrible (1533–1584), destroyed the remaining power of the Tartars in southeastern Russia and annexed most of their territory. He also began the conquest of Siberia and cowed for a while the turbulent Russian nobility. Ivan's Oriental-style despotism was not overly influenced by Western models.

It was not until the reign of the Peter I, the Great (r. 1689–1725), that Russia turned fully to the West. The giant (six foot, nine inches) czar restored order to Russia after a time of weak rulers. He adopted Western-style bureaucratic systems in both central and local government. Western customs such as shaving, drinking wine, smoking tobacco, and wearing low-cut dresses were forced upon the Russian nobility. The czar personally barbered the members of his court. When the patriarch of the Russian Orthodox church opposed the czar's authority and adoption of Western customs, Peter abolished the office of patriarch. He placed a Holy Synod at the head of the church, composed of a committee of bishops and presided over by a lay procurator-general. The church, therefore, became an instrument of the state, as advocated by Marsilius of Padua in the thirteenth century and Thomas Erastus (d. 1583), a professor of medicine at Heidelberg, in the sixteenth century.

FRENCH-STYLE ABSOLUTISM

In France, Cardinals Richelieu and Mazarin exercised authority in the name of King Louis XIII (r. 1610–1643), who preferred hunting to governing. Richelieu (1585–1642) was determined to make royal power supreme in France. As first minister, he sent the king's soldiers to destroy the castles of nobles who defied the authority of the crown, disbanded their private armies, and hanged a number of the most recalcitrant. He also waged war against the French Protestants and stripped them of some of their military and political rights.

To make the power of the monarchy felt in all corners of France, Richelieu divided the kingdom into thirty administrative districts called *generalities*, and placed each one of them under the control of an agent of the crown, called an *intendant*. The intendants could override the authority of local governing bodies and often did so. So absolute was the power of the intendants over provincial affairs, even of the most petty nature, that they came to be called the "thirty tyrants of France." They were chosen for the most part from the ranks of the upper middle class and were shifted around frequently lest they become too "sympathetic" with the people over whom they ruled in the name of the king.

Richelieu's policies were continued by his successor as first minister, Cardinal Jules Mazarin (d. 1661). Working closely with the regent queen, Anne of Austria, Mazarin tutored young Louis XIV in the craft of kingship. He advised the young king to be his own first minister and to avoid sharing power with anyone. As king, Louis followed the policy of "one king, one law, and one God."[21] This translated into a brutal campaign of repression and, in 1685, the revoking of the Edict of Nantes, which had been issued by his grandfather, Henri IV. Calvinism was now illegal in France. French Huguenots were ordered to convert to Catholicism and forbidden to emigrate. Thousands managed to do so anyway, and many ended up in Brandenburg-Prussia,

whose ambitious Hohenzollern ruler, Elector Frederick Wilhelm, eagerly welcomed them and their skills.

Believing himself to be a divine-right monarch, Louis XIV never once met his national Estates-General in the seventy-two years of his reign. Neither did his great grandson and successor Louis XV in the fifty-nine years of his reign. Representative government in France would have no national forum until bankruptcy forced the monarch to summon an Estates-General in the spring of 1789 that touched off the far-reaching explosion known as the French Revolution.

Although absolutism was attempted all over Europe, it is important to remember that even the strongest of monarchs in preindustrial Europe had limitations placed on their authority. Spanish monarchs, for example, found opposition not only in the national parliament (Cortes), but also at the local levels. Even the "sun-king" of France, Louis XIV, could not always force independent sea captains to follow his orders. Problems with communications and transportation were compounded by traditions of local authority. It was often far easier for a local magistrate to get a bridge repaired than for an official of the central government to do it. The importance of limiting the power of the state and protecting human rights was one of the great consequences of the period.

As a cautionary tale, the Reformation has also taught us the importance of toleration and the need to live in communities of love despite our differences. As Martin Luther King, Jr., a twentieth-century stepchild of the Reformation, once said: "We must all learn to live together as brothers and sisters or we shall perish together as fools."[22] The need to learn to live together in community despite our differences is also a part of the enormous legacy of the Renaissance and Reformation.

Chronology

1486	Publication of the *Malleus Malefi-carum* (*Hammer of Witches*).
1532	Imperial Law Code makes witchcraft a capital offense in the Holy Roman Empire.
1533–1583	Life of Czar Ivan IV, the Terrible.
1543	Publication of Copernicus's *On the Revolution of Celestial Spheres* and Vesalius's *On the Fabric of the Human Body*.
1563	*Heidelberg Catechism.*
1577	Jacob Andreae's "Formula of Concord."
1580	*The Book of the Concord.*
1583	Near conversion of Cologne to Protestantism.
1610	Publication of Galileo's *The Starry Messenger*.
1614–1702	Life of Margaret Fell.
1617–1673	Life of Margaret Cavendish.
1620	Publication of Francis Bacon's *Novum Organum* (*New Method*).
1624–1642	Cardinal Richelieu in power in France.
1637	Publication of Descartes's *Discourse on Method*.
1641	Irish revolt.
1642	Beginning of the English Civil War.
1643	Beginning of the reign of Louis XIV in France.
1647–1717	Life of Maria Sibylla Merian.
1649	Trial and execution of King Charles I in England; Cromwell's Irish campaign.
1658	Death of Oliver Cromwell.
1660	Restoration of the monarchy in England.
1685	Revocation of the Edict of Nantes by Louis XIV.
1688	Bloodless Revolution brings William and Mary to power.

Further Reading

RELIGION AND SOCIETY

Robin Barnes, *Prophecy and Gnosis: Apocalypticism in the Wake of the Lutheran Reformation* (1988).

Lawrence Duggan, *Bishop and Chapter: The Governance of the Bishopric of Speyer to 1532* (1978).

Carlos Eire, *War Against Idols: The Reformation of Worship from Erasmus to Calvin* (1986).

G. R. Evans, *Problems of Authority in the Reformation Debates* (1992).

Bruce Gordon, *Clerical Discipline and the Rural Reformation: The Synod of Zürich, 1532–1580* (1992).

Stephen Haliczer, *Sexuality in the Confessional: A Sacrament Profaned* (1996).

R. Po-chia Hsia, *Social Discipline in the Reformation: Central Europe 1550–1750* (1989).

———, *Society and Religion in Münster, 1535–1618* (1984).

H. Larry Ingle, *First Among Friends: George Fox and the Creation of Quakerism* (1994).

Robert Jütte, *Poverty and Deviance in Early Modern Europe* (1994).

Robert Kolb, *Confessing the Faith: Reformers Define the Church 1530–1580* (1991).

Bonnelyn Young Kunze, *Margaret Fell and the Rise of Quakerism* (1993).

Richard Muller, *Post-Reformation Reformed Dog-matics*, 2 vols. (1987, 1993).

Heiko Oberman, *The Impact of the Reformation* (1994).

Steven Ozment, *Protestants: The Birth of a Revolution* (1992).

Jill Raitt, ed., *Shapers of Religious Traditions in Germany, Switzerland, and Poland, 1560–1600* (1981). Fine essays by diverse contributors.

———, *The Colloquy of Montbéliard: Religion and Politics in the Sixteenth Century* (1993).

William Russell, *Luther's Theological Testament: The Schmalkald Articles* (1994).

Gerald Strauss, *Luther's House of Learning: Indoctrination and the Young in the German Reformation* (1978).

Bruce Tolley, *Pastors and Parishioners in Württemberg During the Late Reformation, 1581–1621* (1994).

Marriage and Family Life

Kristen Gager, *Blood Ties and Fictive Ties: Adoption and Family Life in Early Modern France* (1996).

Beatrice Gottlieb, *The Family in the Western World from the Black Death to the Industrial Age* (1993).

Joel Harrington, *Reordering Marriage and Society in Reformation Germany* (1994).

Steven Ozment, *When Fathers Ruled: Family Life in Reformation Europe* (1983).

Lyndal Roper, *The Holy Household: Women and Morals in Reformation Augsburg* (1989).

Thomas Max Safley, *Let No Man Put Asunder: The Control of Marriage in the German Southwest* (1984).

Lawrence Stone, *The Family, Sex and Marriage in England 1500–1800* (1977).

Jeffrey Watt, *The Making of Modern Marriage: Matrimonial Control and the Rise of Sentiment in Neuchatel, 1550–1800* (1992).

Women and Gender

Susan Amussen, *An Ordered Society: Gender and Class in Early Modern England* (1988).

Judith Brown, *Immodest Acts: The Life of a Lesbian Nun in Renaissance Italy* (1986).

Patricia Crawford, *Women in Religion in England 1500–1720* (1993).

Natalie Davis, *Women on the Margins: Three Seventeenth-Century Lives* (1995). Fascinating comparisons of a Jewish merchant, a nun, and a botanist.

Amy Ericson, *Women and Property in Early Modern England* (1995).

James Farr, *Authority and Sexuality in Early Modern Burgundy, 1550–1730* (1994).

Craig Harline, *The Burdens of Sister Margaret* (1994).

Olwen Hufton, *The Prospect Before Her: A History of Women in Western Europe, 1500–1800* (1996).

Anne Laurence, *Women in England, 1500–1760: A Social History* (1994).

Carole Levin and Patricia Sullivan, eds., *Political Rhetoric, Power, and Renaissance Women* (1995). A multidisciplinary collection of essays by various authors.

Phyllis Mack, *Visionary Women and Ecstatic Prophecy in Seventeenth-Century England* (1993).

Patricia Ranft, *Women and the Religious Life in Premodern Europe* (1996).

Margaret Sommerville, *Sex and Subjection: Attitudes to Women in Early Modern Society* (1995).

Joy Wiltenberg, *Disorderly Women and Female Power in the Street Literarture of Early Modern England and Germany* (1992).

Witchcraft and Magic

Carlo Ginzburg, *Ectasies. Deciphering the Witches' Sabbath* (1990).

———, *The Night Battles: Witchcraft and Agrarian Cults in the Sixteenth and Seventeenth Centuries* (1983).

Joseph Klaits, *Servants of Satan: The Age of Witch Hunts* (1985).

Alan Kors and Edward Peters, eds., *Witchcraft in Europe 1100–1700: A Documentary History* (1972). Valuable sources.

Christina Larner, *Enemies of God: The Witch-hunt in Scotland* (1981).

Brian Levack, *The Witch-Hunt in Early Modern Europe* (1987).

H. C. Erik Midelfort, *Witchhunting in Southwestern Germany* (1972).

E. William Monter, *Witchcraft in France and Switzerland* (1976).

Lyndal Roper, *Oedipus and the Devil: Witchcraft, Religion and Sexuality in Early Modern Europe* (1994).

Keith Thomas, *Religion and the Decline of Magic* (1971).

THE RISE OF SCIENCE

Mario Biagioli, *Galileo, Courtier: The Practice of Science in the Culture of Absolutism* (1994).

H. Floris Cohen, *The Scientific Revolution: A Historiographical Inquiry* (1994).

Stillman Drake, *Galileo: Pioneer Scientist* (1990).

Amos Funkenstein, *Theology and the Scientific Imagination* (1989).

Marjorie Grene, *Descartes* (1985).

David Lindberg and Robert Westman, *Reappraisals of the Scientific Revolution* (1990).

Robert Mandrou, *From Humanism to Science, 1480–1700* (1978).

Harold Nebelsick, *The Renaissance, the Reformation, and the Rise of Science* (1992).

Patricia Phillips, *The Scientific Lady: A Social History of Women's Scientific Interests, 1520–1918* (1990).

James Reston, Jr., *Galileo: A Life* (1995).

Edward Rosen, *Three Imperial Mathematicians* (1986).

David Ruderman, *Jewish Thought and Scientific Discovery in Early Modern Europe* (1995).

John Russell, *Francis Bacon* (1979).

Londa Scheibinger, *The Mind Has No Sex? Women in the Origins of Modern Science* (1989).

Michael Sharratt, *Galileo: Decisive Innovator* (1994).

Pamela Smith, *The Business of Alchemy: Science and Culture in the Holy Roman Empire* (1994).

Bruce Stephenson, *Kepler's Physical Astronomy* (1990).

POLITICS

Randolph Head, *Early Modern Democracy in the Grisons* (1995).

Quentin Skinner, *The Foundations of Modern Political Thought*, 2 vols. (1978).

Malcolm Thorp and Arthur Slavin, eds., *Politics, Religion, and Diplomacy in Early Modern Europe* (1994). A fine collection of essays dedicated to De Lamar Jensen.

William Wright, *Capitalism, the State, and the Lutheran Reformation: Sixteenth-Century Hesse* (1988).

THE CONSTITUTIONAL STRUGGLE IN ENGLAND

Julian Davies, *The Caroline Captivity of the Church: Charles I and the Remoulding of Anglicanism* (1992).

Jerome Friedman, *Blasphemy, Immorality and Anarchy: The Ranters and the English Revolution* (1987).

———, *The Battle of the Frogs and Fairfield's Flies: Miracles and the Pulp Press during the English Revolution* (1993).

Pauline Gregg, *King Charles I* (1984).

Christopher Hill, *God's Englishman: Oliver Cromwell and the English Revolution* (1970).

William MacDonald, *The Making of an English Revolutionary: The Early Parliamentary Career of John Pym* (1982).

Conrad Russell, *The Causes of the English Civil War* (1990).

Kevin Sharpe, *The Personal Rule of Charles I* (1992).

David Underdown, *Pride's Purge: Politics and the Puritan Revolution* (1985).

Dewey Wallace, *Puritans and Predestination* (1982).

Austin Woolrych, *Commonwealth to Protectorate* (1982).

ABSOLUTISM

Evgenii Anisimov, *The Reforms of Peter the Great: Progress through Coercion in Russia* (1993).

William Beik, *Absolutism and Society in Seventeenth-Century France* (1985).

Joseph Bergin, *The Rise of Richelieu* (1991).

James Collins, *The State in Early Modern France* (1995).

Jonathan Dewald, *Aristocratic Experience and the Origins of Modern Culture: France 1570–1715* (1993).

J. H. Elliot, *Richelieu and Olivares* (1984).

Richard Golden, *The Godly Rebellion* (1981).

J. Russell Major, *From Renaissance Monarchy to Absolute Monarchy* (1994).

———, *Representative Government in Early Modern France* (1990).

David Parker, *The Making of French Absolutism* (1983).

OTHER TOPICS

John Bossy, *Giordano Bruno and the Embassy Affair* (1991). Was the philosopher also a spy? A fascinating detective story.

Jonathan Brown, *Kings and Connoisseurs: Collecting Art in Seventeenth-Century Europe* (1995).

Peter Burke, *Popular Culture in Early Modern Europe* (1972).

———, *The Art of Conversation* (1994).

Frank Dobbins, *Music in Renaissance Lyons* (1992).

Ronald Hutton, *The Rise and Fall of Merry England: The Ritual Year 1400–1700* (1994). A study of the rituals which marked the passage of the year.

Joyce Irwin, *Neither Voice nor Heart Alone: German Lutheran Theology of Music in the Age of the Baroque* (1993).

Michael Macdonald and Terence Murphy, *Sleepless Souls: Suicide in Early Modern England* (1991).

Ian Maclean, *Interpretation and Meaning in the Renaissance: The Case of Law* (1992).

Roger Manning, *Hunters and Poachers: A Social and Cultural History of Unlawful Hunting in England 1485–1640* (1993).

Carol Menning, *Charity and the State in Late Renaissance Italy: The Monte di Pieta of Florence* (1994).

Sergiusz Michalski, *The Reformation and the Visual Arts: The Protestant Image Question in Western and Eastern Europe* (1993).

Ruth Pike, *Penal Servitude in Early Modern Spain* (1983).

Peter Wallace, *Communities in Conflict in Early Modern Colmar* (1995).

Notes

1. Cited in R. Po-chia Hsia, *Social Discipline in the Reformation: Central Europe 1550–1750* (New York: Routledge, 1989), p. 35.
2. Cited in Julia O'Faolain and Lauro Martines, eds., *Not in God's Image: Women in History from the Greeks to the Victorians* (New York: Harper and Row, 1973), p. 202.
3. Cited in Gerda Lerner, *The Creation of Feminist Consciousness: From the Middle Ages to Eighteen-Seventy* (New York: Oxford University Press, 1993), p. 101.
4. *Malleus Maleficarum*, ed. and trans. by Montagu Summers (London: Hogarth Press, 1928), pp. 41–42.
5. Cited in William Monter, ed., *European Witchcraft* (New York: John Wiley, 1969), p. 87.
6. Ibid., p. 114.
7. Cited in G. R. Elton, ed., *The Renaissance and Reformation 1300–1648*, 3rd ed. (New York: Macmillan, 1976), p. 63.
8. Cited in De Lamar Jensen, *Reformation Europe: Age of Reform and Reconciliation*, 2nd ed. (Lexington, Mass.: D. C. Heath, 1992), p. 382.
9. Cited in John Hale, *The Civilization of Europe in the Renaissance* (New York: Atheneum, 1993), p. 352.
10. Cited in Jensen, *Reformation*, p. 382.
11. Cited in Bonnie Anderson and Judith Zinsser, *A History of Their Own: Women in Europe from Prehistory to the Present*, 2 vols. (New York: Harper and Row, 1988), vol. 2, p. 29.
12. Cited in Elton, *Renaissance and Reformation*, p. 67.
13. Ibid., p. 356.
14. Alexander Pope, "An Essay on Man: Epistle III," line 148.
15. Cited in Anderson and Zinsser, *A History of Their Own*, vol. 2, p. 87.
16. Cited in Jensen, *Reformation*, pp. 387–388.
17. See Ernst Cassirer, *The Philosophy of the Enlightenment*, trans. Fritz Koelin and James Pettegrove (Princeton, N.J.: Princeton University Press, 1951), pp. 51–52.
18. Cited in Elton, *Renaissance and Reformation*, p. 143.
19. See Julian Davies, *The Caroline Captivity of the Church: Charles I and the Remoulding of Anglicanism* (New York: Oxford University Press, 1992).
20. Cited in Jensen, *Reformation*, p. 438.
21. Cited in John Wolf, *Louis XIV* (New York: W. W. Norton, 1968), p. 383.
22. Quoted in a speech at Michigan State University, April 1966.

Index